*Christmas
2003
Nell – To whet your
appetite for your
adventure*

THE AUTHOR Dr ▮▮▮▮▮▮▮▮▮▮▮▮▮▮ th Pacific and New Zealand, and tau▮▮▮▮▮▮▮▮▮▮▮▮▮ ege in New Zealand's North Island. ▮▮▮▮▮▮▮▮▮▮▮▮▮ as from universities on three conti▮▮▮▮▮▮▮▮▮▮▮▮▮ ▮y. His last positions were Senior Lec▮▮▮▮▮▮▮▮▮▮▮ ▮▮stitute of Technology and Visiting Professor at th▮ ▮ity College of the City University in New York. More than a hundred of his articles have appeared in professional journals in New Zealand, Australia, Britain, Canada, South Africa and the United States. This is his sixth book, the previous being *A Traveller's History of Australia*.

SERIES EDITOR Professor Denis Judd is a graduate of Oxford, a Fellow of the Royal Historical Society and Professor of History at London Metropolitan University. He has published over 20 books including the biographies of Joseph Chamberlain, Prince Philip, George VI and Alison Uttley, historical and military subjects, stories for children and two novels. His most recent books are the highly praised *Empire: The British Imperial Experience from 1765 to the Present* and (with Keith Surridge) *The Boer War*. He has reviewed and written extensively in the national press and in journals and is an advisor to the BBC *History* Magazine.

Other Titles in the Series

THE TRAVELLER'S HISTORY SERIES

'Ideal before-you-go reading' *The Daily Telegraph*

'An excellent series of brief histories' *New York Times*

'I want to compliment you ... on the brilliantly concise contents of your books' *Shirley Conran*

Reviews of Individual Titles

A Traveller's History of France

'Undoubtedly the best way to prepare for a trip to France is to bone up on some history. *The Traveller's History of France* by Robert Cole is concise and gives the essential facts in a very readable form.' *The Independent*

A Traveller's History of China

'The author manages to get 2 million years into 300 pages. An excellent addition to a series which is already invaluable, whether you're travelling or not.' *The Guardian*

A Traveller's History of India

'For anyone ... planning a trip to India, the latest in the excellent Traveller's History series ... provides a useful grounding for those whose curiosity exceeds the time available for research.' *The London Evening Standard*

A Traveller's History of Japan

'It succeeds admirably in its goal of making the present country comprehensible through a narrative of its past, with asides on everything from bonsai to *zazen*, in a brisk, highly readable style ... you could easily read it on the flight over, if you skip the movie.' *The Washington Post*

A Traveller's History of Ireland

'For independent, inquisitive travellers traversing the green roads of Ireland, there is no better guide than *A Traveller's History of Ireland*.' *Small Press*

A Traveller's History of New Zealand and the South Pacific Islands

For Joy Chambers: author of historical novels of compassion

A Traveller's History of New Zealand and the South Pacific Islands

JOHN H. CHAMBERS

Series Editor   DENIS JUDD
Line Drawings   JOHN HOSTE

Interlink Books
An imprint of Interlink Publishing Group, Inc.
New York • Northampton

First American edition published 2004 by

INTERLINK BOOKS
An imprint of Interlink Publishing Group, Inc
46 Crosby Street, Northampton, Massachusetts 01060
www.interlinkbooks.com

Text copyright © John H. Chambers 2004
Preface copyright © Denis Judd 2004
Cover design by Mark-making Design
Line drawings John Hoste
Maps by John Taylor

The front cover shows 'Lake Wakatipu with Mount Earnshaw' 1877–1879 by Eugene von Guerard by kind permission of the Mackelvie Trust Collection, Auckland Art Gallery Toi o Tamaki, purchased 1971

Library of Congress Cataloging-in-Publication Data
Chambers, John H.
  A traveller's history of New Zealand and the South Pacific islands/
by John H. Chambers.—1st American ed.
    p. cm.—(The traveller's history series)
Includes bibliographical references and index.
ISBN 1-56656-506-5 (pbk.)
1. Oceania—History.   2. New Zealand—History.   I. Title.
II. Traveller's history.
DU28.3.C468 2003
995—dc21

                    2003000627

Printed and bound in Great Britain

To order or request our complete catalog
please call us at **1-800-238-LINK** or write to:
Interlink Publishing
46 Crosby Street, Northampton MA 01060-1804
e-mail: info@interlinkbooks.com
www.interlinkbooks.com

Contents

Acknowledgements

Two books read in my early teens provided my first understanding of the South Pacific. *A Brief History of the British Commonwealth since Waterloo* by C.H. Currey highlighted the work of the great New Zealand figures and suggested a useful structure for understanding events. And *Among the Natives of the Loyalty Group* sent to me by my Aunt Cissie and written by Emma Hadfield, her sister-in-law, who had been a missionary, gave insights into the Loyalty Islands which lie on the cultural cusp of Melanesia and Polynesia. I have both books still.

Many people and work in many places have helped in writing this book, which blends the history of these two fascinating geographical areas, New Zealand and the South Pacific Islands.

Victoria Huxley, then of the Windrush Press, first recognized the possibilities, and in her always efficient manner has been instrumental in seeing the work to its completion. Dr Graeme Dunstall of the University of Canterbury, New Zealand, and Professor Ron Crocombe of the University of the South Pacific in Fiji, gave of their detailed historical expertise and experience, and physicist Dr John Campbell also of Canterbury helped with the Appendix on firewalking and the section on Ernest Rutherford. None of them is responsible for any of my errors or personal interpretations which remain.

Libraries and librarians in Brisbane, Wellington, Christchurch, Suva, Honolulu and London have been most generous. I should mention in particular the wonderful facilities at the National Library of New Zealand, and the support of the University Librarian, Janine Schmidt at the University of Queensland. Also helpful were Stan Sorensen, Historian in the Office of the Governor, American Samoa, and Joanne

Perry at the library in New Zealand House, London. H.S. Payne, John England, Patricia and Graham Muller, Ngaio and Les Hanson, Captain Scott Marina, Sir Llew Edwards, and Beatriz Llenin found some of the sources and/or commented on several of the chapters, or arranged personal contacts. My wife Maria has been consistently supportive during the writing of this book, which included our research and travels in New Zealand and the Pacific.

I should acknowledge the generous welcome and important insights given by many delightful New Zealand colleagues when teaching in North Island years ago. There have also been innumerable helpful encounters with other New Zealanders, and other Polynesian and Melanesian people over the years in many of the islands mentioned here.

Several of the most fascinating examples are drawn from Professor Crocombe's massive and enlightening book *The South Pacific*.

John H. Chambers January 2003

Preface

New Zealand is about as far away from Britain and a world away from Washington as it is possible to get. It also lies in a region, the South Pacific, that is as different from Europe as can be imagined. This lucid, wide ranging, well researched and wholly enlightening book paints a vivid picture of an exotic area that, even today, remains both distant and profoundly alluring.

I suspect that most readers will be unprepared for the sheer scale and potential complexity of the subject matter. As John Chambers points out, the South Pacific Ocean is 'massive, covering about a fifth of the whole surface of the earth. When European navigators first sailed into the vast region we now call Polynesia, they were astonished. Not merely were there myriads of islands but, immense distances from the nearest continents, they were populated by brown-skinned strikingly built men, and graceful and comely women. Equally startling were the exotic cultures of these Islanders, blessed by eternal summer, with their strange gods and practices ... and, most disconcerting of all, on many islands, a guilt-free and enthusiastic sex life – the opposite of the crabbed constraints of Christian Europe.'

Many of these early impressions are still embedded in Western perceptions and culture, typified in the rather self-conscious musical *South Pacific* and in the stereotype of the warm blooded, smooth skinned, flower garlanded, Polynesian maiden, alluring and available. Merely to let some of the islands' names roll off the tongue was sufficiently magical: Samoa, Tahiti, Tonga, Fiji and so on. The region was also seen as the ultimate refuge for alienated or questioning Europeans, and it is no accident that creative geniuses like Paul Gaugin and Robert

Louis Stevenson went there for inspiration and the experience of an environment that was almost otherworldly.

The flip side of this was less productive for the indigenous population, in that the arrival of the Europeans brought not merely varying degrees of imperial control but also diseases that far too often devastated communities lacking natural immunity. Not that whites had it all their own way: Captain Cook was killed on Hawaii and the first Christian missionary to land on Erromango in the New Hebrides (now Vanuatu) was promptly eaten by his potential converts.

Two-thirds of the book is devoted to New Zealand, which apart from its developed economy and regional significance, is also the goal of most travellers and tourists. New Zealand has a strong and internationally recognised image, and a reputation (not always justified by a close scrutiny of its colonial history) of cordial relations between the dominant white settler majority and Maori minority.

New Zealand's attractions are manifold. First there is the sheer physical beauty of the landscape, a glorious fact of nature that has recently been presented world wide through the stunning settings of the award winning films *The Lord of the Rings*. The mountains, shores, forests and open spaces of New Zealand are as crisp and wholesome as any locally produced apple. Then there are the increasingly sophisticated urban centres like Auckland, Christchurch and Wellington. New Zealand wines have become world famous, as have local writers, filmmakers and artists. Sporting success is there in abundance from the legendary triumphs of the All Black rugby teams, to the athletes and cricketers.

This book provides an excellent guide through the shoals and thickets of this whole extraordinary region. After reading it, not merely does one know exactly what happened to the mutineers of Captain Bligh's *Bounty*, and the difference between Polynesia and Melanesia, but also that New Zealand was the first English-speaking state to introduce serious social welfare reforms a century ago. Above all, one's appetite is whetted for a journey to a part of the world that seems to have just about everything.

Denis Judd
London, 2003

Waterworld

The South Pacific Ocean is massive, covering about a fifth of the whole surface of the earth. When European navigators first sailed into the vast region we now call Polynesia, they were astonished. Not merely were there myriad islands but, immense distances from the nearest continents, they were populated with brown-skinned, strikingly built men, graceful and comely women. Equally startling were the exotic cultures of these Islanders, blessed by eternal summer, with their strange gods and practices, their generally bountiful natural provisions, and, most disconcerting of all, on many islands a guilt-free, enthusiastic sexual life – the opposite of the crabbed constraints of Christian Europe.

Farther west lay the islands we now term Melanesia. Here the people were darker and smaller in stature. Whereas most Polynesians were fascinated by strangers, the Melanesians were often deeply suspicious, many murderously Xenophobic.

The very existence of such Islanders, together with their startlingly different cultures, posed profound intellectual puzzles. How did the people get there? We know there have been many periods when ocean levels were much lower and people in parts of the west Pacific could migrate across land bridges. Even during periods of high sea levels like the present time, many of the high islands of Melanesia can be seen one from another. It would have been comparatively simple for people to migrate island to island. But the Polynesian islands are hundreds, even thousands of miles apart, far from populated mainlands, across terrifying stretches of open ocean, and this would still have been so even in periods of low ocean levels.

How was it possible for ancestors of these Polynesians to reach such isolated specks of land using unsophisticated sailing vessels? Had they stumbled upon their island homes, lucky to survive starvation and dehydration after being lost and blown far off course? Or had they purposefully performed some of the most marvellous feats of navigation in the history of the world?

The peoples of Polynesia inhabited an area as large as Africa. Yet, from the Maoris of temperate New Zealand in the far south-west, to Tuvalu and Tokelau near the torrid Equator, to the forlorn isolated

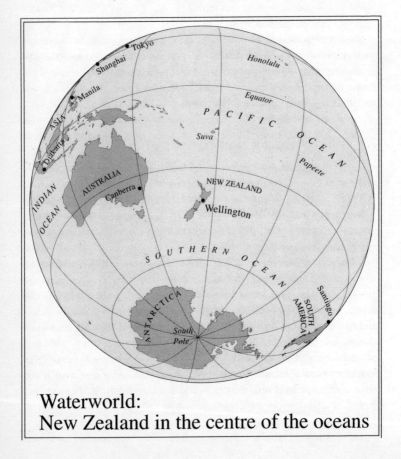

Waterworld:
New Zealand in the centre of the oceans

Easter Islanders 5,500 miles to the east, these people shared much the same culture and spoke closely related languages (the same point applies to the Hawaiians). Why was this? Conversely, why were the Melanesians so diverse, though they inhabited a much smaller region?

Why and how did the ancestors of the New Zealand Maori arrive in their islands, so far away from the balmy Polynesian tropics? How did the Maori, the most distinct of all the Polynesian sub-groups, evolve? And how, five hundred years later, did the British, another nautical and island people, also come in small ships to colonize New Zealand on the opposite side of the world from their homelands?

To such questions and many others this book tries to provide answers, most well-established by scholars and scientists, some more debatable. One thing is certain: 2000 years before the Vikings of Europe, the Polynesians (and many of the Melanesians) were already peoples of the sea.

Region covered by this book

As shown in the map on page 5, following the scheme first devised by the French savant, Dumont D'Urville in the early 1800s, the islands of the Pacific are traditionally divided into three ethnogeographic regions. These are Polynesia (many islands), Melanesia (black islands), and Micronesia (small islands). The South Pacific Ocean, here interpreted as the Pacific Ocean *south of the Equator*, includes all Polynesia except for the Hawaiian Islands, and all of Melanesia. It excludes most of Micronesia. Division at the Equator makes political as well as cartographical sense. This is because the main North Pacific islands, the Hawaiian Islands, the islands of Micronesia (Marshalls, Carolines, etc.) and the Aleutians are all either a US state, parts of a state, or territories closely associated with the USA.

About two-thirds of this book is devoted to the primary topic, the history of New Zealand. On the basis of almost every criterion it is the most significant land mass and nation in the South Pacific Ocean★ and

★ The Australian continent washed by the Pacific Ocean in the east and the Indian Ocean in the west is not IN the South Pacific. Australia is considered in a separate volume in the Traveller's Histories, written by the present author.

the destination for the overwhelming number of travellers to South Pacific islands. Other Polynesian island groups considered are Samoa (formerly Western Samoa) and American Samoa, Tonga, French Polynesia (Tahiti, the Marquesas, etc.), Easter Island, and the Cook Islands. (The tiny Cook Islands attract about five times their total population in tourists per year.) Less significant Polynesian islands such as Niue, Pitcairn, Tuvalu, and Tokelau are mentioned in passing.

All these islands share much early Polynesian history with New Zealand. Some share colonial history; Samoa, the Cook Islands (as well as Niue and Tokelau) were dependencies of New Zealand for almost fifty years, and all have political and economic ties. These islands have also provided significant numbers of migrants to New Zealand in recent years.

The Melanesian island of Fiji is treated in detail. Over the years many of Fijians have arrived in New Zealand. Other Melanesian states, Papua New Guinea, Solomon Islands, Vanuatu, and New Caledonia, are also considered to some extent, their recent history in particular. All five have ancient historical links to Polynesia, and Fiji is the second, and New Caledonia the fourth (after French Polynesia) most popular South Pacific island destination.

Note: nouns used to refer to the peoples of New Zealand

Modern Maori (and New Zealanders generally) normally refer to themselves and their tribes (iwi) without use of the definite article. Thus they would say, 'Maori/Ngati Ira arrived here in ...' rather than 'The Maori/Ngati Ira arrived here in ...' Modern 'Pakeha' New Zealanders also follow this usage. In accordance with normal world-wide English usage the present book uses the definite article in front of 'Maori', except where reasons of euphony, style, or syntax would omit it. It also uses 'Maori', as do all New Zealanders, for both singular and plural.

In New Zealand the word, 'Pakeha' means New Zealander of European descent. It is a Maori word. It is used by both ethnic groups, so most modern New Zealanders see their country as populated by

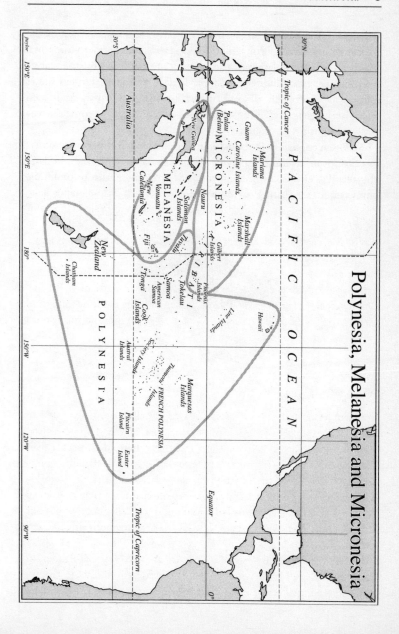

Maori and Pakeha (and others, mainly Asians). This usage, whereby the majority and more economically powerful and formerly imperial ethnic group unremarkably uses a term given them by the native people is perhaps unique in history. It is as if modern United States citizens of European descent, naturally and unself-consciously in everyday language were to call themselves 'Palefaces' or some native-American term.

To lessen confusion for non–New Zealand readers the words 'settler' or 'European' are mostly used here rather than 'Pakeha'. In later chapters 'Pakeha' is occasionally adopted when it appears to make the point better than 'settler' or 'European'.

CHAPTER ONE

A Brief History of the Physical Environment

Extraordinary Variety of South Pacific Islands

The South Pacific Ocean, the site for this story, is vast – about 32 million square miles. It could swallow all of Europe, Asia, North America and much of South America. From the eastern Australian coast to Chile is about 9,000 miles (14,480k).

Viewed from the air the well-known, compact, high islands such as Tahiti and Bora Bora show a core of bright green mountain ringed with shining sand, girdled in turn by a turquoise lagoon – itself enclosed by an outer circle of surf-splashed reef. And around all this stretch the amethysts and sapphires of the deep ocean.

There are other kinds of islands too, for within this mighty half-ocean islands exist in immense variety. New Guinea is the second largest island in the world after Greenland. The North and South Islands of New Zealand, at 45,000 sq.miles/116,500 sq.k (somewhat larger than Ohio) and 58,000 sq.miles/150,000 sq.k (say, Greece or Michigan), are amongst the largest in the world. In contrast, some of the Cook Islands are less than a square mile each – you can hike across some in ten minutes.

The size of other well-known South Pacific islands varies widely. The main island of New Caledonia is 9,000 sq.miles/23,000 sq.k (as big as Wales), Viti Levu, the largest Fijian island, covers about 4,000 sq.miles/10,000 sq.k – a little smaller than the US state of Connecticut or the old English county of Yorkshire; Tahiti is 400 sq.miles/1000 sq.k, similar to New York City or Greater London or Sydney; Easter Island, and Tongatapu (the largest of the Tongan islands) are each about 60 sq.miles/155 sq.k.

The physical form also varies enormously. Islands range from South Island with its 300-mile-long high snowy mountain chain of the Southern Alps; to the low flat coral atolls of the northern Society Islands and Tuamotus; to Bora Bora and Tahiti, with their spectacular sculpted volcanic mountains; or the perfect volcanic cone of Kao in Tonga, rising 3,400 feet (1109m) right from the ocean – one the most beautiful sights in all the Pacific. Also in Tonga lies freakish Fonuafo'ou or Falcon Island; at irregular intervals this volcanic island rises above, and then disappears below sea level. Its greatest recorded height was around 500 feet (152m) in the later 1890s.

Flora and fauna seem to have originated overwhelmingly in South-East Asian archipelagoes. Although all Pacific islands were originally heavily forested, and most still are, the farther east one travels the less favourable are the islands to human habitation, with fewer edible plants and animals. New Caledonia has some 3,500 species of vegetation, but, more than 3,000 miles to the east, the Society Islands (Tahiti) have only about 1,000 species; and far-flung Easter Island, 1,500 miles farther to the east again, had only 47, mostly sedges, ferns, and grasses ('had' because most were destroyed by the early Polynesians). Or consider the example of land birds. In the Solomon Islands (off the coast of New Guinea) there are some 127 known species, 54 in Fiji 1,000 miles south-east, 17 in the Society Islands another 2,000 miles on, and there were merely 6 land birds on Easter Island. Such statistics show that mother nature colonized these islands (with a few exceptions) from the west.

High islands support diverse plantlife, atolls have little, mainly drought-resistant species such as coconuts and pandanus. Despite their lush appearance, even high islands are poor in comparison with the riotous plant-life of the islands of Indonesia or the Philippines. Naturally, the ecology of the smaller and more easterly islands is extremely fragile, a fact which travellers to these precious pearls should remember.

Island temperatures (excluding New Zealand) range from warm to hot, with those nearer the Equator such as Samoa a little hotter than those farther south such as Tonga, but the ever-present sea moderates humidity and there are usually sea breezes. First-time visitors from temperate lands find this climate difficult and enervating. The sun sets around 6pm all year and there is little twilight.

Windward slopes of high islands receive more rainfall from the prevailing south-east trade winds than do leeward sides.

How the Pacific Islands were Formed

The surface or crust of the planet Earth consists of about a dozen major rigid 'plates' and numerous smaller ones. Thousand mile-long fissures in the ocean floor allow new crustal material to force its way from below. As this material spreads sideways from the fissures, the plates are slowly forced into continuous movement (typically 1 in./2.5 cm a year, though reaching 8 ins/20 cms in places in the South Pacific) across the planet's surface, and as a result collide in several different ways with complex local variations. The ways which concern us are 'subduction', which occurs when one plate thrusts under another; and 'crustal shortening', where two clashing plates push material upwards into ridges and mountains.

Most plates are made of old crust, mainly continental but with parts of adjacent ocean floor, but some plates consist of mostly younger ocean-floor crust.

The two plates in our story are the Indo-Australian Plate and the mighty Pacific Plate, the world's largest. The Indo-Australian Plate consists of two sections of continental crust with some ocean floor between. The Pacific Plate is predominantly oceanic crust, but carries some continental crust such as the underwater Campbell Plateau south-east of New Zealand.

All the present-day continents once formed an enormous landmass known as Pangaea (all Earth). About 200 million years ago a huge piece, Gondwana or Gondwanaland, split off and was for a time centred over the South Polar region of the earth. As Gondwana moved it further divided into Africa, South America, Antarctica, India, and Australia. There was also a continually changing mass which, slowly separating from Australia, and at times mostly under water, eventually became the islands of New Zealand.

New Guinea, Vanuatu, New Caledonia, western Fiji and Tongatapu (the main island of Tonga) either ride on the Indo-Australian tectonic plate or on mini-plates of their own. The remaining islands of Fiji, Tonga, the Samoas, the Cook Islands, the Society Islands, the Tuamotus and the Marquesas rest upon the Pacific Plate. Riding above and/or near the clashing plate boundary, New Zealand exists in an ambiguous category of its own.

Traditionally, Pacific Islands have been classified as Continental or Oceanic. Continental Islands such as New Zealand and New Caledonia were formed in large part by the movements and interrelated collisions of the tectonic plates. Oceanic Islands were formed by volcanic material thrusting up through cracks or fissures in the moving plates.

CONTINENTAL ISLANDS

Continental Islands ring the broad western Pacific margin and consist mainly of metamorphic rocks, sediments, and andesitic volcanic material; these contrast with the basically basaltic volcanic material of the Oceanic Islands of the central and eastern South Pacific.

Collision of plates in subduction or crustal shortening, coupled with volcanic upthrust, have produced the long islands or strings of islands of New Guinea, the Bismarck Archipelago and the Solomon Islands, New Caledonia, and New Zealand, with their long mountain chains. Faulted and folded, these mountains reach greater altitudes and their upthrust crustal rocks have produced richer soils than the smaller Oceanic Islands farther east. These Continental Islands are separated from the Oceanic Islands by deep ocean trenches formed along the borders of the clashing tectonic plates.

The deep Tonga Trench east of most of the Tongan Islands has been formed as the thinner Pacific Plate has thrust under the Indo-Australian Plate. Many Tongan islands are thus rising while Samoan islands, near the edge of the subducting Pacific Plate, have been sinking. In fact the first settled Samoan areas are now underwater. In contrast, just east of New Caledonia the Indo-Australian Plate is thrusting under the Pacific Plate. As a result New Caledonia is slowly sinking on the east and the islands of Vanuatu are rising. And the impressive Vanuatu volcanoes belch lava – the result of the monstrous grinding and heat generated by the moving plates. Fiji, stranded in the middle of this activity, remains surprisingly quiet geologically.

OCEANIC ISLANDS – HIGH VOLCANIC ISLANDS AND LOW CORAL ATOLLS

As the Pacific Plate moves in a generally north-westerly direction, it passes across many so-called 'hot-spots' in the earth's crust but, relatively speaking, the hot-spots remain in the same place beneath the plate. Hot-spots are so-named because it is there that volcanic material is continually being pushed up. Over the aeons, some of this volcanic material has forced its way through fissures in the Pacific Plate, to build the volcanoes which have been the source of the multitude of South Pacific Oceanic Islands.

Many of these volcanoes have failed to reach the surface of the ocean and have become what geologists and oceanographers call 'seamounts'. (Prior to the development of the geological explanation of Plate Tectonics in the 1960s and 1970s these were especially puzzling undersea phenomena, for they are usually found in long lines.) Many volcanoes however continued to erupt, and so rose far above sea level. As volcanic material kept accumulating these formed what are called High Oceanic Islands, or High Islands

So, over tens of millions of years a chain of new seamounts, or volcanic islands, or a mixture of both is formed. Examples are the long north-west oriented chains of the Cook Islands, the Austral Islands, and the Society Islands. The world's best-known chain is perhaps the Hawaiian Islands in the North Pacific.

Young volcanic Oceanic Islands such as Tahiti and Bora Bora (in the Society Islands), and Tutuila (in American Samoa), stand in splendour high above the ocean. But with the passing of time all such islands begin sinking under their own weight and are worn down by erosion. This is why islands at the north-west end of such chains are low and flat, many having become atolls. Consider the long chain of Tuamotus and Gambiers in eastern Polynesia. Because of their great age, the Tuamotu Islands are all low islands such as Manihi and Rangiroa Atolls. The latter, about 220 miles/354k north-east of Tahiti, encloses a massive 47 × 16 miles/76 × 26k lagoon – famous for its scuba divers who come to swim with the sharks. But the Gambiers to the south-east, having passed over the hot-spot more recently, are high islands. At the south-east end of the Austral Islands a seamount known as MacDonald is now only 164 feet (50m) below the ocean surface and growing at about a cubic mile per century.

Sometimes, after long geological ages, submerged coral islands are again uplifted above the surface by volcanic action, or to balance the massive weight of a volcano pressing on the seabed. Niue, and Henderson in the Pitcairn Islands are examples. The best known of all re-uplifted islands is low, flat, southward-sloping Tongatapu, upon which the Tongan capital Nuku'alofa stands.

CORAL REEFS AND THE MAKING OF CORAL ATOLLS

Coral reefs are created by the accumulation of billions of limestone skeletons left by millions of generations of tiny coral polyps, most no larger than a pinhead. Polyp skeletons are generally white, but living polyps are multicoloured. Coral thrives in clear salt water where the temperature remains at 65°F (18°C) or above. The solid base for polyp growth must not be less than about 160 feet (49m) below the surface. The colony of coral polyps grows slowly upward, building upon the skeletons of earlier generations, until it reaches low tide mark. It then continues to grow, but outward. Healthy reefs can spread several inches per year.

Reefs are one of nature's great realms of ecological diversity and extravagant life, rivalled only by tropical rainforests. When a snorkeller slips into the turquoise waters of a lagoon, paddles across the yellow sand and approaches the reef, the scene is an immense colourful fantasy. Thousands of fish of hundreds of species individually and in schools dart in and out of the diverse coral formations: damselfish, butterfly fish, soldierfish, triggerfish, and so forth. On the lagoon floor and ensconced in the innumerable lower nooks and crannies live a startling variety of invertebrate creatures, large and small crabs, sea cucumbers, shrimps, seasnails, colourful nudibranches. And, mostly at night, out come the moray eels, barracuda, and other predators. Parrot fish, pike, jackfish, stingrays, and small sharks patrol the larger lagoons.

Lengthy reefs have formed along the coasts of several Pacific

Continental Islands. New Caledonia has massive reefs along each coast, the 335-mile-long (539k) NorthWest Barrier Reef and the 370-mile (595k) SouthWest Barrier Reef. The Great Sea Reef of Fiji stretches about 160 miles (257k). There are substantial barrier reefs around many high Pacific Oceanic islands.

Coral reefs have also been crucial in the geological creation of the low Oceanic Islands called 'atolls'. Atolls are the final stage in the 20 million-year story of the growth and decay of Oceanic Islands. This explanation was first worked out by evolutionist Charles Darwin (1809-82) during his epic voyage in the *Beagle* in the 1830s. (His captain during that voyage, Robert FitzRoy, was later made governor of New Zealand.) Darwin's idea that Pacific Islands evolve is now accepted by the whole geological community.

The sequence is as follows (see diagram). A volcano spawned by a hot-spot bursts through the surface of the ocean and eventually forms a high island. A fringing coral reef slowly builds around the coast of this island. After growing to its maximum height and being carried away from the hot-spot by the moving plate, the volcano becomes extinct. The island slowly erodes, but, more important, it begins to sink under its own great mass. The growth of the fringing reef keeps pace with the sinking. The reef also acquires sand, driftwood, vegetation, and debris. As the island continues its subsidence the coral reef becomes detached and an ever-widening and deepening lagoon forms between island and what has now become a barrier reef. Finally, the island disappears from sight to leave an approximately circular blue lagoon surrounded by what is now a coral atoll which marks the original boundary of the volcanic island. Such lagoons may be many miles wide but the land of the atoll islets is normally only about 200–400 yards/metres wide. The beaches of such atolls are formed by the powerful Pacific surf which pounds the coral, shells and assorted debris into tiny fragments – the pristine white of the travel posters.

The French Polynesian islands of Tahiti, Moorea, and Bora Bora are good examples of volcanic islands partway along this sequence. Here high extinct volcanoes are surrounded by circular reefs enclosing blue–green lagoons. All are sinking at about a centimetre a century. Tahiti, the youngest, has a narrow lagoon and the highest peak at 7352 ft/2241m;

The creation of a coral atoll

A new volcano rises
from the ocean floor.

Volcano becomes extinct and
acquires a fringing coral reef.

The volcanic island erodes and begins to sink.
The reef continues to grow upward to surface and outward,
acquires sand, debris, and vegetation to form islets.
A lagoon is left between sinking island and reef islets.

The island continues to sink entirely below the ocean surface,
leaving the ring of reef islets, which now circle an enclosed lagoon.
A coral atoll has been created.

jtaylor

Moorea has a slightly wider lagoon and a 3369 ft/1,207m peak; Bora Bora, the oldest, has a much wider lagoon and a lower 2385 ft/727m peak. Time travel to all three in 20 or so million years and only circular coral atolls enclosing lagoons will remain. About 250 miles/400k to the north-west, the islands of Bellingshausen and Scilly are already atolls.

By drilling into the 800-mile-long chain of atolls of the Tuamotus to the north-east of Tahiti, oceanographers have confirmed the sequence of reef growth from high island to atoll. In islands at the younger south-east end of the chain the coral rock is 1148 ft/350m thick; in the middle at Hao Atoll it is some 1970 ft/600m; and at the north-west end at the great atoll of Rangiroa the coral rock is about 3280 ft/1000m thick.

Physical Features of New Zealand

GEOLOGICAL HISTORY

Hundreds of millions of years ago most of the original area of the various continents consisted of rigid central sections of rock called shields. As these shields slowly eroded, the sediments produced settled along the continental margins. Volcanic and plate movements transformed and uplifted this marginal material, adding it to the shields. These processes were repeated many times and in this manner the continents grew in area.

From some 600 million years ago to about 200 million years ago much of the material that would become the islands of New Zealand formed part of the margins of the then contiguous continents of Antarctica and Australia within Gondwana. Let us call this material 'proto-New Zealand'.

As plate tectonic movement drifted the continents into their present positions, proto-New Zealand was at first attached to Australia. About 85 million years ago proto-New Zealand severed from Australia; by 60 million BC the Tasman Sea had opened, and proto-New Zealand was eroding away. By 30 million BC proto-New Zealand was now close to its present position, but much of it lay under the ocean, with little more than an archipelago of flat islands reaching above sea-level. These flat islands formed extensive coastal swamps and large areas of peat. In the

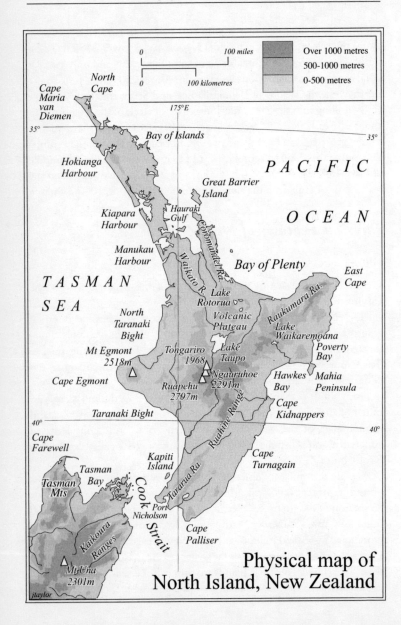

0   100 miles

0   100 kilometres

Over 1000 metres
500-1000 metres
0-500 metres

Cape Maria van Diemen

North Cape

175°E

35°   35°

Bay of Islands

Hokianga Harbour

PACIFIC

Great Barrier Island

Kiapara Harbour

Hauraki Gulf

OCEAN

Manukau Harbour

Waikato R.

Coromandel Ra.

Bay of Plenty

East Cape

TASMAN

Lake Rotorua

SEA

North Taranaki Bight

Volcanic Plateau

Raukumara Ra.

Lake Waikaremoana

Mt Egmont 2518m

Tongariro 1968

Lake Taupo

Poverty Bay

Cape Egmont

Ngauruhoe 2291m

Ruapehu 2797m

Hawkes Bay

Mahia Peninsula

Taranaki Bight

Cape Kidnappers

Ruahine Range

40°   40°

Cape Farewell

Kapiti Island

Cape Turnagain

Tasman Bay

Tasman Mts

Tararua Ra.

Cook Strait

Port Nicholson

Cape Palliser

Kaikoura Ranges

Mt Una 2301m

jtaylor

Physical map of North Island, New Zealand

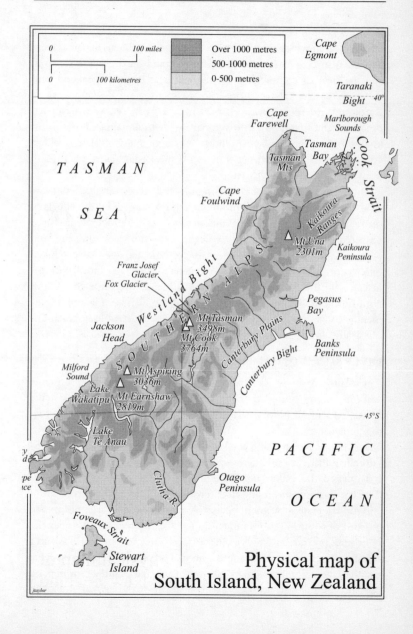

0   100 miles
0   100 kilometres

Over 1000 metres
500-1000 metres
0-500 metres

Cape
Egmont

Taranaki
Bight   40°

TASMAN

SEA

Cape
Farewell

Tasman
Bay

Marlborough
Sounds

Cook
Strait

Tasman
Mts

Cape
Foulwind

Kaikoura
Ranges

Mt Una
2301m

Kaikoura
Peninsula

Franz Josef
Glacier
Fox Glacier

Westland Bight

SOUTHERN ALPS

Pegasus
Bay

Jackson
Head

Mt Tasman
3498m
Mt Cook
3764m

Canterbury Plains

Banks
Peninsula

Milford
Sound

Mt Aspiring
3036m

Canterbury Bight

Lake
Wakatipu

Mt Earnshaw
2819m

Lake
Te Anau

PACIFIC

Clutha R.

Otago
Peninsula

OCEAN

Foveaux Strait

Stewart
Island

Physical map of
South Island, New Zealand

jtaylor

next few million years there was slow subsidence. The swamps became shallow seas in which sand and mud eroding from the higher areas were deposited to cover the peat, limestone formed on the ocean bottom, and the heat of compression turned the peat into the coal, oil, and natural gas, which have proved so useful to New Zealanders since European settlement. In the last 20 million years renewed uplift has produced the islands we know today, with mountain-building most intense about four or five million years ago. New Zealand's oldest volcanoes, such as the extinct cones on Banks Peninsula, were erupting from about 15 million years ago.

During these changes the evolving bits and pieces and shape of New Zealand have been radically modified and rearranged: by the effects of many ice ages which varied the ocean's depth and extended and retracted shorelines; by mighty volcanic explosions covering the land deep in volcanic debris, and by plate tectonic activity that produced uplift and subsidence and massive lateral slippage. Fiordland, for instance, in the far south-west of South Island, was once contiguous with northern Nelson in the far north of the island – a lateral movement of over 300 miles (500 ks)! As a result modern New Zealand is physically almost as complex as a continent.

DIVERSITY: VOLCANOES TO GLACIERS

The islands of New Zealand now ride above several very unstable sections of the boundary between the Indo-Australian and Pacific Plates. As a result New Zealand is still evolving geologically – in two different ways.

Just east of North Island the Pacific Plate is sliding beneath the Indo-Australian Plate in a subduction zone. In the ocean floor this movement has opened the Hikurangi Trough and the even deeper Kermadec Trench. Earthquakes result after tensions build to critical proportions and sudden plate movement occurs. As the subducting plate plunges to a depth of about 50 to 60 miles /80 to 96k, the rock melts under the enormous pressure and rises to the surface as magma. In North Island a number of impressive volcanoes, thermal areas, and depressions have resulted, the volcanoes being vents for the magma. A line of former and current volcanic activity reaches from north of the city of Auckland through the Volcanic Plateau to the centre of the island. Auckland itself rests upon about 50 cones of extinct volcanoes, and Rangitoto Island in its harbour erupted only 600 years ago. Another volcanic line reaches from active White Island in the Bay of Plenty and across the same Volcanic Plateau to Mt Ruapehu. On the Volcanic Plateau are highly active thermal areas of steam, fumaroles, geothermal springs, geysers, and boiling mudpools. These are centred on Rotorua, and the picturesque blue Lake Taupo, New Zealand's largest.

In the year AD 177 in the Taupo region, greater than Krakatoa, louder than the Tunguska Event, there occurred earth's mightiest explosion of the last few thousand years. Fortunately there were then no Maori inhabitants to be obliterated by this volcanic blast. Debris was flung an estimated 40 miles/64k into the atmosphere, and a rapid flow of pyroclastic material rushed in every direction for fifty miles or more. This plasma-like liquid even climbed up the slopes of adjacent volcanoes such as Tongariro. The vast hole and lake produced by earlier explosions were made even larger and, filled with fresh water, became Lake Taupo. From the lake spills the country's longest river, the beautiful Waikato, which caresses its way through 265 miles/425k of now lush green farmlands.

Farther south rear the spectacular active volcanoes of Tongariro, Ngauruhoe, and Ruapehu 9176 ft/2797m, and the smaller Pihanga. Ruapehu produced regular significant eruptions during the 1990s. New Zealanders were reminded of the dangers of Ruapehu on Christmas Eve 1953. The crater lake at the top burst and the resulting watersodden avalanche washed away a railway bridge on the Main Trunk Railway to the south. Minutes later a crowded express train plunged into the abyss, killing 153 people. To the west lies a line of three volcanoes of which Mt Taranaki/Egmont at 8260 ft/2518m, the Fuji of New Zealand, is the highest. Taranaki is dormant at present, having last erupted about 350 years ago.

Relatively recent uplifts of land produced by plate movement occurred during the 1855 Wellington and 1933 Napier earthquakes. The land of the present airport and plains around Napier rose from the ocean, and in Wellington, a proposed sheltered boat anchorage became a playing field.

The landmass of the South Island is growing in a different manner. Below the island the two plates are smashing into each other in the process called 'crustal shortening'. In this region the rock material of the Pacific Plate is not thin oceanic crust but thick continental crust. This refuses to plunge in a subduction zone but has slid past the Indo-Australian Plate and has uplifted material to form the mighty, still-rising 300-mile (480k) mountain spine of the Southern Alps. The steep sides on the west of the Alps are evidence of geologically recent uplift. Mt Cook (Aoraki) (12,300 ft/3755m), the country's highest peak, stands in the Alps, together with 16 other peaks above 10,000 ft/3050m. Midway along the west coast is a short and narrow coastal plain, the alluvium of a few mossy, fast-flowing rivers.

Reminding us that geological change is never ending, in December 1991, a monstrous section of Mt Cook's top ripped away to produce a massive landslide which altered the shape of the mountain forever. Something like 170 million cub.ft/14 million cub.m of rock were flung across adjacent glaciers. For, over the aeons more than 300 glaciers have formed in the Southern Alps. The largest are the quickly moving Tasman (18 miles long), Fox, and Franz-Joseph. Earlier geological periods have also produced long, deep lakes such as turquoise Wakatipu and Te Anau. Their beds were scraped out by former expanding glaciers, and filled with water as the glaciers retreated.

To the east, alluvial deposits washed down from the Alps have formed the gently sloping fertile Canterbury Plains. Poking into the ocean, elevated Banks Peninsula near Christchurch and Otago Peninsula near Dunedin consist of several extinct volcanoes each. Originally separated from the mainland, they were the product of earlier volcanic activity produced at the plate boundary.

In the south-west corner lies mythic Fiordland. Here, former glaciated U-shaped valleys have become flooded by the ocean to distances of 10–20 miles (16–32k) inland. In such places as the superb Milford Sound, the fiord walls can drop sheer for thousands of feet into the sea. Fed by almost 300 inches (7,600mm) of rainfall a year, hundreds of cascades rush down them, and the air is sharp with clean invigorating oxygen.

Fiordland in New Zealand, with the sheer cliffs of Milford Sound

CLIMATE

All other Polynesian islands except the Chathams lie within the broad belt of the north-east and south-east trade winds. New Zealand, in contrast, lies far to the south, between the stormy waters and changeable weather of the Tasman Sea and the problematic 'Roaring Forties' winds of the Southern Ocean/South Pacific south of latitude 40 degrees. The 800 mile/1290k long, almost north–south islands, together with the contrasting altitudes of mountain, hill, and plain, have produced some climatic diversity.

Other Polynesian islands have a tropical climate, but New Zealand varies from the Alpine climate of the Southern Alps and cool-temperate climate of southern New Zealand to the warm temperate lands of much of the North Island and the almost sub-tropical region of Northland.

The prevailing winds being trapped by the Alps, rainfall is heaviest on the west coast of the South Island, with most of the coast reaching levels comparable to Milford Sound. In contrast the Canterbury Plains in the east receive only 25 inches. In the North Island rainfall is more evenly distributed, though again the precipitation on the west coast and the western sides of the volcanoes is a little higher. Auckland in the north receives about 47 inches (1200mm), Wellington in the south a little less, with the island as a whole averaging about 50 ins./1300mm. Such levels of rainfall and fertile soils encourage the pristine greenness which so startles the visitor.

FLORA AND FAUNA: A LUSH BIRDLAND

Lush, sub-tropical forest thrives in Northland, cool deeper green temperate forest in higher parts of the South Island, tussock grassland in central Otago, and verdant pasture introduced by the settlers in Canterbury and much of the North Island. In many places during the twentieth century fast-growing introduced pine trees have commandeered the landscape.

Australia and proto-New Zealand separated from the rest of Gondwana prior to the evolution of mammals. (Fossils of dinosaurs, from some 65 million years ago have been dug up in the Hawkes Bay region.) The only New Zealand mammal which existed prior to human settlement was the bat – and that was obviously immigrant rather than native.

In proto-New Zealand in the absence of higher animal life, birds took over and filled many of the evolutionary niches occupied by mammals on the continents (birds are descended from dinosaurs). Somehow, despite all the massive geological and harsh climatic changes, the ancestors of today's New Zealand birds survived on their travelling proto-New Zealand land 'rafts'. A handful of other peculiar species seem to have survived the journey too – amphibians such as earless frogs which do not croak, primitive tiny reptiles like small lizards, strange wingless crickets called wetas, and the craggy, squirrel-sized, iguana-like tuataras, which may be 200 million years old.

New Zealand, the world's largest oceanic archipelago, became history's greatest Birdland. For the larger birds, in the absence of most predators, flight was no longer an advantage and they evolved to become ground-foraging and flightless. By the time the first Polynesians arrived, about a third of all birds were either flightless, or had difficulty flying. Some, such as the kakapo, learned to climb trees. The various species of moa, which over the aeons even lost their wings, were the evolutionary equivalent of horses and deer. The largest of them probably needed to eat as much vegetation a day as does a buffalo. The great New Zealand eagle, *Harpagornis*, which could have a ten-feet wingspan and preyed on the moa, filled the evolutionary niche of the absent predator mammals such as jaguars and tigers – and it too spent a lot of time scavenging on the ground. In place of the cow was the takahe, a large grass-eating wading bird. The penguins, pukekos (still in the process of losing the use of their wings, i.e., they fly but awkwardly), keas, and kiwis were the equivalent of wolves, foxes, and dogs. Kiwis, flightless foragers of forest floors, were and are bizarre. Uniquely, they have nostrils at the end of their prodigious Pinocchio beaks, feathers more like hair, a body temperature similar to mammals, and lay an egg that may be a fifth of the bird's body weight. The kea is a ferocious forest parrot. Today, adapted to a new environment, it tears open the backs of sheep as easily as it rips the rubber from the windows of cars. There were also shags and albatrosses. (Today, the most northerly habitat of the latter can be observed in a protected area on Otago Peninsula at the entrance to Dunedin Harbour.)

Over millions of years the New Zealand birds created their own unique but fragile ecology. That is why introduced species have done untold damage. The Polynesian rat brought by the early-Maori began the destruction. In the nineteenth and twentieth centuries, the rabbits and hares of the European settlers continued it. And the weasels, stoats, and ferrets introduced to control the latter when their numbers rocketed caused even more damage. For it was much easier for them to trap New Zealand's flightless birds than it was to catch rabbits! Chamois and Himalayan tahrs and the hoofs of ten species of deer destroyed unique alpine flora, and the Australian opossum brought in to begin a fur trade munched through much of the temperate forest. Today, dedicated New Zealanders are fighting a rearguard action to preserve the remaining bird populations.

Let us now find out how these human beings arrived in New Zealand and the scattered Pacific Islands.

CHAPTER TWO

Early South Pacific Cultures

The Melanesian Islands are an extension of the mainland of South East Asia, but the Polynesian islands lie at extreme distances from the populated continents of Australia, Asia, and the Americas. Yet, with sailing vessels which must have been constructed from the simplest of natural materials, Polynesian colonization spanned a vast open ocean. Prior to the development of the world-wide empires of Spain, Britain, and France after 1500, the Polynesians were the most widespread racial or ethnic group on earth – even more than the Mongols. Noting this, Captain James Cook wrote in his log in 1774: 'It is extraordinary that the same Nation should have spread themselves over the isles in this vast Ocean from New Zealand to this Island [Easter Is.] which is a fourth part of the circumference of the Globe.'

Despite being so massively dispersed, the cultures and languages of the various Polynesian island groups remained similar. But the cultures of Melanesia, though covering an area much smaller than Polynesia, are very diverse. Such facts raise fascinating questions. How, when, and why did the Melanesians and Polynesians ever reach all these islands, near galactic in number?

Melanesian Colonization

The questions about the Melanesians and Melanesian colonization are relatively easy to answer. Melanesians originated in South East Asia. Settlement seems to have occurred in several stages of a long-term movement. The first involved the 'Papuans', who are now the main inhabitants of the New Guinea Highlands and Solomon Islands.

Archaeological evidence shows that some of these Papuans were well established before 50,000 BC.

Early Melanesian settlement was achieved at first by crossing the land-bridges in existence until about 16,000 BC when the polar ice began melting and oceans rose. Farther to the east 'island hopping' was possible as many large islands lie within sight of one another. Colonization would have proceeded from the New Guinea mainland, through the Bismarck Archipelago (New Britain, etc.) and the northern Solomons. Much later it seems to have continued on to Vanuatu, the Loyalty Islands, and so on.

A hostile environment of cyclones/hurricanes, foetid jungles, deadly snakes, crocodiles and a multitude of other dangers, together with belief in sorcery, produced a suspicion of strangers and the isolation of the various island cultures. Isolation encouraged cultural differentiation and diversity, increased by the immense length of time Melanesia has been settled. There are for instance at least 1,200 different languages in Melanesia.

As might be anticipated, the Polynesian/Melanesian distinction is not clean and clear. The Loyalty Islanders, for instance, just to the east of Melanesian New Caledonia, show a blend of Polynesian and Melanesian cultural features. Fiji also exhibits aspects of each.

Early Melanesian Material and Intellectual Culture

Less than a third the area of Polynesia, Melanesia contains a diverse range of cultures. Its languages comprise about a quarter of the world total; its peoples' skin colours range from deep black to light brown.

The great size and corrugated nature of Melanesian New Guinea, its impenetrable jungles, malarial swamps and permanently snow-capped mountains, ensured that hundreds of distinct tribes and languages would evolve. In that huge island patterns of settlement varied widely, lasting antipathies were encouraged, and bizarre practices and beliefs developed – such as ritual headhunting, and the idea that dreams and real life are a continuum. On the coastlands and in the plains of the wide Sepik River, large relatively permanent villages of about a thousand people grew up. Though the fertility of highlands

New Guinea made for comparatively dense populations, settlements were smaller.

Most Melanesians did little travel after ancestral occupation of an island or hilltop or valley. They lived in villages with others of their extended families, and might inter-marry with neighbouring villages. The Melanesian islands are mostly much larger than those of tropical Polynesia, so dissatisfied people also had the opportunity to establish new villages. Melanesians were deeply suspicious of strangers: Xenophobia was a common state of mind.

Rivalry was endemic, with sporadic warfare (skirmishes and raids) in reprisal, over women, infringement of territory, and belief in sorcery practised by neighbouring tribes. Personal status could be enhanced by success in war. In the highlands of Papua New Guinea there evolved a tradition of ritualized warfare. A custom unique to Melanesia and one which engendered fierce conflict was (and is still in a few districts) headhunting. Trophy heads were believed to increase spiritual protection and success.

Horticulture, agriculture, hunting and fishing were the chief sources of food. In New Guinea agriculture developed very early (root and tree crops, such as sago palm and sugarcane) by 10,000 BC. Techniques varied according to type and area of territory controlled.

Though with few exceptions, Melanesian tribes were self-sufficient in food, many liked to trade. In the Solomon Islands, for example, inland tribes exchanged horticultural products for the fish, shell-fish, eels, and seaweed of coastal tribes.

Trade in specialist items was usually by way of innumerable short links between adjacent islands. There were also a few tribes who gained a reputation for trading and seafaring, such as the Siassi of Papua New Guinea's north-west coast, who organized exchanges of pottery, pigs, and dogs between the coast and New Britain. Ceremonial exchange also existed, as in the famous and fascinating 220 mile/350k diameter Kula Ring, of the Trobriand Islands, D'Entrecasteaux, Louisades, etc., off the south-east coast of New Guinea, which has continued for perhaps 500 years. Here red shell disk necklaces move clockwise around the islands, while white shell armbands or bracelets move anti-clockwise. Specially constructed canoes, painted in red black and white designs, are used. The traders deal with the same partners throughout their lives. The number and quality of the shells possessed decides a man's status in the network.

In Melanesia, men and women occupied separate domains of activity. In contrast to Polynesia, women's political influence was negligible. Personal adornment also was almost everywhere a male prerogative. Elaborate male personal display might appear, in different islands, on any part of the body, even the genitalia. Decoration for the ritual warfare of the New Guinea Highlands involved massive head-dresses of feathers and plants. There was often equally remarkable physical separation of the sexes as well, with exclusive longhouses as a focus of male and military solidarity.

Sacred objects were kept in these longhouses, and the initiated males used the houses as the centre of their communal work, chatting, chewing betel nut, and sleeping. In their longhouses the males also believed themselves secure from the proscribed female pollution of menstruation and child-birth. These invoked special tapus (taboos) because they were universally considered unclean. In different islands women had to remain in their huts, or retire to special places outside the village. The latter would be lower in altitude, or lower down the local stream, so that women's blood would not pollute and bring supernatural harm upon the community.

INFLUENCE THROUGH FOOD: THE 'BIG MEN'

Slash and burn (sometimes called 'swidden') cultivation was common throughout much of Melanesia. A tribe would clear an area of forest and cultivate this for some years; when fertility declined they would just move on a mile or two and repeat the process, and eventually return to the original site. A fallow period of 7 to 12 years allowed time for soil to recover its fertility. Some tribes in New Guinea and New Caledonia had permanent gardens, and New Caledonians used irrigation to cultivate swampy species such as taro. Marsupials and birds were hunted, and pigs domesticated.

Melanesians had various ways of preserving food, but all had limitations, which restricted the accumulation of wealth. Intriguing social–political developments related to rapidly distributing any surpluses before they perished. The most interesting of these was (is) the so-called 'Big Man', whose social position rested upon economic and political success in competition with other Big Men. This involved obligations such as arranging alliances and marriages and distributing fat pigs. In New Guinea Vanuatu, and other parts of Melanesia, monumental feasts (mokas) with ritual exchange of goods demonstrated the wealth and status of the Big Men, and became fundamental to inter-village and tribal relationships. Big Men had high social and economic status, some concomitant political influence, but limited political power. Their rivalry channelled energy which might otherwise have resulted in aggression.

The nature of Melanesian political power varied. There were tribes with hereditary chiefs, groups without any hierarchy except the immediate family, and various shades between. In small villages the Big Man was merely the most significant person in the men's house. In large tribes and confederations the Big Man behaved more like a Polynesian chief.

SORCERY AND SUPERSTITION

Religious and superstitious beliefs involved innumerable local, capricious, often malevolent spirits who supposedly interfered in human affairs. Rituals were required to divert their influence or to channel it into something practical such as encouraging a crop or catching fish. Such rituals of spirit supplication or aid were usually part of the common knowledge of a tribe or village and there were few priests. In Melanesian religion there was little of the veneration and worship so typical of Christianity and Islam. Indeed there was little specialisation – all the men built houses, or collected betel nuts, or went on a raid to destroy another village. A few complex skills such as canoe making were the preserve of specialists.

Sorcery, universally believed, caused many problems and was the most obvious aspect of such beliefs. It achieved its aims without the need to coopt a helping spirit. Natural disasters such as a house struck by lightning, an epidemic, a crocodile attack, most deaths, and other events were attributed to sorcery.

Sorcery could be worked nearby or over long distances. There were two kinds. The first was either deliberate but unacknowledged, or attributed to a person but denied by him. In this situation there were few sorcerers as such. In the second kind, the sorcerer acknowledged his status and people went in fear of him. A supplicant would plead with a sorcerer to use his powers, such as bringing misfortune upon an enemy. Expensive gifts would be brought. To achieve a death, even something as valuable as a large double canoe might be given. This deliberate use of sorcery, either to bring about a result or to protect oneself from disaster, continues today. Modern New Guinean businessmen and politicians have been known to resort to it.

Unlike in Polynesia, no great sea barriers interposed themselves between the Melanesian islands. This fact allowed an enormous variety of plant, animal, bird, and insect life, useful and deadly, to travel both ways and to infest the various archipelagoes. Besides the dangerous animals there were millions of species of pests and insects. The latter carried vile parasites and endemic diseases such as dengue fever and malaria.

Melanesian life was lived under constant threat from real human and animal enemies, and from imagined human and spirit ones. Melanesians worked hard, lived in fear, and died young. Many still do.

Polynesian Origins and Colonization

EXPLANATIONS OF POLYNESIAN ORIGINS

Since the questions of origins were first asked, the consensus has been that the ancestors of the Polynesians had to come from the island chains off South East Asia. Assuming such an origin, the two obvious routes of colonization would have been through Micronesia or Melanesia.

During the first half of the 1900s there were several attempts to explain Polynesian origins in more detail. Since World War II and especially in recent decades wonderful discoveries in archaeology, linguistics, and genetics have made the answer fairly clear.

Because Melanesian culture with its enormous diversity is much older than Polynesian, the first suggestion was that there had been a rapid movement of people from the Philippines and/or Indonesia, which merely *skirted* the Melanesian islands, rather than passing through them, and so remained largely uninfluenced by Melanesian culture. Is there any evidence for this claim?

Yes there is. For modern linguists have discovered that the people of the island chains of South East Asia all speak languages from a family known as Austronesian. What is exciting is that the Polynesian languages are Austronesian too! Moreover, we find that the language map of New Guinea and the Bismarck Archipelago shows Austronesian languages in pockets along the north coast of New Guinea and into the Bismarck Archipelago to the east, but non-Austronesian, Papuan languages in the remainder. So this first explanation was correct in suggesting that there was some skirting of New Guinea by early eastward-moving Austronesian-speaking people. But we also now know that they were not Polynesians *as such*, not Polynesians in their present ethnicity.

A second theory was that the route of the same people from the Philippines and/or Indonesia passed further north, through the islands of Micronesia. This explanation was suggested by the eminent New Zealand Maori scholar, Sir Peter Buck. He believed he detected some cultural similarities between Micronesia and Polynesia which pointed to a common origin. Today we know that this ingenious speculation was incorrect.

A third theory proposed that the Polynesians came from North or South America! It had a famous supporter, self-publicist, and 'puffer' in the Norwegian adventurer, Thor Heyerdahl. In 1955, just by drifting in the ocean currents and using favourable winds, he managed to sail his raft, the *Kon Tiki*, from off the South American coast all the way to the Tuamotu Islands in eastern Polynesia. Of course, this proved nothing except a possibility. Heyerdahl was disproportionately impressed by the presence in Polynesia of the sweet-potato, a plant of American origin, but he ignored the fact that the overwhelming proportion of Polynesian plant life is of South East Asian origin. We now know that all domesticated Polynesian animals originated in Asia too. Heyerdahl acquired a widespread popular audience, though scholars were always sceptical. Almost all scientists and historians agree that South East Asia was the source of Polynesian ancestors, though they

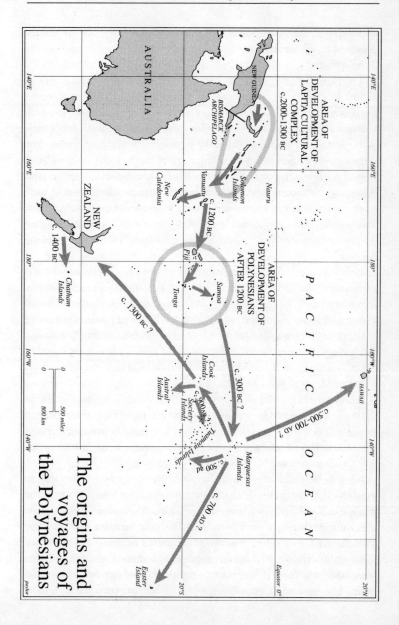

The origins and voyages of the Polynesians

AUSTRALIA

AREA OF DEVELOPMENT OF LAPITA CULTURAL COMPLEX c.2000-1300 BC

NEW GUINEA

BISMARCK ARCHIPELAGO

Solomon Islands

Vanuatu

New Caledonia

NEW ZEALAND c. 1400 BC

Chatham Islands

c. 1200 BC

Nauru

AREA OF DEVELOPMENT OF POLYNESIANS AFTER 1200 BC

Fiji

Tonga

Samoa

c. 300 BC ?

c. 1300 BC ?

Cook Islands

Austral Islands

Society Islands

c. 900 BC ?

Tuamotu Islands

Marquesas Islands

PACIFIC OCEAN

c. 500 AD

HAWAII

c.500-700 AD ?

c. 700 AD ?

Easter Island

0   500 miles
0   800 km

Equator 0°

20°N

20°S

allow that some small South American cultural influence may have occurred at a later date, involving transfer of a few plants such as the sweet-potato.

The fourth view, first proposed in 1959 by the anthropologist Kenneth P. Emory, is that the Polynesians *as such* did not come from anywhere. *Polynesians evolved from a small population of mixed Austronesian origins in the western Polynesian region of Samoa and Tonga.* There they developed their unique culture, and from there they spread in stages (see map) to other parts of the South Pacific. This is now the view accepted by almost all scholars of the Pacific people, historians, anthropologists, archaeologists, linguists, and geneticists. It is continually being confirmed by new evidence and discoveries. Two further facts about this 'small population of mixed Austronesian origins' which evolved in the Samoa and Tonga region should be noted.

One is that the first Polynesians recognizable as such shared what is now called the Lapita Culture. The Lapita Culture spread relatively rapidly through Fiji and western Polynesia. Lapita Culture is named after a simple but characteristically decorated form of pottery, produced without a wheel and first detected by archaeologists in New Caledonia. Archaeologists unearthed the fact that the Lapita Culture originated in New Britain in the Bismarck Archipelago, and had reached Fiji, Samoa, and Tonga, by about 1200 BC.

The second fact derives mostly from linguistics. It is that the Lapita Culture was carried by various Austronesian-speaking peoples who originated in Taiwan and the Philippines, and possibly northern parts of the Indonesian islands, the peoples who made the small coastal settlements in north coast New Guinea.

So the best current answer to Polynesian origins is this. Some Austronesian-speaking descendants of peoples from Taiwan, the Philippines and perhaps Indonesia developed the Lapita Culture in the Bismarck Archipelago off eastern New Guinea. Around 1200 BC they took their Lapita Culture to Tonga and Samoa, and also to Fiji (which has a predominantly Melanesian population today). They then seem to have had little contact with their origins, and for perhaps a thousand years this interacting population consolidated in Tonga and Samoa.

They voyaged still, but within the 'Fiji–Tonga–Samoa Crescent'. During this consolidation these Lapita Culture people evolved into that special racial/ethnic group we call Polynesian. The evidence for this explanation as *the main source* of modern Polynesians is now overwhelming. This does not rule out the possibility of other minor sources, perhaps even from Japan. There is still lively debate among the specialists.

WHEN AND WHY WAS THE REST OF POLYNESIA SETTLED?

The similar culture of all the Polynesian islands has suggested to scholars that their colonization must have been relatively rapid, and that historically speaking it took place relatively recently. Had it occurred over a longer historical period, much greater cultural differences would have had time to develop.

A phase of rapid eastward colonization began around AD 1 by people from Samoa now clearly Polynesian. These Polynesian colonizers appear to have settled the Marquesas first, and to have been well established there by the AD 300s as the earliest validated archaeological dates are all in those islands. Linguistic research also supports this view. Later Polynesian groups travelled north and south from the Marquesas, and possibly also again from Samoa, and had settled the Society Islands (Tahiti), Cook Islands and Hawaii between 500 and 700, and Easter Island by circa 700. And, probably around 1300, Polynesians most likely from the Society Islands first settled New Zealand to the far south-west – the Cook Islands are another possible origin. Prior to the 1990s, much earlier dates were suggested for New Zealand settlement, but these are now considered overestimates. Certainly New Zealand was the last major region of the Pacific to be peopled. Given that it lies well outside the tropical wind systems, this is to be expected. *If* there were other colonizations of New Zealand at later dates, as explained in Chapter 3, this was *not* because the first arrivals returned home to alert their countrymen of New Zealand's existence.

That Polynesia was settled at all is itself the most remarkable fact of Polynesian history. Just how did these non-literate, non-mathematical, non-scientific, and non-metallurgical people reach what we now call

Polynesia? For the evidence shows that the main pattern of settlement spread *from west to east*, i.e., *against the prevailing winds*, which are *from the south-east*. Moreover ocean currents are also from east to west in these Southern Hemisphere tropical latitudes. Historians at first assumed that Polynesians would have had to sail or paddle hard into the wind, but in recent decades scholars have pointed to the significance of the irregular summer *westerly* winds.

The Polynesians may have slowly tacked into the wind, or they may have waited for the right time of year to use the brief periods of westerlies. With either method, if they became lost, or were running short of food, they could then use the south-easterly winds to blow them home again – or somewhere near to home. Later expeditions travelled across, north and south, adapting the prevailing south-easterly winds.

The relatively rapid spread of settlement together with the presence of the same useful plants and domesticated animals support the idea of premeditated colonization. The consensus today is that most successful colonizations derived from expeditions which were deliberate and well-equipped. Rational reconstruction of ideas during the last 100 years, together with construction of Polynesian canoes and imitation voyages undertaken from the 1960s onwards, have made this conclusion inevitable. The Polynesian colonizing expeditions carried women, food, tools, seeds, plants, domesticated animals, warriors, and priests. Most canoes were a little cross-section of Polynesian society. Some scholars believe that colonizing expeditions were preceded by deliberate scouting voyages.

Voyaging was made possible by the Polynesian economy. Besides the beneficence of mother nature, the Polynesians discovered how to preserve and store food and create some surpluses, so gained the time to build canoes and to voyage. Voyaging may have occurred for a multitude of reasons: overpopulation, disputes, oppression, wars. But the *persistence of voyaging* over so long a period and across so vast an area makes it unlikely these suggestions are sufficient. More likely, many voyages resulted from sheer intellectual curiosity, that desire to know about the world, to find what lies over the horizon, the curiosity which makes us human. In time this urge to voyage, to discover and to settle, seems to have became a syndrome, a fundamental characteristic of Polynesian culture, just as the endless pursuit of scientific and technological knowledge have become fundamental to Western culture in the last few hundred years.

Evidence and argument also suggest *some* accidental discovery. Drift voyages by fishermen or inter-island travellers blown off course or lost cannot explain the extent and success of Polynesian settlement, but they may explain some. Indeed, drift voyages are still quite common. Each year stories of drift voyages appear in Polynesian newspapers. For instance, a boatload of people from Papua-New Guinea in 1995 was blown off its intended course to a neighbouring island. After a gruelling three-month journey the boat washed up in Tuvalu 800 miles (1,300k) away. The people had lived on raw fish and rainwater. Successful colonization requires women. With rare exceptions fishing trips would not include women, but inter-island travel often would. The best example of successful accidental settlement may be Easter Island.

There would have been loss of life from faulty navigation, especially in the earlier stages, and also from summer typhoons, waterspouts, and cyclones/hurricanes. Some deliberate colonizers would soon have perished on their new islands. Others, such as the people who settled Henderson Island in the Pitcairn Group, remained for several decades or centuries before departing or dying out. From Tahiti to the Marquesas to New Zealand, the myths preserved in oral storytelling suggest long ocean voyages as the source of ancestors. Myth and oral tradition are of course problematic evidence for producing hard history. In this case, however, they receive support from science. Over the decades and centuries there also would have been various kinds of cross-fertilizations of people and culture.

It is possible that Polynesian stature may also be the result of the long voyages. Many Polynesians have large, even intimidating physiques. It has been speculated that these resulted from 'survival of the fittest' on the long ocean voyages. Larger people with more body fat may have been better able to survive the constant chill of evaporating sea spray. And it would be the survivors who passed on their genes. Computer simulations comparing racial/ethnic groups have supported this view.

Alternatively, it has been suggested that the large body size results from a high carbohydrate diet.

METHODS OF NAVIGATION

Polynesian methods of navigation were fascinating. Because of the Western world's newly found respect for indigenous cultures, there is a tendency these days to turn the Polynesian navigators into supermen. They were not. Over centuries they learned by trial and error, and ocean-going knowledge was discovered and lost. The New Zealand Maori are an example of the latter. Presumably because they no longer had need of them, within a short period of time the Polynesian ancestors of the Maori forgot all their deep-sea skills. It is also easy to overestimate the Polynesians' precision and efficacy.

Their methods were intelligent, but empirical, rather than scientific. They worked – more or less. Polynesians learned to navigate, but they did not *understand navigation* in the sense we do today. Their techniques were derived from observing nature. From watching the skies over generations they learned to construct mental star-maps. These consisted of constellations and individual stars well separated in time and direction so that at least one or two were always visible at any hour of the night. Constellations which rise or set in the same part of the horizon were noted. In equatorial latitudes the stars seem to follow an almost straight path from east to west each night.

To sail north (to Hawaii) or south (to New Zealand or Easter Island) posed more difficult problems. As we move into higher latitudes the apparent paths of the stars become increasingly parabolic, and only on rising and setting do they provide a reliable directional guide. The Pole Star, which indicates due north, would be useful on the outward voyage north. But any return voyage became problematic. And in travelling south, to New Zealand, there was no equivalent of the Pole Star.

The Polynesians also *sensed* their way across the ocean. They learned to distinguish the long ocean swells of the deep, which are flatter and longer in amplitude than waves produced nearer to islands. They would have learned the nature of the prevailing ocean currents. Like any good ocean-going yachtsman today they could detect reefs from the colour of the water above them, and recognize the presence of land by the shape, colour, and movement of clouds: clouds above land appear to be more stationary, clouds above the lagoons of atolls often have a green tinge. The smell of jungle and plants was brought to them by off-shore breezes. Land birds were recognized: noddies and terns can go perhaps 20 miles/32k out to sea, boobies 40 miles, and frigate birds as far as 75 miles. The regular patterns of migrating birds that fly north or south would have suggested land in those directions.

CANOES

We know there was an evolutionary progress in boat-building in the South East Asian archipelagoes, and Polynesian boats evolved from these. First there was the dug-out canoe which was paddled. Then a rudimentary low-set sail was fixed to a mast on the canoe – but taller sails made the canoe unstable. The Lapita people's and thus the Polynesians' solution to this problem was the ingenious 'outrigger' float added to one or both sides. The dug-out was improved by adding a single board to the top of each side, either sewn or tied on. Next, entire canoes were made of planks sewn or tied to a V-shaped dug-out hull. Longer craft were constructed by sewing boards in sequence along the hull. An inside structural framework was provided by a series of naturally curved pieces of wood. Everything was held together by

A reconstruction of a Polynesian double canoe

lashings/cords of 'sennit'. Sennit was produced from patiently plaiting grass, coconut fibres, or palm leaves, and needed replacing periodically. Such techniques provided the flexibility needed in ocean sailing. Caulking between boards was sennit impregnated with the gum of breadfruit. Of course, such canoes were not watertight and they needed regular bailing!

Decades or centuries later these conceptions evolved into two large V-hulled canoes joined by wooden crossbeams with a large platform on top. Such great canoes, steered by a huge oar or oars at the stern, were now suitable for long-distance travel – and were the world's first true ocean-going craft, able to cross thousands of nautical miles in a month.

Sails evolved too. By the 1500s, when European contact was first being made, a new sail was being developed in western Polynesia. The Fijians and Tongans were using huge fore-and-aft inverted triangular sails with the point downwards, similar to the lateen of the Arabs. This sail had long been standard equipment in Micronesian craft, from where it reached first to Kiribati and then to Fiji and Tonga. By the early 1700s, produced by sewing together large pandanus leaves, it was in use far to the east in Tahiti and the Tuamotus.

The Tongan Tongiaki double-hulled canoes commented upon by the European navigators of the 1700s could carry between 30 and 100 men. Though, unlike the case of Viking longships, there are no surviving examples of early vessels we can assume that the original Polynesian voyaging canoes were smaller and less efficient versions of the Tongiaki.

Early Polynesian Material and Social Culture

Because Pacific lslanders were non-literate, there are no written accounts of early Polynesian life. We can however gain some general idea of the life of former times by deduction from the Polynesian culture first encountered by the European explorers and savants, from the first Polynesians who were taught to write in the early 1800s, and from the exacting work of archaeologists and other modern specialists.

Because of their great distance from the settled continents, and from the islands of Melanesia, the Polynesian islands were generally free from pests and diseases. There was however the dangerous life of the ocean which Polynesian fishermen and seafarers continually faced, with its sharks, sea urchins, jellyfish, stonefish, and other problematic creatures. Some also inhabited the land. One was the coconut crab. This fierce crustacean can crack coconuts with its claws! It can also give nasty injuries.

SIMILARITY OF LANGUAGES

To compensate for their lack of literacy, Polynesians developed wonderful traditions of memorized myth, oral 'chronology', and story-telling. Specialists committed to memory immensely long genealogies.

Polynesian languages were rich in practical detail. They had a complex vocabulary of terms crucial in navigation, names for the different stars and clusters, for types of ocean currents, winds, directions, landforms. Different grammatical forms indicated direction of motion towards or away from the speaker. As the languages evolved, some consonants went missing, producing a softer sound. For instance, in Tagalog (Philippines) coconut is *niog*. In Polynesian languages this becomes *ni*, *niu*, or *nu*. Elevated vocabularies existed for addressing aristocrats.

A similarity of vocabulary and grammar exists amongst all the Polynesian languages. Some specialists talk of 16 languages, others with different criteria for languages and dialects, of rather more, up to 32. Consider the resemblances in the table below from Tonga in the west to the Marquesas in the far east of Polynesia:

English	Tongan	Samoan	Tahitian	Maori	Marquesan
house	fale	fale	fare	whare	hae
island	motu	motu	motu	motu	motu
priest	tufunga	tufunga	tahua	tohunga	tau'a
man	tangata	tangata	taata	tangata	enata
woman	fefine	fafine	vahine	wahine	vehine
land	fonua	fanua	fenua	whenua	henua

COCONUT CONTAINERS AND SHARKSKIN POLISHERS

These people developed an amazing variety of fishing techniques. They used poison, basket traps, lines and nets made from jungle creepers, spears, even fishing lines dangling from kites. They also produced some amazing lures and traps. One trap used the cobwebs of the banana spider, which would entangle the tiny teeth of the long tom fish. Fish hooks, in a society without metals, were made of human and animal bone, and in some isolated islands such as Easter Island and Pitcairn, even from stone.

Like the Australian Aborigines, Polynesians were hampered by lack of metal and beasts of burden. So from the available products of nature they ingeniously developed tools and utensils of stone, bone, plants, and wood. Laboriously, stone tools were used to shape wooden implements for gardening, and also to make other stone tools. Coconuts and shells were used for containers, coconut palms and banana leaves for weaving baskets and for clothing and matting. In Samoa the long leaves of the screwpine or pandanus were woven into mats, the most prized being used as gifts on important occasions such as funerals, weddings and the appointment of chiefs.

Joseph Banks on Cook's first expedition reported that Tahitians used stone axes shaped like an adze, chisels or gouges made of human bone, a file or rasp of coral, and the skin of stingrays and sharks and coral sand to polish with. These were, he said, 'a sufficient set of tools for building a house'. He admired their carpentry: 'I have seen them dubb off the first rough coat of a plank at least as fast as one of our carpenters could have done it; and in hollowing, where they were able to raise large slabs of the wood, they certainly work more quickly, owing to the weight of their tools.'

CHIEFS AND COMMONERS

Over the centuries social distinctions and hierarchies developed, largely based on heredity. The number of ranks correlated roughly with size and fertility of the island. On small islands social distinctions were minor. On large, populous islands chiefs and priests were often despotic, chiefs possessing the power of life and death.

Still, politically astute chiefs took into account the advice of other aristocrats and tried to promote the general wellbeing of the people. Not to do so might result in assassination or civil war. Political power was most commonly inherited from the father, social status often from the mother, but not inherited by direct primogeniture. Though eldest brother or eldest son might make the front running, chiefly candidates could be drawn from various relatives of the dead chief – brothers and sons, uncles and nephews. Aristocratic consultations and meetings were held to make the decision, in which mana and warrior ability weighed heavily. Women might play important parts and sometimes outranked their brothers. Behind the scenes they could wield enormous influence, as was so in Tonga and Tahiti in the 1700s.

Political units varied in size from comparatively large in the Tongan archipelago, with thousands of warriors, and perhaps 30,000 people; through middle-size polities of perhaps 5,000 in Tahiti, and of one or two thousand of the Maori tribes in New Zealand; to tiny groups in the Cook Islands and the atolls of the Tuamotus or Tokelau, with a few tens or hundreds of inhabitants. So it is remarkable that in such small populations distinctions between classes may have been as marked as in other former more intensely populated civilizations of the world, say, the Inca Empire, or the African lands ruled by their god-kings.

On High Oceanic Islands polities and land claims often took a wedge-shape, based upon a valley and stream, stretching from a long oceanfront, along lateral ridges and watersheds to an imagined point on the central inland mountain – natural boundaries in time of warfare.

There were no towns. Houses were scattered amongst the crops. Sometimes, in the vicinity of temples, marae, or chiefly houses which were built upon raised platforms of earth or stone, there might be a somewhat higher concentration of houses that we could loosely call hamlets.

Sex roles were mostly distinct. Women worked in the home and with other women, while men dealt with outside issues, like construction and fishing, and were the protectors and decision-takers. People often worked hard, much of the work was communal, and even the athletic contests encouraged warrior skills and values. Contrary to popular fantasy, the Polynesian way was not a lotus-eating life of lazing in the sun.

Standards of living differed from island to island. The means of life were more easily procured on fertile islands with regular rainfall like Upolu and Tahiti but precarious on tiny atolls and islands of variable rainfall in eastern Polynesia. Still, we may suppose that the standards of living and the happiness of most Polynesians would not have been any lower or less and probably compared favourably with that of contemporary Europeans, Africans, and Asians. Food was often literally at hand, shelter was easy to construct, fresh air and ocean were endless, there was an absence of diseases and insect pests, and a generous sex life was available to all except certain unlucky aristocrats elevated and constrained by mana and tapu (taboo) far above their contemporaries. Polynesian men possessed great seafaring abilities, and swimming was second nature; most women too could swim. Surfing developed early, both canoe and body surfing. While in Tahiti in 1769 James Cook observed: 'I could not help concluding that this man felt the most supreme pleasure while he was driven so fast and so smoothly by the sea.' To the early European visitors Polynesians seemed to be almost amphibious.

WAR

There was on–off warfare of four sorts, between neighbouring tribes and islands. Most common were small raids and skirmishes over real and imagined petty annoyances like theft; then there were battles caused by infringement of tribal boundaries; there were conflicts and battles over succession; fourthly, and rarely, were the deliberate invasions of neighbouring islands or archipelagoes for tribal expansion and chiefly mana. On 13-square mile (21 sq.k) Nauru, which today one can drive around in twenty minutes, there were 13 often mutually hostile tribes. About six months before Cook arrived in 1769 there was a vicious war between the tribes of 'Big Tahiti' (the larger end of the hour-glass shaped island) and 'Little Tahiti', and women and children were included in the general slaughter. Weapons were clubs of many kinds, slings, and spears. At times stones thrown with astonishing precision became weapons. Captain William Bligh left us a terrifying description of stoning, recorded during his harrowing open-boat journey after the 1789 mutiny on the *Bounty*.

The incident occurred at Tofua, a volcanic Tongan island. The Tofuans became increasingly brazen as they realized Bligh had no ship. Dozens grew to hundreds gathering cynically along the beach. Sporadically at first, some islanders began to clap large stones together in a hard rhythm. Bligh had heard this sound before when he voyaged with Cook, and he recognized the rhythm of death. As more and more Tofuans took up their stones, Bligh ordered his men to return to the boat as nonchalantly as possible but before the sailors were all aboard, the Tofuans began hurling. The first stone smashed into Bligh's shoulder, drawing blood as he ran into the water. Intended to bring him down, accurate stones cut at his ankles and knees. Battered and bloody under the non-stop barrage, the sailors pulled away, but not before the gallant quartermaster in cutting the mooring rope was bashed to death. Canoes pursued, and the Englishmen survived only because Bligh distracted the Tofuans by casting pieces of clothing into the ocean, which were precious for Polynesians because of the rarity of European cloth.

Warfare being endemic on so many islands, some Pacific tribes constructed fortifications of earth, wood, and stone. From about AD 1500 New Zealand Maori produced the pre-European Pacific's most structured and effective hill fortifications, with a succession of elaborate fences, ditches, and ramparts. They developed these to even greater sophistication in the Musket Wars and New Zealand Wars of the nineteenth century.

Falling prisoner of war was usually fatal, or at best led to slavery. Finau, an early nineteenth-century chief who expanded his territory to include much of what is now Tonga, tied his prisoners naked to palm trees to burn and dehydrate to death in the sun. Or they were bound hand and foot, tied to leaky canoes and towed out to sea, to drown if they were lucky, or to be gutted and gobbled by sharks. Prisoners of war also provided a source of cannibal protein.

CANNIBALISM

Cannibalism occurred in the South Pacific, but its incidence varied greatly. Whereas it was commonplace in Fiji and the Marquesas, and certainly occurred in New Zealand, it was rare in Tahiti. Two important reasons for the practice were to acquire the mana of the victim, and to exact supreme revenge. In many islands dead bodies were tapu and to be touched only in particular ways by particular people. But cooking was believed to destroy all tapu. It therefore made possible the quintessential disrespect of eating the person. Motives of mana and revenge could also became blurred with a third – dietary convenience. As cannibalism reminds us, Polynesians had their own characteristic cosmological and religious values.

RELIGION

As almost everywhere else in history prior to the development of Western rationalism and democracy, religion was the handmaiden of Polynesian rulers. Reminding one of the ancient Greeks, eastern and central Polynesian religions were polytheistic, with many 'departmental' gods who were concerned with special aspects of human life. The list varied from island to island, but sky, sea, forest, and war were typical: Tangaloa, Rongo, Tu, and Tane. As time passed, such gods could acquire additional responsibilities. They were also believed to be progenitors of human beings, ancestors as much as divinities. There were local gods and spirits. Tonga and Samoa in the west had a smaller number of great gods but more spirits involved in lesser roles, and attached to kinship groups.

All islands had myths and legends to explain the existence of men. women, and their world. The great demi-god Maui was the most interesting figure in Polynesian mythology. He supposedly caught the sun to give fire to mankind, and lifted many islands, including North Island New Zealand, out of the ocean with his fish hook.

Some Polynesian origin myths showed interesting similarities to the biblical account. It was said that Samoa was created by the sky god Tangaloa who then produced rock, commanding it to split into clay, coral, cliff, and stones. When the rock broke up, earth, sea, and sky came into being. From a piece of rock there emerged a spring of fresh water. Tangaloa then worked on creating minor gods to deal with other human wants, those of agriculture, forest, fishing, war. Then at Asua in the Manua Islands of Samoa, Tangaloa created a man and a woman, and commanded them to be fruitful. He then produced day and night, sun and moon.

Polynesian religion had nothing to do with salvation or morality. Paralleling relations amongst people, relations between men and gods were reciprocal. Gods gave men wealth, support, protection. Men sacrificed to the gods to receive these. To promote this communication, Eastern Polynesians erected great numbers of temples and monuments, shown in the numerous ruins today. The most outstanding were the moai of Easter Island. The temples, the marae, often had surrounding walls and standing stones, and raised platforms (ahu) of coral and basalt. Other significant events also occurred there, such as a council of war, celebrating a victory, installing a chief. Occasionally human sacrifices took place. Western Polynesian marae, e.g., in New Zealand, were less ceremonial.

MANA AND TAPU (TABOO)

Conceptions of creation were related to the two crucial supernatural, metaphysical-cum-religious ideas which derived from the god-ancestors and controlled Polynesian life: mana and tapu. Crucial to control, mana and tapu were central to the rule of chiefs and priests – the chiefly mana in some mysterious manner suffused through the tribe. But, derivatively, lesser mortals could also possess mana, and objects, foodstuffs, and places could be tapu. Mana was the more active and positive form of control, and tapu exerted a more negative control. Every aspect of social, political, and economic life might at one time or another be affected by them: language, trade, government, places, construction of houses and fortifications, landholding, agriculture, eating, social relations, sexual relations, and birth and death.

We in the modern West can distinguish between influence, authority, power and prestige, but all these and more were fused in the amorphous concept of mana. Fundamental in leadership, this occult, ubiquitous, arbitrary, and amazingly effective form of control could inspire respect, awe, terror. It could be increased or reduced by one's own actions and those of others. Because the presence of mana could be recognized only through its effects, in practice there was endless confusion over cause and effect. A philosopher might argue that the whole conception was an illusion, redundant.

It was believed that aspects of mana of chiefs could be dangerous to commoners unless proper precautions were taken to avoid, or divert it. In Tahiti, if a chief entered the house of a commoner, it had afterwards to be burned down to prevent the supposed ill effects of mana.

Tapu too was enormously powerful, regulating, restricting, prohibiting contacts among people and among people and things. Essentially, tapu was a protective device, not a curse or a power in itself like mana. Mana or some other supernatural force sacred or cursed was always the authority for tapu – tapu protected mana and *supposedly* maintained tribal well-being: in the Marquesas all canoes were tapu to women – a belief which functioned to empower men and keep women at home. Words, people, places, and things which were tapu had to be avoided. As societies became more hierarchical tapus increased. In Tahiti and the Society Islands generally it was tapu to utter the chief's name, and pork and dog were tapu to the lower classes. In Tonga all members of the elite were the object of numerous tapus which controlled their lives and which commoners had to avoid infringing. In Tahiti, New Zealand, and many other islands, tapu extended to the chief's ornaments, weapons, clothes, drinking vessels, and head. One New Zealand missionary reported seeing a chief choking on a fishbone, but his family would not aid him because his head was tapu.

Monolithic sculpture on Taiohae island, North Marquesas in French Polynesia

There were strictly enforced penalties for violation of tapu – avoidance, ostracism, clubbing to death, strangling. Mana and tapu together, like religions elsewhere, formed a wonderfully interrelated, self-justifying belief system, subject perhaps to slow evolution, but in the eyes of believers closed and beyond disproof.

The priests–cum–wise men were the repositories of knowledge about tapu and mana. They performed the religious ceremonies necessary to install a new ruler, to moderate the anger or adapt the power of a relevant god, or to expunge a tapu. Besides being the experts on religion, they preserved the practical knowledge about such matters as medicine and navigation and the growing of crops. Possessing such a combination of the arcane and the utilitarian they were powerful beings.

SOCIAL VALUES AND SEX

Motives and motivations tended to be practical and expedient. Pleasure and pain, strength and weakness, success and failure, mediated through mana and tapu, justified, guided, and controlled what people did.

Polynesian attitudes to sexual activity were in general straightforward. Sexual and sensual matters generally were less elaborate than in Europe and Asia, though more so amongst the higher classes. There were of course courtship rituals and courting etiquette. As clothing was minimal, it could scarcely have a major role in courtship and sexual relations, either as encouragement or as inhibitor. In general there was no *pathological* concern for or against sex such as developed in Asia, Christian Europe and Islamic lands. There was nothing which could function like pornography. But in Maori art, for instance, there was some stylized representation of genitalia, and words chanted in the haka (Appendix 3) can be obscene by Western standards. Anyway, where was the need for sublimation, substitution, or elaboration when the thing itself was so available?

Erotic dancing was commonplace. Cook wrote about 'a very indecent dance which they called Timorodee, performed by eight or ten young Tahitian women, singing the most indecent songs and using most indecent actions in the practice of which they are brought up from the earliest childhood.' Ingenuously, he adds, 'In doing this they keep time to a great nicety.' Sexual life was enthusiastic, vital, fixated. Cook reported that in Tahiti 'both sexes express the most indecent ideas in conversation without the least emotion [concern] and they delight in such conversations beyond any other'. Cook also remarked on the casualness of sexual activity in public. When European sailors wanted to retire into the woods, Tahitian girls were highly amused. The arioi, a religious caste unique to Tahiti, practised what might be likened to free love. In accord with the general sexual openness, children in many islands were allowed sexual play. In the Marquesas, even with very young children the emphasis on sexuality was such that it begins to look pathological.

Menstruation and child-birth invoked the same range of special tapus as in Melanesia. Homosexuality seems to have been reasonably common in Polynesia amongst young men though mostly rejected in adulthood. In the Society Islands it was/is institutionalized in the form of the mahu, in Samoa as the fa'afafine, a homosexual man who performed/performs many female tasks, and had/has a special status.

FOOD AND FEASTING

The early Polynesian settlers lived largely by hunting and gathering. There existed a plenitude of natural foodstuffs in field and forest. As natural resources were destroyed, they began gardening and cultivating. The major cultivated foods were taro, yam, sweet-potato, coconut, breadfruit, and bananas. Sweet-potatoes (kumara) became the staple in temperate Easter Island and in cooler New Zealand's North Island, bananas and breadfruit in stony Samoa and in Tahiti, yams in the easily cultivable soils of Tonga, and taro in the irrigated valleys of the Cook Islands and the Society Islands. Many plants were used as medicines. Pigs, dogs, and chickens were the only domesticated animals.

On atolls and on the coastal lowlands of high islands, the coconut palm was the most significant plant, and not merely for food. It was perhaps the most versatile tree in history. The kernel, the copra, provided food and oil; the milk supplied drink; the shell, vessels; the husk, fibre; the leaves, material for roofing and for weaving, wrapping and carrying.

Around AD 1 the Polynesians ceased producing pottery, perhaps for lack of a suitable clay. So they no longer boiled their food, and instead developed underground ovens for baking and steaming. In parts of New Zealand such as the Rotorua region, Maori were able to make use of thermal cooking sources.

There were local delicacies. One was the balolo or palolo worm. Twice a year for about an hour in the reefs of Samoa (also in Fiji) tens of thousands of these worms emerged from the coral and wriggled to the surface of the lagoons to propagate. People gathered in those sections of the coast where the worms were most likely to appear. On the night of their rising, dip nets were used to scoop them urgently from the water as people stood on the sea bottom or reached down from canoes. Baskets filled rapidly with thousands of worms and their extruded eggs seething in slimy masses. The worm is still regarded as a delicacy. To the Western palate it tastes like oyster spinach.

Food had great cultural significance in many islands. The mana of a village could be affected by the nature and amount of food presented during inter-village meetings and festivities. Here is a description of a massive royal feast in Tonga in 1938, which was also a matter of mana. This one was in honour of the then British High Commissioner for the South Pacific.

> The guests sat on mats on the ground, and ate with their fingers. In front of each group of guests rested a huge tray about 6 feet by 2, made from large banana leaves stretched between branches. Food was piled high upon it, especially pigs – pigs of all lengths and girths, ages and shapes. They had been cooked in ground-pits on a lining of red-hot stones. About 200 guests sat in long lines on either side of the trays, and the Commissioner thought there might have been 200 pigs too. There was a cornucopia of chickens cooked in coconut milk, freshly caught crayfish and crabs, mussels resting on little leaf pads, and turkeys steamed in banana leaves. Slices of hot, white and purple yam substituted for bread. Any spaces on the trays were plugged with the Tongan dessert of balls of a starchy dumpling-like substance rolled in leaves. Each guest had a personal salt-shaker of leaf, edges neatly trimmed. On completing the banquet, guests washed their hands in kava carried in wooden bowls held by the Tongan queen's maids of honour, and dried them on napkins of tapa.

On many islands gourmandizing by Polynesian chiefs was expected, though not in the case of the battle-hardened chiefs of New Zealand.

Joseph Banks mentions that an average chiefly meal on Tahiti consisted of several breadfruit, a number of fish raw or cooked, and twelve or more bananas. Chiefs were expected to be overweight, ability to ingest monstrous amounts of food being symbolic of their superior status. This tradition has continued. In the late twentieth century, King Taufaahau Topou IV of Tonga was massively obese at 440 lb/200 kg and even after a long-term serious reduction diet and exercise, still weighed 290 lb/132 kg.

ARTS AND CRAFTS – TAPA AND TATTOO

Polynesian arts were integrated into the way of life. They were not individual, but communal expressions. Conformity was expected and even the accidental slip of a chisel was anathema and punishable. There were elaborate wood carving, carving of monumental stone figures with stylized torsos, weaving of mats and clothing, ceremonial drinks such as kava/ava, and the art of tattoo. Polynesians, unlike Melanesians, did not carve masks, and few works were painted. The most striking real and pseudo-apparel of most Pacific Islands were (and are) made from tapa (not in New Zealand) and created by tattoo (tatau).

Tapa is barkcloth. Made from the inner bark of paper mulberry and other trees, tapa is one of the most ancient and distinctive products of the Pacific. Where tapa-making flourished it was an important means of women's self-expression; in the Marquesas and Easter Island men also produced it for ritual objects and loincloths.

But tattoo was Polynesia's most unique ritual and art form (Appendix 4). It remains valued today because it survived the onslaught of Western culture, in particular all efforts of missionaries to extinguish it. Among the first Europeans to see a tattoo was Dutchman Jacob Roggeveen and his crew in the 1720s. They failed to recognize it for what it was. One of his crew described it as 'artfully woven silk tights or knee breeches'. Over the years this description has given great amusement to those Polynesians who have learned of it. In fact the Dutch misunderstanding is normal, because we all bring our present preconceptions to every new experience. At first we see what we know rather than know what we see. Until the new thing or experience is explained or taught to us, we inevitably force it into our old way of seeing and understanding. The Dutchmen's misconception would have been repeated many times across the Pacific by European seamen until knowledge of tattoo became general in Europe.

The tattoo masters used fine-toothed chisels fashioned from boar's or shark's teeth or bird bones to break the skin as the tool was tapped along the surface. A dye mixed from the charcoal of various trees, e.g., the candlenut in Samoa, was then used. To tattoo an area about as big as a hand took hours. Tattooing took its most extreme form in the Marquesas, where the whole male body might be covered, and tattooed women were ashamed to have sex with an untattooed man. In the modern Pacific Islands new tattoo patterns are being created alongside traditional ones.

TRADE

There had always been trade or exchange within archipelagoes, of local items, more easily produced in one island than another. In the Marquesas, for centuries, there was an important internal exchange network. There was also inter-archipelago trade. The most elaborate was a 'trade' in Samoan and Fijian spouses for high-ranking Tongans, together with accompanying ceremonial goods such as fine tapa mats from Samoa, and bowls, drums, and headrests from Fiji. Tongans sailed to the eastern islands of Fiji to obtain the large trunks of the vesi tree which they needed for their ocean-going canoes. They also acquired some of the accoutrements such as rope and mat sails. Fijian pottery was also in demand. Tonga was usually the intermediary in Fiji–Samoa trade, in pottery, and sandalwood. To the east, there were highly developed exchange/trade networks amongst the many Society Islands, the northern Tuamotus, and the Australs.

CHAPTER THREE

Special Cases: Easter Islanders, Fijians, Maori

Differences in physical geography and location, and separation over time brought South Pacific cultural diversity. In this chapter the early history of three of the most interestingly different areas is considered. First we examine what until the last decade or so were the immense mysteries of the Easter Islanders. Then we discuss the Fijians, the most easterly of the Melanesians, who show affinities to the Polynesians. And thirdly we look at the Maori of New Zealand, and how they evolved in a cool-temperate environment very different from that of other Polynesians, to produce what many outsiders think is the most fascinating of the Polynesian cultures.

The Lost Polynesians of Easter Island

In 1722 Dutchman Admiral Jacob Roggeveen and the crews of his three ships were amazed when, on Easter Sunday, they stumbled upon the lost people of Rapanui, which they called Easter Island. The islanders were all by themselves in the eastern Pacific, more than 2000 miles/3220k from South America and 1400 miles/2250k from the nearest inhabitable island of Pitcairn. The Easter Islanders were equally astonished by the visitors. Isolated for a thousand years, these people may have believed they were the world's only inhabitants.

For the next 260 years the islanders and their hundreds of huge stone statues and their barren, birdless, treeless landscape remained one of the world's great enigmas. The islanders had no seagoing vessels and Roggeveen was met by men who *swam* to his ship or came in tiny fragile leaking canoes 'compelled to pass half their time in bailing'. Where then had the Easter Islanders come from, and how had they reached this most lonely inhabitable island in the world? How and why, without wheel or steel or engine, had they carved and raised their huge stone statues? With its volcanic soil and mild climate Easter should have been a precious little green paradise. So why was the land so barren and impoverished that the Dutchmen on first viewing it from the sea thought it was an island of sand?

To solve the enigma became one of history's great detective stories. Questions were finally answered only during the 1980s and 1990s by scientists in linguistics, palaeontology, archaeology, pollen analysis, and radio carbon dating, with persistent field work on the island itself.

Easter Island is a 64 sq. mile sub-tropical oceanic high island, formed by successive underwater volcanic eruptions. Three extinct volcanoes mark the corners of its triangular shape. It has no harbour, and its forbidding ocean cliffs sometimes as high as 1000ft/305m make it impossible to come ashore except at a few narrow beaches. There are now no permanent streams, though rainwater collects in the crater lakes of the volcanoes.

LANDFALL BY LINGUISTICS

Through analysing vocabulary differences, modern linguists showed Easter Island Polynesian to be a dialect related to the speech of the island of Raivavae in the Australs (now part of French Polynesia) about 2,000 miles/3,220k away. The linguistic diversion has been dated at about AD 700. Radiocarbon dating of rubbish tips has suggested a similar time for first landfall. There are however alternative possibilities for Easter origins such as the Gambias, or other islands along the southern fringe of East Polynesia. The success of this late colonization such a long way from other Polynesian islands points to a planned expedition. The difficulty of deliberate navigation points to chance. Either way the expedition would have been perilous. Archaeological digs suggest that the original handful of settlers had become perhaps 7,000 during the island's most prosperous period.

POLLEN ANALYSIS AND ARCHAEOLOGY REVEAL RICHES

Had the island always been as barren as in 1722? Careful pollen analysis helped tell the true story. Columns of sediment were cored from the bottoms of the crater lakes, radiocarbon methods used to date the

An Easter Island 'Long Ear' woman with a reed hat, as seen by the artist William Hodges during Cook's visit in 1774. Cylindrical wood 'earrings' were usually worn

different layers which had accumulated. Painstakingly the pollen grains were analysed under microscopes to determine the plant species that produced them. A stunning new picture of ancient Easter emerged.

For at least 30,000 years before human settlement Easter Island was indeed covered with a thick forest of trees and low shrubs, ferns, and herbs. Tallest of all were the Easter Island Palms, related to today's Chilean Palm which reaches over 80 feet and 6 feet in diameter (24 × 2m). Within the forest grew the hauhau tree (for rope) and the totomiro, good for firewood. The Chilean Palm produces nuts and a sap which is made into sugar, syrup, and wine. Presumably the Easter Palm was a similar source of food.

Archaeological excavations revealed other surprising foodstuffs. Lack of coral reefs, and high cliffs make coastal fishing difficult. As a result, less than a quarter of the bones dug from the ancient garbage heaps were fish.(In the rest of Polynesia the proportion is more than 90 per cent.) Almost a third of the bones were dolphin! (The proportion is less than 1 per cent in other islands.) Dolphins in such numbers would have been speared deep at sea, far from the island. So those now extinct Easter Island Palms must have been used to make sea-going canoes!

Also discovered were remains of six land bird species such as parrots and owls – all destroyed before Roggeveen's time. The early Islanders ate seabirds too, for isolated Easter was a haven for breeding albatrosses, boobies, frigates, fulmars, petrels and others. More than 25 nesting species were identified by archaeologists – again all gone by 1722. The local small rats were another food source. Easter is the only Polynesian island where rat bones outnumber fish bones! All these creatures were cooked using firewood from the forests.

So how had this pristine piece of Polynesia become the near desert of 1722? Again the pollen record gave the answer.

PARADISE LOST

Destruction of the forests was considerable as early as the year 800. Grass began to replace trees. Sometime in the 1400s the palms were extinct, chopped down too often, their propagating nuts gnawed by the rats. As the forest disappeared the native landbirds died out too, and the seabirds ceased to come. The whole ecosystem went into terminal decline.

Dolphin bones no longer appear in the garbage after the 1400s – for there were now no large trees to make canoes. But the chickens (brought by the first immigrants) increased in number. And, ominously, after that date another kind of bone began to appear in the archaeological garbage heaps – human. In this island cut off from all contact with the world, people became a source of protein. As told to the early European seamen who followed Roggeveen, one favourite jibe was, 'The flesh of your mother sticks between my teeth!' In 700 years of settlement the fertile green island became its own little hell on earth.

THE MOAI STATUES

What is the explanation for the huge statues which made the island so mysterious to outsiders? Carving in stone and wood and placing carvings upon large stone platforms were common throughout Polynesia.

The puzzle of Easter Island was the great size of the statues, the Pacific's largest, their huge number (almost a thousand), the endless repetition of face and torso, and how they had been transported and erected in such a barren landscape with no obvious means and with so few people.

The facial repetition is to be expected. It stemmed from the mind-killing isolation, the insularity that comes from the lack of stimulation of ideas brought in from the outside. Paradoxically, the statues are striking in their monotony. There they stood, staring stoically across their narrow world, with their backs to the ocean, metaphorically like the people of the island.

Their cutting and construction were the product of an enormous communal enterprise, inch by inch, day after day. In recent decades archaeologists have enlisted local people to do some carving and lifting. Easter Island volcanic stone is not hard. It has been estimated that 20 people working with local obsidian chisels could have carved even the largest statues within a year.

With sufficient rope from the hauhau tree, teams of several hundred could use Easter Island Palm logs as sleds or rollers or bipods to transport the moai, and poles of palm as levers to raise them. In 1964 Thor

Two of the mysterious Easter Island statues found in the quarries of Rano Raraku. There are almost 400 in all

Heyerdahl organized 12 local men to erect a fallen statue using only stones and levers to slowly lift it. Small stones were replaced one by one by larger and larger stones and, resting upon its ever-growing stone ramp the statue gradually rose up. It took them 18 days.

In mediaeval Europe cathedral stone masons anticipated that in the next world they would be rewarded for their labours; in Easter Island, platform and moai workers probably also expected supernatural rewards. And everyone assumed that the mana of the statues which represented deified ancestors brought great benefit to the villages which possessed them. Around AD 1000 the people began building larger platforms (ahu). The halcyon days of statue making occurred after about 1200. Finally there were about 300 platforms, mostly along the shore, facing inwards towards their villages. About half eventually carried moai.

Two major confederations of clans appeared, and society became stratified into nobles, priests, practical experts, commoners, and slaves. There was a royal line and an hereditary chief centred on the village of Anakena, a role more religious than political, both repository and source of mana. As wits have said, he was 'to the *mana* born'. Different districts specialized in fishing or cultivation, or were the sites of crucial resources such as obsidian, reeds, or volcanic tuff.

When increasing clan competition produced ever larger statues and platforms, a new form of rivalry was invented – ten ton top-knots or crowns. These were cut from a different pink–red lava and placed on top. It seems that during these centuries the islanders were at peace. Energy expended in warfare in other islands was here sublimated into statue and platform construction. Then suddenly statue rivalry ceased, for by 1500 the palms were all gone. Having no tree cover, the springs and the few streams dried up. With scarcely a tree, in an increasingly bare landscape the soil washed and blew away, its nutrients were leached, and crop yields declined.

BIRDMEN AND RONGORONGO SCRIPTS

In the despairing, declining society, radical religious and political changes followed. Rejecting the religion of deified ancestors, the islanders came to worship the creator god, Makemake, with fertility rituals and chants. Hereditary privileges were lost as warrior leaders gained control, and rivalry became conflict. Two loose confederations developed, a western and an eastern. There were clan battles. No more wooden houses could be built and people lived in caves. Population plummeted to less than 2,000. Vindictive enemies began to topple one another's statues. Top-knots rolled, heads broke off. Eventually not a single statue would be left standing. (Those upright today have all been re-erected in recent decades.)

At some point there evolved an extraordinary social–political system, and no creator of a fictional society has ever written anything more astonishing. Its *inspiration* was religious, but the *function* prevented conflict in this now small and precariously placed population. Island leadership came to alternate between local groups, on the basis of a bizarre ritual race for an egg! The winner of the contest became the sacred 'birdman' for a year.

The centre of this birdman cult was the old ceremonial village of Orongo, on the rim of the largest crater, Rano Kau, perched above a 1000-foot vertiginous drop to the ocean. Here in early spring each birdman candidate gathered and chose a youth to represent him. The youths clambered down the precipice and, using reeds as flotation, swam 1.25 miles/2k to Motu Nui, the larger of two islets. Here they waited, perhaps for weeks, for the arrival of the first migratory seabirds, the sooty terns, and the laying of their first brown-speckled egg. Once a youth found the first egg, he shouted his success to his master and swam back with it in his headband. The man now became the sacred birdman, and lived in splendid isolation for a year. As the god Make-make's earthly embodiment, his group were recipients of supernatural blessing.

When the Belgian Catholic lay missionary Eugene Eyraud landed on Easter in 1864 he discovered the existence of hundreds of long wooden tablets and staffs incised with thousands of small hieroglyphic figures. Apparently believing them the work of the Devil, he burned all he could find. But 25 somehow survived and became the source of another Easter Island puzzle. What was the meaning of these unique 'rongorongo' as they were called, with their lines of tiny glyphs written upside down on alternate lines – for no systems of writing evolved elsewhere in the Pacific Islands. The keenest Victorian minds such as famous zoologist Thomas Huxley (1825–95) tried to decipher the glyphs. Some of the best minds of the twentieth century tried too. Building upon earlier and contemporary studies by ethnologists and epigraphers, Steven R. Fischer finally found the solution only in the 1990s. Rongorongo repeat procreation chants. Mostly they follow the structure of ancient Polynesian procreation chants/genealogies, namely: 'X copulated with Y: there issued forth Z'. Rongorongo examples are: 'Ant copulated with Pura Yam: there issued forth the ant' and 'All the birds copulated with fish: There issued forth the sun.'

Rongorongo were also relatively modern. It seems that Easter's priests were inspired by the 'treaty of annexation' drafted in front of them by the Spanish on their brief 1770 visit. During this ceremony the Spaniards encouraged the Island leaders to 'sign' the document by making their marks in ink. This was powerful mana and the Islanders later began to invoke this mana by producing rongorongo. Their rongorongo glyphs were derived from an obvious source, the glyphs of their own rich local carved rock art of sun, birds, ants, fish. The chants are written from left to right in imitation of Spanish, and the regular reversal helps to avoid confusing the lines. The priests who composed rongorongo were creating procreation stories to fit the evolving religion of Makemake.

Fijians: 'Polynesian Melanesians'

The Fijians are today generally regarded as Melanesians, but in the past they formed a borderland or cultural bridge between Melanesia and Polynesia.

Physically, Fiji is more like such Melanesian islands as Vanuatu and the Solomon Islands. It has always been heavily forested. Even today, in sharp contrast to Easter Island, almost half of the total area remains so. From a plane flying over central Viti Levu, the interlaced trees look like some monster green moss.

MELANESIAN LOOK, POLYNESIAN CULTURE

Our conventional racial and cultural boundary between Melanesia and Polynesia made no sense in earlier times. Fiji together with Tonga and

Samoa was then part of the region in which proto-Polynesians and their culture first evolved from the original Austronesian-speaking Lapita people who arrived in the Fiji Islands around 1500 BC. Probably with continual infusions from Vanuatu, the Fijian racial type developed at the same time as the Polynesian type was itself evolving in Tonga and Samoa. The word 'Fiji' is a Tongan corruption of 'Viti', the original name for the islands.

Despite the fact of their overwhelmingly Melanesian appearance today, modern Fijians and their culture still share features from the quasi-Polynesian past, such as their large stature, though their darker skins link them to other Melanesians.

It is in their social and political arrangements that the Polynesian connection is most obvious. As in Polynesia people specialized. There were priests, warriors, craftsmen, fishermen, even special fishermen for different kinds of sea creatures. And there have long been relationships between the scattered Lau Islands chain of eastern Fiji and the Tongan Islands. In recent centuries ties have been in trade and marriage alliances. Ties were often aggressive. Tongan warriors fought in Fijian wars.

At several stages in the early Fijian archaeological record, about 700 BC and about AD 1100, for example, new types of pottery appear, the latter like the Mangaasi ware of Vanuatu. Their arrival suggests further waves of migration into Fiji from Melanesian islands to the north-west. Such immigrants presumably helped to produce a Fijian physical type different from their evolving Polynesian neighbours in Tonga and Samoa.

During the first millennium of the Christian era there seems to have been considerable coming and going between Fiji and the nearby evolving Polynesians. A whole chain of related dialects evolved, stretching from the western Fijian islands and into Samoa and Tonga, one or more of which became the basis for the early forms of the Polynesian languages.

CHIEFS, CANNIBALISM, AND CONFLICT

Kudos and mana could be gained by generous distribution of food, but not to the extent of the 'Big Man' of New Guinea and Vanuatu.

Rather, the Fijian political style, like the Polynesian, tended to emphasize status and authority by descent, and gaining greater power through diplomacy and war.

Perhaps these immigrations/invasions encouraged conflict. For around AD 1100 large numbers of fortifications of earthworks were built on the two main islands of Viti Levu and Vanua Levu, and on Tavenui, which points to regular warfare. In fact Fijian traditional and oral history is full of tales of callous and cruel fighting. Suicide was preferable to capture.

Chiefs were powerful, with unchallenged power of life and death over commoners. A chief dwelt in a large house. When its corner posts required replacing, rotted by the rain and humidity, commoners were sacrificed. Several of them became human foundations. When a chief or a great warrior died his wives were sacrificed, or buried alive alongside him. No European ruler ever possessed such absolute rights. Regarded as the living embodiment of the ancestor god and of the tribe as a whole, chiefs saw themselves as *personifying* the tribe both present *and* past. In a way they still do. The following quotations from the 1947 proceedings of a government enquiry into fishing rights show this belief. The Ratu of Verata and the representative of Bau are disputing historical claims:

> *Ratu of Verata*: I have never heard of our meeting at Naivonini in 1750 . . . I don't know any Bau Herald named Sainisakalo that you say I killed at the beach at Walu [in the late 1830s] . . . I do not know of any set of 10 whales' teeth that you claim were offered on my behalf by Nagalu to Ratu Cakobau and Ratu Mara [in the 1850s] . . .
>
> *Representative of Bau*: From long ago until 1750 you were the owner of all the reefs we are disputing here, but I won them from you in 1750 when I defeated you in the war at Naivonini . . . I know that I destroyed you the third time I took your town.

Fiji's drua, 100 ft/30m-long double-hulled catamarans were the fastest, strongest, most manoeuvrable in the Pacific. Their construction was in the hands of master craftsmen with hereditary status, and they took years, some as many as seven, to construct. The amount of food available was significant for this skilled but hard work. There was a saying amongst such men, 'The chopping is in the belly.' Their key importance in war demanded ceremonial and symbolism when they were launched. Again people were sacrificed, preferably prisoners-of-war. Tightly bound, they became screaming human rollers over whom the drua would be hauled to the water.

Other ceremonies too required piles of freshly slaughtered human beings. A normal ritual greeting for a commoner to a paramount chief was the abject, 'Eat me!' Commoners were expected to bring the earliest yams and taro as supplication to the chief. In return, tradition demanded that he present them with the bodies of enemies or outsiders for their own feasts. A similar ritual occurred when a chief married. Whether such cannibalistic rituals evolved in Fiji or came with the earliest colonists is not known, but clearly they were ancient, for there is evidence of cannibalism in Fijian middens of food-waste from as early as about 2,500 years ago.

After a battle, bodies were either eaten on the field or returned to the village spirit house, offered to the god of war, butchered and baked, and the meat served up on plaintain leaves. The victory was celebrated with music and dance, men performing the death dance, women the 'dele' or 'wate' in which they sexually abused corpses and prisoners. For later eating, strips of human meat were preserved by smoking, like pieces of beef jerky. Because their hands and lips were tapu, Fijian chiefs normally could not touch their food, and were fed by female attendant. But at cannibal feasts chiefs fed themselves with sacred, carved, lon -pronged wooden forks. These forks had names and it was believed, personalities, and were preserved in the spirit house.

Hairpins, ornaments, and ear decorations were made from human bone; the coastal tribes of Viti Levu used leg bones as needles for thatching and sail making. The skull of a special enemy might be used as a kava drinking bowl. Bones were also placed as trophies outside the spirit house.

Temperate Climate Polynesians: early-Maori and Maori of New Zealand

New Zealand is easily the highest, largest, longest, widest, most physically and climatically diverse landmass in Polynesia. Even counting the

Hawaiian Islands, New Zealand takes up about 90 per cent of Polynesian land. It is also by far the coldest Polynesian country. When the ancestors of the Maori arrived, they faced some generations of exploration and difficult climatic adaptation.

THE FIRST LANDFALL

Though the dates of arrival are debated, New Zealand was certainly the last landmass in the Pacific (Polynesia, Melanesia, or Micronesia) to be settled. Most linguists and archaeologists now agree that settlement of New Zealand was from eastern Polynesia, probably the Society Islands. Recent archaeological digs in Huahine, near Tahiti, suggest a specially close affinity to Maori culture. There may have been only one original canoe, or there may have been several. Recent DNA analysis points to perhaps 70 women in the first landfall(s). It has been suggested that during the first century, driven by a high protein intake from eating moa, the population doubled every 30 years. Had this rate continued the population would have been more than 86,000 in 1769. This number has recently been estimated by the modern New Zealand historian James Belich, for the year in which the English navigator James Cook first arrived. But lean years and starvation hit the population hard after the moa were exterminated, leading to severe population decline. Earlier estimates of population have been much higher, but it is now widely agreed that they (and the estimated population in other Polynesian islands) have been widely exaggerated – 'wild guesses, or uncritical regurgitations of wild guesses' as, Bellich puts it.

Probably around AD 1300, on a summer's day the first Polynesian catamaran canoe(s) landed in uninhabited New Zealand, on the northeast coast of the North Island. Archaeologists have shown that except for the high mountains, all of New Zealand had been occupied within about a century, though some areas were very sparsely peopled. A search for the best areas for hunting and horticulture presumably produced this dispersal. By the time the first Europeans arrived in the late 1700s the whole country was claimed by one tribe or another, the claim resting upon historical occupation, use of the land, or conquest. Aware of no other race, the Maori thought of themselves just as *tangata whenua*, 'the local people'.

The first arrivals had been lucky. Favoured by the weather, somehow they had avoided the winds of the regular depressions blowing from the west. They therefore escaped being lost in the vast open ocean between New Zealand and South America, or forced east and south into the great waters which stride through 2,000 empty miles all the way to Antarctica. And suppose instead, sailing farther west they had landed in eastern Australia or on an island off its coast, what would have been their future?

The first colonizers of New Zealand were young and strong, the expedition apparently planned – in the sense that they hoped to find new land. The women had a precious stock of plants. These included coconuts, yams, taro, gourd seeds, paper mulberry cuttings, sweet-potatoes (kumara) and colocasia tubers. Perhaps there were also plaintains and bread fruit, which would have been planted immediately and carefully cultivated. Dogs survived the voyage, as did an unwanted stowaway, the Polynesian rat!

There may have been later arrivals of Polynesians – but most likely *not* through any *knowledge* of the existence of New Zealand carried back to them. The complete absence of New Zealand artifacts in tropical Polynesia, including valuable ones such as greenstone, and the absence in New Zealand of the prize Polynesian food animal, the pig, strongly suggests there were no return or round-trip voyages to the island(s) of origin. The Tahitians, who had knowledge of many Polynesian peoples, had none about New Zealand. The Tahitian Tupaia (Tupia) accompanied Cook on his first voyage to New Zealand. Tupaia's Polynesian language was sufficiently similar to Maori for him to be able to converse. He was sharp, and raised a serious objection to some Maori claims to have made a round-trip voyage. Joseph Banks quotes his retort thus:

> And you have no hogs among you? said Tupia. – No. – And did your ancestors bring none back with them? – No. – You must be a parcel of Liars then, said he, and your story a great lie for your ancestors would never have been such fools as to come back without them.

DIFFICULTIES OF ADAPTATION

The newcomers soon found that open-sided tropical houses had to be replaced by warmer-walled ones, and began to insulate the walls with bullrushes. They quickly learned the need for more clothing. In the temperate climate, many of their tropical plants failed. There were no local breadfruit, bananas, or pawpaws (papayas), but the kumara survived. This last fact suggests that the landfall must indeed have been in the north of the North Island, because only there could the first plants have lived through the more rigorous New Zealand winter where frosts occur throughout the islands except for the extreme tip of Northland. Only after much trial and error would they have found a way to grow kumara further inland and further south. The colonists discovered that kumara tubers needed to be stored underground and carefully tended. The paper mulberry, taro, and gourd also survived – but scarcely flourished.

Fortunately, the surrounding ocean teemed with fish, and in the tidal reaches there were many different kinds of shell-fish in a much greater variety than on the Pacific's tropical islands. Seals and sea-lions in immense numbers gathered in rookeries all along the coast. With a little ingenuity they could be surprised and clubbed to death. The newcomers found no native four-footed animals, but birds in their billions – rails, geese, ducks, swans, countless seabirds, and many small flightless birds like the kiwi.

We know from skeletal evidence that the males among the settlers were tall by mediaeval world standards, averaging 5ft.7ins/1.7m. We also know that both sexes shared the duty of paddling, as shown by a groove in the collarbone of skeletons.

Arthritis was common. Pneumonia and infections caused by decaying teeth seem to have been significant killers. Gum diseases often occurred – which shows that the vitamin-rich fern root, which later became a staple, was not eaten by the earliest settlers. This reluctance is understandable because fern root in other parts of Polynesia was a famine food, a last resort. These early-Maori people lived on the average perhaps 35 years.

EXTERMINATING THE MOA

The moa is the other flightless bird for which New Zealand is famous. After New Zealand separated from Gondwana, the Moa evolved independently of its 'cousins' the emu, the ostrich, and the cassowarry, stranded on other southern landmasses. All apparently developed from a common Gondwana ancestor, the ratites.

Moa ranged in size from that of a large turkey to the massive Great Moa, of 440 lb (200 kg), with a back some 6ft.6ins/2m high, and a neck it could stretch to perhaps 10ft/3m, though this is only an educated guess because no one knows the way moa held their heads and necks. Though moa inhabited all the different New Zealand landforms except for the high mountains, they bred slowly and population density was low. Even where they were most prolific, such as in eastern South Island, density was no more than 2 to 5 per sq.mile/2 per sq.k. Their only enemy was the huge *Harpagornis* – the largest eagle known to history. Its 30 lb/13.5 kg of muscle and 12 ins/30 cm tiger-like claws plummeting from its perch in high tree or cliff provided an efficient killing machine – like a pack of bricks falling from an eight-storey

The now extinct Great Moa and a Kea parrot

building. Yet, having evolved together, eagles and moa remained in ecological balance.

The arrival of the ancestral Maori, sometimes called the Moa Hunters, ended all this. For the moa soon became their primary food. There are about 300 moa archaeological sites, of two sorts: sites where moa perished from natural causes in caves and rocks, mud deposits, volcanic ash, glacial ice, sand dunes, and swamps; and the butchering sites of the Moa Hunters.

The great swamps revealed huge deposits of bones when they were being drained for farming by nineteenth-century settlers. At Glenmark Swamp, first examined by famous Canterbury geologist, Julius von Haast, there might have been a thousand skeletons of moa trapped when they fell through the deceptive semi-floating covering mat of vegetation. The killed moa were brought downstream by reed boats from the hunting grounds, and over the years the larger sites saw many thousands butchered, cooked, and consumed. The large moa eggs would also have been popular, the shells used as containers for water. Moa eggs at up to 15 lb/7kg were the equivalent of perhaps ninety or more hens' eggs.

How early-Maori killed moa remains a mystery. Oral tradition did not record it. Surprisingly, there are no hunting weapons at sites. They had no bows and arrows, and moa ran faster. The best guess is clubs, spears, dogs, and fire, together with snares. Snares were certainly used to catch other flightless birds, and would have made capture less dangerous, for moa had disproportionately massive clawed feet. The bones of the moa were themselves fashioned into various artifacts for harpoons and spear heads, fish hooks, needles, and awls. It has been suggested that moa meat may have been preserved in its own fat, held in bags made of taha and kelp.

Hunting seems to have reached its greatest in the late 1300s. As von Haast was the first to point out, the hunters were extraordinarily wasteful: '[They] must have had such an abundance of game that they selected for their food only the most valued portions of the birds.' Such profligacy, combined with the human population now in the several tens of thousands, and with clearing the moa habitat of brush and forest for horticulture, began a rapid decline. Probably few moa remained after about 1500, with extinction soon after. These early-Maori were no better than today's human beings at environmental preservation. Besides the twelve species of moa, they wiped out about twenty other bird species and burned off about a third of the native forest prior to European arrival. The more accessible seals and sea-lions on the large islands also were hunted to extinction. Naturally, the moa's chief predator, the great eagle, also passed from the earth. Perhaps the cute kiwi survived because it was nocturnal.

TROPICAL POLYNESIAN CULTURE ADAPTS TO NEW ZEALAND

With their previous experience limited to small islands, New Zealand must have seemed a continent to the newcomers. Puzzled by the unfamiliar plants, they were forced to coin new names, consisting of compounds of botanical terms they had previously used separately.

Novel geographical entities such as snow and lakes also strained linguistic abilities. The white stuff glistening upon the highest mountains of the North Island was called fuka (foam). The large lakes too were outside all previous experience. Some, such as Taupo in the North Island and Wakatipu in the South Island were as large as the islands from which they came. They called such lakes either roto (lagoon), or moana (sea/ocean), the first depicting a body of water which was really too small, and the second one much too large. Their word 'moa' was equally unsuitable. 'Moa' was the old Polynesian term for chicken!

There were no pandanus plants to weave into baskets and mats, but there were varieties of New Zealand flax which could be used. Tedious hours of tiring finger work by the women produced a sort of flax twine which could be woven into cloth. The tall New Zealand trees, totara and kauri proved superior to tropical Polynesian timber, and strong houses and splendid long canoes could be constructed.

The long summer days were also a surprise, contributing to the name eventually given to the new land – Aotearoa (long daylight).

Amongst the first settlers there must have been at least one person well versed in Polynesian myths, for Maori oral tradition is as rich as any other in the Pacific, and much resembles others such as the

Marquesan. Naturally, in their new environment Maori produced some changes.

TRIBES

Over a period of several hundred years the early-Maori evolved into the Maori, their way of life modified by their new temperate environment. They also developed into tribes (iwi), clans (hapu) and extended families (whanau). By Cook's visit in 1769 something like fifty tribes or confederations of tribes existed in a state of intense rivalry, and warriors defended their territories to the death. Powerful tribes which developed included the Nga Puhi of the Bay of Islands, the Waikato of the Waikato and Waipa valleys and the coast north of Kawhia, the Ngati Maniapoto of the King Country further south, and the Te Arawa group further east. The most important South Island tribe was the Ngai Tahu.

Tribes had chiefs (ariki), commonly the senior son of the senior family, and an aristocratic class (rangatira). Also within the aristocrats were priests (tohunga). The common people were called 'tutua'. Some tohunga were concerned with spiritual matters, others with practical expertise. Maori traced and trace ancestry through both male and female, though the complexity is lessened by the importance given to chiefly lines. As with almost every other race or group in the history of the world, Maori also kept slaves (taurekareka) – usually prisoners captured in war.

A tribe's lands would usually support several villages, with much temporary dwelling at the site of main sources of food. Construction of a large object such as a long fishing net, a fortified village (pa), or a large war canoe, required the cooperation of the whole clan or tribe. The tribe or clan was united not merely by kinship and shared values, but by communal ownership of land. A core value was obligation to kin, which showed itself in sharing of resources and jealously preserved relationships.

WAY OF LIFE AND ARTS

Tribes which owned the more fertile northern regions with a settled agricultural base were larger in numbers than tribes in South Island, which mainly hunted and gathered. By the time of Cook's visit probably more than 85 per cent of population lived in the North Island.

Like other Polynesians, the early settlers and their descendants lived a New Stone Age life, making weapons, tools, and utensils from animal and human bone, stone, and shells, and cooking food in earthen ovens. The most important stone for knives was obsidian, volcanic 'glass' found in the north of North Island, with some trade between regions. On the western side of the Southern Alps greenstone was found in the riverbeds. Greenstone is a high-quality jade which Maori learned to shape and sharpen to a fine cutting edge. Superb fighting clubs and carving chisels, and a whole range of ornaments were also made from greenstone. South Island tribes travelled through the mountain passes to gather greenstone. Much of it was then traded across Cook Strait to northern tribes.

The arts were central to Maori lives and religion. Even with their limited tools the decorated boards of tribal meeting houses (whare tapuna) and the bows and sterns of war canoes were marvellous. *Te Toki a Tapiri*, the 82 ft/25m, 100-man war canoe in Auckland War Memorial Museum constructed circa 1836 from a single totara log, is a superb example. Maori carving was the most fully developed in Polynesia. (British steel chisels, acquired from the early 1800s, further improved Maori technique.)

Similar to the carvings on wood were the carvings on the human body – tattoo, or in Maori, 'moko' – scratched with a scalpel-sharp bone implement. After these stoically endured wounds healed, a blue-stained dye design remained permanently (Appendix 4).

There were many different dances which were accompanied by songs and music. There was the grimacing, intimidating haka (Appendix 3) of the men, with its rolling eyes, protruding tongues, slapping thighs, stentorian shouts, and stamping feet. And there was the gentle, flowing poi dance of the women – accompanied by a sprightly refrain and as its core the complex twirling of the poi. The poi was a small flax ball stuffed with the down of the raupo (bullrush) flower. It was attached to a short or long string and whirled, thrown, caught, and tapped to the music and song.

Though some Maori women of aristocratic birth could be very

Maori tattoo or 'Moko'

influential, most women seem to have been controlled by their men-folk. Though Reverend Samuel Marsden said he never saw a woman maltreated, Johann R. Forster wrote that women were 'perfect slaves' of their men, and Richard Cruise who visited Northland in 1820 said that husbands, 'considering women as beings infinitely inferior to themselves, often treat them with great brutality'.

Women were popular prisoners of war and became the sex-slaves or low-status wives of their captors. In general women were 'second class citizens'. They possessed no rights of address in tribal forums. Little everyday distinctions make the point: though women were the best at catching crayfish, it was men who consumed the best crayfish caught. Subordination to men ought to be expected. It is the general pattern through history on every continent but the variation comes in the degree of ill treatment. Still, there were and are several basic practices in which both sexes are equally important, though playing separate roles. And there were and are some, such as the call (te karanga), by which a woman welcomes visitors onto the marae, to be returned by a woman from the visiting group, which are crucial and without which there can be no gathering.

Maori children helped in the home and the field, and from their mothers and fathers learned to become wives or warriors. They also had many amusements: flew kites, span tops, walked on stilts, and played games similar to knucklebones and cat's cradle.

MURU AND UTU: RAIDS OF RETRIBUTION

In Maoridom, infringements and disturbances of social order in almost all cases invoked the principle of 'utu'. Social/political relationships between individuals, hapu, and tribes involved an implicit 'accounting system' of positives and negatives. A favour involved returning the favour in the future. This helped stability within hapu and tribes, and underpinned trade.

Utu restored the balance and preserved or restored mana to avoid the ancestor gods' displeasure. In restoring the balance utu involved payback, recompense, revenge, for insult or harm real or imagined, which could result in some kind of conflict. Within tribes or hapu, utu dictated that offences and infringement of mores brought retribution in the form of 'muru' – socially accepted compensating plunder of persons and their property. Muru turned violent only when the victim resisted.

For serious offences such as murder, or an attack by another tribe, the reprisals of muru necessarily turned equally deadly. Much tribal, clan, and family history turns on revenge and murder. Occasionally a woman might refuse marriage until her suitor had avenged her kinsman's death. Helping perpetuate disputes and making matters more bloody was the fact that extended families, clans, and tribes tended to become the focus of vengeance rather than merely the guilty individuals.

MANA AND TAPU

New Zealand beliefs were similar to those of Polynesia generally. There was never-ending rivalry to acquire mana. Mana among one's extended family and sub-tribe came first; second was mana among one's tribe; then came mana among neighbouring tribes related by marriage and tradition. Rivalry could become overt competition, but when this threatened the general welfare it was recognized as counter-productive and mana suffered. Mana could also be acquired by co-operative and constructive achievement. The Maori cared little what strangers thought. But strangers served their purpose, and a successful campaign against a distant tribe could raise one's mana among kin and among neighbouring tribes if they agreed with the act.

Were, say, a chief insulted or fields trespassed upon, a tribe was compelled by utu to exact muru, otherwise they believed loss of mana and fatal spiritual retribution would follow. Food and death tapus were particularly powerful, whose infringement could be extirpated only by more deaths, or battle.

WARRIOR VALUES AND WAR

Warrior values were displayed in these struggles within and among tribes, for the same motives as in other parts of Polynesia. Making the sequence unending, death in battle had to be avenged. Jean Roux, one of Marion du Fresne's officers, described a duel he accidentally wit-nessed in the Bay of Islands in 1772, while hunting, probably between Ngati Pou and Nga Puhi warriors. For perhaps six minutes the two Maori combatants exchanged vicious blows with long two-handed hardwood weapons called taiaha (blade at one end, spear-point at the other). They demonstrated amazing skill and astonishing reflexes and agility, after which they simultaneously changed to one-handed short clubs (patu) which they drew from their wide flax belts. When they then fell to it again with equal vehemence Roux realized this was no practice match. He rushed to intervene, at which point one of the men, probably distracted, had his head split open, and dropped dead while the other sprinted away. The head, said Roux, 'was cut open at the level of the eyes as if by a blow from a cutlass'.

From about AD 1400, perhaps coinciding with the decline of the moa, there seem to have been endemic tribal wars, though lack of sophistication in the weapons helped restrict bloodshed. Tribes and clans began to construct elaborate hill-forts (pa). These were both community centres and strong defensive points. About 6,000 sites have been identified. (There are stories of lost/shipwrecked Spanish ships, and that Maori learned how to construct the palisades of pa from their crews! Some people turn the least likely possibility into the most likely. Let us at least give Maori credit for being able to develop palisades for themselves.) Many of these pa are in reasonable preservation, the terraces clearly visible through the green grass cover. Several well-preserved examples, such as One Tree Hill, stand boldly within the built-up area of Auckland, New Zealand's largest city.

Their complexity surpassed all other Polynesian fortifications. There were banks, ditches, palisades, trenches, fighting stages. Inside the pa was again partitioned for further defence. The age-old, worldwide battle rule of defending from height and the high ground was applied wherever possible. Pa were so well constructed that after a few days besiegers generally gave up. Successful attacks were almost always the result of ruse, surprise, or deceit, and ambush became a well-used Maori military tactic.

Though war was of supreme value, Maori were practical people. There would not be much fun in fighting if everyone were starving. So when kumara crops had to be planted, husbanded, harvested, these tasks usually took precedence over war. Fighting traditionally began following the planting of kumara in October and November – though this was also better weather for fighting!

CANNIBALISM

As elsewhere in the South Pacific, and depending on circumstances, eating someone could be just a part of diet, or the ultimate in religion-driven revenge. The eating of prisoners of war on the campaign trail is an instance of the first; the eating of Frenchman Marion du Fresne, now to be considered, is an example of the second. The death of Marion (1737?–72) is the earliest verified cannibal report. It also provides a marvellous example of the inescapable power of tapu.

Marion du Fresne was visiting the Bay of Islands in 1772. He and his crew spoke a little Tahitian Polynesian and were able to communicate to some extent. According to the local Ngati Pou, Marion and his crew had been warned not to fish in a cove that was now tapu because several of the chief Te Kauri's relatives had recently drowned there. For some reason Marion and his men fished and ate the fish. This was a sort of double infringement of tapu. For the fish might have nibbled the bodies of the drowned Ngati Pou, and to eat them was like eating the corpses of the tribe, and thus an attack on both the tapu of the corpses and on the mana of the tribe's gods.

There may also have been some tribal rivalries involved, but in any case the Maori killed Marion and fifteen of his crew and ate them, thus deliberately destroying their life force and mana. Their bones were turned into forks and flutes. The Ngati Pou also tormented the French by wearing the clothes of Marion and other dead officers, shouting something like, 'Te Kauri ate Marion!' Jean Roux, who witnessed the duel described earlier, was one who survived. In retaliation he and the other Frenchmen attacked three villages and shot perhaps 100 tribespeople. In ignorance of the real motives, each side had been appalled by the behaviour of the other and took vengeance according to its own conceptions of justice.

FOOD SCARCITY

Loss of all sources of moa and seal protein was serious. Skeletons in archaeological sites have shown clear evidence of recurring famine.

This was despite the fact that the Maori had made valiant efforts to make up for the shortfall: by migrating to less populated areas; by intensifying their horticulture; by extending hunting of birds and rats, and gathering of wild fruits, berries, fern tips, roots, and shoots; by innovative techniques such as taking honey from flax and making cakes of raupo pollen; and by warfare to take resources from others. One huge problem was that some of the easier-to-obtain 'bush food' had little food value. It has been estimated that for an adult Maori to survive on cabbage-tree pith 42 lb/18.8 kg a day would be required! Fernroot had to be dried for two weeks before the hard work of pounding could begin, and then needed baking. Some foodstuffs were poisonous in the raw state and required special preparation. In any case even the taro and kumara fields required hard digging with long-handled ko, a pointed wooden 'spade', like a stilt with a cross-bar for thrusting with the foot, about 18 ins/46 cm from the bottom.

When Europeans first arrived at the end of the 1700s, the staple elements of diet were difficult-to-digest fern roots (a food which wore teeth flat), fish, and shell-fish, and difficult-to-produce kumara. It is

likely that the introduction of the white potato by early European
explorers such as Cook saved many Maori from starvation.

We now describe the arrival of the European navigators who would
eventually change this Maori way of life, and also link the scattered
archipelagoes of the South Pacific into a geographical whole.

CHAPTER FOUR

Contact and Commerce: the South Pacific Islands to around 1900

In the late 1400s and early 1500s Western Europe broke free from the Muslim strait-jacket which both constrained it and controlled eastern and far-eastern trade through the Middle East. Europeans now went in search of the sources of this trade. Made possible by improved ships, coupled with an inquisitiveness to discover the nature of the world, first the Portuguese outflanked the Muslims by sailing around Africa, and a few decades later the Spanish repeated the process in the opposite direction around the south of South America. As a result, in the 1500s and 1600s European navigators began to arrive in the South Pacific. The complex relationship, which to this day continues to evolve, had begun. The Pacific Islands and Europe both being aggressive, militaristic cultures, the surprising fact is that clashes were not more common.

In the late 1700s and 1800s, in the wake of the ocean explorers came traders and Christian missionaries, and a little later European settlers and large trading companies, and after decades of informal piecemeal colonization, European and American domination. The earliest of these outside influences was the commerce of whaling and other extractive trades.

This chapter describes the first sea explorers and the early traders.

Early European Navigators and Savants

MAGELLAN, THE PATHFINDER

Ferdinand Magellan (1480?–1521) was a great Portuguese navigator in the pay of the Spanish Crown. The difficulties of Magellan and his crew, the first Europeans to enter the Pacific, are worth describing.

In 1520, when Magellan sailed into the Southern Sea he renamed it *el Pacifico*, the Pacific, because it seemed so calm. He thought it might take a week or two to sail across to his planned destination, the Spice Islands in the Indies (Indonesia). The actual distance is about 10,000 miles! Underestimation of the size of the earth, overestimation of the size of Asia, compounded by navigators' difficulties in accurately calculating longitude grossly misled him about the width of the Pacific. Borne by the south-east trade-winds, day after day, week after week, to Magellan's increasing consternation, his three tiny ships sailed north-west but sighted no land.

Early in January 1521, men began to die of malnutrition and illness. The biscuits were rotten with weevils, the flour stained yellow with rats' urine; the remaining food was foul. Amazingly, Magellan missed seeing every one of the eastern Pacific's vast archipelagoes of atolls and high islands. Though their route passed close, they saw neither Sala y Gomez, nor Easter Island, nor Pitcairn nor most of the islands of what is now French Polynesia.

In late January, they stumbled onto an atoll, probably Pukapuka in the northern Tuamotus, and for a week replenished their water, and gorged themselves on turtle eggs till sick. In early February they saw another flat atoll, possibly Caroline Atoll in the Line Islands. Still they sailed north-west and Dame fortune kept playing her tricks. They missed the northern Cook Islands, and all the islands of Tuvalu and Kiribati. Now they were reduced to eating the hides which bound the rigging. 'And of the rats which were sold for half an ecu apiece, some of us could not get enough', writes Antonio Pigafetta, the Italian gentleman who accompanied Magellan. More men died from scurvy. Scurvy, a vitamin deficiency disease, caused gums to swell, teeth to fall out, which together made chewing virtually impossible, and stiff joints which finally made movement impossible too.

Then on 6 March they made landfall at the island we call Guam, in Micronesia. Ten days later they were in the archipelago of the Philippines which they named after their king. They had taken almost four months to cross. Pigafetta's judgment on the journey was: 'And I believe that nevermore will any man undertake to make such a voyage'! This peculiar, incalculable mix of determination, privation, and good and bad luck, was typical of all the early Pacific expeditions.

Victims of hunger, thirst, and disease especially scurvy, crews died in great numbers, and those who survived were deeply fatigued. Ships and their equipment rotted away, and many had to be scuttled. There were problems of discipline and morale in sick, tired, bored crews years away from home, and mutinies occurred. And not least were the immense difficulties of finding one's way for there was no accurate method of calculating longitude. They had to rely on 'dead reckoning', an estimate of the distance travelled each day. Problems of longitude were the main reason why islands were discovered and then lost. As one geographer wistfully put it, 'There are in the South Sea many Islands, which may be called Wandering Islands.' Even Magellan had not reached the Spice Islands, and was killed before his ship, now captained by Juan del Cano, finally did so. The problem remained until Englishman John Harrison (1693–1776) invented the marine chronometer in the mid-1700s.

SEEKING SPICE AND '*TERRA AUSTRALIS*'

Driven by avarice and the desire to seize the spice trade from the Portuguese, curiosity and a profound desire to convert the heathen to Catholicism, Magellan's Spanish were first into the South Pacific. Five years later they followed with seven ships captained by Garcia de Loaysa, piloted by Juan del Cano. Only Garcia's flagship reached the Spice Islands, but both he and del Cano were dead by that time.

The next South Pacific endeavour was led by Alvaro de Mendana de Neira (1541–96) in 1567–68. He departed from Spain's Pacific colony of New Castille (Peru), searching for *Terra Australis Incognita*, the great Unknown Southern Land. Ancient Greek philosophers, contemporary geographers, and commonsense believed this continent must exist to balance the northern continents. Mendana found the Solomon Islands instead. (There was a legend that the gold of Old Testament King Solomon came from these islands.) In 1595 a much older de Mendana with the Portuguese Pedro Fernandez de Quiros (1565?–1615) set sail again and once more crossed the whole of the tropical South Pacific.

Quiros was the first to claim to have found *Terra Australis*, and as he said he 'took possession of the site of the New Jerusalem'. Actually it was the island of Espiritu Santo in Vanuatu. In 1605–6 de Quiros and the Portuguese Luis de Torres (1565?–1610) found the south coast of New Guinea, but no *Terra Australis*. Disease and constant hostilities ended a Spanish attempt to colonize the Solomons, and Spanish interest moved to the more receptive climes of Micronesia and the Philippines.

Next came the Dutch, moving east into the Pacific from their East India Company colony in the East Indies (Indonesia). They sought trade and hoped to find it in *Terra Australis*. In 1615 Jakob Le Maire unsuccessfully searched for *Terra Australis*, and one summer December evening in 1642 Abel Janszoon Tasman (1603–59) believed he had found one corner of it. In fact Tasman had stumbled upon a piece of New Zealand. Tasman anchored in what is now called Golden Bay (gold was later found there) in the north of South Island. Two Maori canoes of the Ngati Tumata-kokiri tribe approached, and hailed his ship. The Maori sounded an instrument 'like a Moorish trumpet'. Tasman's crew waved, and one, who could play the trumpet a bit, improvised some tunes. Perhaps the Maori interpreted this reply as a challenge. For next day war canoes surrounded Tasman's ships and four Dutch sailors in a ship's boat were killed. Tasman called the place 'Murderers' Bay'. Though he sailed away without landing, it was he who gave the new land the name by which the world would come to know it. At first he referred to 'Staten Land', and only later, 'New Zealand' after the coastal province of Zeeland in his Netherlands.

Tasman's fortunes improved in the islands of Tonga further north. He visited many and gave them Dutch names. On Tongatapu Tasman was entertained by the claimed thirty-second Tui Tonga and the seventh Tui Ha'atakalua, and was presented with a beautiful wooden bowl. He found the islands peaceful and the Tongans industrious and ready to trade. They deeply coveted European iron – a metal which would eventually help change the way of life of the whole Pacific.

In 1722, after rounding Cape Horn, Jacob Roggeveen reached remote Easter Island. Roggeveen was followed by the Frenchmen

Louis-Antoine de Bougainville in 1768 and La Perouse in 1787, and by Spaniards in 1770.

There were also the English. Sir Francis Drake (c.1540/43–96), in 1577–80, also searching for the South Land, sailed the far eastern Pacific, touching the coast of the Americas in what became buccaneering raids against the Spanish colonies, and crossed the North Pacific before completely circumnavigating the world by 1580. Three-quarters of a century later the gifted observer William Dampier (1651–1715) led a proto-scientific expedition into Melanesia for the British Admiralty. His book *A New Voyage around the World* (1697) popularized the idea of a great southern continent. In 1743 George Anson (1697–1762) sailed across the South Pacific before capturing the Spanish silver galleon from Acapulco. Exemplifying the dangers of Pacific voyaging, he lost five of his six ships and 1000 men not in battle, but to illness and hazards of the journey. He then completed his own circumnavigation of the world.

The Pacific had already become a place of mystery and legend, and writers were able to use it as a setting for exotic adventures. Jonathan Swift's (1667–1745) hero, for instance, in *Gulliver's Travels* (1726) has adventures in various parts of the Pacific, and his best-known adventure occurs in diminutive Lilliput. The latitude and longitude Swift gives, place Lilliput in the area of *bone dry* Lake Torrens (!) in the present state of South Australia, which was then an unknown blank on world maps. Daniel Defoe (1660–1731) in his enormously popular *Robinson Crusoe* (1719) sets down his hero on an uninhabited island on the opposite side, in the eastern South Pacific.

WALLIS AND TUMESCENT TAHITI

By the 1760s intellectuals were persuading the French and British governments that more systematically organized searches for *Terra Australis Incognita* should be mounted. The British were the first. In 1764 Commodore John Byron (uncle of the poet) went searching. He found some minor islands in the Tokelau, Tuamotu and Gilbert Islands (modern Kiribati).

In 1767 Captain Samuel Wallis (1728–?) and his crew in the *Dolphin*, also searching for the Southern Continent, were the first Europeans to see exotic Tahiti. During Wallis's five weeks' visit the voyagers found

Tahiti idyllic, though not at first. When his two ship's cutters tried to find an anchorage, they were attacked. For several more days the Tahitians opposed a landing, with perhaps 500 canoes and several thousand warriors.

By turns the Tahitians would be peaceful, offering to trade, then suddenly renew hostilities. They had attempted to lure the sailors in the cutters ashore by displaying 'a good many fine girls on the beach', as the *Dolphin*'s Master, George Robertson, demurely pointed out. And later, observing that the girls 'attracted our men's fancy a good deal ... the natives made the girls play many droll, wanting [wanton?] tricks, which drove all our people upon the Gunwells to see them'. Once Wallis's men could safely go ashore, relations altered dramatically. Given Tahitian hospitality, Wallis's crew like most Europeans in following decades were extremely reluctant to leave. Before doing so, Wallis annexed Tahiti in the name of King George III. He then continued the search for *Terra Australis* for several months.

THE NOBLE SAVAGE AND THE EUROPEAN ENLIGHTENMENT

It was with Wallis's encounter with the Tahitians that the exciting legend of the noble savage and his nubile women first began to mesmerize the European mind.

Two years after Wallis, the Frenchman de Bougainville, also on the trail of *Terra Australis*, arrived in Tahiti. (He too annexed it – in the name of Louis XV!) His ship was soon surrounded – by canoe-loads of bare-breasted young women offered by the Tahitians for sex in exchange for cloth, rope, and iron. Though he stayed merely 13 days, de Bougainville was convinced the Tahitians lived an idyllic life, and his elegant report, *Nouvelle Cythere*, played a major role in convincing educated Europeans of Tahiti's pristine innocence. The tales of love told by his sailors added to the legend.

Jean-Jacques Rousseau had written his *Discours sur les Arts et les Sciences* in 1749. It criticized Western civilization and praised the simple life which followed nature. So a (superficial) knowledge of Tahiti came at just the right time for the philosophers of the European Enlightenment – Rousseau, Diderot, Voltaire, Bouffon, Montesquieu, and the

The French explorer, Chevalier de Bougainville

others. Here, they falsely believed, was an example of unaccommodated man, a society where the unnecessary complexities of government, artificial conventions, antipathies of class, conflicting religious dogmas, constraints on sexual expression, and hatreds of Europe were all absent. With its seemingly joyous, forthright, and guilt-free attitude to life, its bountiful natural foods from ocean and forest, and its sunny climate, Tahiti appeared to the philosophers to echo Paradise before the Fall. It looked like an example of what Rousseau and the other philosophers called the 'state of nature', life *supposedly* as it had been prior to civilization. To return to it should be the aim of all rational politics and philosophy.

The Tahitian, Omai (c.1753–c.80), who had been wounded in a skirmish during Wallis's visit, was the first Polynesian to sail to Europe and return to his native land. The toast of society, he created a sensation in England and contributed to the myth. His portrait was painted by the famous Sir Joshua Reynolds. The novelist, Fanny Burney

(1752–1840) was completely infatuated by this Polynesian paragon, 'this lion of lions' as she gushed, who was continually jumping up and kissing ladies' hands. In discussing him, she, like many others, lost her critical faculties entirely. Omai seemed, she wrote,

> to shame education, for his manners are so extremely graceful, and he is so polite, attentive and easy that you would have thought he came from some foreign court ... I think this shows how much more Nature can do without art than art, with all her refining, unassisted by Nature.

Philibert Commerson, Bougainville's naturalist, an instant authority like the modern tourist who stays in a place a few days, wrote that Tahitians were a people without vice, without prejudice, without wants, without discord!

In time a more realistic assessment of the Polynesians emerged. Reports of human sacrifices, cannibalism, and massacres reached Europe. When the utopian Rousseau learned of Marion du Fresne's fate he was incredulous: 'Is it possible that the good Children of Nature can really be so wicked?'

The reports by Wallis, and Bougainville and Cook, and the others, formed part of a larger enterprise. For it was Enlightenment Europeans who first conceptualized the Pacific as a whole, i.e., as a place distinct from but in relation to the rest of the world's continents and oceans.

Learning about the South Pacific was merely one part of the mighty Enlightenment agenda, which was to seek and gather objective knowledge of the whole of the human world. The first step in understanding the South Pacific was to describe and catalogue what was there. Various categorizations were suggested, but the Frenchman, Jules-Sébastien-César Dumont d'Urville's (1790–1842) division into Polynesia, Melanesia, and Micronesia, of the 1820s, became accepted, eventually even by the Islanders themselves. Then came painstaking attempts to explain the existence of the Islanders: how they had reached their island homes and why Melanesians and Polynesians were so different from one another and other world cultures. From early tentative speculations, and the observations of perceptive explorers such as James Cook the modern subject of anthropology was born. Anthropology was a Pacific Islands baby.

James Cook, Explorer Extraordinary

James Cook (1728–79) began the true disciplined exploration of the Pacific. His Pacific journals form the foundation of our knowledge of the geography, anthropology, and culture of four of the main Polynesian groups: New Zealand, Tonga, Society Islands and Hawaii, and of the Melanesian islands of New Hebrides (Vanuatu) and New Caledonia, and of eastern Australia. Cook and his crew were probably also the first Europeans to see, and he and his officers certainly the first people to map accurately the last four places. He is often said to be the greatest of all the explorers of our world.

Though of humble origins, Cook's intelligence, application, and charisma caught the attention of his superiors. His experience as cartographer in Canadian waters in the Seven Years' War (French and Indian War) and the glowing reports of his commanders, recommended him.

THE FIRST VOYAGE: TAHITI, NEW ZEALAND, AUSTRALIA

As a result Cook was selected to lead the first thoroughly financed and carefully coordinated British scientific voyage into the Pacific. The ship he chose was the sturdy, former collier, *Endeavour*, 368 tons (334 tonnes) and just under 98 feet long! This is about half the length and a tenth the displacement of a modern private 'super yacht'. Joseph Banks (1744–1820), a wealthy young botanist and man-about-town, headed the scientific and civilian personnel. He was accompanied by astronomers, botanists, and artists. There was a social gulf here, a potential for disaster in the cramped spaces of *Endeavour*. But from the first there developed a genuine affection between the dour Yorkshire captain and the lively London naturalist.

In all Cook made three voyages which revolutionized mankind's understanding of the Pacific. And thanks to his insistence on regular doses of sauerkraut (rich in vitamin C – a concept unknown to Cook's time), not a single man died from the dreaded scurvy. Had this been his only achievement he would have been a significant historical figure.

The first voyage, 1768–71, took him directly to Tahiti, which rises out of the ocean like a mighty piece of crumpled dark green velvet. At

Matavai Bay Cook built a fort and stayed ashore for four months, to observe and note the behaviour of the islanders. During this time his scientists performed their astronomical and botanical work. Cook was fair but worked his men hard. This was not merely because he knew that mischief tempts the idle, but because his success depended upon continual maintenance of his ship. Only on Sunday afternoon after church were the crew allowed off duty. They made the best of this short time to dally with the obliging young Tahitian women.

Cook and Banks were impressed by the friendship, conviviality, and commonsense of the high-ranking Obarea, whom Parkinson, the surveyor and artist, called, 'a fat, bouncing, good-looking dame'. Banks certainly succumbed to the charms of the girls she offered him. But there is nothing to suggest that Cook took a mistress. As always, he had to set an example, and though he accepted the love-making all around him with equanimity, he himself had to be above it.

Tahitians proved to be past masters at pilfering, or as Cook put it, 'they showed a great inclination to pick our pockets', and, 'in this they are prodigious expert'. Two early items were a snuff box and a 'spy glass'. Amazingly, at one point someone even managed to prise two glass ports out of the *Endeavour*'s hull! Some of these items were recovered, some never. The visitors tried to be tolerant. But one morning a heavy box, with sides about a foot and a half, had disappeared from its tent in the middle of the fort, despite having been guarded all night. This was disastrous, for the box held the ship's sextant, which was crucial if the Englishmen were to continue their voyage. It was also fundamental to the unique observations of the planet Venus passing across the face of the sun, which would not occur again until 1874, which the astronomers had come 12,000 miles to make. A desperate Cook was considering options when a chief, Tubourai, told Joseph Banks he knew the offender. Armed only with pocket pistols, a search party of Banks, the astronomer Charles Green, a midshipman, Tubourai and several tribesmen set off into the mountains in anxious pursuit. After four sweaty miles a new problem arose – they needed to travel about three more miles, but this was through the territory of another tribe. They had almost reached their destination when one of Tubourai's men who had gone ahead returned with a *part* of the sextant. One by one the pieces appeared – and some other stolen goods as well. Several pieces were damaged, but Green was later able to repair them.

Some of Cook's sailors had their arms tattooed, becoming thereby fathers to the tradition of the tattooed mariner. Not to be left out, the youthful Banks also acquired a small tattoo, becoming the first of what must indeed be a very select historical group, namely, tattooed scientists!

The transit of Venus was successfully observed, Cook and his crew had reluctantly to depart, and the Tahitians were equally saddened to see them go. Eyes streaming tears, Obarea and the chiefs came aboard to say farewell, many canoes paddled alongside *Endeavour* out of the bay, and sorrowful Tahitians filled them. Banks climbed to the highest lookout and remained waving as long as the Tahitians lay in sight.

The second of Cook's instructions was systematically to search for the fabled Southern Continent, which might offer rich possibilities for trade. The zig-zag route he followed showed that if *Terra Australis* existed it was much farther south than anticipated. As part of the search he sailed west to New Zealand, which Tasman had suggested was a corner of the continent. Circumnavigating the New Zealand islands in six months and producing the first detailed map, he showed Tasman's idea to be a fiction. They had sailed hopefully down the south-east coast of New Zealand but what they found south of Stewart Island was open ocean – a deep disappointment. Cook's charting of New Zealand kindled British interest and eventually led to annexation and the development of modern democratic New Zealand.

Next Cook headed for unmapped eastern Australia, then known as New Holland, and charted the whole east coast. In so doing he established for the first time the western margin of the South Pacific Ocean, and began the chain of events which led to the foundation of the vibrant mostly British-heritage democracy we call Australia.

SECOND AND THIRD VOYAGES: FILLING IN THE PACIFIC MAP

On the second voyage, 1772–75, Cook had the advantage of excellent chronometers, one an accurate copy of John Harrison's masterpiece, which had changed the face of navigation. It kept precise time despite the continual buffeting of the small ship, and together with improved sextants allowed accurate calculation of longitude. In command of two ships, Cook virtually circumnavigated what we now know as Antarctica, reaching as far south as 71 degrees 10 minutes, thereby destroying completely any remaining idea that *Terra Australis* might exist. There was no great southern continent and no trade! He and his crew were the first men to enter the great southern icefields and survive. Cook entered in his log the observation:

> Thick fogs, snow storms, intense cold and every other thing that can render Navigation dangerous one has to encounter ... the Country ... doomed to lie for ever buried under everlasting snow and ice ... [if a ship should penetrate to] the ports which may be on the Coast ... she runs the risk of being fixed there for ever, or coming out in an ice island [iceberg].

Again Cook visited New Zealand and Tahiti, renewing acquaintances. In Dusky Sound in Fiordland, the innocence of New Zealand birds was emphasized, when one perched on the end of a naturalist's musket-barrel! Cook firmly established the location of Easter Island, rediscovered the lost Marquesas, visited Tonga, and sailed past the reefs of Fiji, before finding, naming, and mapping the New Hebrides (Vanuatu) and New Caledonia. On the way east to Cape Horn and home, he again sailed deep into southern Pacific latitudes to disprove several earlier claims of land being sighted there.

Cook found the Polynesians fascinating. They found him and other European navigators equally so, even bizarre. The account by the New Zealand Maori chief Horeta Te Taniwha is revealing. As a small boy in 1769 he had been given an iron nail by Cook on the first expedition. He kept it all his life, and as an old man recalled:

> When our old men saw the ship they said it was an atua, a god, and the people on board were tupua, strange beings or goblins... As our old men looked at the manner in which they came on shore, the rowers pulling with their backs to the bows of the boat, the old people said, 'Yes, it is so: these people are goblins; their eyes are at the back of their heads; they pull on shore with their backs to the land...' As we could not understand them we laughed, and they laughed also...

In the third voyage Cook was mainly concerned with the North Pacific, searching for a north-west passage between the Atlantic and the Pacific. (We now know this is impossible for sailing ships – but not for ice breakers and nuclear submarines.) He visited Tahiti for the last time in 1777, and sailing north, chanced upon another great Polynesian outpost, the Hawaiian Islands in 1778, until then unknown to anyone but their inhabitants.

Cook perceived better than any other European navigator the serious future consequences for the native peoples of European penetration of the Pacific. He also showed a modern sympathetic awareness of their culture. So it is ironic that, like the hero of a Shakespearean tragedy, he was killed by some Hawaiians during a fracas over a ship's boat, when his impeccable timing and judgment of human nature for once failed him.

Bligh and the Bounty

THE MUTINY & CHRISTIAN'S HIDEAWAY ON PITCAIRN

Captain William Bligh's (1754–1815) escape from the Tofuans' stones was described above. In 1789 Bligh, who had sailed with Cook, was given the seemingly mundane task of sailing to Tahiti to take on board nutritious breadfruit plants to be transplanted to the British West Indian Islands.

On the way to Tahiti he had acquired some pineapples in Brazil and these became the source of Tahiti's crop. Soon after leaving Tahiti with the breadfruit, the famous mutiny against him took place under the leadership of the Master's Mate, Fletcher Christian. Bligh and eighteen loyal crew members were turned adrift in the ship's longboat. Though Bligh had a foul temper, the crucial factor in the mutiny was probably the lure of Tahiti's exuberant sexuality in place of harsh shipboard life. These extraordinary events have become the stuff of legend – a number of very successful books, and five Australian and Hollywood films with a string of famous actors have portrayed Bligh and Christian.

Some mutineers returned and stayed in Tahiti. Christian, eight others, and their Tahitian women, anticipating that the Royal Navy

1789: Mutiny on the *Bounty*

might some day come searching for them sailed off in the *Bounty* to find an island where they could be safe. In 1790 they chanced upon the little isolated, two square mile Pitcairn, 1,350 miles (2,170k) southeast of Tahiti. For a time inhabited by Polynesians, it was now deserted. There they remained hidden from the world until found by some American whalers in 1808. To this day fifty or so of Fletcher Christian's descendants still inhabit Pitcairn. The melding of Tahitians and Anglo-Saxons proved to be propitious. More than 200 years of genetic inbreeding have produced no signs of serious defects, though over the years there have of course been occasional genes left by visiting vessels. Cousins have continued to marry cousins: Allan Christian marries Eva Christian and the Magistrate is Edgar Christian. Since 1877 the islanders have been strict Seventh-day Adventists.

BLIGH'S EPIC 3,600-MILE OPEN-BOAT VOYAGE

Presumably the mutineers hoped Bligh and company would perish at sea or be stranded. Bligh determined they would not. The men in the boat with Bligh were a fascinating little group. One of the eighteen was 42-year-old William Peckover, a gunner, perhaps the most interesting unknown figure of Pacific exploration. He sailed on all three of Cook's Pacific voyages and spoke Tahitian well. By the date of the mutiny he had seen more of the Pacific Ocean, from the Antarctic to northern Alaska (actually the Arctic Ocean), than anyone else in history.

Bligh knew a British settlement had been established at Sydney in 1788, but he did not know if it had survived, so he headed for the next nearest European port, Coupang in Dutch-controlled Timor. The route was dangerous and he knew they could not count upon acquiring food (the Tofua stoning proved him correct). With the food allowed by the mutineers, Bligh therefore worked out how much each man could have per day. Other than food they might catch, and rainwater, it was 2 ounces (0.125 of a pound/0.06kg) of food and half a gill of water (0.25 pint/0.12 litre). Every man agreed to go on.

The 3,600 miles (5,800km) journey is one of the great epics of the seven seas, not because of the navigation, which was relatively straightforward for the experienced Bligh, but because of the dangers, the lack of food, and perseverance under such privation. The wet sea cold of the open boat froze the bones at night and the sun scorched the skin in the day; there were throbbing cramps and open sores; Bligh and his men retched from raw food – for just occasionally they were lucky to catch a fish or a seabird. One day a little noddy perching on the yardarm was grabbed. Bligh's cutlass slashed it into 19 pieces (including the entrails and claws). For hundreds of years sailors of the Royal Navy after shipwrecks, and sinkings in battle, had drifted hopefully in small boats on the open ocean, and a standard procedure for fairly sharing food had evolved. One of the sailors was told to turn his back to Bligh who pointed to a piece at random and asked, 'Who shall have this?' The sailor replied with some man's name, and the piece was passed to that person. 'Who shall have this?' continued Bligh, pointing to a second piece ... So the tiny bloody raw scraps of bird were slowly distributed to all including Bligh, and devoured.

The 18 Men in the Boat with Captain Bligh

William Cole (in his 30s) Boatswain

William Elphinstone (aged 36) Master's Mate

John Fryer (37) Master

Thomas Hall (40) Cook

John Hallet (17) Midshipman

Thomas Hayward (22) Midshipman

Robert Lamb (23) Butcher

Lawrence Le Bogue (41) Sailmaker

Thomas Ledward (24) Surgeon's Mate

Peter Linkletter (32) Quartermaster

David Nelson (40) Botanist

John Norton (36) Quartermaster

William Peckover (42) Gunner

William Purcell (38) Carpenter

John Samuel (26) Clerk (Bligh's Secretary)

George Simpson (29) Quartermaster's Mate

John Smith (38) Captain's Steward

Robert Tinkler (17) Midshipman

Two months later, after nearly starving to death, being pursued by fierce Fijians, almost destroyed by a waterspout, and attacked by Aborigines in northern Australia, emaciated, dehydrated, suffering scurvy, they arrived at Coupang, where David Nelson, the botanist from Kew Gardens, worn out by the ordeal, died; he had been recommended to Bligh by Joseph Banks.

Further Exploration

'The Age of Exploration', as it is called by historians, continued. Others copied Cook's approach of deep attention to detail and daily sauerkraut for the men to prevent scurvy. Before the close of the 1700s there were several more scientific expeditions to the South Pacific.

Jean-Francois de La Perouse (1741–88?), perhaps a Cook in the making, led the main French expedition. In 1788, in one of navigation's great coincidences, La Perouse encountered the founding British

First Fleet in Botany Bay, just as it was departing to establish the first European colony in Australia at Sydney, ten miles to the north. La Perouse later perished in a shipwreck in the Santa Cruz Islands, and Antoine de Bruni d'Entrecasteaux (1739–93) went unsuccessfully searching for him. Captain George Vancouver (1757–98), who had sailed with Cook, led a British expedition in 1791–95, sailing to New Zealand, the Chathams, Tahiti, and the North Pacific. Early in the 1800s there was a major Russian expedition, and in the following decades further French and Russian voyages.

Even the youthful USA joined the hunt for Pacific scientific knowledge, with the 1838–42 expedition of Charles Wilkes (1798–1877), formerly in charge of the United States Naval Observatory and Hydrographic Office. Besides visiting South Pacific islands, he sailed along the Antarctic ice barrier, noting land at several points subsequently known as Wilkes Land. He returned to New York having circumnavigated the world.

British nineteenth-century voyages were mainly surveying expeditions making maps for future naval use. One such was the voyage of the *Beagle*, captained by Robert FitzRoy (1805–65), on which Charles Darwin circled the world and acquired evidence which helped him develop his explanation of biological evolution. FitzRoy later became Governor of New Zealand.

Cook had given the great map of the South Pacific a basic structure. The navigators just described provided more details. But it would be very different men who filled in further gaps. For the detailed knowledge they would discover was only incidental to their purpose – the extractive trades. They were sealers and whalers, and gatherers of sandalwood and beche de mer. To their fascinating and very dangerous activities we now turn.

Commerce

Commerce was responsible for the next sweeping changes to the lives of the South Pacific Islanders, and began the long period of informal penetration by Europeans and Americans. Conflicts of interest between the traders and the Islanders arose almost immediately – but not because of serious misunderstanding. Even though they held much property in common, Polynesians also knew all about private property. They immediately recognized the usefulness of Europe's iron and cloth and tried to get them by means fair or foul. As early as 1792, Vancouver observed that Tahitians had almost entirely replaced native items with imported iron tools, utensils, and cloth. Polynesians (and to a lesser extent Melanesians) wanted Western goods, but unlike the spices of the Indies or China's tea, they had little to trade. After the hectic decades of sandalwood and beche de mer or sea cucumbers ended, all they had was exotic scenery, replenishment of food and water, and hospitality. The situation is similar today.

WHALING

The first impact was made by sealing. It was of considerable importance during the late 1700s and early 1800s, particularly in New Zealand and other southern islands such as the Chathams. But the greatest commercial impact was made by whaling, because until modern times it was easily the largest, most widespread, and most long-term Pacific trade. The first sperm whale was harpooned in 1789 by one, Archelus Hammond, from the British whaler, *Emelia.* Four more were taken on that epochal day. The earliest South Pacific fleet was five small British vessels out of Sydney in 1791 (they had been convict transports) which pursued whales in the Tasman Sea. During the next decade tiny transient shore stations were set up in Tasmania, along the eastern Australian coast, and in New Zealand, where the blubber was rendered down into oil.

Until the discoveries of underground petroleum, there was an increasing demand in Europe and North America for whale oil, for cooking, to light street and household lamps, and for lubrication. The fine oil in the head of the sperm whale was most valuable. Whalebone (baleen) was used in chair seats and ladies' corsets and horse whips. And there was the rare and astonishing, waxy ambergris (mostly cholesterol!) which is secreted by the sperm whale's intestine. Whether it is normal or pathological is unknown. Very occasionally it was found within a whale, or floating in the ocean. It was exceedingly valuable because it was used as a spice in East Asia, and to fix the scent of perfumes in

Europe. On one occasion the New Zealand whaler *Splendid*, out of Dunedin, found a piece so large it depressed the world price and the captain and crew were paid only £25,000 rather than the anticipated £89,000 (millions today).

There were two kinds of whaling, ocean or pelagic, and bay or shore whaling. Ocean began in the 1790s and bay whaling in the 1820s. Bay whaling, which hunted the docile, easily floating southern right whale, was most important in New Zealand. Ocean whalers pursued the fast square-headed sperm whale and the aggressive humpback. The main whaling regions of the South Pacific were the south-west Pacific and New Zealand, and the south-east Pacific and off the South American coast.

The 240-ton *Beaver* was the first United States whaler into the Pacific, in 1791. From the 1820s whaling became overwhelmingly American, mostly out of New England, especially the busy islands of Nantucket and Martha's Vineyard off Cape Cod in Massachusetts. In the Pacific as a whole there were about 200 US ships in the later 1820s, and nearly 600 at the height of the industry ten years later. This growth was itself a reflection of the expansion of the American nation generally. The average whaler carried 33 crew. As the American numbers increased, so French, British, Australian, and New Zealand vessels withdrew.

It was a life of extremes. Weeks of depressing routine aboard ship were followed by days of terror in tiny boats; after months of salt pork came cornucopias of fresh tropical fruits; four months of temperance at sea might be followed by four days of unending alcoholic binge in port. The work was dirty and dangerous. Harpooning was done from a six-man, lightweight cedar boat with a steersman, harpooner and four oarsmen. Successfully harpooned, a whale might tow a boat for miles if the rope held, if the boat were not overturned, or if it were not pulled under before the whale became exhausted. When the steersman then tried to kill the whale by churning his long lance in its brain, it might still crush the boat with a reflex flash of its fluke. Towed home, and tied alongside the mother-ship, the whale would be stripped of its blubber, which was then rendered down for the oil in huge cooking pots. Meanwhile in the blood-thickened water, dozens of sharks would attack the floating whale in a feeding frenzy. Whaling was not a job for the fainthearted.

Young Polynesian men joined the whalers to see the world. They were also useful as interpreters. Given that most whaling voyages lasted three or four years, many Polynesians never again saw their homes. The longest was the eleven-year voyage of the *Nile* from New London, Connecticut. So Pacific island ports were needed to refit the ships and to refresh the crews. Tonga, suffering from civil warfare during the great days of whaling, was almost untouched, as was Fiji because of its cannibals and great reefs. Papeete in Tahiti developed from a tiny Polynesian village into a busy little European port, and became the main whaling haven of the South Pacific.

Local gardeners in New Zealand and elsewhere began to provide foodstuffs such as the white potato, and local girls provided sex. Indeed, sex preceded and then accompanied whaling as South Pacific commerce. Although there had been no prostitution *as such* in Polynesia, women were in many circumstances a Polynesian *commodity*. They were crucial in tribal alliances. Their favours were given as hospitality to visitors. Moreover they appear to have been willing participants in most of these actions. From their point of view it seems to have been a small move from giving themselves sexually to Polynesian visitors, to giving themselves to sailors in exchange for iron, cloth, or money.

PORK, SANDALWOOD, AND BECHE DE MER

Within fifteen years of its foundation the British convict settlement at Sydney in Australia was a going concern. Freed convicts and free settlers established businesses, built small ships, and began to trade with New Zealand and other Pacific islands. At times the settlement's government joined in. In 1801 Governor Phillip G. King (1758–1808) despatched HMS *Porpoise*, a small Royal Navy vessel, to collect a cargo of salted pork from Tahiti. This trade continued for 30 years and became Tahiti's key source of British and European manufactured goods.

Another considerable early trade was in fragrant sandalwood, popular as incense in China. Early in the century, stands of sandalwood were found in Fiji and for about ten years ships called there to trade with the chiefs who had cornered the market. The wood was exchanged for iron tools and other hardware, tobacco, cloth, and muskets shot and powder for tribal wars.

As the Fijian wood became depleted new stands were discovered in the faraway east Polynesian Marquesas, and the first sandalwood cargo from there reached Sydney in 1815. In both Fiji and the Marquesas trade was extraordinarily dangerous, for these were the two Meccas of Pacific cannibalism. Later, smaller stands were discovered on some other islands, such as New Caledonia and the Loyalty Islands just to the east. There too, given local cannibals, and the sharp practice of the merchants, trade could be problematic. In 1849 the whole crew of the American ship *Cutter* were killed and eaten by the Pouma tribe of north-east New Caledonia. Still, as one trader put it, 'You cannot trade with these people and fight them too.' During such trading some islanders acquired new wants like smoking. Complex sequences of exchange could result. As a contemporary pointed out, traders were 'teaching islanders to smoke tobacco so that Chinese could burn sandalwood, so that Australians could drink China tea'.

About ten years after the end of sandalwood in Fiji a new intensive extractive trade began there, the gathering of beche de mer/trepang/ sea cucumber which inhabits tidal reefs. Again it was for the Chinese as an ingredient in soup. Silk and chinaware joined tea as items of exchange.

The demographics of beche de mer were the reverse of whaling involving many locals and a handful of traders. Beche de mer trade strengthened the power of the Fijian chiefs because only they could dragoon the large numbers needed to gather the trepang from the reefs, to clean and boil them, to cut the wood for the fire trenches and drying sheds, and to package and load the ships. In return the chiefs acquired the same range of products as with the sandalwood trade. Over some decades several thousand muskets entered the island of Bau alone.

Once again though the profits for some traders could be enormous, the trade was extraordinarily dangerous. It was practised against a background of Fijian civil wars, the chiefs might renege on their deals, the exploited commoners might revolt, and the trading partners might cheat. And of course chiefly celebrations still needed human meat.

BLACKBIRDERS, PIDGIN, AND PERUVIAN SLAVERS

Later there was the trade in human beings. There were two kinds. The first was stigmatized by missionaries as 'Blackbirding'. It began in 1863 and consisted in tempting young men to work in the sugarcane and cotton fields of tropical Queensland, Fiji, and Samoa. In the early years they came mostly from New Caledonia and Vanuatu, and later from the Solomon Islands and New Guinea as well. Some of the first thousands who came failed to understand their contracts of indenture and were in effect kidnapped. Still, once this indenturing trade became established and regulated, it was rare for the misunderstandings of early days to occur, and a period working on overseas plantations to earn money became a *tradition* in many Melanesian families and villages.

One fascinating side-effect was the development of Pidgin English. Given the dozens of different Melanesian languages spoken by these workers, there was a need for a *lingua franca*. An informal blend of English and native languages resulted, called Pidgin. Today there are three main varieties, in Papua New Guinea, Solomon Islands, and Vanuatu, with the Solomon version slightly closer to standard English. Given the power of grammatical structure over our thinking, Pidgin combines English-derived words and Melanesian grammar and uses few pronouns, adverbs, and prepositions.

The second trade was the South Pacific slave trade – short but vicious. Seeking cheap labour for Peruvian plantations and guano islands (Peru had become independent in 1821), slave raiders sailed to the Cook Islands, Tokelau, Kiribati, and the Tuamotus and Australs. Their activities were devastating. In 1862–63, in the Cook Island atoll of Penrhyn, for example, four native Polynesian Christian missionaries helped the slavers, believing they were arranging temporary and worthwhile work. The grateful Peruvians ironically dubbed Penrhyn 'the island of the four evangelists'. From Penrhyn's 700 population about 470 slaves were landed in Lima, and 130 in Tahiti. The entire chiefly line disappeared, and Penrhyn is today the only Cook Island with no paramount chiefs.

In 1862 eight Peruvian slave ships arrived in unlucky Easter Island, capturing perhaps 400 (about half the population), killing others, while some escaped only by diving into the sea from the cliffs. Amongst those carried off were the chief and almost all the leaders of the community. Similar disasters hit other islands.

Eventually yielding to pressure from Britain and France, years later the Peruvians repatriated surviving slaves. But so many had died from overwork and diseases or from smallpox on the return voyage that a mere handful reached home. The Easter Islanders brought a smallpox epidemic with them which reduced the population to about 100 lost souls. The island's culture had been obliterated. Even today, the name of Peru is loathed in many Pacific Islands.

BEACHCOMBERS AND CASTAWAYS

Shipwrecked and deserting American and European seamen, drifters, shore-based sealing and whaling seamen deserted by their captains, escaped convicts from the Australian penal settlements, idealists and *roués* searching for their illusory tropical paradise tried to make a living in the islands. Such men became beachcombers (they originally set themselves up on the beach) who provided small services to chiefs, captains, and traders – translating, repairing muskets, doing carpentry and blacksmithing. Some married into island life. Some eventually became small traders. Some even became chiefs.

The Swede Charles Savage was wrecked in Fiji in 1808. He managed to retrieve muskets and ammunition from the wreck, and these were used to great effect by the chief of the fierce island of Bau. In return for this and for his help in Bau's wars he was given many privileges, including Fijian wives, and fought for Bau for about five years before dying in battle. His skull became an honoured kava bowl. Another white man, Paddy Connel, was almost equally helpful to Bau's chief enemies, the tribes of Rewa.

CHANDLERS, LARGE COMPANIES, AND POLYNESIAN PORTS

Within a few decades, the beachcomber phase of trading was replaced by more intense and intentional business organization. Besides Papeete, other little port towns of Europeans and Americans began to grow up on the most convenient harbours and along nearby beaches, to serve the whalers and traders. The chief were Levuka on the Fijian island of Ovalau, Apia and Pago Pago in Samoa, and Kororareka in the Bay of Islands in New Zealand. In these little ports the earlier informal repair and provisioning of ships was now replaced by permanent ships' chandlers. The dangerous extractive trades and traders and the whalers were also supplanted in the 1860s and 1870s by a new class of resident European and American traders and their large-scale permanent companies, supported by growing amounts of capital. This commerce was now based on regular commodities such as coconut oil and involved long-term planning. As we shall see in the following chapter, effective German, British, French, Australian, and American trading companies existed by the mid-1850s, in Fiji, Tonga, Samoa, and Tahiti. Polynesia was being dragged into the world economy.

CHAPTER FIVE

Christianity and Colonization: the South Pacific Islands to around 1900

Arrogance in their beliefs, and lack of understanding of the culture they wished to convert, mixed with denigration or worse, have characterized proselytizers of all religions throughout world history. The missionaries of the South Pacific were no exception: they went to the Pacific with the avowed intention of changing Polynesian and Melanesian society.

The Spanish lived in a theocracy. An aim of all their voyages and colonies was conversion to Roman Catholicism. In strong contrast to their success in the Americas and the Philippines, they had little in the South Pacific. The later French Catholic missionaries had more.

At first the Protestants also failed. But perseverance paid, especially in Polynesia. Much of the Protestant success when it did come, can be attributed to the *nature* of their Christianity, the medium as much as the message. For the beliefs of these evangelical missionaries were embedded in Luther's Protestant Reformation and the British Wesleyan/Methodist revival of Luther's conceptions. For them the foundation of all Christian understanding was not a priesthood and an all-knowing Church but personal salvation and faith through grasping God's written word in the Bible. This meant that converts needed to be able to *read the Bible for themselves*. To help his countrymen understand this, Luther himself had produced a robust translation of the New Testament in German. So, fundamental missionary tasks became to produce Polynesian scripts, to translate the Bible into them, to print these Bibles, and to teach the people how to read them. These were mammoth tasks and much more complex than the first missionaries realized. For instance, until they could have their own presses sent out, the translated writings had to be shipped for printing to Sydney, or even all the way back to Britain. Literacy was fascinating and powerful to Polynesians, and would eventually become *a key attraction of Protestant Christianity*. To produce written Polynesian languages, for the first time in history, was one of the splendid side-effects of Pacific missions. Soon Islanders were also writing down and so preserving their genealogies and traditions. The religion which deliberately and accidentally destroyed so much Polynesian tradition also helped to preserve some of it.

In the second half of the 1800s, European penetration unconnected to Christian missions resulted from the ever-increasing demand for tropical products in Europe and the United States. After mineral oil was discovered in the USA in the 1850s, there was no longer a need for large volumes of whale oil. That trade was soon replaced by South Pacific coconut oil for the developing European and American market.

Coconut oil began to be exported from Samoa in the late 1850s, and large plantations of coconuts, sugarcane, cocoa, and cotton were developed there and in other islands in the 1860s. Cotton growing boomed during the American Civil War when supplies from the world's main source were cut off by Northern blockade. Acquiring land through methods legitimate and devious, and with varying amounts of aid from the metropolitan governments, European, American and Australian planters located themselves in Samoa, Fiji, and Tonga, and later in New Caledonia and the New Hebrides (Vanuatu) and set up their own informal governments. Where the native people were reluctant, the indentured Melanesian labourers described above under 'Blackbirding' were brought in to work the plantations in Samoa and Tonga, and Indians into Fiji.

Each of the main Polynesian island archipelagoes will be considered separately. The Melanesian islands will not be discussed here, other than Fiji which experienced modern trends much earlier than the others. For most of Melanesia was plagued with malaria, authority was diffused among thousands of villages, the people were warlike, xeno-phobic, and in some cases cannibal, and Christianity was much more difficult to establish. In New Guinea, for instance, until well into the 1900s it hardly penetrated beyond a few coastal tribes. In most of

A church in modern Samoa

Melanesia, Christianity has never been as accepted. Colonization too was in general a much later and less effective arrival.

Tonga

TU'I TONGA, TU'I HA'ATAKALAUA, & TU'I KANOKUPOLU

In a situation unique in the Pacific, in the Tongan archipelago, for hundreds of years before Tasman commented upon it, there had existed some degree of centralized authority under the rule of the Tu'i Tonga. ('Tui' or 'Tu'i' is equivalent to 'king'.) Though we may regard details of the early claims with some scepticism, Tongan genealogies suggest a beginning of political consolidation in the tenth century, and AD 950 is the conventional date for the beginning of the reign of the supposed first Tu'i Tonga. Until about a hundred years after Tasman the stability continued. The Tongan state was sustained by royal mana, protocol, tapu, and fierce punishments for infringements. 'Police state' has recently been used to describe it!

Over the centuries the Tu'i Tonga became so untouchable, his person so sacred and tapu, his role attained a status completely out of reach of ordinary Tongans. His function now entirely religious and ceremonial the Tu'i Tonga no longer took part in political control. Political administration fell into the hands of a new office filled by a new chiefly line – the Tu'i Ha'atakalaua. It appears that early in the 1700s the Tu'i Ha'atakalaua in turn became either too sacred or lost political power, his duties taken over by a third office – that of the Tu'i Kanokupolu! When Captain James Cook visited Tonga on his second voyage he found the politics too complex to be understood. For, further complicating the issue was the following situation.

TU'I TONGA FEFINE AND TAMAHA

It had become the custom for the eldest daughter of the Tu'i Ha'ata-kalaua to be taken as the principal wife of the Tu'i Tonga. Two possibly unparalleled historical facts of female precedence followed. The eldest daughter of this match became the Tu'i Tonga Fefine, who ranked higher than either her father or her brother who would be the next Tu'i Tonga. Her status was so godlike, no human male was allowed to marry her! If she did produce a child by secret liaison, this was not shameful, rather the opposite, for the child, if female, was regarded as a sort of virgin birth, called Tamaha, 'the sacred child', and treated as the earth's most exalted being. No one, not even the Tu'i Tonga Fefine could eat in her presence, and she had her own royal–religious court on the island of Ha'apai. What had thoroughly confused Cook was to see the Tu'i Tonga himself do homage to the Tamaha.

Tongan politics at that time of Cook's visit were also changing; the accepted roles and rules of succession were breaking down. Many Tongan leaders had become sceptical of their religion; warrior chief-tains again became important as they had at the very beginning of the sequence which established the Tu'i Tonga; civil wars broke out and continued sporadically in the early decades of the 1800s. Among the chief players in the game of state at this time were four generations of chiefs Finau Ulukalala, the treacherous, powerful and sadistic lords of the island of Vava'u.

KING GEORGE TUPOU AND CHRISTIANITY

In 1820 Taufa'ahau Tupou (1797–1893) became ruler of the island of Ha'apai. Finau Ulukalala IV had designated Taufa'ahau as his successor, so in 1833 Taufa'ahau became ruler of Vava'u as well. In 1845 on the death of his great-uncle he succeeded to the once again effective title of Tu'i Kanokupolu and so was now possessor of the three most powerful titles in the Tongan archipelago. He had however to subdue several reluctant Tongatapu chiefs before he could finally claim to control the whole archipelago in 1852. His foresight, forcefulness, and charisma succeeded. To demonstrate his new status as supreme ruler of Tonga and in admiration of the British monarchy he took the title of King George Tupou, and established the dynasty which still reigns. From conviction King George had converted to Christianity in 1834 – but he also saw that Christianity made political good sense. The old gods gone, a new social/political cement was needed in his islands.

Fired by the enthusiastic Evangelical revival occurring in Britain, the earliest missionaries to Tonga were members of the London Missionary Society (LMS), a composite organization of several different groups. Because they thought it a good idea that their people should possess practical skills the first nine missionaries to arrive in Tonga in 1799 were not ordained ministers but conscientious carpenters and blacksmiths, which was an unfortunate choice. For carpenters were the lowest class in the Tongan social scale, who, it was also widely believed, lacked souls! Beings without souls were trying to save those with souls. Three missionaries were murdered, the mission was an unmitigated disaster, and the LMS fled Tonga in disarray. An 1826 mission eventually took root and its success was in the long term due to the remarkable 30-year efforts of John Thomas (1786–1875), who translated much of the Bible into Tongan by himself.

Even before he had united the islands, King George saw the need for uniform laws. He produced the Vava'u Code in 1838. With its biblical basis, it began the merging of church and state in Tonga, and prevented chiefs from mistreating commoners. To maintain his independence from the great powers, King George sought constitutional advice from New Zealand and New South Wales and even travelled to Sydney in 1853. As a result his new Constitution of 1862 considerably extended the Vava'u Code: education for children was made compulsory; 'serfdom' was ended; land was no longer to be sold to foreigners; and all males over sixteen years gained the right to land. Though the monarch was still supreme, a parliament was set up. For its time and place, this was a remarkable piece of work.

KING GEORGE TUPOU AND REVEREND SHIRLEY BAKER

A new era began with the arrival in 1869 of Rev. Shirley Waldemar Baker as head of the Wesleyan Mission. The king liked him immediately. And for thirty extraordinary years Baker, of limited education, but alert and self-confident, would be the king's right hand, slowly accumulating great influence and power. In the following decades three issues would exercise their minds: further constitutional reform, relations with the great powers, and the status of the Tongan Church.

Over the years a state seal was produced, a national anthem written, a national flag designed, and the attractive timbered white-walled, red-roofed Royal Palace constructed in Nuku'alofa. Meanwhile the enlightened land laws of the 1862 Constitution had encouraged Tongan commoners to produce cash crops. Over a decade or so this trend attracted European merchants to the islands, giving additional urgency to the king's political thinking. So in 1875 after years of work an improved Constitution appeared. As King George said at the time:

> ...the form of our Government in the days past was that my rule was absolute and that my wish was law and that I could choose who should belong to the parliament ... but a new era has come and it is my wish to grant a Constitution and to carry on my duties in accordance with it.

Though the king remained the final source of authority, and appointed the tiny cabinet, parliament now had half its members elected, judicial procedures were tightened, and a clear line of monarchical succession was stated. With few alterations, the constitution remains the same today. The king's son Tevita (David) Unga was made first prime minister.

Meanwhile merchants such as Godeffroys of Hamburg arrived, and King George welcomed the presence of the newly formed German navy as a counterweight to pressures on him by France and the USA. In 1876 and 1879 Tonga signed treaties of friendship with Germany and Britain and King George was recognized as the ruler of an independent nation.

Baker's persistent loyalty to Tonga and its king and his long-time favour in the latter's eyes earned the antipathy of Tonga's chiefs, annoyed his fellow ministers and missionaries, and antagonized Tonga's small group of settlers. And the British and American consuls believed he favoured the Germans! At last all these enemies triumphed, the Wesleyan Conference dismissed him, and Baker sailed despondently to New Zealand. But all was not over. When the king's son the prime minister died in 1880, the king turned again to his old friend and made Baker prime minister.

As always 'Tonga for the Tongans' summed up Baker's approach. He set up government schools and developed further egalitarian policies. The chiefs saw him as a usurper, the settlers were upset, and some of the commoners objected to his morality laws. The Tongans remained overwhelmingly Wesleyan, and with his new powers and the king's support Baker was able to split with the Australian Wesleyan Conference, and established a Free Church of Tonga in 1885. Wanting to be master in his own realm, King George enforced the change and those not with him were assumed against him. Dissent was suppressed, government officers were sacked, and those continuing stubborn, including his own daughter Salote, were exiled.

Baker was rightly and wrongly blamed for the excesses. There was an attempt to assassinate him and after a secret trial four accused Wesleyans were exiled and six hanged. In the hot-house atmosphere after the trial, Baker made the greatest error of his career. He claimed, without evidence, that the British consul had been privy to the plot against his life, and launched a belligerent verbal attack on the British High Commissioner for the Western Pacific in Fiji. This was too much for the

British officials in the region. Sir John Thurston, the High Commissioner, put pressure on the ageing King George, who agreed to dismiss Baker, and appoint the youthful Sir Basil Thomson, a senior civil servant from Fiji, as temporary prime minister.

In recent years of office Baker had become so engrossed in personal disputes that he failed to keep proper financial records, and Thomson found complete disarray. The difficulties are suggested in the following conversation which Sir John Thurston recorded following Baker's departure. Sir John is talking to Junia Mafileo, the Tongan Minister of Finance, an aged nephew of the king:

> Sir John: 'What is your office?'
> Junia Mafileo: 'I am Minister of Finance.'
> Sir John: 'What is the revenue of Tonga?'
> Junia Mafileo: 'I don't know.'
> Sir John: 'But what is your office?'
> Junia Mafileo: (warmly) 'Minister of Finance.'
> Sir John: 'Well, who knows what is the revenue of Tonga?'
> Junia Mafileo: 'Mr Baker.'
> Sir John: 'Who takes care of the money?'
> Junia Mafileo: 'I do.'
> Sir John: 'How much do you have in the treasury?'
> Junia Mafileo: 'I don't know.'
> Sir John: 'But you are Minister of Finance?'
> Junia Mafileo: 'Yes. I have told you that I am.'
> Sir John: 'Well, where's the money?'
> Junia Mafileo: 'In the safe.'
> Sir John: 'Who knows how much there is?'
> Junia Mafileo: 'Mr Baker.'
> Sir John: 'Yes, but he's gone. Can't you go and count it?'
> Junia Mafileo: 'No. I do not have the key.'
> Sir John: 'Why, who keeps the key to the Treasury?'
> Junia Mafileo: 'Mr Baker.'

King George died in 1893 at the patriarchal age of 96. The contrasts with his youth were startling. He was the chief factor in the change from a country of warring, illiterate, pagan islands to an organized, educated, and peaceful Christian kingdom, from autocratic chiefly rule to a written constitution and the beginnings of parliamentary government.

By 1901, as will become clear by chapter's end, the South Pacific was a European/American lake, and it was only a matter of time before Tonga would succumb to one great power or another. The young king King George Tupou II (1874–1918) agreed to being protected by Britain. Britain's action was self-interested in so far as it would prevent Germany or another European power from seizing the best harbour in the western Pacific, within striking distance of Fiji. But the treaty of friendship was not intended to destroy the independence of Tongans, rather to preserve it in the only manner then possible. Britain controlled foreign policy, but in everything else the Tongans were allowed to get on with their self-governing. In 1951 they would enthusiastically celebrate the anniversary of the treaty.

Fiji

BAU AND CAKOBAU

As we have seen, serious fighting and tribal rivalry had been endemic in Fiji for centuries. In the 1700s and early 1800s smaller tribes were subdued, amalgamated, or exterminated, until five core tribes or tribal 'federations' emerged. Three of these existed on or near the main island of Viti Levu. The smallest in area was Bau, a tiny island of just 23 acres (9 hectares) off the east of Viti Levu, wedged between the large confederations of Verata in the north and Rewa in its rich river delta in the south. On the second large Fijian island, Vanua Levu, the tribes of Cakaudrove had established themselves, extending their control into the islands to the south-east. To the east, the rulers of the scattered Lau chain of islands were also making a bid for power.

For more than a century the warriors of Bau had been terrorizing the archipelago, and it was Bau and the confederation it eventually formed which rose to supremacy. Bau itself was intensely developed, covered with the houses of its 3,000 people. But more important, like the contemporary British who would soon become so important in Fiji, Bau made shrewd use of naval power. Indeed, its small size forced it so to do, because, as with Britain, Bau's greatest rivals were land powers. In Bau's case, the outmanoeuvring of the enemy was achieved with the highly mobile fore-and-aft sailed, twin-hulled catamarans called druas. Bau was encircled by stone jetties which protected these craft. The power of Bau's navy of druas, together with the muskets acquired from the sandalwood and beche de mer trade allowed its rulers to strike their enemies unexpectedly. So Bau was able to extend its hegemony over the islands and territories along the western and eastern edges of the Koro Sea. And today Bauan Fijian is the country's main language.

By the 1840s Bau and Rewa had become the most powerful of the tribal states. They then fought the greatest war in Fijian history between 1843 and 1855. Allies were drawn from most of the islands but the main theatre of war was in the Rewa Delta. In several areas the war was devastating.

Into this dangerous situation, requested by several chiefs, had come Wesleyan missionaries from Tonga in 1835. The first important chief to convert, in 1849, was the Tu'i Nayau, paramount in the eastern Lau Islands, but the great chief, Cakobau (1815–83) of Bau, claimed hegemony over Lau. We may therefore imagine Cakobau's rage at this apparent challenge to his authority and support for pacifist ideas. He threatened Christian Lau with war if it did not revert.

Remembering that the Tu'i Nayau was supported by fierce Tong warriors, in a cool moment Cakobau decided to let him alone. T s decision probably saved Cakobau from defeat, and was a turning point in Fijian history. For, as we have seen, this was the time when King George Tupou of Tonga was growing powerful. Had Cakobau lost to Lau and the Tongans, King George would have been tempted to take Cakobau's territories into his own and the political balance of the whole western South Pacific would have changed. En route to Sydney in 1853 on his constitutional fact-finding voyage, King George visited Cakobau and warned him, 'It will be well for you, Cakobau, to think wisely in these days,' and advised him to convert to Christianity. The warning came on the heels of a series of disasters, humiliations and rebellions. In April 1854 Cakobau converted. Soon after, and it must have seemed miraculous, his fortunes began to change. The people of Rewa sued for peace and Fiji's longest war was over.

CAKOBAU AND THE ALLEGED AMERICAN DEBT

Meanwhile there began three interrelated developments which would concern Cakobau and Fiji for the next 20 years: the increasing numbers of European settlers; the presence of King George's powerful nephew Ma'afu in the Lau Islands; and what may be called 'the alleged American debt'.

While Cakobau and other chiefs had been distracted by the protracted Bau–Rewa wars, the Tongan, Ma'afu, had extended his control in the Lau Islands. Ma'afu was clever, his islands were well-governed, and he encouraged Europeans to settle and trade. However, the majority of Europeans were settling in and around the town of Levuka on Ovalau Island, off the east coast of Viti Levu, which had grown with the extractive trades. In the disorganized political climate they had been able to buy land from various chiefs and to begin cotton and coconut plantations.

Then there was the commercial agent of the United States government, one John B. Williams, who arrived in Levuka in 1846. A recent Pacific historian calls him 'petulant, belligerent, and self-seeking'. Somehow Williams's ship *Elizabeth* caught fire and ran aground, and (of course) the local Fijians looted what remained. During his Fourth of July Celebrations three years later, through his own negligence Williams's house caught fire, and this too was looted! For both actions he blamed Cakobau. By 1855 he and other Americans were demanding a huge $43,000 ($18,000 for Williams) compensation and pressing the claim with increasing threats from visiting US ships. Cakobau possessed nothing like that kind of money. In 1858 a disturbed, desperate Cakobau offered the whole Fijian archipelago to Britain if she would pay the alleged debt! No doubt Cakobau also saw this as a way of forestalling the growing power of Ma'afu. In 1862 Britain declined.

SETTLERS, BRITAIN, AND GORDON

Meanwhile Cakobau was only nominally in charge of Fiji, and various unsuccessful attempts at forming a government of the islands were tried, some with Cakobau as king, others involving Ma'afu, others dominated by settlers. To add anxiety to angst, American ships again appeared pressing the old claim. The distraught Cakobau was finally rescued by a consortium of Australian businessmen from Melbourne. In these years Melbourne was riding high on the revenue from the Victorian gold rush as the great new city of the Southern Hemisphere. The Melbournians paid the American debt, gave Cakobau a large amount, and in return received 200,000 Fijian acres, much in the Suva area, and, as the Polynesian Company, the right to trade in and develop Fiji.

As a result European settlers poured into Levuka and other places and parts of Viti Levu became anarchic. Pressured by the Levuka settlers Cakobau tried a revised version of an earlier plan of government, but the settlers remained difficult to control. They imported 'Blackbirded' labourers into the islands and racial conflict increased. The lawless state of Fiji was becoming a South Seas scandal, especially in the eastern Australian colonies. The Australians, as part of the British Empire, pressed Britain to annex Fiji.

Cakobau again offered Fiji to Britain. After long negotiations the islands became a British colony in 1874, though some hill tribes rebelled. The town of Levuka was made capital. With financial encouragement from Australian settlers on the Suva Peninsula in the south-east, the government moved the capital to Suva in 1882.

Sir Arthur Gordon (1829–1912) was installed as governor. Gordon was aware of the disastrous recent Maori–settler conflict in New Zealand and was determined to prevent any recurrence in Fiji. Instead, his plan was to protect Fiji and the Fijians from further settler exploitation, and to help Fiji enter the modern world. The tribes in rebellion were pacified and pardoned. Then Gordon developed a brilliant four-pronged plan for governance.

His first and crucial move was to involve the Fijians in government. To reduce costs and introduce them to modern civil administration he adapted the hierarchical Fijian native system of paramount and lesser chiefs, turning them into village, district, and regional government officers. The paramount chiefs belonged to the Great Council of Chiefs, which was involved in government. They retained much of their customary authority but this was being channelled into a modern bureaucratic form with properly maintained government records.

Secondly, the settlers needed labour for their plantations, and Gordon needed prosperous plantations to produce taxes to make the colony self-supporting. But to turn the Fijians into a plantation-labouring proletariat was opposed to his overall goals. Indian emigration to tropical colonies which needed labour had occurred in Mauritius and the West Indies, and Gordon decided to encourage Indians to come as indentured labour for a specified period, assuming that most would return at the end of their contracts. None of us can read the future, and Gordon was not to know that most would stay and plague Fiji with a vast new political problem.

The settlers had desired annexation so their land purchases would be validated and further land become available. Gordon could not agree. Like that of his contemporary, Rev. Baker in Tonga, his view was that Fiji belonged to the Fijians. To the chagrin of the settlers, in 1879 he established a Native Lands Commission which ruled on the status of pre-annexation purchases. Land acquired legitimately was retained. Land taken by sharp practice was returned. All subsequent sale of land ceased, though land not used by Fijians could be leased.

The fourth move was to give Fijians productive employment which would involve them in the tax base and give experience of a cash economy. Gordon encouraged them to farm this land which the government had protected, and keep much of their traditional social organization. To control British subjects in the other islands, Gordon was also made High Commissioner of the Western Pacific.

In the next few years a horrendous measles epidemic hit. Something like a quarter of the population perished.

CSR AND BURNS PHILP

Australians were the largest group among the plantation owners. The greatest of the settler enterprises was the Colonial Sugar Refining Company (CSR) of Australia, founded 1855, which drew and grew upon the sugar plantations of the settlers and to a lesser extent of the Indians and Fijians. Sugarcane growing and processing became the South Pacific's greatest industry outside New Zealand's farming. It was

Fiji's dominant industry, and its taxes the mainstay of the economy, and so it became influential in government decisions. In the 1880s CSR established four sugar mills around the coast, and a fifth in the 1920s. The colonial government supported the Company and helped organize the long-term leasing of land, and indentured labour. CSR expanded into the ownership of plantations, but later moved to sub-contracting the sugar growing to European plantation owners. In 1894 the Company started to lease land to formerly indentured Indians, some of whom became very prosperous. Its handsome green and gold cans of sugar and syrup became a key kitchen item throughout the South Pacific, Australia, New Zealand, and Britain.

Much of the shipping to the islands was increasingly under the control of an Australian company, Burns Philp of Sydney. By the end of the century the company was working nine steamers and forty-one sailing vessels in Pacific Island trade.

Gordon had laid the foundation for Fijian prosperity and constructed an administrative system, which soon became largely self-regulating.

Samoa

CHIEFS AND STATUS SYMBOLS

Power in Samoa was diffuse, with many significant chiefdoms throughout the islands. But wars and alliances over earlier centuries created four powerful chiefly families akin to four royal lines, and reminiscent of the three lines of Tonga: the Malietoa, Tupua Tamasese, Mata'afa, and Tu'imaleali'ifano. These families remain influential in (independent) Samoa to this day. Chiefs competed for four leading titles which gained the possessor immense status. By acquiring lesser titles a chief could work his way towards the higher. Character, prowess, warrior ability, oratorical power – all these qualities were important in achievement of a title. He who finally possessed all four became Tafa'ifa. The Tafa'ifa was not king of Samoa, but rather the most prestigious person. He possessed political power only in his own tribal area.

By the 1830s the competition for Tafa'ifa had been corrupted by a certain Tamafaiga, who attained to the title mainly by force and cunning. He was assassinated and civil war broke out. This was the 1830s, and at this point Christianity entered the archipelago and the anarchy. The remarkable LMS missionaries Rev. John Williams (1764–1839) and Rev. Charles Barff arrived in the western island of Savai'i with eight Tahitian missionaries. A few years later A.W. Murray landed on Tutuila (now the main island of American Samoa) and others went later to the eastern Manua Group.

Christianity was so successful that today almost all Samoan social activities are church oriented or organized. Conversion was rapid perhaps because Samoan religion was less institutionalized than on other islands, and because Christianity was seen as the culmination of a self-fulfilling prophecy made hundreds of years earlier. This predicted that some day a new religion would arrive and destroy the old gods. Moreover, the biblical Genesis story and many Christian values in fact nicely matched local culture and legends. Samoan converts then went as missionaries to other islands. For the next hundred years, most missionaries in the Pacific, perhaps a thousand or more, were Polynesians and Fijians.

He who finally won the four titles and became Tafa'ifa was Malietoa Vai'inupo from central Upolo. He soon converted to Christianity – a good political move given the way the new religion was sweeping the islands. Because at Apia he possessed one of the two good harbours in Samoa (the other is at Pago Pago in Tutuila) he was in a favourable position to become a King George or a Ratu Cakobau. Perhaps he would have, had he not died early, in 1841. At his death he dispersed the titles among four contenders to begin again the traditional competition. This move was backward-looking; it diverted Samoan attention from the political changes being wrought by settlers and Christianity.

SETTLERS, GODEFFROYS, GERMANS, AND AMERICANS

Civil wars rocked the islands from 1848 to 1856 just as the settler population was increasing rapidly, especially in Upolo. From time to time, settlers abetted by commanders of American and British warships tried to form governments, but as there was no one to coordinate the

Samoan response, these failed. Apia was a tough town, and superseded Kororareka in New Zealand as 'the Hell of the Pacific'. Hell anywhere results when there is no rule and there are no rules. And the settlers and the Samoans at this time badly needed the rule and rules of central government.

Two related developments during the next twenty years brought the Samoans closer to government by foreigners. One was the arrival in Apia of the German trading company of Godeffroy and Son of Hamburg in 1857. The other was another civil war from 1869 to 1873.

Godeffroys' capital, organization, efficiency and discipline made it formidable. Whereas the first 50 years of South Pacific trade involved individual merchants seeking quick rewards from non-renewable products, Godeffroys developed a permanent trade in a renewable product, with long-term rewards. In so doing they changed the commercial history of the region. Their product was coconut oil, required in ever-increasing amounts for the candles and soap of USA and Europe. Godeffroys engaged agents to collect the oil from the multitudinous island archipelagoes and bring it to Apia where it was cleaned and graded, and whence it was shipped in large consignments to the Northern Hemisphere.

Godeffroys were blessed by innovative managers in Apia. First was August Unshelm, but he drowned at sea before his extraordinary plans could develop, then came the ambitious and brilliant twenty-year-old, Theodor Weber, who somehow achieved the impossible and in 1864 persuaded some Samoans to sell Godeffroys several thousand acres of land. Weber had realized that oil from coconut plantations on Upolo, owned by Godeffroys and worked by labour imported from other islands, would be more cost-effective than oil from individual agents scattered across half the islands of the South Pacific. Over a period of about ten years this plan went into effect. But shipping leaking barrels of oil across the world had its own problems.

Weber's next move was even more innovative. He slowly phased out the plantation oil and moved into shipping plantation copra and opening plantations in Fiji. After all, the oil came *from* the copra, the inside flesh of the coconut. Now the copra was shipped in bulk to Germany where large efficient machines pressed out the coconut oil.

The second development which made foreign government inevitable was a side-effect of the civil war of 1869–73. The Samoans pursued this war with such vehemence to pay for arms that the old refusal to sell land disappeared. The same land might be sold by different sellers to different buyers. After the war total foreign claims to title seem to have been several times the land area of all the Samoan islands! It was now more necessary than ever that there be stable government to determine claim and counter claim. But for the next 20 years unending rivalries, factions, and jealousies local and international among USA, Germany and Britain resulted in 'governments' patched together by shifting coalitions of Samoan and settler leaders, and in civil wars and rebellions. The most successful of these 'governments' was the quasi-dictatorship of the mysterious American, Colonel Albert B. Steinberger (1840–94), from May 1875 to February 1876. A confidence man, plausible, personable, good at forging compromises, he claimed to represent President Grant of the USA. When it became known that his connection to Grant was fictitious, support deserted him.

Finally the great powers concluded that Samoa could be governed only by international agreement and conferences were held in the period 1885 to 1889. Warships were sent to Apia. A modern Samoan writer suggests the three great powers were at that point 'like three large dogs snarling over a very small bone'. Had the Samoans done less snarling amongst themselves in previous years the bone might not have been available.

In March 1889 Apia was struck by one of the South Pacific's greatest typhoons/hurricanes. Three German warships and three American were wrecked in the harbour. But the captain of HMS *Calliope*, the only British ship, decided to escape just as the storm hit, fought her way out of port and survived. To clear the harbour *Calliope* had to pass between the USS *Trenton* and the reef. The *Trenton*'s engines were now dead and she floundered helpless, her decks swarming with sailors. As the struggling *Calliope* passed close to them the Americans cheered, which buoyed the British to new effort.

King Malietoa Laupepa of Samoa

Probably the disaster helped, for later that year the three powers agreed on a formula. Samoans being considered incapable of agreement were not consulted. Samoa became a single kingdom with the king and top officials selected by the neutral king of Sweden, and consuls of the three governments allowed advisory powers. So for a few years and in a strange manner Samoa was independent under King Malietoa Laupepa.

The Samoans again became disputatious, the king was continually challenged by the leading Mata'afa, so a new Tripartite Treaty was drawn up in 1899. The Germans gained western Samoa and the USA the eastern islands, and Britain withdrew. From that year forward the history of the two artificially separated Samoas has continued to diverge.

Tahiti and the Society Islands

For hundreds of years Tahiti and other main islands in the archipelago had been divided into antagonistic tribes. At one stage there were nine tribes on Tahiti, each with a ruling family, an attendant upper class, common people, and the serf-like servants. Strict tapus existed. No woman dared to eat in the presence of a man. Because there were no transport animals chiefs travelled their domains carried on the shoulders of servants. There was also a privileged priesthood, the arioi, of both men and women, with several different grades distinguished by dress and tattoos.

THE RISING GOD ORO AND THE RED FEATHER GIRDLE

In Tahiti during the second half of the 1700s the chiefly balance of power changed dramatically, and here it was intertwined with religion. To the confusion and consternation of contemporaries, the power of the traditional Tahitian gods, Tangaroa, Rongo, Tane, and Tu was challenged by the followers of a new god, Oro.

Oro rose to supremacy on the island of Raiatea, 125 miles northwest of Tahiti, long the religious centre of the Society Islands. The most sacred and renowned of all marae was there. Raiatea was to Society Islanders as Rome was to contemporary Roman Catholics or Mecca to Muslims. An opportunist Tahitian chief and his priests realized Oro's potential and promoted the new cult. Oro's appetite for human sacrifice was great. The terror this inspired in rivals and the subtle development of a new and elevated chiefly title associated with Oro disturbed the former political equilibrium among the many Society Island chiefdoms. The new title came to be marked by the possession of a striking girdle of red feathers. Red was a rare colour in the Pacific and red objects held mystical powers. Red feathers came to be used to attract Oro's attention.

By the 1760s the family of the chief, Teu, which became known to history as the Pomare family, was seeking possession of the girdle, but alliances of rivals thwarted him. Tue's son Tu was similarly frustrated. At this point the family's aspirations became entangled with the first visits by the European ships of Wallis, Cook, and the others.

THE *BOUNTY* MUTINEERS, THE POMARES, AND THE LMS

Bligh's legacy again enters the story. On the captured *Bounty*, the mutineers returned to Tahiti. About half remained there with their

Tahitian women, and, as told above, the other half escaped to Pitcairn Island. Cook, Bougainville, and the other early mariners had resisted appeals by their Tahitian hosts to help them in local wars. But the mutineers could not be so circumspect, and went to work for the Pomares. This was history's first example of a group of Europeans taking sides in a South Pacific war. (At one point, bizarrely, because of its mana, some red hair from Richard Skinner, the mutinous ship's barber, had been stitched into the red feather girdle!) For several years the mutineers' muskets proved critical, the Pomare mana rose, and the family was able to take over more of the island. Then the British navy returned as Fletcher Christian had anticipated, and captured the mutineers.

Shortly after, Protestant missionaries from the LMS landed. They were not the first Christian mission to arrive. The Spanish, immediately after learning of Wallis's discovery, had tried from 1772 to 1776 to convert the Tahitians. They failed and left.

The people of Tahiti were noble savages to the philosophers, but ignoble to the missionaries. So in 1797 twenty-five devout tradesmen, four LMS clergy, and a few wives and children landed on the black sand beach of Point Venus in Matavai Bay, near to where Cook had built his fort. These Europeans, imbued with the work-ethic, and convinced that they alone knew what was moral and why, now found themselves in an island full of sensualist pantheistic pagans.

As would later happen in Tonga and Fiji and New Zealand and for the same reasons, their faith was tested endlessly, they had no success, and they departed disillusioned. Some returned in 1801 and for years, despised by Tahitians and visiting European whalers and traders, bravely they pressed on. They tried to set an example in their own Christian lives, learned to speak Tahitian, and worked on the herculean task of producing a written version of the Tahitian language.

Because almost all European visitors anchored in the bay in Pomare territories, the family gained great prestige, and Pomare II (c.1782–1821) was able to acquire more chiefly titles and more muskets and considerable power over other tribes. But in 1808 his rivals combined their armies and defeated him in battle, and he retreated to nearby Moorea. In exile Pomare II began to question the power of the god,

Oro, and the point of the red girdle, and sought salvation and success through the alternative teachings of the Christians.

He converted, and as his influence increased, so did that of the LMS. His rivals resented his growing strength, and, supported by his Leeward Island kinsmen he went into battle. At the celebrated Battle of Feipi in 1815, Pomare's forces triumphed. Christian ethics also: for perhaps the first time in the Society Islands, the victors did not massacre the prisoners or destroy their villages, or even plunder them. Afterwards, Pomare II was able to put his own people to rule over other Tahitian tribes.

THE CONSTITUTIONAL RULE OF GOD

Christ now took over from Oro and there were mass conversions. Tahiti now relatively pacified, Pomare's mind turned to constitutional issues and he asked the missionaries for help. They attempted to explain the Western European principle that Church and State were two different realms. As this was a conception which had developed only with the Protestant Reformation and the European Enlightenment, it is hardly surprising that Pomare II found it difficult to comprehend. So, based on biblical principles the Code of Pomare was enforced in 1819. This was the first written code of laws in the South Pacific Islands.

Pomare II died in 1821, and was succeeded by his boy son, Pomare III, with the LMS missionaries as his official tutors and regents. A new Constitution with missionary input was promulgated in 1824, which had the astonishing provision for the time, of a parliament and manhood suffrage. The child king died in 1827, to be succeeded by his seventeen-year-old sister, who took the title Queen Pomare IV.

QUEEN POMARE IV AND THE FRENCH CONQUEST

Queen Pomare made alliances with nearby islands, and extended her contacts to the Austral Islands. In fact she ruled for 50 years – long enough to see her realm fall to France.

For Catholic France did not just accept the Protestant triumph. The Roman Catholic Church had become established in the Gambiers from 1834 (below) and, more tenuously, in the Marquesas – in spite of the cannibals. In 1836 the French navy deposited Fathers Honore Laval and

François Caret to do a bit of clandestine conversion. When they took themselves to Papeete the queen had them deported. *Quelle insulte!* To deport French Catholic men of God was a stain upon the honour of France. And by a tiny South Pacific country at that. Apologies were demanded. Threats were made. 'The bourgeois king', King Louis Philippe, at this date beginning the conquest and settlement of Algeria, was not pleased. Unfortunately for Queen Pomare, she had little freedom of manoeuvre and her appeals for British protection went unanswered.

Finally the French decided to act directly. Admiral Abel du Petit-Thouars was dispatched in *La Reine Blanche* to Papeete. In 1842 he trained his guns upon the little town and the queen surrendered. French troops and French Fathers landed. As the official tourist website for French Polynesia today euphemistically puts it: 'in 1842 a French Protectorate was established'.

George Prichard, Queen Pomare's British missionary advisor, was deported, but the queen still clung to the hope of British help. In 1844 she fled to Raiatea. Though guerrilla warfare began against the French in Tahiti and Moorea, by 1846 France was in control. Resigned to the new political facts the queen returned in 1847. She was now a French puppet.

FATHER LAVAL'S LITTLE THEOCRACY

Meanwhile, now supported by the French state, the Catholic Church consolidated wherever possible, especially in Tahiti, the Marquesas, and the Gambias. Some missionaries became virtual dictators of their islands.

Perhaps the best/worst example of this was Father Honore Laval, missionary to the Gambier Archipelago between 1834 and 1871. This is as far from Tahiti as it is possible to be and still remain in French Polynesia. As if to recompense himself for his humiliation by Queen Pomare, he established the Church in the Gambiers with an obsessive passion.

Laval's Congregation of the Sacred Heart was set up in 1834 and rapidly the whole population converted. Laval's memoirs recount his delight in smashing the old idols and marae and every possible remnant of the old religion and its culture. He and his assistant Caret then seem to have taken control of everything.

Until complaints reached Tahiti decades later and he was recalled, for 35 years Laval ran the place like a mediaeval baron's fief. The population went into reverse from a probable 5,000 or 6,000 when Laval arrived to 463 when the first official census was taken in 1887. Two explanations have been given. One is that the island population was already in decline from diseases left by whalers and traders, and Laval and Caret had little to do with it. The other is that Laval worked the island population to death constructing monuments to his vanity and beliefs.

The tiny declining population constructed roads, lookout towers, monuments, chapels, nine churches, wharves, a 'palace' for the last king, a convent, even a prison. His greatest achievement was the Cathedral of St Michael. Today it stands as monumental as ever, and can accommodate more than the whole archipelago population of about 1,100. With twin towers, and 180 feet (54m) long, it took work gangs of Islanders nine years to build.

CONCLUSIONS

Queen Pomare was succeeded by her son, Pomare V, who had little interest in being a puppet king, and in 1891 drank himself to death. Meanwhile Laval's Gambier Archipelago was annexed in 1881, the remaining Society Islands in 1888, and the Australs in 1900–1. France now had an empire in Oceania covering an ocean territory almost as large as Western Europe.

So by 1900 the '3 Cs' of contact, commerce, and Christianity, often combined with agitation by settlers, had undermined the control of the indigenous rulers and had led, with various degrees of enthusiasm or reluctance, to European and American annexation, i.e to the fourth 'C', colonization. With the exception of Tonga, every Pacific island was now either controlled by or claimed by a non-native government.

Here we ought to mention a fifth 'C', unlike the others, unintentional: contagion. For perhaps the most devastating result of outside contact for the South Pacific Islanders was imported diseases, Western diseases for which they had developed no immunity. Chickenpox, influenza, measles, tuberculosis, venereal diseases, and whooping cough were unwittingly introduced. Over decades, they hit in recurring waves of pandemics.

Mortality had its own idiosyncrasies and ironies: in part it depended on frequency of visiting ships, and Tonga for instance, relatively isolated, suffered much less; mission schools with pupil boarders spread disease, especially TB! The Islander populations perished in tens of thousands. We have already noted the measles epidemic in Fiji, which struck perfect conditions in 1875. In the Australs in 1826 alone through virulent fever, the numbers dropped from about 3,000 to about 120. Samoa's population perhaps fell by 50 per cent during the 1800s. Tahiti's estimated 25,000 population at contact was only about 8,000 in 1900. But all significant islands recovered during the twentieth century, and today it is only emigration which prevents horrendous over-population in most South Pacific islands.

We now turn to the fascinating history of New Zealand. In its native Maori, early trade, settlers, and acquisition by a European power, it parallels the histories of the islands just described, but in a somewhat different sequence, on a very much larger canvas, and with strikingly different results.

CHAPTER SIX

Maori Musket Wars, Christianity, Colonization: New Zealand to 1840

Perhaps because it was so much larger in area, New Zealand lacked the native trend to centralization of Tonga, Tahiti, and Fiji. Nevertheless, it experienced much the same pressures from contact, commerce, Christianity, and colonization, which they and the other South Pacific islands such as Samoa encountered. But in New Zealand there was full-scale *planned* European colonization which accelerated the changes. As a result, by the end of the century, although many Maori probably regarded themselves as colonized, New Zealand itself would become a colonizing power.

Informal Early European Settlement

James Cook had placed New Zealand on the world map, and from the late 1700s the islands were visited with increasing regularity by British, British–Australian, French, and American ships hunting the sperm whale. They would moor in the spectacularly green and tranquil Bay of Islands, or Hauraki Gulf and other northern harbours, to refit and to trade with the Maori.

There were seal hunters too. In 1803 a Sydney company sent a schooner to Dusky Sound in the far south. Soon, the southern beaches and coasts were the scene of bloody seal massacres. The sealers would make temporary settlements, harsh hamlets of tents, or rough flax-walled huts, or merely upturned ships' boats. They would work the region with a promise of being picked up at a later date; and for months and sometimes years such men would live a difficult dangerous and monotonous existence. Sometimes the ships would not return at all, and sealers' lives would hang upon the hard chance of rescue by a passing vessel, or the hospitality or enmity of local Maori tribes. Some of these men formed liaisons with Maori women, to become the first permanent European inhabitants of these spectacular islands.

The economic power behind most of these sealing visits was the trading and business communities which had rapidly grown up in Australia in the British convict towns of Sydney (founded 1788) in the colony of New South Wales, and Hobart (1803) in Van Diemen's Land (later, Tasmania). It was these groups which first saw the commercial possibilities of New Zealand, and for some decades New Zealand was in effect an Australian frontier. Without the planting of these colonies, it is unlikely that any trade in flax, timber, or sealskins could have developed. The American and French sealers came too, the American ships in increasing numbers. In 1806 a US vessel landed a huge cargo of 60,000 New Zealand seal skins in Sydney.

In the first decades of the 1800s, some coastal Maori tribes were inevitably brought into regular contact. They helped cut timber for masts and spars, they dragged huge kauri tree trunks and loaded them aboard ships, and from British shipwrights they learned how to construct boats and small ships. As crew, Maori sailed in the whalers. Particularly in the Bay of Islands considerable trade developed. Here, Maori white potatoes, pork, and the services of women were given in exchange for blankets, knives, and iron implements. Maori would trade anything to get iron, and as time went on, just like the Fijians, increasingly and disastrously for muskets. From the early 1800s chiefs looking for trade, or to widen their horizons, visited Sydney. Some chiefs hoped to ally themselves with the British governors of New South Wales.

Some visiting ships infringed Maori lore, ignored tapu, and kidnapped Maori men and women. In 1809 one such kidnapped Maori was at last returned home by his captors, the crew of the schooner *Boyd*. He persuaded his kinsmen to take vengeance: every crew member of the *Boyd* was killed and eaten. Deserters, and escaped convicts from the Australian settlements, came to live with Maori tribes. Many of these Europeans and Americans were of poor character, the flotsam of the sea-going life, and were in turn victimized by the traders. In 1834, one of them, James Worser wrote [his italics]:

... but we could *not get any money for our work*, instead of money we had to take Sugar Soap Tobacco Spirits Clothing ... the Merchants sent down their Vessels for the produce of the place, and gave Orders to the Captain not to give any Passage to Sydney without charging an enormous price ... *so they could keep us Here* ... the reader may see how we got robbed by the merchants and agents ...

In 1839 J.D. Lang, the senior Presbyterian in Sydney, said that New Zealand Europeans consisted mostly of 'the veriest refuse of civilized society'. The early missionaries provided similar descriptions. We should remember however that these men of religion held puritanical moral views. One US trader, John Knights, said he preferred to deal with the 'barefaced villains' than with the missionaries.

Still, the stories of the savage white men, when added to the fearsome reputation of the Maori gained for New Zealand during the early decades of the 1800s, the reputation of the most dangerous place in the Pacific, an earlier version of the anarchy of Fiji described above. This was all in fascinating contrast to New Zealand's well-merited present-day peaceful international image.

Christianity Cometh

Just as early missions had little success and contributed to tensions and culture clashes in other Pacific islands, so they did in New Zealand. The first mission was not of the LMS, but the effort of the British Anglican Church Missionary Society (CMS).

Reverend Samuel Marsden (1765–1838) of Sydney, Australia, took Christianity to New Zealand. Solid in physique, unshakable in views, he was chaplain to the convict settlement. That he acquired the sobriquet 'the flogging parson' (for he was also a magistrate) suggests he felt more pity for the 'poor benighted heathen', as he called the Maori, than for the underclass of his countrymen. Marsden had met some visiting Maori chiefs in Sydney, and was deeply impressed with their manliness. Here were worthy subjects for Christian conversion. The chief Ruatara invited Marsden to come to New Zealand under his protection. Agreeing with the prevailing view about the best form of Christian missions, Marsden believed success would be more likely if the Maori could be Europeanized so like the LMS in Tonga he wanted there to be tradesmen among the first missionaries, who could teach their skills to the Maori. But no British clergymen were prepared to risk their lives in this far land. So the first three missionaries Marsden brought with him were: carpenter William Hall, John King, a shoemaker who also made rope, and Thomas Kendall (1778?–1832), a humble schoolteacher. ·

On Christmas day 1814, the gospel was preached for the first time in New Zealand. Marsden's text was 'Behold I bring you good tidings of great joy.' Just what the listeners heard is a matter for speculation because Ruatara translated (shortened and reinterpreted) Marsden's sermon. Marsden then returned to Sydney.

Missionaries who arrived some years later were also mostly tradesmen. Far from European comforts, inadequately trained in their religion, mentally unprepared for dealing with Maori with values so very different from their own, they had little chance of success. They disagreed, they bickered, they despaired, they gave up, they 'went native'. It took eleven years before the first success – a deathbed conversion at that.

THOMAS KENDALL, TORMENTED MISSIONARY LINGUIST

The mission of Kendall, Hall, and King was given the protection of the main chiefs of the Bay of Islands, Hongi Hika and Ruatara, in late 1814. The most interesting of the three, a man who left his linguistic stamp on New Zealand history, was Kendall. Of only basic education, he possessed much drive, commonsense and foresight. Unlike many of his contemporaries he realized that he would have greater success if he acquired a detailed knowledge of Maori language and culture, and humbly he set himself that gargantuan task.

Lack of funds forced closure of his Maori school in 1818. That in the same year his chiefly friend, Hongi Hika, with 800 men from the district went on a murderous rampage down the east coast in an early campaign of the Musket Wars, suggests the difficulties such missionaries faced. Paradoxically, it would be the horrors and dislocation caused by the Musket Wars which in time helped many Maoris to yearn for the peace of the Christian message.

Kendall's failure to convert anybody was balanced by success in understanding the culture. In Sydney in 1815 he published the world's first book in Maori: *A korao no New Zealand: the New Zealander's first book; being an attempt to compose some lessons for the instruction of the natives.*

In 1820 Hongi Hika persuaded Kendall to sail with himself and a younger chief, Waikato, on a whaler to England. This exotic threesome were invited to the great houses. James Barry painted them and Hongi Hika had an audience with King George IV (1762–1830), who presented him with two muskets, a suit of chain mail, and a helmet which later saved his life.

Through Kendall's efforts, the three men were able to work with the gifted linguist Professor Samuel Lee of Cambridge University to compile a Maori grammar, which resulted in the publication of *A Grammar and Vocabulary of the Language of New Zealand.* This text was of incalculable importance for the future history of the country, its ramifications today more significant than ever. For it established the foundations of the Maori written language. It was this, not his Christianity, which makes Kendall so significant.

Like other Polynesians, the Maori were frank and open about sex. Maori women saw no virtue in virginity. Sexuality and childbirth were an integral part of Maori cosmology. Both fascinated and repelled by such things, Kendall began to see the world through Maori eyes. As he explained in 1822, 'I have been so poisoned by the apparent sublimity of their ideas that I have almost completely turned from a Christian to a heathen.' He had an adulterous affair with a young Maori woman, Tungaroa which also gave him access to the knowledge of her father, an elderly tohunga (priest/expert). These actions and his forthright opinions brought dismissal by Marsden.

Kendall's life in New Zealand was an epic attempt to understand Maori culture, a body of beliefs which men such as Marsden saw as heathen superstition. Eventually Kendall seems to have assumed the origins of Maori religion to be in some mysterious manner related to biblical scripture. But it would be almost two decades before Christianity took root and changed Maori life and culture.

MISSIONARY SETTLERS AND MAORI CONVERTS

Wesleyans arrived in 1822, but not until the Roman Catholics came in 1838 was there much doctrinal antipathy. In 1843, Anglican Bishop Selwyn (1809–78) asked a famous Taupo chief, Te Heuheu Tukino II (?–1846), why he would not become Christian. The chief stretched forth three fingers and said, 'I have reached a crossroads, with three ways – the English, the Wesleyan, and the Roman. Each teacher says his own way is the best. I am sitting down and wondering which guide I shall follow.' Before Te Heuheu could decide, many of his tribe, his wives, and he himself had been buried in a vast mud landslide. Others were more shrewd or cynical. His descendant, Te Heuheu Iwikau (?– 1862) informed another Anglican missionary that when the latter was present he was Anglican, with the Wesleyan missionary he was Wesleyan, and 'when the RC priest calls, I am a Papist'. He also said that when no Europeans were around, he was heathen.

Bishop Selwyn saw his mission in very different terms from the sedentary life of an English bishop in his Palace. Within ten days of his arrival he was on a six months' journey of 2,300 miles around his new domain. He learned Maori and preached in it, actively sought Maori converts, and aided by those already converted, went exploring. He reports on part of an 1843 journey:

> We then came to a tributary of the Whanganui River which gave us more trouble, the natives being very unwilling to cross. Foreseeing that there would be more rain, I blew up my air bed, which is my 'state barge' on such occasions, and the natives having made a frame of sticks for it, Mr. Taylor (who cannot swim) crossed safely upon it.

He describes the problems of traversing dense forests in 1847:

> We were very much entangled amongst the sides of the steep and thick scrub, sinking deep at almost every step among layers of ancient fallen trees all more or less rotten … so that sometimes the Maori as well as myself would sink down so far – crashing through the rotten timber, and yet without touching the earth – that we could not extricate ourselves without assistance … when we finally halted [exhausted] we remained just as we were until daylight.

Selwyn also took to the ocean in his small but sturdy schooner, *Undine*, which he not merely navigated but could work like any seaman.

Charles Darwin (1809–82), of evolution fame, who visited New Zealand in 1835 on his epic round the world voyage on HMS *Beagle*, saw much to be admired in the missionaries' material achievement. He described the mission settlement at Waimate in the Bay of Islands as follows:

> There were three large houses ... near to these the huts of the native labourers. On an adjoining slope fine crops of barley and wheat in full ear, and others of potato and clover ... with every fruit and vegetable which England produces, and many belonging to a warmer climate ... the lesson of the missionary is the enchanter's wand. The house has been built, the windows framed, the fields ploughed, even the trees grafted by the New Zealander [i.e. Maori]. At the mill a New Zealander may be seen powdered white with flour, like his brother miller in England.

The Protestant missionaries themselves certainly put down roots. Twelve of the earliest had something like 84 children. And when the dubious early European purchases of land were first investigated by the New Zealand government in the 1840s, some missionaries owned large acreages. The well-known Henry Williams claimed to own more than 11,000 acres (4,500 hectares)!

Sometimes the clash of cultures could be farcical. Ake was an old Maori who, in the hot sun, liked to work nude in the fields and Bishop Selwyn's colleague Rev. Richard Taylor (1805–73) tried continually to turn him to Church morality. Says Taylor,

> I repeatedly spoke to him but in vain. One day however, when I was going over the river to the town with my wife and daughter, I saw old Ake in his usual state. I ran on before and bid him go into a house and put on his mat; he refused, I said he should, he declared he would not, I pushed, he resisted, at last I saw there was no alternative but force, so I put my arms around him and fairly pushed him into a house, to the great amusement of the natives who stood by. He was conquered, but I dearly paid for the victory; Ake's skin had been anointed with red ochre and oil, which, I found to my cost, had completely destroyed my best black coat.

New Zealand's first artists were the Maori carvers of canoes and meeting houses with allegorical and mythological features, and the incisers of Moko (Appendix 4). Their art adapted Christianity as much as adapted to it. In 1845 a great Maori artist, Patoromu carved 'the Maori Madonna' in which, to the consternation of the orthodox, Mary and Jesus have full moko. Much conversion also, at least in the 1830s and 1840s was a means to an end: of gaining mana, of leaning to read, or of acquiring books. In 1842 a man in Taranaki offered a missionary a pig for a bible; in 1849 a Wairau woman offered herself. Still, Christianity was a success, and by the 1850s something like 60 per cent of Maori called themselves Christian, and in some sense meant it.

As we shall see in later chapters, in the shape of prophets like Te Kuiti, Rua, and Ratana, the Maori eventually produced their own unique and fascinating combinations of Christian and indigenous ideas.

The record of the first sixty or so years of missions in New Zealand and the other South Pacific Islands was mixed. Though missionaries preserved native languages by giving them written form, they suppressed native culture unassimilable to Christian ethics and metaphysics, or too different from European conceptions of what was normal for human beings. In confusing things European with things Christian, missionaries almost without exception rejected some harmless values, but also helped end much suppression of women, as well as cannibalism. They taught helpful medical practices, but also unintentionally introduced diseases. They acted as mediators in local conflicts, and civilized negotiations between Islanders and traders and colonists. In their own lives many demonstrated an ethical sincerity and selflessness completely unknown in these regions, but some took the opportunity for personal monetary advancement. Christianity helped in the unification of Pacific Islands and New Zealand regions, especially when a great chief converted. Though Christianity brought peace, and to its believers the sublime value of salvation, it contributed substantially to the dislocation of the Pacific islands in the first place.

The Maori Musket Wars 1818–40

By the time the missionaries first arrived on New Zealand shores, the Maori tribes had begun to slaughter one another in the prelude to the brutal, unremitting Musket Wars.

POLYNESIA'S WORST WARS?

The Wars proper took place in the period 1818 to 1840, though battles prior to this date had later repercussions. The chief of these was Moremonui, which occurred in 1807. Fighting was desultory from 1807 until 1818, intensified to 1836, being most bloody in the early 1830s. Fighting continued at a lesser intensity from the mid-1830s to 1840, after which there was sporadic fighting till 1845. Something like 3,000 battles, sieges, and raids took place in the 1818–40 period, many as parts of long campaigns.

These wars produced the greatest amount of slaughter in the whole history of Polynesia. Possibly, more New Zealanders were killed in them than in all the other wars fought by New Zealanders in the last 200 years combined, World Wars I and II included. Something like 3,000 Maori, British soldiers, and settlers were killed in the better-known New Zealand Wars of the 1840s and 1860s. But it is possible that at least ten times that number of people were killed in the Musket Wars – mostly in battle, but also through disease and starvation, through being worked to death as prisoner-of-war slaves, or being eaten as part of cannibal victory feasts or as walking food supplies along the trails of the war parties. Some missionary estimates put the dead at 80,000, an unlikely figure. Nevertheless, the missionaries were in the heartland of the great slaughterer, Hongi Hika, and they were the only people keeping figures.

From the little we know or believe about Maori population growth, at the time the wars began it seems to have been negligible. If 30,000 perished in the Musket Wars then, from an estimated Maori population of, say, 100,000 when the wars began in earnest in 1818, *proportionately* these were among the most devastating wars in the recorded history of the world.

CAUSES

Like any war, the New Zealand Musket Wars developed out of a complex set of earlier circumstances. By the 1700s, war, warriors, and their mana had become the central values of Maori culture. Though some regions seem to have been relatively peaceful for long periods, and apparently even without fortifications, others were the scene of continual warfare. In such places there had been decades, even centuries of shifting tribal rivalries and animosities, kept alive by the negative aspect of the second core Maori idea of 'utu' (reciprocity/ payback). And two new factors, one godlike and life-giving, the other devilish and life-taking, now made possible an unprecedented degree of bloodshed.

The first was the spread of white potato growing. This had been introduced by James Cook and, though the point is often forgotten, solved the Maori food problem. Traditionally, the season for war began after the kumara crops had been planted in October and November. But potatoes could be planted earlier and, unlike kumara, needed little attention. So although the potato was nutritional salvation, there was now also more leisure time for fighting. The second factor was the arrival in New Zealand of the Europeans and Americans trafficking in cheap trade muskets. Had Westerners not sold muskets, the wars could never have taken such a bloodcurdling form. Possession of muskets enhanced the mana of warriors, and provided a superior way to settle old scores and, increasingly as the wars progressed, to gain control of territory. As Maori obtained muskets in increasing numbers new reasons for revenge multiplied. It was Maori values: the pursuit of mana and utu, which made the Musket Wars happen. It was muskets which made the Musket Wars horrendous.

From about 1810 some northern tribes made raids south, but details are obscure, and it is generally agreed that weapons were traditional Maori ones, not muskets. But from 1818 the balance of power was radically altered. Tribes whose territories enclosed harbours accessible to traders and their muskets now had the means to conduct lengthy and successful campaigns far from home. North Island tribes eventually ravaged South Island, 400 and more miles from their home territories. Raids increased as chiefs realized they could preempt attack by striking before rivals acquired too many muskets. The Musket Wars were similar to the musket warfare which, as we have seen, destabilized other South Pacific islands such as Tahiti rather earlier, Fiji around the same time, and Samoa somewhat later. But in New Zealand they were on a larger scale.

Given the tradition of shifting alliances between tribes and sub-tribes, the Musket Wars were immensely complex, and there is a lack of documentary evidence. Still, the general outlines are clear, and certain battles and figures rise above the melee. The careers of the two best-known figures will now be described.

HONGI HIKA'S BLOODCURDLING CAMPAIGNS

In 1807 an exhausted 500-strong raiding party of the Nga Puhi tribe from the Bay of Islands decided to rest at the valley of Moremonui. The valley led inland from the beach just north of today's town of Darga-ville in Northland. The Nga Puhi did not know that a war party of the Ngati Whatua tribe lay in the flax and toetoe bushes waiting to ambush them.

Fierce fighting left some 150 Nga Puhi dead on the beach and in the valley and many Nga Puhi prisoners were taken. The few muskets possessed by the Nga Puhi had been insufficient to protect them. In Maori folklore the battle became known as Te Kai-a-te-Karoro, 'the Seagull's Feast'!

One of the defeated warriors who escaped was a lesser chief called Hongi Hika (1772–1828), who as we have seen was friend to the missionary Kendall, and who would become perhaps the best known of all the Wars' warriors. Because his two older brothers were killed, Hongi Hika became a leading chief. He always remembered the humiliation of the Seagull's Feast, deeply resented the Ngati Maru of the Coromandel Peninsula and the Ngati Paoa who lived at Mokoia (now Panmure, a suburb of Auckland) and for all three tribes waited long years for revenge. In the following decade he helped to weld all the different tribes and sub-tribes of his Nga Puhi people into a confederation ranging across about 70 miles of territory north to south.

In 1818, his warrior reputation growing, from his pa at Kerikeri, Hongi led a war party of about 800 on the second great campaign of the Musket Wars – an eleven-month journey all the way down the east coast of North Island to near modern Gisborne. (The first campaign south was led by his Nga Puhi rival for leadership Te Morenga, a month earlier.) By this time Hongi had acquired about 50 muskets, and

A *haka* during the Maori Musket Wars c. 1840

because most of the tribes he met had little experience of them, he was extraordinarily successful. Some enemy warriors just fled in terror. Hongi claimed he had burned 500 villages, no doubt an exaggeration, but many chiefs and hundreds of warriors were killed. According to the missionaries, perhaps 1,000 prisoners were brought back as slaves, while one canoe alone held 70 severed heads. Slaves had never been taken in such numbers. Hongi needed slaves to produce his wheat, flax, pork, and potatoes, which he exchanged for still more muskets from European and American traders. Hongi also wanted more victories to circumvent the leadership challenge by Te Morenga.

From the voyage to England, mentioned above, and from Sydney on the return, Hongi bought about 300 muskets. Instantly the Nga Puhi had become the most powerful fighting force in the country, and he continued buying. (Around 1820 in New Zealand, the cost of one musket was something like 200 baskets of potatoes or 15 pigs.)

In 1821, planning vengeance, Hongi organized another war party for the south. The local missionaries estimated there were 2000 warriors with perhaps a thousand muskets. His first targets were the two large Ngati Paoa pa at Mokoia and Mauinaina, set in their fertile fields 100 miles away. Because the battle at the first pa continued after the Ngati Paoa chief was killed, Hongi constructed a wooden tower from which to fire into the enemy pa. So thorough was the slaughter of Ngati Paoa that the Auckland isthmus was almost depopulated.

Now Hongi marched on to the Ngati Maru tribe's pa, near today's town of Thames. Stalemated after two days heavy fighting, Hongi made a treacherous peace and then attacked at night. Perhaps 1000 people were slaughtered and 2000 taken prisoner. Such levels of captured and casualties were something new in Maori history. Returning home, Hongi horrified the missionaries with days of cannibal feasting upon the prisoners. He had now taken revenge in excess upon the Ngati Paoa and the Ngati Maru.

Still the battles continued. Because Hongi's son-in-law had been killed in the fighting, he led 3000 warriors to exterminate surviving Ngati Paoa and Ngati Maru, who had fled south to the protection of their ally the Waikato. But in fighting the Waikato, Hongi's warriors killed an allied chief of Te Arawa, which then brought war with that tribe and its allies. A great war party of Nga Puhi departed for Te Arawa territories in February 1823, led by Hongi and several other famous chiefs. On learning of Hongi's approach all the major tribes and sections of Te Awara gathered on their supposedly impregnable Mokoia Island in the middle of Lake Rotorua, itself at an altitude of 920 ft/280m on the Volcanic Plateau.

After paddling something like 225 mls/360k to Tauranga in the Bay of Plenty, Hongi's troops had the prodigious task of paddling, portaging and climbing with their great canoes, the largest perhaps twenty-five tons, to the level of the Lake Rotorua. Unlike their invaders, the Te Arawa had few muskets. The Te Arawa chief fired a musket ball as Hongi was stepping ashore, hitting him on the helmet acquired from King George IV. Hongi collapsed into his canoe – but was merely stunned. Soon after that moment of potential disaster the Nga Puhi muskets rapidly turned the one-sided battle their way. Hundreds were killed, and soon Te Arawa were fleeing in all directions across the lake. Rev. Samuel Marsden, who happened to be in New Zealand, recorded the return to the Bay of Islands of the hundreds of prisoner slaves, the heads, and the stacked human meat.

Hongi's leadership was now being challenged by younger chiefs, and early in 1825 he decided to take his revenge for the Seagull's Feast. But there was now less enthusiasm and his small war party had difficulty defeating the Ngati Whatua at Te Ika-a-Ranganui.

By the end of 1825 Nga Puhi dominance was waning because most other major tribes now had muskets, and everyone was learning to construct 'musket-proof' or 'gunfighter' pas. These involved series of trenches, embankments of earth, and thicker palisades. Within a few years Hongi suffered a series of family disasters, his tribespeople detected a loss of mana, and skirmishing within the Nga Puhi federation itself began. In early 1827 Hongi was shot through the lung and paralysed. By March 1828 he was dead. The great days of Nga Puhi dominance were over.

THE CHAKA ZULU OF NEW ZEALAND: TE RAUPARAHA'S CONQUESTS

Te Rauparaha (?–1849) of the Ngati Toa was the second greatest warrior of the wars. But in territorial conquest, in winning allies, in turning his small power base into a large one, and in trading and treachery he outdistanced Hongi. In some districts of New Zealand where descendants of his victims live his name is remembered with loathing. In contrast, some people believe that while hiding from pursuers as a young man he composed the most famous haka, *Ka mate* (*'Tis death*) (Appendix 3), which New Zealand international rugby teams perform prior to their matches.

While Hongi Hika was devastating the north, Te Rauparaha, after suffering attacks by the Waikato tribe led his small Ngati Toa people to the 'promised land'. From their home region of Kawhia half-way down the west coast of North Island they journeyed on a tortuous migration first into Taranaki and then farther south, where he planned to capture the whole Horowhenua region north of Wellington, the home of the Muaupoko. (The Muaupoko had made a treacherous but failed attack on Te Rauparaha in 1822.) By early in 1823 Te Rauparaha's Ngati Toa, and allies from Taranaki were raiding into the Horowhenua.

The Muaupoko retreated to special pa they had constructed on six artificial islands in Lake Horowhenua. These they formed by driving stakes into the lake bed, tying manuka between them and filling the space between these walls with soil and sand carried by canoe in endless journeys. (In 180 years these formerly brush-clad islands have sunk into the lake and can no longer be seen.) Determined on muru and land grabbing, Te Rauparaha's warriors dragged their canoes up a narrow stream and into Lake Horowhenua. They attacked at dawn and as at Mokoia Island the slaughter was terrible. After seizing other Muaupoko pa, the Ngati Toa remained feasting and ransacking food stores. While there, they were in turn attacked by allies of Muaupoko, from farther south. The Ngati Toa triumphed again, but with many casualties.

Meanwhile, Te Rauparaha's mind turned to seeking a truly secure fortress refuge for himself. After mounting several testing raids, he decided upon the Muaupoko's Kapiti Island, a few miles off the west coast. There were already several pa which could be further strengthened; much of the coast was cliffed, especially the west – almost inaccessible; it was near the Cook Strait shipping lane with its general and musket trade; and as a long term goal it could be used as a base from which to capture the north of South Island and its trade in greenstone. Strategically, Kapiti was a choice of genius. Because Te Rauparaha was engaged in the Horowhenua, the invasion of Kapiti was led by his uncle and advisor, the hereditary Ngati Toa chief, Te Pehi Kupe (?–1828). Te Pehi Kupe took the relaxed Muaupoko garrison by surprise.

After the capture of Kapiti, Te Rauparaha defeated his rivals, extended his conquests, acquired more allies, and led numerous raids into South Island against such tribes as the unfortunate Ngai Tahu. He soon came to dominate the south of North Island and the north of South Island, and was the real ruler of these regions. He acquiesced in the founding of Wellington, New Plymouth, and Nelson by the New Zealand Company in the 1840s, intending to manipulate the settlers for his own ends. The modern historian, James Belich calls Te Ruparaha's domains 'the nearest thing New Zealand could boast to an African-style "conquest state".'

DESTRUCTION OF THE MORIORI

Another notorious Musket Wars example concerns the unfortunate Moriori of the Chatham Islands. Around AD 1400, several canoes of early-Maori chanced upon the Chatham Islands, about 500 miles east of South Island. Just as the Easter Islanders lost contact with other Polynesians, so these Moriori, as they came to be known, lost contact with New Zealand. On their isolated islands the Moriori *technically regressed*, developing a peaceful hunting and gathering existence, in which social distinctions were negligible. To prevent overpopulation and famine, they castrated some male children.

In 1835 their peaceful lives were shattered, because members of the Ngati Mutunga and Ngati Tama tribes had learned of their existence from Maori who had sailed on European sealing vessels. They also learned that the Moriori had no warrior tradition. Now dwelling in the Wellington area, the Ngati Mutunga and Ngati Tama had both suffered defeats by Te Rauparaha, and lived in fear of him. The islands of the Moriori seemed the ideal place to colonize. They forced the captain of the brig, *Lord Rodney*, to ship them to the Chathams. The first voyage brought about 500 warriors and families, mostly Ngati Tama, a second some 400 people, mostly Ngati Mutunga, and seven war canoes. Being first to arrive, the Ngati Tama were able to claim the best land.

Moriori traditions were peaceful, they had no weapons except clubs to kill seals, and instead of resisting decided to offer to share the islands peacefully, but the Maori attacked. During several callous days, hundreds of Moriori were bludgeoned and shot, many cooked and eaten, and the living who remained enslaved. One of the conquerors explained their behaviour in this way, 'We took possession ... in accordance with our customs and we caught all the people ... some ran away ... these we killed, and others we killed – but what of that? It was ... our custom.' The invaders then battled one another to claim the best land. In 1835 there had been perhaps 1600 Moriori; in the 1840s there were believed to be about 160. In 1870 the New Zealand Native

Land Court recognized that the two invading tribes had a right to more than 90 per cent of the land.

THE WARS COME TO AN END: THEIR RESULTS

By the mid-1830s emphasis was increasingly placed on defence. Pa which incorporated protective banks of earth, firing trenches, and angles for crossfire, became too dangerous to attack. Battles became inconclusive. There was often enormous expenditure of ammunition for few casualties. Even though the poor quality trade muskets were increasingly changed for powerful military ones, and even though chiefs acquired ships' cannon, the latter were usually incorporated into pa so there was still a balance on the side of defence. The Musket Wars had finally come to exemplify a universal principle of warfare: new weapons and tactics of aggression eventually produce defensive reactions which nullify them.

Many tribes were becoming war weary. Others were too depressed to take up arms. Despair and illness kept death rates high even after the Wars had ended. Christian ideas became influential. One reason some chiefs welcomed the 1840 Treaty of Waitangi between Maori and Briton seems to have been that they wanted peace and saw a British presence as a way of achieving this.

Unlike the wars which led to greater unification in other Pacific Islands such as Tonga, Tahiti (and Hawaii in the North Pacific too), and Fiji, the Musket Wars were mostly destructive, with little trend to political centralization. Though there were innumerable examples of extreme stoicism, immense heroism, altruism and self-sacrifice, and at times chivalrous treatment of enemies, they were fought not for unification under a single ruler, nor for belief in some uplifting political ideal, but to increase mana and exact utu. Even Te Rauparaha's unification of much territory on both sides of Cook Strait was temporary.

Besides the serious decline in Maori population, tens of thousands were displaced, great swathes of country emptied. At least forty tribal migrations resulted and tribes who reoccupied empty lands brought about later legal disputes, some of which still continue. Except in much of the less-populated South Island, tribal boundaries were radically altered – sometimes erased. In the three important later British settlement areas of Auckland, Wellington, and Canterbury, the wars seriously reduced the numbers of Maori. The Musket Wars thus made British colonization of New Zealand easier. Though for another twenty years Maori were more powerful militarily than the settlers, Maoridom as a warrior force was seriously reduced.

As the Wars ended, instead of fighting, tribes began commercial rivalry. Some chiefs had their own trading schooners by 1840 purchased with products that would have been sold for muskets five years earlier.

Absent-minded British Acquisition of New Zealand

What to do about New Zealand, a land without Western law and order, perplexed the governments of the Western countries whose citizens traded there. The British especially were concerned. The colonial British government in New South Wales (based in Sydney) and the British home government in London wanted to protect British citizens from Maori attacks. But this was also the age in which the world's first humanitarian movements began, as enlightened Europeans started to question the right of one country or people to rule another. Increasingly, such conceptions influenced British policy, so the governments in Sydney and London also wanted to protect the Maori from the immoral and lawless amongst the British, European, and North American whalers, sealers, and traders. There ensued a long, and tortuous tussle between politicians and humanitarians on one side and the reticent British Colonial Office on the other. The former wanted *some* level of British control or annexation; but the Colonial Office was itself torn between those who believed that Britain already possessed enough responsibilities and troublesome colonies around the world and were exceedingly reluctant to take over, and those who believed some control needed to be exerted in New Zealand.

The commissions of the early governors of the colony in Sydney included a vague authority over 'adjacent' islands – over Norfolk Island, for instance, which lay almost as far from Sydney as did New Zealand. Most governors interpreted their commission as including some undefined responsibility for New Zealand. Following the *Boyd* massacre, ships which left Sydney to trade in the 'South Seas' were forced to deposit £1000 as good behaviour bond. Rev. Thomas Kendall was made Justice of the Peace. Such measures had little effect on Maori or settler.

But after an infamous Musket Wars incident in 1831 when Captain Stewart shipped Te Rauparaha from Kapiti to Banks Peninsula to slaughter Ngai Tahu, Governor Darling at Sydney persuaded the British government to appoint a British Resident in the Bay of Islands. In 1833 James Busby arrived at Kororareka. The fact that he had authority but no power to back it up rendered his efforts impotent: a 'gunboat without guns'. And the British government was reluctant to provide him with power because that would have challenged their belief that the Maori chiefs held sovereignty.

Busby attempted to confederate the northern Maori tribes. He had some success, but his 'United Tribes of New Zealand' was a conception too radical for the Maori. However, a flag was designed, the British government recognized it, and for a time New Zealand-based trading vessels sailed under it. It flew at Busby's home until 1840.

So, politically New Zealand remained problematic. In 1837 about 200 missionaries and settlers petitioned King William IV for protection from the Maori, and even Busby's life had been threatened by an attack on his home.

By 1839 perhaps 2,000 Europeans lived in New Zealand, about 1,400 in North Island. Some 500 or more of these lived in and around the Bay of Islands, where Kororareka, New Zealand's only town, had grown up. Up to 30 ships with a complement of 1,000 men might at one time lie at anchor there. The European residents of New Zealand formed three contrasting groups. There were the missionaries and the inhabitants of their mission stations, orderly, organized, of civilized manners and middle-class morals. There were the whalers, former whalers and sealers, ex-convicts, and adventurers, of wild and unciv-ilized ways. And there was a group of professional men and traders. There resided Busby, an American Consul, and a medical doctor. There were also a blacksmith, several sawyers who organized the timber trade, sundry tradesmen who helped build houses and repair visiting ships, and merchants and traders who owned warehouses. These latter men victualled visiting ships, and their own small vessels traded up and down the coast and across the Tasman Sea to Sydney.

THE TREATY OF WAITANGI

In 1839 the British government decided it was time to recognize officially that settlement by British subjects was occurring whether Britain liked it or not. This decision of the British Colonial Office was finally forced by the intentions of several private groups of colonizers, in particular the New Zealand Association (later the New Zealand Company) which it knew planned a colony. The government also knew that the Company planned to purchase huge tracts of land from the Maori for speculative exploitation. Its fears that this implied more settler–Maori problems and that the Company might not deal fairly with the Maori were well based, as we shall see in the next chapter.

A reconstruction of the signing of the Treaty of Waitangi in 1840

Captain William Hobson had visited New Zealand in 1837 and thought that the level of British labour and capital already invested made annexation appropriate. In 1839 he was appointed as a kind of consul to the chiefs and first British Lieutenant Governor, and instructed to proceed towards British control of all or part of the islands. But Britain recognized that sovereignty presently lay with the various Maori chiefs. Consequently Hobson's job was to try to seek 'the free and intelligent consent' of the Maori chiefs to a general British suzerainty so they could be protected from the excesses of settlers, while leaving them to control their own lands. New Zealand would be the first of the Pacific islands to fall to a European power, but certainly without any British government enthusiasm.

Hobson organized the Treaty of Waitangi in 1840. It was named 'Waitangi' after the hamlet in which the agreement was made. During several days, with the help of Busby and his own secretary James Freeman, Hobson hastily drafted a written treaty. Invitations to attend a gathering at Waitangi on the Bay of Islands on 5 February 1840 were sent to chiefs who had been in Busby's confederation, and later to other chiefs. Meanwhile a translation into Maori had been produced by the leading missionary Henry Williams and his son, Edward. The first printed versions ran off the mission press at Paihia on 17 February 1840, after the signing. Maori were granted legal equality with the settlers and 'full, exclusive and undisturbed possession of their lands, forests, fisheries, as long as they wish to retain the same' (Appendix 2). Land sales were to be only to the government.

On 5 February in a large marquee, the Treaty was presented to a gathering of some hundreds of Maori. Present were Hobson and his people, local English and French missionaries, and some settlers. It is possible that verbal explanations embellished the text to make it clearer to the Maori. The chiefs under the Catholic French influence of Bishop Pompallier were more sceptical. By the end of the day, however, chiefs who supported the British missionaries seem to have convinced a majority to agree. That night the Treaty was further discussed by the chiefs in private. The next day, 6 February, forty-five chiefs agreed, the first being Hone Heke Pokai (c.1808–50), one of the chiefs of the Nga Puhi. Later there were some fifty Treaty meetings in different parts of the country, organized by Major Thomas Bunbury and the missionaries, and by September over 500 chiefs had signed. Five women signed. Other women who were refused by Maori custom, pointed out that the real party to agreement on the British side was a woman, Queen Victoria! Some chiefs refused outright, which meant the exclusion of whole tribes such as the Te Arawa of Rotorua, who had been slaughtered by Hongi in 1823.

The situation in sparsely populated South Island was different. Signatures were collected from chiefs at five places along the east coast. But before Hobson could be informed of this, he felt himself forced to proclaim British sovereignty 'by right of discovery by the late lamented Captain Cook'. For by this time the first British settlers of the New Zealand Company had arrived at Port Nicholson (Wellington) and French colonists were heading for Akaroa (now near Christchurch) probably to claim the island for France. Hobson believed he had the duty to exert British government authority over the British settlers and to preempt the French.

The Maori version was somewhat different from the English version. This difference was not intended to deceive, but derived from haste and difficulties of translation. There was, for instance, no precise Maori equivalent of the word 'sovereignty'. The nearest the translators could arrive at was *kawanatanga* (a made-up word for governorship), meaning something like 'government authority/complete government over'. Perhaps the chiefs interpreted the agreement as something like a lease of their lands (though there was also no Maori word for 'lease') rather than as ceding sovereignty. In other words, it is not clear that Maori chiefs who signed agreed that they were giving up their traditional authority. One chief assumed that 'the shadow of the land will go to him (Hobson), but the substance will remain with us'. Within a few years of the signing and ever since in varying degrees, the Treaty has been contentious, in recent decades perhaps more than ever. The differences in opinion are over its interpretation – and not all Maori interpret it the same way either.

To the extent that any thought had been given to the matter, it had been assumed by the British that a slow blending through assimilation of the two races would occur. This would come about through the natural processes of contact and trade, through growing knowledge of the other's culture, and through formal legal equality.

Validity of current tribal boundaries was an unexamined assumption of the Treaty, and the lost rights of tribes dispossessed by the Musket Wars went unnoticed. Though descendants of the losers still experience the consequences, even if Hobson had been aware of this issue it is difficult to see what he could have done. So even today the Wars have relevance – especially for the claims and massive redistributions of money and land awarded by New Zealand's contemporary Waitangi Tribunal.

Meanwhile in January 1840 some weeks before the signing at Waitangi, the advance ship, *Tory*, and some weeks later the first immigrant ship of the New Zealand Company, had sailed into Port Nicholson (Wellington Harbour). And now the 1834 Busby flag of independent New Zealand tribes was flying above the new settlement as well! Hobson reasoned that the settlers were presumptuously seizing the prerogatives of the British Government. Disturbed by exaggerated tales of the settlers' attitudes, he decided he had to do something forceful.

Hobson soon established the capital at Auckland (there was no pre-existing Maori village) about 110 miles/180k south of Waitangi. This was to the immense displeasure of Hone Heke who wished it to be at Kororareka in his territories on the Bay of Islands. Trouble would come of that too.

CHAPTER SEVEN

Settlements and Wars: New Zealand to 1872

During a period of a dozen years British colonial towns were established around the coasts of North and South Islands. From 1840 Auckland 'just grew' as Governor Hobson's instant capital on a volcanic isthmus between two large harbours. Wellington, squeezed between a magnificent harbour and close precipitous hills, was at first the botched result of plans laid by the New Zealand Company on the other side of the world. A decade later, though Dunedin and Christchurch were both in South Island, and like Wellington were 'Wakefield-inspired' settlements, they differed. Dunedin was built on hilly countryside, Christchurch on swampy plain, the former the aspiration of determined Free Church Scots, the latter of enterprising English Anglicans.

North Island towns also had to take the Maori into account. For some decades Auckland settlers benefited from living reasonably close to many hard-working Maori who could supply fresh fruit, fish, pork, and potatoes. This Maori–settler relationship was central to the development of Auckland's early identity. So it is historically appropriate that today Auckland has the largest Polynesian population, both native Maori and immigrant Pacific Islanders, of any city in the world. But in the 1850s Wellington and Auckland (and in the early 1860s Auckland again) felt threatened by settler–Maori conflict. In contrast, Christchurch and Dunedin developed without any such tensions. South Island Maori population had always been small, and the attacks by Te Rauparaha made it even smaller. The lesser New Zealand Company towns of Nelson, New Plymouth, and Wanganui also developed their own personalities. As case studies of the settlers' lives, the early years of Wellington and Christchurch will be considered in some detail.

Wakefield, the New Zealand Company and Formal British Settlement

The story of planned settlement in New Zealand begins with the problematic, dogmatic, restless figure of Edward Gibbon Wakefield (1796–1862). While in prison for abducting a fifteen-year-old girl (he had already eloped with a sixteen-year-old who died four years later) he thought and wrote about penal reform and the inefficiency of convict colonies. Out of prison, he discussed his ideas with other men who were interested in developing colonies and in solving contemporary problems of British overpopulation and unemployment, and began to advocate a new and very different system of settlement. Unlike the ever-expanding United States, Canadian, and Australian frontier societies, Wakefield wanted settlements to be tidily agricultural, and centred on a well-organized town.

In place of allocating large free land grants and leases as had occurred in eastern Australia, Wakefield advocated the sale by the government of small lots of land to men of capital, close together, at a 'sufficient price'. This was a price which was supposed to achieve equilibrium among land, labour, and capital. Landowners would have a town lot and less expensive country lots. Only relatively wealthy people would be able to afford the 'sufficient price' for such lots, so labourers would need to work for some years before they could themselves accumulate funds to purchase their own land. Money from land sales would be used to bring further immigrants to maintain the supply of labour in the colony, and at the same time help to solve the British unemployment problem. So the new farming settlement would be socially balanced and grow in a disciplined manner. As soon as practicable self-government was to be allowed the colonists.

Wakefield's scheme had already been tried in 1836 in founding Adelaide and South Australia and had come close to disaster. He hoped for better in New Zealand, though, and it was characteristic of the man, that he did not modify his theory in accordance with this experience. In 1839 Wakefield's New Zealand Company was floated as a joint stock company to establish a new colony somewhere in the Cook Strait region. Within a month investors had bought the 1,000 purchase-orders, lured by the chance of winning a valuable waterfront property. The lottery held in London in July 1839 determined the order in which land sections would be chosen in 1840 in the colony itself.

Wellington

Wellington, today the capital city, was the first New Zealand colony to implement Wakefield's ideas. Wellington too would suffer from problems similar to those of South Australia, compounded by a difficult location (except for the magnificent harbour) and the presence of resident Maori.

WILLIAM WAKEFIELD AND THE PURCHASE OF MAORI LAND

During the Musket Wars the Wellington region had been invaded six times and the land and harbour acquired several new masters by force. By the early 1830s the Te Ati Awa were in the ascendant, but reluctantly sharing with Ngati Mutunga and Ngati Tama. The latter two, seeing a way out of the imbroglio, and as already described, transported themselves to the Chatham Islands, and transferred their 'rights' to the Te Ati Awa. Complicating matters further, the Ngati Toa, led by Te Rauparaha, were nominally allied to the Te Ati Awa. But as we have seen the Ngati Toa had already captured great swathes of North and South Islands and the Te Ati Awa lived in fear of them.

Te Rauparaha now possessed the powerful trading post and fortress of Kapiti Island just off the west coast, where European, Australian, and American trading ships sheltered, and a thousand slaves scraped flax to support his economy and pay for his muskets. Squabbles and skirmishes kept everyone tense. It was therefore a moot point which tribe 'owned' the Wellington land and harbour in 1840.

Into this confusion in 1840 the New Zealand Company ship *Tory* suddenly appeared in Port Nicholson at the end of its long journey. On it was Colonel William Wakefield (?–1848), chief New Zealand Company administrator and brother of Edward Gibbon Wakefield, and he was extremely anxious to purchase Maori land!

Rejecting the striking Marlborough Sounds portion of South Island as unsuitable, Wakefield crossed to Port Nicholson and quickly negotiated with the chiefs Te Puni and Te Wharepouri of the Te Ati Awa. Te Puni was very willing to sell, and Te Wharepouri manipulated the sale to his advantage, for, themselves opportunists, both saw the sale as a way of getting manufactured goods and increasing their mana. (Two and a half years later, Te Puni admitted to a government inquiry over disputed land that the land had not been his to sell!)

The legal status of these actions was dubious in British law and problematic in Maori lore, but with immigrants shortly to arrive, Colonel Wakefield was not interested in niceties. He then sailed to Kapiti Island to bargain with Te Rauparaha who scolded him for dealing with chiefs whom Te Rauparaha considered at best vassals and at worst usurpers. Wakefield finally claimed he had purchased an enormous 31,000 square miles (80,000 sq.k) of land lying on both sides of Cook Strait.

Soon after the *Tory* departed England, the New Zealand Company had despatched a surveying party in the *Cuba*, followed in short order by the other six ships, which carried 647 emigrants in steerage and 157 in cabins. The *Cuba*'s surveyors beat the first immigrants into the harbour, but by only 18 days! To the newcomers the lack of preparation was a debilitating shock. As one disheartened settler wrote,

> A strong and favourable wind soon carried us inside the heads of Port Nicholson. The passengers were all on deck straining their eyes to catch a glimpse of civilization. Little was said, although disappointment was visible on the countenances of everyone.

There was no 'civilization' to see. Nothing was ready for the settlers. On the north of the harbour where they landed there was a narrow foreshore with rugged forested slopes behind. Soon the immigrants were camping on the bits of flat land, while around them lay confused heaps of their goods from pots to pianos.

They struggled but they did not starve. The harbour teemed with fish and shell-fish, and the local Maori grew ample supplies of European vegetables. There were also multitudes of birds. Soon settlers were happily blasting away at any bird that came in sight. These were acts of liberation as much as hunting. For in 1840s Britain this would never have been allowed, countryside birds being the preserve of the land-owner.

Superior access to shore soon persuaded Wakefield to move the settlement around to Lambton Harbour in the south-west corner of the bay – which would become the core of the future city. But the hard topography still faced by the settlers is clear to every visitor to Well-ington today who takes the steep cable car from Lambton Quay to the gardens atop the ridge. The town was named after the Duke of Wellington, hero of Waterloo, and former prime minister, who had supported the Company.

In June 1840 Willoughby Shortland with five mounted policemen, a lieutenant, and thirty troops landed in Wellington. He had been des-patched by Governor Hobson, concerned at the reportedly anti-government attitudes of the new settlement. The officious manner in which Wellington's subordination to Hobson was made clear raised the settlers' hackles, and the antipathy which would exist for several decades between the northern settlements and Wellington began on that day. In retaliation a local bullock-driver named his animals after Hobson's delegation, and to the amusement of the Wellingtonians, profanities shouted to the beasts *Shortland*, *Cole*, and *Best* echoed around the little settlement.

Though Te Rauparaha had agreed to the settlement, the handful of local Maori protested, and surreptitiously removed the survey pegs at night. Still, by the end of July 1840 the town sections had been surveyed and were balloted. But outside the town was not properly surveyed for years. At the end of 1841 the Ngati Rangatahi tribe came south to join the Ngati Toa in the Hutt Valley to the north of Wellington, and so settler expansion in that direction became prob-lematic. Te Rangihaeata (?–1855), the nephew and lieutenant of Te Rauparaha, who dwelt about 10 miles to the north-west in the fer-tile region of Porirua, would soon prove to be an even greater threat.

SOCIAL DEVELOPMENTS

The settlers made the best of their difficult situation. Within a couple of months Wellington was home to two social clubs, a cricket club, and horses were being raced on Te Aro Flat. New Zealand's first recorded cricket match took place in May 1840 when the Gentlemen of Thorndon played the new Pickwick Club. Several lodges were established. There were soon a dozen small pubs which doubled as meeting places, the best known being Barrett's Hotel and the Thistle Inn. When the formidable Te Rauparaha occasionally parked his war canoe on Thorndon Beach and strode into the Thistle, nobody dared ask him to pay.

Two sections of town evolved. The Thorndon area consisted of Wakefield's large verandahed house, the wealthier migrants, the immigration and military barracks and Barrett's Hotel, and was considered the official quarter. To the south was Te Aro Flat which developed as the commercial area of traders, wharves, pubs, and workmen's cottages. The children also divided into two gangs, Thorndon's 'Sharps' and Te Aro's 'Flats'.

In 1843 James Marriott converted part of a pub into a theatre and staged Wellington's (and New Zealand's?) first plays. His success was immediate and persuaded him to construct a new theatre, the *Royal Victoria*. Comparisons with Australia began early: for the *Wellington Gazette* boasted that, 'to the playgoing public Port Nicholson now presents all the attractions to be found at Hobart Town or Sydney'. But the report of a visitor at the time suggests frontier town boisterousness rather than drama: 'The first actor who made his appearance was greeted with such a shout, and underwent such an impertinent cross-examination as to where he had procured his red striped pantaloons, how the moustache was stuck on, &c., that he could not proceed.'

WIND, EARTHQUAKE, FIRE, AND FLOOD

The weather which gave the town its sobriquet 'Windy Wellington' quickly made itself felt. In August 1840 in a fierce southerly, several small boats got into difficulties in the harbour and those who went to save them also drowned – nine men in all.

Fire was a continual hazard in a settlement of closely built wooden shops and houses and inadequate preparations to combat it. Within six months of the first landing, fire devastated about 14 cottages, destroying precious possessions which had survived the longest colonizing voyage in the history of the world. Two years later a fire began in a bakehouse at the north end of Lambton Quay (still the main street today). Fed by Wellington's howling winds, it raced through forty wood and raupo structures.

Worse were the earthquakes. Though they had no notion of the existence of the moving tectonic plates beneath their feet, Wellington's citizenry were soon aware of their effects. A mere four months after they arrived the settlers experienced a sharp shock just after midnight. Unfamiliarity led to novel reactions. Shaken from their beds and thinking they were being robbed, or attacked by Maori, some drew their swords, or ran out in night-shirts firing pistols. The resident Maori to whom earthquakes were commonplace were much amused.

There were so many minor tremors, some twenty-five or more from the time of arrival to 1846, that residents became accustomed to such visitations and their tendency to knock things over. The matter of fact attitude has continued. The 1848 earthquake was more severe. Its toppling of chimneys and public and private stone buildings strongly suggested that structures should be built of wood. It was fortunate that many people did thereafter use wood, because the 1855 earthquake would be the most powerful ever recorded in the country.

Around 9.17 pm on 23 January 1855 at a depth of 16 miles (26k) below Cook Strait, about 25 miles (40k) south-west of Wellington, a large section of the crust of the earth was suddenly ruptured. For decades monstrous pressure had been mounting as the western 'edge' of the vast Pacific Plate pushed underneath the eastern edge of the Indo-Australian Plate, just east of North Island. A shock wave a thousand times the strength of the atomic bomb dropped in World War II on Hiroshima raced outward in all directions.

In Wellington proper the quake raised most of the harbour shoreline by more than 3 feet/1m, uplifted beaches into a platform which today supports Marine Drive and Hutt Road, and changed the little harbour that was planned as a sheltered anchorage, into the flat land that is now Basin Reserve playing field. In Petone on the north of the harbour land rose more than 6 feet/2m and the sea flooded inland over 300 feet/ 91m. Farther to the north a piece of country about 50 miles × 19/80k × 30 was permanently uplifted. Its edge, the fault-line on the west of the Wairarapa Valley, was raised between 2 feet/0.6m and 19 feet/6m in different sections, forming fissures which swallowed cattle. In 1856 the visiting Sir Charles Lyell (1797–1875), one of the founders of the science of geology, described the fault-line as an almost vertical wall 9 feet/2.7m high 'which could be followed for the amazing distance of 90 miles [145k]'. In open country it is still clearly recognizable.

STAGNATION AND THEN SHEEP

The lack of suitable land and the difficulties of surveying caused the failure of the New Zealand Company's plans for an agricultural colony and led to economic decline. People departed for Australia and else-where, and immigration to Wellington almost ceased by the end of 1842. By mid-1845 only 7000 acres/2800 hectares of the purchased 110,000 in the Wellington region had been surveyed.

By 1843, in desperation, Colonel Wakefield had sent settlers inland to the disputed Hutt Valley to make their own farms. Though a response to the needs of the real world, such spread of settlement was anathema to the Company's utopian intentions. It was also annoying to some of the local Maori, and when settlers died in the Wairau Incident of the same year in South Island, a frisson of fear passed through these Wellington colonists. By 1848 only 85 of the *original* 436 settlers with capital would remain!

What saved Wellington was the introduction of sheep farming. In 1844 Frederick Weld (1823–91) and others edged their flocks of sheep along the beaches and into the empty Wairarapa Valley. Wool exports of about 8,600 pounds (3,900kg) in 1844 had reached a significant 112,000 pounds (51,000kg) by 1848. *That* was never envisaged in Wakefield's theory.

In 1865 Wellington, then a little town of about 5,000 people, was made capital of New Zealand. This brought a new kind of prosperity. The move was made because Wellington was more centrally located, and because there were fears in North Island that the gold-rich South Island settlements might want a separate colony if the capital remained so far away.

Harbour reclamation began, which has proceeded on and off ever since, to provide more commercial space: the names of modern streets Thorndon Quay and Lambton Quay which now stand well inland make the point. Public buildings transformed the town in the 1870s, especially in Thorndon, which began to take on its present government character. There was an elegant gabled and towered parliament house (replaced in 1922), and a huge wooden Government Building on the reclaimed land, which in itself showed the increasing importance of central government. Further inland, the villages which are now the centres of the towns of Hutt and Upper Hutt were developing. There were important commercial initiatives. Joseph E. Nathan (1835?–1912) established the mercantile Nathan and Co. in 1873. This was the parent company which would eventually spawn Glaxo, now the largest pharmaceuticals company in the world. By the end of the 1870s, Wellington was taking on some of the characteristics which today make it the nation's chief banking and finance centre.

Christchurch and Canterbury

MOA HUNTERS, MAORI, AND WHALERS

The early-Maori who travelled south from their landings in North Island were the first people into the region now called Canterbury. At that time the coastlands and most of the now open Canterbury Plains were thickly forested with matai and totara. These early-Maori burned and cleared much of that forest for horticulture, and hunted the moa. In the 1500s and 1600s their lands were invaded by North Island tribes, mainly the Ngati Mamoe and, subsequently, during the 1700s, groups who became known as the Ngati Tahu who either merged with or killed them.

The first Europeans in the region were sealers, flax traders, and whalers. By the time Wellington was founded there were probably about 80 Europeans settled on Banks Peninsula, the volcanic outcrop which pokes into the South Pacific. Much-reduced numbers of Maori, perhaps 500, also lived in Canterbury. These were all who remained after a deadly civil war in the 1820s and the murderous invasions by Te Rauparaha and his North Island Ngati Toa.

In August 1840, on Hobson's instructions, Captain Owen Stanley raised the British flag at Akaroa on Banks Peninsula, barely ahead of a group of 80 French colonists. Though soon outnumbered by the English, the French left their influence locally, developing the charming little town of Akaroa.

The first permanent European settlers on the Plains were two Scottish brothers, William (1817?–51) and John Deans (1820–54) and their families in 1843. Disappointed by their New Zealand Company land in Wellington and Nelson, the Deans found Canterbury to their liking, built the first European house, and named their farm Riccarton, now a Christchurch suburb.

WAKEFIELD AND THE CANTERBURY PILGRIMS

The real founding of the province of Canterbury took place some years later. In England in 1847, the enthusiastic, idealistic, young Anglican, Anglo-Irish lawyer and classical scholar, John Robert Godley (1814–61), met Edward Gibbon Wakefield, that brain behind the Wellington colony. Wakefield's plans had proved problematic in South Australia and Wellington, but he still believed his theory had not been properly tried. Godley was convinced, and the two worked energetically to plan a further settlement in New Zealand. Their well-organized Canterbury Association was formed in 1848, encouraged and supported by many powerful English Anglicans: peers, MPs, and the Archbishop of Canterbury. The capital of the new colony was to be called 'Christ Church', the name of Godley's college in Oxford, and the colony itself 'Canterbury'.

Though Canterbury would never become the success Wakefield wished, it did come closer than the others to his idea of transplanting a cross-section of English society overseas. Twelve shiploads of settlers were planned, and the first four ships departed in September 1850. There were 773 colonists, ranging from aristocrats and Oxford graduates, to barbers and bricklayers, and shop keepers and shepherds. The Anglican Church even made a grant to purchase 2,000 volumes to begin a colonial library. After the farewell banquet to the 'Canterbury Pilgrims', as they became known, an enthusiastic *Times* reporter was moved to write that, 'A slice of England, cut from top to bottom was despatched to the Antipodes.' It was almost true.

SURVEYING AND SETTLING

Meanwhile Governor Grey had been instructed by the Colonial Office to send a commissioner, Henry Kemp, to purchase Maori land for the Pilgrims. The usual misunderstanding and disagreement occurred, but sixteen Ngati Tahu elders signed 'Kemp's Deed', selling most of their land, for a ridiculously low price. Promises were broken, for instance the proposed Maori reserves were never established, and soon enough the small numbers of Maori were overwhelmed by arriving settlers. Neither people could have anticipated the events of the 1990s when the Waitangi Tribunal would award so much compensation to Ngati Tahu who claimed descent from the early Ngati Tahu invaders and occupiers, that they would suddenly become a significant force in the South Island economy.

In contrast to Wellington, preparations were made. Using local Maori and labourers from Wellington, the rudiments of a por including an immigrants barracks, were established at the deep harbo r of Lyttelton on Banks Peninsula – though communications over or around the hilly country between it and the main settlement proved to be a problem for years. John Robert Godley had been appointed first leader of the Anglican colony, and arrived in April 1850. As a wit has put it: 'In the beginning was Godley.'

A Wellington pioneer, Captain Joseph Thomas (1803–80?) and his aides performed an efficient job of surveying the swampy site of Christchurch, but when his chief assistant suggested that some of the streets be crescents (as at Bath in England) Thomas dismissed this idea as mere 'gingerbread'. As a result, Christchurch, perhaps the most English of all the world's colonial cities, was laid out mainly as a grid like Melbourne, Toronto, Chicago, and all those others in the New World.

'THE FIRST FOUR SHIPS' AND THE FIRST FEW YEARS

The 'First Four Ships' of colonists acquired a mystique in Christchurch, and today many are proud who can claim descent. It is extraordinary that after travelling *separately* across the world, these sailing ships all arrived in Lyttelton within hours or days of one another. *Charlotte Jane* arrived on 16 December 1850 in the morning, *Randolph* mid-afternoon! *Sir George Seymour* docked the next day, and *Cressy* ten days after. Godley and Governor Grey greeted them.

Life was rough. In the second year Dr Alfred Barker (1819–73), who was beginning to record the colony's progress in photographs, encountered a newcomer who was forcing his way through the tall native flax in what was to become Cathedral Square in the city's heart. The man asked Barker to direct him to Christchurch! But gradually houses were built, a newspaper was begun, the Christchurch Cricket Club was formed, and the prosperous Riccarton farm of the Deans encouraged others. By the end of 1851 there were 3,000 British in the area, many moving into the plains to the west.

Very quickly Godley had recognized that Wakefield's conception of a closely knit market town surrounded by agricultural farms would have to be modified. Perhaps learning from Wellington, he, and his successor from 1853, another Anglo-Irishman James Edward Fitzgerald (1818–96) realized that the Canterbury Plains were ideal for sheep farming. In 1852 the Canterbury Association allowed generous leases, using a sliding scale for rent as flocks increased. In such ways, the Canterbury settlement was much more practical and experimental than Wellington and more immediately successful.

In 1853 the British government established provincial government in New Zealand: six elected Provincial Councils each with a Super-intendent. Canterbury's able first Superintendent was Fitzgerald, founding editor in 1861 of *The Press*, a newspaper which is still published.

Experienced pastoralists from Australia were soon taking up sheep 'runs'. Despite periodic setbacks such as the flight of young men to the goldfields of Victoria, Otago, and the West Coast in the 1850s and 1860s, Christchurch developed. It became a market town, partly for agriculture as Wakefield had hoped, but much more for the sheep runs spread far across the Plains, and the province rapidly developed a staple export – wool. Compared with a few years earlier, wool exports had doubled to £90,000 by 1858 and doubled again to £189,000 by 1860. Excise duties, and sale and lease of the up–country runs provided the new Provincial Council with its first important revenue. Some was spent on public works, such as the splendid Provincial Council Buildings, which still stand.

CATHEDRAL, TUNNEL, AND COLLEGE CLOISTER

During the first decade or two Christchurch and Canterbury evolved their own English–antipodean values. The developments which epitomized these were the cathedral, the railway tunnel, and the university.

Christchurch is a city built around a cathedral with a spire which until the architectural depredations of the 1980s dominated the skyline. Appalled at the prospects of pioneering, the first Anglican bishop-designate scurried back to England after only six weeks. Rev. Henry Harper (1804–93) arrived as bishop in 1856 with his expanding family. Energetic and dedicated, Harper reorganized church finances and got the cathedral constructed – eventually. When in 1858 it was agreed that the cathedral should be built, Christchurch had an adult male population of about 450. Its population was thus much smaller than that of towns which began cathedrals in mediaeval Europe.

A foundation stone was laid on a wet windy day in 1864, and construction of the foundations rapidly completed – but nothing more could be afforded for a decade, and it appeared it might never be. Work recommenced under a resident architect, Benjamin Mountfort (1825–98), who had trained amongst the pioneers of the Gothic Revival in England. Local timber and stone were used. In 1881, amid town–wide celebrations, the nave and tower were finished first so the church could hold services. Transepts, chancel, and sanctuary took over 20 years more, and all was completed in 1904. Christchurch has had its share of earthquakes which damaged the cathedral and other buildings – the stately new 1863 stone town hall was so badly hit in 1869 that it had to be demolished.

A statue of John Robert Godley in front of Christchurch Cathedral

The railway tunnel to link Lyttelton's deep-water harbour to Christchurch through the frustrating barrier of the Port Hills sparked international interest because it was driven through the walls of an extinct volcano (perhaps a world first). A Melbourne company contracted, the provincial engineer Edward Dobson (1816–1908) supervised, and after nine years the two drives met in the middle in May 1867. The port was now linked to the other little railway lines leading inland from Christchurch. Some years earlier the *Lyttelton Times* described the first railway opening:

> The project has survived all opposition, though the promoters have been opposed by the heaviest intellects in the colony [a reference to Fitzgerald] ... On and about the platform paraded a crowd of elegantly dressed ladies and gentlemen, and everybody seemed impressed with the necessity of shaking hands as frequently as possible ... passenger carriages are four, two first, two second class, comfortable rather than expensively fitted; they are built of Australian timber.

The men who designed and built the University of Canterbury, Canterbury College as it was first called, thought that buildings too should broaden minds. They chose handsome Gothic Revival cloistered structures, and the best arts and science professors they could entice from Britain. Within two decades the college would produce Ernest Rutherford, one of history's greatest scientists.

This exciting period of pioneer developments in South Island was marred in North Island by the continuing New Zealand Wars, fought mainly because settlers wanted land and many Maori wanted to keep it.

The New Zealand Wars

The New Zealand Wars were a series of struggles in North Island between various Maori tribes on one side, and on the other, in varying combinations, regiments of the British army, New Zealand colonial militias, and Maori tribes who for a mixture of reasons supported the government – including paying back old scores from the Musket Wars. Tribes supporting the government, or neutral tribes, *far outnumbered the others*. Clashes arose over land claims, and different interpretations of the Treaty of Waitangi in 1840. Whereas the British governors and settlers believed that British authority was paramount in such matters, many Maori tribes believed that they still possessed local autonomy.

Earlier terms describing these conflicts were 'Anglo-Maori Wars', 'Maori Wars' and 'Land Wars'. The Wars can be grouped conveniently into three: (1) the local limited conflicts of the 1840s; (2) the much later core of the wars, the 1860–64 clashes between Empire troops and (mostly) the tribes supporting the Maori King movement; (3) the small, sporadic, and widely dispersed fighting of 1864–72, on one side colonial militias supported by Maori allies, and on the other the followers of the main Maori prophets.

Casualties were tiny, about 3,000 Maori and Europeans killed. In fact the greatest loss of life in a single day did not occur in battle. In February 1863 the steam corvette, *Orpheus*, hit the deceptive Manukau bar, and 189 officers and men, British reinforcements for the Waikato War, were drowned. Still, the New Zealand Wars are of deep significance in New Zealand because they retarded economic growth of

North Island, tragically harmed race relations, and ended the hopes of some Maori for independence.

LOCAL CONFLICTS: HONE HEKE'S NORTHERN WAR OF 1844–45

The first war, 'Heke's War', was fought in the Bay of Islands region. Its immediate cause was the actions of Hone Heke Pokai, like his uncle Hongi Hika, one of the chiefs of the Nga Puhi, and, ironically, as we have seen, the first person to sign the Treaty of Waitangi. Some Nga Puhi such as Kawiti Te Ruki (?–1854) supported Hongi, some helped the British, others were neutral.

Heke had been disillusioned by the manner in which British authority was being extended (as in customs duties) and deeply resented that the settlers' capital had been moved out of his territory south to Auckland. Such things reduced his trade and undermined his mana.

We have seen how Kororareka in the Bay of Islands was the first true settlement of non-Maori. Heke's discontent was enthusiastically encouraged by the Americans living there, and he attached a US flag to his war canoe. From a flagpole in the tiny town there flew a British ensign. In July 1844, Hone Heke chopped it down. In January 1845 the flagpole was twice re-erected and twice chopped down by Heke. A fourth flagpole was sheathed in iron and erected inside a blockhouse.

In a carefully orchestrated attack at 4 o'clock one morning Kawiti's 300 men engaged the town's gun battery, while Heke and 150 followers rapidly captured the flag blockhouse and chopped down the pole for the fourth time! After some fierce fighting the gun battery garrison withdrew. In this little early battle of the Wars the Maori had won, with 3 Maori killed and 20 British. Knowing little of the fighting ability shown in the Musket Wars, Governor Fitzroy (1805–65) and the settlers were astonished.

There were some indeterminate skirmishes and several pa were destroyed. When Hone Heke and another chief began to fight each other Colonel Henry Despard (1784/5?–1859) took advantage and attacked the pa of Kawiti at Ohaeawai. To Despard's surprise, his cannon were largely nullified by the fortifications, the result of extraordinary foresight by the Maori, who achieved a significant victory.

During the next few years the technique was brilliantly developed by the Maori until what has been termed 'the modern pa' had evolved into something new in defensive warfare. The modern pa consisted mostly of earth, not wood as in the 'gunfighter pa' of the Musket Wars. It had a low profile and was constructed at strategic points away from the Maori population. Its crucial features were bunkers of earthworks dug into the ground and covered by soil, massive logs, stones, and flax mats to absorb the cannon fire, firing trenches, and normally one side from which the defenders could retreat into thick bush. Campaigns in which the Maori proved most successful all employed the modern pa.

Despite Heke's War, Governor Fitzroy respected the Maori and acknowledged their land rights, and after Ohaeawai began peace negotiations. At that moment he received news that he was being replaced by Sir George Grey (1812–98), previously governor of South Australia which he had rescued from the errors of Wakefieldism. Grey is one of the powerful figures of New Zealand history. He would be made governor a second time when war broke out again in 1860, and was also an early premier of the country (1877–79). He arrived in 1845 and immediately mounted an indeterminate punitive campaign which resulted in a handful of casualties on each side. Heke and Kawiti retained their independence. A footnote to the war: Kawiti's son reerected the famous flagpole in 1858!

SOUTHERN SKIRMISHES OF THE 3 W'S (1843–47)

The 1840s also saw three small conflicts in the Cook Strait area, the region Te Rauparaha had made his own: at Wairau in Nelson, Wellington, and Wanganui. All involved the Ngati Toa and Te Rauparaha, and were sparked by settlers trying to assert control over certain districts.

At Wairau in 1843 in a small confused encounter over disputed land, Te Rauparaha and his nephew Te Rangihaeata (?–1855) easily defeated an inexperienced settler party by 6 deaths to 22, most of the settlers being killed after their surrender. To the disquiet of settlers, far away in Auckland Governor Fitzroy felt powerless and made no attempt at reprisal. His was the correct political decision, for so uneven was military power between settler and Maori at that date, that had Te

Sir George Edward Grey, Governor of New Zealand, 1845–53 and 1861–67
and Premier 1877–79

Rauparaha felt inclined he could have destroyed the Wellington and
Nelson settlements.

At the end of the Hone Heke clash, Governor Grey moved most
troops to Wellington. There the power relations were changing. In
1846 land squabbles occurred in the nearby Hutt Valley and there was
skirmishing with Maori led by Te Rangihaeata and the Wanganui chief
Te Mamaku (?–1887). Other Maori remained neutral or supported the
government. Under British pressure Te Rangihaeata retreated north.
The climax was the capture and imprisonment of Te Rauparaha, which
destroyed his mana and did much to raise 'settler mana', i.e., to establish
government and settler authority in the region. Released in 1848, the
old warrior died the next year.

Minor skirmishing broke out north-west of Wellington in the

Wanganui district in 1847, characterized as much by Maori support of the settlers (by the lower river tribes) as by their opposition (the upper river tribes). There were some casualties and for a time Wanganui town was blockaded by Te Mamaku. The conflict showed that each side was determined to defend what it considered its legitimate areas of settlement.

HEALTHY COOPERATION OF 1840 TO 1860

This early fighting should not be overestimated. During periods of conflict in one region there was always much cooperation in other parts of North Island, and except for Wairau there were no South Island clashes. Thus the period from 1840 to 1860, despite the engagements of the 3Ws, was mainly one of cooperation between the two races, especially the long peaceful period of the 1850s.

The British settlements around the coast of North Island and the Maori interior became economically interdependent. To have a settlement on or near their lands raised Maori mana and helped them economically. Maori were in fact the main suppliers of food to the settlers until the 1860s. They also exported to the Australian colonies. Not only did they grow wheat, as in the Waikato valley, but some chiefs owned flour mills – these too were a matter of mana. The chief, Paratene of the Waikato, was New Zealand's first commercial dairy farmer. Many were very prosperous. The Waikato tribes for example took large quantities of flour, maize, pigs, potatoes, kumara, flax, timber, vegetables, and fish to the markets of Auckland. The shortage of labour also drew them into the settlers' pastoral activities in both islands. In contrast to later fighting over land, Maori also helped surveyors and explorers.

By 1850 British settlement controlled perhaps 20 per cent of New Zealand, Maori the rest. But in time, just as Maori became concerned to keep control of their own affairs, so Maori opposition to the selling of land increased, and in the period 1854–58 a quasi-nationalist movement developed, the so-called King Movement. If the British could be so powerful, and were loyal to a single monarch, perhaps the Maori should support the mana of one leader too: this was the thinking upon which the King Movement developed. Centred on the upper

Waikato River Valley where several of the Waikato tribes had withdrawn, it also had strong support from Taranaki and central North Island tribes such as Ngati Maniapoto and Tuwharetoa. The King Movement's central principles were to resist further selling of land to settlers, and to develop institutions of Maori governance. The position of king of this group of tribes was finally accepted by the great warrior Te Wherowhero (?–1860) who took the ceremonial name Potatau I in 1858. The Kingites wanted meaningful partnership and equality with the settlers, not rule.

The Movement's significance can be overrated. With a total population several times greater, all the northern, east coast, and southern Maori tribes, and the Maori of South Island remained aloof. After the British 1852 Constitution Act, which provided self-governance for settlers but *in effect* excluded Maori, these tribes too became concerned at the settlers' increasing power. Without the king idea, they formed inter-tribal assemblies and councils of their own and pursued similar strategies for similar ends.

Relations deteriorated in the late 1850s as the settlers' desire for land increased, and the Maori learned how the value of land they had sold had risen through inflation and speculation – but also from the settlers' use of previously undeveloped land.

1860–64 CLASHES: TARANAKI AND WAIKATO WARS

The new governor Thomas Gore Browne (1807–87) and many settlers found Maori independence and the King Movement disquieting. At this point a minor chief, Teira, despite the disapproval of his superior chief Wiremu Kingi (?–1882) mischievously offered 600 acres of land for sale south of the Waitara River near the small settlement of New Plymouth in Taranaki. Though the British settlers possessed land sufficient for their then needs in New Zealand as a whole, New Plymouth was an exception, and, pressured by the settlers, Governor Browne felt he had to accept the offer. Wiremu Kingi resisted the surveying parties. In March 1860 war broke out. Within weeks Kingi was receiving support from other Taranaki tribes and from the King Movement. (The similar names 'Kingi' and 'King Movement' were a coincidence.)

The Maori constructed many easily expendable pa. By using sapping, the British captured many of them, then built redoubts to hold the territory. Eventually the Maori laid siege to New Plymouth, full of settlers fleeing their farms, and about 100 people died of disease. The siege ended when the Maori went home to plant crops. Eventually Governor Browne realized the Maori could not be defeated in Taranaki and he negotiated a truce. While he was considering possible alternatives he was dismissed and replaced – again by George Grey. From 1862 Governor Grey systematically prepared for possible conflict by constructing the Great South Road from Auckland towards the Waikato River Valley. The road reached the borders of the Kingite lands. Grey had exaggerated the threat and received reinforcements. A telegraph line was constructed and steamers were acquired from Australia to outflank the Maori by using the river. Different views of sovereign rights perhaps made war inevitable, and it broke out again in 1863.

An initial British success and advance were halted by Maori raids on General Sir Duncan Cameron's (1808?–88) lines of supply, and by the large pa at Meremere – where however the Maori defenders without fighting just evacuated into the bush. Several British successes followed late in 1863. After winning at Rangiriri, Cameron pushed on and captured the Kingite capital of Ngaruawahia. A tactically brilliant night-time outflanking march through bushland allowed Cameron to bypass the several pa at Paterangi which defended an important agricultural district and supply base and, with minimal casualties, he captured it. This was a serious blow to Maori independence.

In March 1864 occurred the memorable Battle of Orakau. The Maori defenders of the pa repulsed three assaults. Acknowledging Maori bravery, Cameron asked their leader Rewi Maniapoto (?–1894) to surrender, but the response given and often attributed to him was, '*E hoa, ka whaiwhai tonu ahau kiakoe ake ake!*' (My friend, we shall fight you forever, forever!) A few days later in an engagement notable for the contribution by the Forest Rangers, the attackers took advantage of Orakau's one weakness – it could be surrounded. In a desperate effort the Maori evacuated through the British lines and suffered perhaps 80 killed to the British 17.

As the war continued, the British troops and officers became more and more disillusioned, asking why they were fighting this war on behalf of the settlers. At best it seemed only partly justified, and the Maori were an enemy they respected both as people and as warriors. The British troops later erected a memorial to the gallant Orakau defenders in the little church at nearby Te Awamutu.

The war in the Waikato now stalemated. Though Cameron had captured much Kingite territory, the rest was independent. The clash shifted to Tauranga on the Bay of Plenty, to stop its use as an entry point for Kingite supporters from the east coast. The Maori won a victory at Gate Pa and the British at Te Ranga, and the 1860–64 War petered out.

DIVERSE SKIRMISHING AND MAORI 'CIVIL WAR', 1864–72

From late 1864 the Maori resistance began to take a guerrilla form, under the leadership of several religious leaders or prophets: (1) Te Ua Haumene (?–1866) in north Taranaki, who developed his Pai Marire (good and peaceful) religion, later called 'Hauhau'; (2) Kereopa Te Rau (?–1872) who further developed Pai Marire in Hawkes' Bay and the centre of North Island; (3) Riwha Titokawaru (c.1823–88) in south Taranaki, whose struggle was at first successful; and (4) Te Kooti (?–1893) and his Ringatu religion in Poverty Bay. Because these prophets challenged tribal authority, they antagonized other Maori as much as they provoked the government and settlers. For this and a multitude of varying local reasons the numbers of Maori directly supporting the government increased. There was much confused skirmishing and raiding, some due to Maori resistance to the confiscation of land of 'rebellious' tribes. From 1864 British troops withdrew and the sporadic fighting until 1872 was taken over by colonial militias supported by loyalist Maori.

Te Kooti is the most fascinating of the four prophets. Escaping with followers in a schooner from imprisonment in the Chatham Islands, in 1868 he attacked Maori and European settlements in the Gisborne area. Maori and colonial troops pursued him. He hid, lost battles, made an extraordinary fighting journey which circled Lake Taupo, escaped to the Urewera Mountains, and finally took refuge in the King Country, establishing a peaceful Ringatu religion. Thus ended the New Zealand Wars.

CONCLUSIONS

British and colonial commanders such as General Cameron encountered difficulties not because they were arrogant or incompetent, but because the Maori leaders and warriors were so skilful. The Maori warrior tradition, together with their intelligent strategy and tactics, in particular the development of the modern pa, were extraordinary. Had the governors and settlers been more aware of the previous centuries of Maori warfare, they might have anticipated this ability. Militarily, neither side had won.

But Maori lands were increasingly taken over by the government and settlers. Much occurred through the operations of the Native Land Court established in 1862. Established to protect Maori interests, with time the Court's operations too often ignored the spirit of the Treaty of Waitangi and became a force for settler coercion. The repercussions of these acts continue: many Maori felt cheated and resentful, and modern members of tribes such as the Tainui (Waikato), harboured discontent into the 1990s, though the reparations of the Waitangi Tribunal and direct negotiations with the government are reversing that attitude.

For decades, although there was some intermarriage, many Maori and settlers lived in largely different worlds. On the other hand many settlers came to respect the native people, and the deeds and culture of the Maori became a celebrated part of the country's evolving national history. The desire for reconciliation was clearly demonstrated in 1867 when the settlers reserved four seats in parliament specially for Maori voters, and by the way in which Maori responded – and this occurred while some Maori were still fighting. But the economic development of North Island suffered, and any Maori hopes of independence were destroyed.

North Island was now ready for the solid and sustained development which had characterized South Island in the previous two decades, which we shall now discuss as part of the country's overall political and economic growth to the turn of the century.

CHAPTER EIGHT

South Pacific Britannia: New Zealand 1861 to the Early 1900s

By the 1880s, merely forty years after the first planned settlement, British New Zealand was a vibrant going-concern, and even more so by the turn of the century. It was a destination, a successful evolving political entity attracting people in their tens of thousands. The most astonishing thing about nineteenth-century New Zealand was the speed with which it became a new polity, in many ways a brand-new egalitarian South Seas Britain.

Political and Economic Development

Under the disunited Maori, the country was neither a nation nor a state. 'The state' as such came to New Zealand with the arrival of William Hobson. At first New Zealand, as with most other British colonies, was a crown colony with executive power vested in a British-appointed governor and his self-chosen executive council. Inevitably the governor tended to be rather autocratic. Having come from a society in which they contributed to government, the most politically active members of the various settlements were dissatisfied at the rate of political progress and began to challenge the governor. In particular, residents in Wellington, and in South Island believed the governor in faraway Auckland was neglecting their interests. A few even uttered the well-worn rhythmic refrain 'no taxation without representation'. They were less happy still when they learned that Governor George Grey, correctly suspecting settler self-interest, had recommended that representative responsible government for settlers be postponed until they showed a more sympathetic awareness of Maori needs.

The appointment in Wellington from 1847 of a Lieutenant-Governor, Edward John Eyre (1815–1901), of exploring fame in Australia, was intended to give the settlers there a greater share in decisions. Because Eyre and Grey disagreed on so many issues, differences with the Governor were only magnified, and the Wellingtonians remained dissatisfied.

In 1852 the British parliament passed the New Zealand Constitution Act. It established six provincial governments with settler assemblies: Auckland (centred on Auckland town), Taranaki (New Plymouth), Wellington (Wellington), Canterbury (Christchurch), Nelson (Nelson), and Otago (Dunedin). Crucially for the country's future political development as a nation, the Constitution Act also set up a central parliament for all New Zealand. This British act of parliament combined with the Treaty of Waitangi was the nearest New Zealand came to having a written constitution until the New Zealand Constitution Act of 1986. Like the mother country, New Zealanders from that point saw parliament itself as politically supreme.

Local politicians now had ample opportunity to voice their opinions. But no one could read the future and know that war would break out again in 1860, so on the basis of a constitution heavily influenced by Grey and Wakefield, responsible government was allowed the settlers in 1855. So in 1856 executive authority was largely transferred from Governor Gore Browne to Premier Henry Sewell (1807–79), New Zealand's first premier. The words 'largely transferred' are used because, concerned at the settlers' desire for land, the Governor reserved executive control over Maori affairs to himself.

New Zealand was a country without any aristocratic elite, and in its absence the well-to-do middle class became the most influential political class and filled provincial and central parliamentary and executive positions. Political parties did not develop until the 1890s. Prior to that time, governments were shifting coalitions of men with similar interests or problems, grouped about a temporary leader. As a result there were 24 premiers in the first twenty-one years of government.

GOLD DISCOVERIES IN OTAGO AND WESTLAND

In 1848 some 278 Scottish colonists under the leadership of William Cargill (1784–1860) arrived in Dunedin harbour in the south of South

Island and established the province of Otago. (It is interesting to note that a small Scottish linguistic element still survives in speech in present-day Southland.) These Scots settlers too were trying to implement Wakefield's ideas. Their common membership of the Free Church of Scotland gave a social cohesion and a unity of purpose lacking in Auckland and Wellington. But they shared the same immediate problem of zero economic infrastructure – no wharves, no roads, no buildings. The whole religious experiment might have ended disastrously had it not been for the self-denying hard work of the settlers, Cargill's inspiration and tenacity, and the resolution of Thomas Burns, nephew of the poet, and minister to the settlement. But Cargill maintained Wakefield's conception of 'sufficient price' of £2 per acre too long, thus stifling immigration. By 1861 Otago still possessed only about 13,000 people, with Dunedin itself still a village of a few thousand – but not for long.

For while North Island was consolidating wool and wheat farming, and still suffering from the New Zealand Wars, gold fever hit the South Island. Significant amounts of gold had already been found in the far north of the South Island in uninhabited Massacre Bay, soon renamed Golden Bay. And tiny quantities of gold had been found in up-country Otago. Gabriel Read (1824/26?–84), who had panned for gold in California and Victoria and engaged in trade in the Pacific Islands, thought there must be larger amounts of gold in Otago. In May 1861, while the Taranaki War was in progress in North Island, in central Otago he made the first considerable discovery:

> In broad tussocky country, at a place where a kind of 'road' crossed a shallow river bar, I shovelled away about two and a half feet of gravel, arrived at a beautiful soft slate and saw the gold shining like the stars of Orion on a dark frosty night.

The new provincial superintendent, J.L.C. Richardson (1810–78), welcomed Read's news. Staid Scottish Dunedin was soon in a frenzy, obsessed by the idea of finding a fortune. Burns wrote to his brother in Scotland, 'Every blacksmith's forge is blown out, the carpenters have bolted, the sawmill is silent.' Gold-hungry miners flooded in from other parts of New Zealand, and Australia. Before 1861 was out, the provincial population had more than doubled and New Zealand's heretofore most underdeveloped province soon had a third of the population.

Soon there were discoveries all across central Otago. Wild and previously unoccupied regions became covered with mining camps. Much of this was hard country, tussock-covered mountains with pneumonia-killing winters. Men died from starvation or were lost in the bush, but others persevered and some splendid finds were made in the alluvial sands of mountain streams.

In the nineteenth century gold was the ally of undeveloped settler colonies. Dunedin boomed. Three pubs became thirty and Dunedin rapidly became New Zealand's largest city. In the new prosperity the country's first concentrated cluster of solid stone public, private, academic, ecclesiastical, and commercial buildings arose. Here at the Antipodes, at the end of the earth from Europe, rose a mirror image of a prosperous Victorian British city. Early buildings still grace its central octagon. By 1869 Dunedin had New Zealand's first university, its buildings modelled on those of Glasgow University. Later, there was New Zealand's first high school for girls. There were several daily newspapers, New Zealand's first cable tramway, and the first sizable reclaimed port area. Of course the social makeup of Otago changed, and the original settlers were not entirely happy as the newcomers expressed their egalitarian and go-getting ideas.

On the fields behaviour was remarkably orderly, for the Otago authorities learned from the mistakes made in Victoria. Purchase of a modestly priced yearly 'Miner's Right' entitled its possessor to search for gold, and larger individual 'claims' were allowed than in Australia. Police were carefully selected and properly paid, and the mounted police escort of gold from the fields to Dunedin was well organized and never robbed. By the time the Otago rush slowed at the end of 1864, it had been the best-behaved gold rush in history. No man was ever lynched on a New Zealand field.

As in all rushes, it was providers more than the miners who did well. Merchants, publicans, builders of carts and wagons, operators of transport, entertainers, ladies of the night – many made a success of supplying the miners. So did the wheat and sheep (mutton/lamb) farmers. Some insurance companies and banks prospered. For the first time New Zealand developed a reasonably secure and systematic financial system. Later, as the more easily attainable Otago gold was gone, there was another gold rush on West Coast, then politically part of Canterbury province.

When the rushes subsided, some workings became towns. One such was Queenstown in north Otago on exquisite Lake Wakatipu, once a stop-over for early Maori on their route to the west to dig greenstone. For the settlers it was at first a sheep-rearing area. Gold was found in 1862, and a rush began. At one stage four paddle steamers were plying Wakatipu bringing people and goods from the lake head. In the twentieth century Queenstown developed as a tourist resort. This now seems inevitable given its superb location. The town stands on fingers of peninsulas poking into the lake, backed on one side by the ragged, jagged Remarkable Mountains snow-covered in winter, a great green hill on another side, and across the turquoise lake sheer mountains plunging straight into the waters. Scenically Queenstown can hold its own with any place in the world. Today it is one of the youthful world capitals of adrenalin-rush adventure tourism.

As the alluvial gold was worked out, mining companies were formed. Large syndicates from Auckland and Dunedin imported expensive equipment or had it made to order in New Zealand, and a new type of mining culture developed. Most miners were now employees rather than individual small entrepreneurs. The most important site was the Clutha River south of Dunedin. Here, steam-driven 'spoon dredges' and later, much larger bucket dredges processed huge volumes of river sand and river bank for specks of gold impossible to extract by hand panning. A dredge consisted of a flat raft-like hull supporting a deck-house to protect the steam boiler and processing machines; dredging buckets extended from the bows of the vessel; a long boom at the stern carried an 'endless chain' which deposited the sifted tailings well astern. By 1900 over 230 dredges were at work in New Zealand, 187 of them on or near the Clutha River, the others mostly in Southland and Westland. Today's environmental lobby would have been horrified by the devastation wrought on the river valley.

There were North Island finds too. The mine at Waihi on

Coromandel Peninsula south-east of Auckland, near to where Hongi Hika had slaughtered his Ngati Maru foes, attracted Australian and British capital.

The Vogel Boom

JULIUS VOGEL'S ECONOMIC IDEAS

By the late 1860s North Island was still mired in the declining New Zealand Wars and the prosperity of the 1840s and 1850s was past. Even the South Island economy, formerly expanding upon pastoralism and gold mining, was in the doldrums. Some kind of radical innovation, or a man for the moment, was needed. That man appeared: Julius Vogel (1835–99).

Vogel is one of New Zealand's great names. He was reared by his mother's prosperous London Jewish middle-class family. Striking out on his own, he migrated to the Victorian (Australia) goldfields in 1852 at 17, then nine years later to the rush in Otago, as a journalist. The same year, aged 26, he founded the *Otago Daily Times*, in Dunedin, a newspaper which still flourishes. Political success came in New Zealand, first as a member of Otago Provincial Council where he became treasurer, and in the same year as MP in the New Zealand parliament. Six years later the premier, William Fox (1812?–93), invited Vogel to join the government as Colonial Treasurer.

Vogel was a man of grand, even grandiose ideas. In 1870, to shift New Zealand out of its economic lethargy, he proposed to parliament that the government should raise a massive loan of £10,000,000 in Britain. The capital, he argued, would be used to boost immigration, and construct roads, railways, and telegraph lines. The immigrants would be employed on these public works until they could find work for themselves. The economy would expand and provide the jobs because of the money being spent by the government and through opening up the land to development. This was an astonishing proposal for a country whose total population was about a quarter of a million. It is difficult to give precise modern equivalents. In 1870 the value of a US dollar was a mere fraction of that of a £ sterling, so in today's money

Premier Julius Vogel – one of New Zealand's great names

the loan would be perhaps several billion dollars US – something like $10,000 per head! Of course there was nothing new in young colonies borrowing capital. How else could they develop their lands? What was radical was the enormous sums.

He had hardly made his proposal than opponents leaped to their feet to condemn him. R. Wood said he had 'never heard of a scheme so wild, so unpractical and so unpracticable'. In 1870s 'politician-speak' H.J. Tancred said it was 'the last throw of a desperate gambler'. Conversely many politicians were enthusiastic, the bill passed, and at the following election the voters supported Vogel. In 1873 he became Premier of New Zealand. In fact about £20,000,000 was borrowed during the decade. Not all went well. These were the days before real cost-benefit analysis, there were scandals over some railways being built to the properties of rich landowners, and waste in construction, and the wealthy southern provinces of Canterbury and Otago did better than most of the more needy North Island.

Nevertheless, the influx of new capital worked. Immigrants were brought out. In the 1870s most people had jobs, development did occur and exports did increase. About 1100 miles/1760k of railways, 2,500 miles/4000k of paved roads, many bridges and about 4,000 miles/6,500k of telegraph line were constructed.

As land was opened up, settlers tried their hand at all kinds of farming, even viticulture. Most early vineyards were in the north: Northland, Auckland Province, and Hawkes Bay, though some of the pioneers made their own wine in other places like Nelson and Central Otago. In the 1870s and 1880s commercial wine making was attempted elsewhere, but only in Hawkes Bay did it survive.

In 1876 the provincial political system was ended, but only after a hard fight to survive by provincial leaders such as the former governor, Sir George Grey of Auckland, and Sir John Hall (1824–1907) of Canterbury. By this date the provinces numbered nine: the original six plus Marlborough, Hawkes Bay, and Westland (between 1861 and 1870 there had been 10, while Southland was separate from Otago). The system served its purpose when the country was beginning, with isolated little settlements and parochial provincial feelings. But now New Zealand was rapidly developing into one economy and needed to stop the wasteful duplication of effort; moreover unification made possible more favourable terms on the London capital market.

Though Vogel's loans increased short-term land speculation and inflation, the borrowing of the 1870s helped massively in the long term, setting up the infrastructure without which it would have been impossible for New Zealand to develop.

IMMIGRANTS

By the end of the 1870s with an additional 200,000 people the population had almost doubled. The resident population had reproduced rapidly, almost 100,000 assisted-passage immigrants had arrived from Britain, and a significant number of people had come from Australia. By the mid-1880s the native-born European population exceeded those born overseas, and natural growth of Europeans and Maori has kept ahead of immigrant numbers ever since.

Who were these people who came to Vogel's call? About two-thirds had assisted passages. They changed the demography of New Zealand because there were few of the lesser gentry, middle class, and professional people who formed much of the population of the early settlements. New Zealand was becoming even more a working man's country.

Large numbers of single women were assisted, most were soon married, family life became more the norm, and drunkenness and petty crime decreased. Most migrants were British, about two-thirds of these English, but there were small proportions of Scandinavians (mainly Danes) and Germans. Many British also arrived from Australia.

And what was the voyage out like?

The Auckland Maritime Museum has an imaginatively organized full-size replica of the living quarters of married people who travelled to New Zealand in 'steerage', the section for assisted passage and poorer immigrants who could not afford cabins. The creaking timbers and the rolling deck are reproduced. Down the middle there is a long narrow table with benches, on the bulkheads (walls) a series of hooks for hanging the passengers' bags which everyone was given to store clothes, utensils, food, water bottles, and so on. Everything else the passengers might immediately need had to be placed in the tiny double sleeping cubicles which stretch along both sides. The trunks which held most of their goods were stored in the hold and were available only at intervals, and sometimes sea water seeped into them. The Museum cannot reproduce the stench, but one gains a good idea of the crowded nature of the quarters and the startling lack of privacy.

Even in the best of emigrant ships disease could rampage. In 1863, 46 people died on the *Brothers Pride* outwardbound for Lyttelton (Christchurch). In 1864 on the *Ganges* with 394 emigrants including 125 children, more than twenty people died, mostly children. In some ships, burials at sea became almost routine.

By Vogel's time conditions were improving. This was because the main way New Zealand (and the Australian colonies) could compete for immigrants with much closer USA and Canada was to subsidize the passage. Assisted passages were in fact the most permanent result of Wakefield's ideas. Having paid for their passage the New Zealand government wanted its migrants to arrive healthy. More attention was therefore paid to shipboard conditions on this long cross-world voyage than was the case on the short but notorious cross-Atlantic run.

By the early 1870s government immigrant officers met every arriving ship and filed a report, some of which became parliamentary papers which led to improved conditions. Many reports were routine, but some could be quite caustic. An 1873 report, describing the arrival of the *Wild Duck*, stated that, 'Water leaking from the upper deck kept the beds in the married people and single women's compartments almost constantly wet, and the hospital arrangements were entirely unsatisfactory,' pointing out that when these immigrants sent back their letters of complaint to their relatives and friends in Britain, 'this would do more to retard emigration than all the costly advertisements ... and highly paid agents do to advance it'.

Nevertheless there were many Britons well satisfied with their passage and their change of location. Especially during the early 1870s with their massive inflowing capital enthusiastic reports were sent back. 'This country is good for living – beef, mutton, butter and eggs, and everything else that is good ... We are happy as the day is long. I would not come back on any account ...' wrote one.

To newcomers New Zealand was geographically and climatically upside-down and socially topsy-turvy. Here it was not merely possible to start anew, but often absolutely necessary because of the common lack of amenities. Those who worked with their hands became the crucial class. Social distinctions were mostly unenforceable, and a degree of equality developed impossible in the Old World. Some of the first middle-class emigrants to Canterbury soon used all their capital and were reduced to working on the roads, while others were employed at daily wages by people whom they had brought out as servants. The author Anthony Trollope, who visited in the early 1870s, noted:

The very tone in which a maid servant speaks to you in New Zealand, her quiet little joke, her familiar smile ... tell you at once that the badge of servitude is not heavy ... she does not consider herself to be of an order of things different from your order ... if we look at this matter from the maid servant's side we cannot fail to find there is much comfort in it.

Communications

BOATS, SAILING SHIPS, STEAM SHIPS AND THE COAL TO POWER THEM

Communicating with one another and transporting people, information, and products between settlements and between New Zealand and the rest of the world were continuing concerns. But nineteenth century New Zealand was heir to all the discoveries made by the European Scientific Revolution and the technology of the Industrial Revolution, so the establishment of efficient communications which took Europe hundreds of years took New Zealand merely a few decades.

Besides the towns mentioned above, other significant settlements were Oamaru 1853, Invercargill, 1855, Napier 1856, Timaru 1859, Hastings and Hamilton 1864, Palmerston North 1866. The last three were inland towns which posed special problems of communication. All the others, and numerous additional scattered outposts around the coasts, could for decades be linked only by sea. Such was also the case with Hokitika and the other West Coast gold towns. Most goods and people came and went by sea. So a little Armada of small ships, schooners, cutters, most built in New Zealand, many owned by Maori, began, from the earliest days of British settlement to ply the coastal routes.

Most of the early settlements were made on substantial harbours, Wellington and Auckland on great ones. But some were unlucky. New Plymouth, Oamaru, and Timaru lay on exposed coasts and settlers, merchants, and merchandise had to suffer wild rides through the surf in long surf boats.

Shipbuilding began early, and a multitude of inlets and harbours had their own little construction yards. The balance of trade and contact had a somewhat different pattern from today. Nelson, now a charming provincial tourist town, was for a decade in the 1850s and more, because of its central position, the preferred first port of call for ships from Australia.

In 1854, to great fanfare, the first coastal steamer arrived from England (it took 104 days). But it proved costly to run, as a surveyor to the New Zealand Company explains:

> ... owing to great expense of coaling, which *as English coal must at present be used* will reach to £50 a day ... the wages of engineers, stokers, firemen, seamen are also at least double what they are in England.

By 1859 people could travel the length of New Zealand, from Dunedin to Auckland, by steamer in about two weeks, including delays in changing ships.

The next worst wreck to that of HMS *Orpheus*, mentioned earlier, was the 1882 sinking of the cross-Tasman liner *Tararua*, which crashed onto a reef off Southland, drowning 131 passengers.

Once bituminous coal was found on the West Coast near Westport and Greymouth, steamship costs reduced considerably. This coal was of the highest quality. Without its discovery the New Zealand economy would have been seriously retarded, for the steam engine was the prime mover of Victorian transport and industry. Transporting the coal from its source was at first difficult until a monster lode was found inland from Westport on the Rochefort Plateau at about 1,800 feet/550m.

The Westport Colliery Co. tapped this wealth by creating the ingenious Denniston 'self-acting incline'. Loaded wagons running down one rail track were connected by cable and pulley to empty wagons rising up the other track. No engines, only gravity, were needed to move the wagons. The surplus gravitational energy from the descending wagons was retarded by an ingenious system of brakes, which adapted the technology of steam locomotives and pushed contemporary technical knowledge to the limit. Joy-riders illegally used the incline too. The little mining town of Denniston grew at the top of the plateau, inhabited from 1879 until the seam worked out in 1967.

The greatest of all the shipping lines was the Union Steamship

Company, begun in Dunedin in 1875. Presided over by entrepreneurial genius James Mills (1847–1936) it used West Coast coal, and grew prosperous on coastal, cross Tasman, and Pacific Islands routes. It would operate until the year 2000.

CABLES, TELEGRAPHS AND COACHES

Communications by telegraph lines were virtually instantaneous over a hundred miles and one of the wonders of the Victorian age. Beginning as local links, between Lyttelton and Christchurch, for example, the New Zealand-wide network, paid for with Vogel money, was completed some decades before railways. Undersea telegraph cables linked the two islands. The central government and business quickly learned to make use of the system. Once the country was connected in this manner a colony standard time was imperative. New Zealand Mean Time was introduced in 1868, based on the meridian of longitude 172 degrees 30 minutes East, which bisects the country, and was eleven and a half hours ahead of Greenwich Mean time. The time was sent by telegraph to all centres daily from the Government Observatory in Wellington. New Zealand was one of the earliest countries after Britain to introduce standard time. In 1876 Wellington was linked to Sydney by undersea cable. As Sydney was connected by telegraph line and cable all the way to London, New Zealand was now linked across the world to the capital of the Empire.

On land, on the rough or almost non-existent roads between settlements goods went by horse, or coach, or, for the very heaviest land-transported items, by crawling bullock dray.

An innovation in land transport occurred with the introduction of 'Cobb & Co' coaches. Easily the best form of early New Zealand land transport, this American firm's coaches came via Australia where they had been very successful on the rough roads of the goldfields. An 1864 traveller reports: 'Got Cobb's coach at 8am at Christchurch post office. It was a wonderful machine, sprung upon leather straps. Its easy swinging motion however is apt to produce upon some a feeling akin to seasickness. We had five horses, driven by Mr. Baker, a veteran American coachman.' But, as everywhere else in history, land transport was always expensive until the arrival of the railways.

RAILWAYS

The railway system began in earnest in the 1870s, also funded by Vogel capital. In time five state railway workshops were established, giving the country a significant heavy engineering industry which manufactured locomotives until 1967.

At first isolated lines were built which ran into the hinterlands of main towns, like that from Christchurch into the Canterbury Plains. Later they were linked to provide a national network. The largest engineering project in NZ in the 1800s was the Main Trunk Line, connecting Wellington and Auckland, begun in 1885. Given the involvement of powerful pastoral interests, whether the line would proceed east or west of the central volcanoes became a thorny political problem. Equally problematic, if west it would have to pass through the Maori King Country, for most purposes independent until well into the 1880s. When approached, King Tawhiao (Te Wheroewhero (?–1894) said he would never allow a railway line to be constructed. This attitude was opposed by other Ngati Maniapoto chiefs who recognized that because of the economic possibilities, a railway traversing the King country was inevitable, but wanted Maori to control the process. They managed to outmanoeuvre King Tawhiao, and held discussions with the government.

Still, several other Maori chiefs in the King Country agreed with King Tawhiao. As a result some surveying teams were obstructed. One altercation was recorded in the *Appendices to the Journals of the House of Representatives* (the New Zealand lower house of parliament) in 1883:

> [the surveyors] were forcibly led about half a mile, and then thrust into a Maori cook house; their feet were chained, and their hands tied with rope behind their backs; they were then left for 41 hours, during which time they were kept without food. They were finally rescued by the Maori who had been with them when they were captured

The toughest and longest section connected Te Awamutu to Marton. From Te Awamutu it had to pass west of pretty Lake Taupo, past the three mighty volcanic peaks, and south into the Manawatu region. Construction began in April 1884. Proceeding from each end, work was hindered by lack of finance and physical difficulties requiring many viaducts and tunnels. On the section to National Park Station the line had to climb 400 feet (122m) in little more than a mile (1.6k), i.e., an impossible gradient of 1 in 13. The problem was neatly solved by constructing the famous Raurimu Spiral, with a loop, a horseshoe curve, and several tunnels, giving a just-acceptable gradient of 1 in 50, a triumph for the surveyors! The link was at last completed in 1908.

Technology and Trades Unions

REFRIGERATION

Though economic development slowed from the beginning of the 1880s, a spectacular new initiative was the beginning of the trade in refrigerated farm produce across the world.

In February 1882 the 1455 ton/1320 tonne sailing ship SS *Dunedin* of the British Albion Shipping Company departed Port Chalmers (port for Dunedin) for London. A huge freezing chamber had been installed in Britain the previous year. It now held 3350 carcases of mutton, 490 of lamb, carcases of pigs, frozen hams, turkeys, sheep tongues, some rabbits, and 245 kegs of butter.

The business risk was immense, and an enormous amount of creative effort had gone into the organization. William Soltau Davidson (1846–1924), the energetic manager of the New Zealand and Australian Land Company, had had long negotiations with the shipping and refrigeration companies and the other New Zealand suppliers of the produce. The New Zealand Agent-General in London notified meat-importing companies. Loading took weeks and special butchers had to be employed to prepare the carcases at the wharf. In December 1881 a crank shaft in the chamber broke and about 1000 frozen carcases had suddenly to be sold. Operations were suspended for an economically disastrous month while a new shaft was found and installed.

On the journey there were continual technical problems, especially in the tropics when the refrigeration often threatened to close down. The freezer produced sparks and at one point set a sail on fire. (No steam-ship had been available for the voyage.) But at last, after more than three months, the *Dunedin* docked in England. Davidson was waiting there and jumped aboard to check the condition of the cargo! The English buyers were pleased with the good quality of the produce, one being of the opinion that 'there was a bright future for' New Zealand lamb and mutton. The London *Times* observed that the voyage had been 'prodigious'.

So began New Zealand's great export trade of meat and butter across the world to Britain. These persistent efforts by an enterprising private company were to change the New Zealand economy. (The contribution of the New Zealand government remained minimal until the early 1890s.) Thanks to taking a gamble on the new technology of refrigeration, the country's previous export staple of wool was now joined by meat and butter, and cheese in later shipments. New Zealand farmers were able to provide for an ever-expanding British market, and Britain would remain by far New Zealand's greatest trading partner until after she joined the European Economic Community (European Union) in 1973.

WOOLLEN MILLS, SWEATED LABOUR, TRADES UNIONS

Joining dairy produce, in the 1870s New Zealand developed a great wheat industry on the Canterbury Plains, but opportunities for expanding other primary export industries such as fishing and horticulture were strangely ignored except for the local market. So, despite a significant mining industry which continues to the present day, for almost a hundred years New Zealand would remain basically a country whose economy was sustained by a multitude of smallish farms and farming families.

Though manufacturing was hindered by overseas tariffs and immense distances to markets, in the 1870s, 1880s and 1890s New Zealanders did develop some secondary industries for local consumption – luxuries such as beer, and necessities such as soap and woollen textiles. The woollen mills of Dunedin, for instance, using milling machinery imported from Britain had success in manufacturing for the local market, and became a little antipodean Yorkshire. As the world over, most of the employees of these mills were women.

The economy was deflating and wages were cut. Women were not paid male wages anyway, and by 1888 in the mills abuses were common. A Dunedin minister, Reverend Rutherford Waddell (1849–1932, exposed these abuses. There were working weeks of 72 hours, exploitation of apprentices, payment of workers in goods rather than in cash, penurious rates paid for piece-work in the home – in short 'sweated labour' as in Europe and the USA. Waddell awoke the moral imagination of the country. The government appointed a Royal Commission of inquiry which agreed that exploitation was widespread; it then planned a new Factory Act.

Encouraged by the climate of opinion, several unions were established, the tailoresses in July 1889, and the first umbrella organization of semiskilled workers, the Maritime Council, consisting of seamen, wharf labourers (dockers/stevedores), railway workers, storemen and coal-miners in October. In 1890 there were strikes by railwaymen and miners, and a wharf dispute in Australia dragged in the Maritime Council. It was not strong enough to withstand pressure from the shipping companies and collapsed, and the first New Zealand union movement was for the time being defeated.

In any case the government and the general public disapproved of strikes. For many New Zealanders strikes by employees were the unacceptable moral equivalent of sweated labour by employers. They were horrified to see their country following the path of industrial confrontations in the Old World and North and South America. At this very time, however, some fine New Zealand minds were developing ideas to reverse this trend.

The Liberals: Ballance, Reeves, and Seddon

Political ideas from Britain and USA were filtered by local pragmatic commonsense and applied in New Zealand, and change was possible because of the country's small population. New Zealand became a kind of social laboratory for the world, and its legislation came to attract the attention of the world's leading political thinkers.

The 1890 election was a landmark. John Ballance (1839–93) became the new premier in January 1891. His statue of white Nelson marble now rises in front of Wellington's Parliamentary Library, on the plinth the words, 'He loved the People'. His proposals were at first rejected. But later in the year, 5 members we would now classify as Labour joined with Ballance's 33 who called themselves 'Liberals' and 7 Independents from farming regions. Together they formed a conglomerate but cohesive governing group. They could easily outvote the 24 'Conservatives' supported by owners of large farms and city merchants and bankers. New Zealand's first true political party then emerged, the Liberal Party. Under the Liberals New Zealand's economy began to recover from the mid-1890s, especially with improved export prices.

EPOCHAL SOCIAL LEGISLATION OF
WILLIAM PEMBER REEVES

Probably partly inspired by the ideas of writers such as John Stuart Mill (1806–73) in Britain and Henry George (1839–97) in the USA, for the next fifteen years the Liberals passed laws to help town workers and farmers. For his Minister of Labour, one of the first in the British Empire, Ballance made a brilliant choice. He selected a man who would become another of New Zealand's greatest names, the Young Turk of the South Island, William Pember Reeves (1857–1932).

Reeves had a first-rate intelligence, and a deep sympathy for the less privileged including the Maori, and was able to persuade others of his ideas. He was born in New Zealand, but as he used to say had only just managed it, because this occurred three weeks after his parents' arrival in Christchurch. From a well-off family, and elected to parliament in 1884, Reeves soon became the party's leading intellectual, and its policy maker in labour legislation.

The Liberals made a good start with the Truck Act of 1891, which forced all employers to pay in cash not goods. The same year they also passed the state Coal Mines Act which authorized the government to buy two West Coast mines. The motive for this act is interesting. It shows the party's experimental and non-doctrinaire approach to government. For the Liberals did not intend this as a first move in a programme of nationalization. Rather, it aimed at bringing more competition to the industry and so lowering prices! They also introduced something citizens have continued to bemoan ever since – an income tax, though a tiny one.

There was a string of legislation in the remarkable year of 1894. John (Jock) McKenzie (1839–1901) shaped land reform with acts making possible loans for farm purchase and development, and set up a Department of Agriculture. (Because they were seen as communal land holders, none of this applied to Maori.) Reeves put through the Shipping and Seamen's Amendment Act, stipulating the proportion of trained seamen on a ship; and his Shops and Shop-assistants Act enforced weekend holidays and turned the country into the 'land of the long weekend', where, until the 1980s scarcely a shop was open after mid-day on Saturday. And to prevent the abuses exposed by Waddell, his Factories Act laid down maximum working hours for women and children and forbad the employment of children under fourteen. The accompanying Department of Labour had the power to enter factories and enforce the rules.

The most innovative piece of legislation was the 1894 Conciliation and Arbitration Act. It offered a legal and peaceful solution, 'a kindly solution', as Reeves put it, to industrial disputes. The Act also stated that it was planned, 'to encourage the formation of Industrial Unions and Associations'. The Act set up local Boards of Conciliation and a national Court of Arbitration. To receive an award (say, a rise in wages) from the Court, workers had to form a union, and employers were forced to recognize it. Most unionists agreed with the Act, many employers disliked it. This was the Act which most grabbed the world's attention, for it was a world first, and would dominate New Zealand industrial relations for ninety-two years. It was soon copied by New South Wales and other colonies and countries.

All these developments strengthened enormously the support of working people and small farmers for the Liberals, and from the time of Ballance gave them twenty-one years in government.

In 1896 Reeves was made Agent-General, and in 1905 High Commissioner in London. This was in no way a demotion, but in fact the best-paid New Zealand government position. In Britain Reeves was a spectacular success. Promoting New Zealand, he delivered hundreds of lunch and after-dinner speeches. He also helped raise loans.

His radicalism was stimulated by his friendships with British socialists such as the playwright George Bernard Shaw, the Fabians Sidney and Beatrice Webb, and the pioneer of cerebral science fiction, H.G. Wells. But Reeves was deeply distressed when his very bright daughter, Amber, ran away to Paris with the promiscuous, already married Wells, and had a child. Reeves's relations with the Fabians cooled, and thereafter he continually denounced Wells, whom, it is believed, he threatened to shoot.

'KING DICK'

Richard John Seddon (1845–1906) was another political giant. Poorly educated, he, like Vogel, migrated to Victoria in 1864 to try his hand on the goldfields. Again like Vogel he shipped to the New Zealand goldfields, but to the new West Coast. There he became active politically and was elected to parliament in 1879. In 1891 Ballance made him Minister of Mines, and on Ballance's death in 1893, to the amazement of the country including many in his own party, he manoeuvred himself into the Premiership, which he held until 1906.

Homespun, rotund, robust, shrewd, loud, he was a great mixer. He promoted himself as an ordinary 'bloke' who understood other ordinary folk, and developed the cult of the ordinary into a political fine art. And he knew how to gain publicity. To one and all Seddon became known as 'Dick'. To Liberal supporters, levelling and egalitarianism were like mana to the Maori. Within a few years he would be called 'King Dick'. Brilliant at political tactics, Seddon talked a lot and said little. Especially in his early years his speeches sometimes almost emptied the House, and he was certainly no original thinker. He left that to people like Reeves and McKenzie.

In fact the Reeves–Seddon relationship was problematic and uneasy from the beginning. They arrived at their concern for working people from entirely different social and educational backgrounds. Reeves wrote poetry and books and was a man of letters; Seddon read newspapers. Reeves thought Seddon was bullying and brash; Seddon saw Reeves as a rival. It is probable that had there been no Seddon, Reeves would have become premier. Reeves wanted to bring in more labour laws; Seddon, aware of the need to keep the support of

Richard Seddon, the long-serving Liberal Prime Minister

rural electorates, wanted to slow down. Finally, as mentioned above, Reeves was 'promoted sideways' and out of the country to London.

Under Seddon the legislation continued, but not at the furious rate of the Reeves years. Collective marketing arrangements brought cooperation between business, farmers, and government in capturing the British market. There were further moves to open up to more intense settlement, the large estates formed in the early days of colonization, and in general the Liberals promoted the numbers and political influence of small farmers.

There were also modest Old Age Pensions, a world first. This move was politically brilliant and it seems to have been Seddon's own idea. He introduced the Bill when challenges from the opposition in parliament and from his own party had him close to resignation; but he made sure the Act was efficiently implemented and administered, it revived him politically, and for the last eight years of his premiership he was New Zealand's most popular person. On observing the first payment of pensions at the Christchurch Post Office, the American H.D. Lloyd wrote: 'Punctually upon the opening of the door at nine o'clock the little corner of the office ... was filled with old men and women. Entering with anticipation and not infrequently anxiety on their faces they came out in happier mood.'

Not everyone agreed with the Liberals, of course, and they could be rather overbearing. Some modern historians have applied the term 'elective despotism' to describe King Dick's 'reign'. Seddon won five consecutive elections. In 1906, soon after the last one, he died aboard ship in the Tasman Sea en route from Australia. On his departure from Sydney he had told his friends that he was on the way to God's Own Country – an epithet he liked to apply to New Zealand. His bronze statue stands beside that of Ballance.

During Seddon's tenure of office, other important social and political developments had taken place. They fitted New Zealand for its twentieth-century role, and to them we now turn.

CHAPTER NINE

Making a Nation: New Zealand to 1918

Before the Liberals lost their hold on the electorate women were enfranchised, leading Maori took new responsibilities, New Zealanders decided to remain separate from the Australian federation, a keen inventive ability which has become something of a defining characteristic of New Zealanders had shown itself, and the country had begun to produce scientists. By the time the First World War broke out government was in the hands of a party whose most powerful group was farmers.

Votes for Women

Another piece of legislation which grabbed world headlines under the Liberal government, this time in spite of Seddon, was women's right to vote, in 1893. In 1879 all New Zealand males had been enfranchised. New Zealand women had always been more accepted in public life than their British, European, and North American 'cousins'. Women had been allowed into the universities immediately on establishment, education for girls had always been considered significant, and female ratepayers were given a vote in local elections in 1875. Many men recognized the inconsistency of preventing women from voting in national elections.

Though success came only after decades of hard work by New Zealand women and enlightened male supporters, women's franchise was almost accepted by parliament on four earlier occasions. The Married Women's Property Act of 1884 helped. It allowed women to own property in their own right. Before that date, as almost everywhere else in the world, on marriage a woman's property became that of her husband.

Women organized huge petitions. The Women's Christian Temperance Union (WCTU) fought for the vote, though its activities confused the issue and encouraged opposition from the powerful beer brewers' lobby. Many able and intelligent women contributed but the greatest of all was Katherine Wilson Sheppard, 'Kate Sheppard' (1848–1934), who fought a tireless campaign for many years, forever organizing, distributing pamphlets, stumping the country on lecture tours,

A cartoon by Ashley Hunter in 1893, summing up the belief that women would clean up the dirty business of politics

and galvanizing the support of male parliamentarians such as former premier Sir John Hall. Many such men supported her because they believed women were morally superior and would raise the tone of elections and parliament.

Seddon's main opposition to women's votes came from his connection to the brewers. He believed that prohibition would come with women's votes. In 1893 the bill finally passed the previously antagonistic upper house apparently because two of Seddon's opponents, themselves opposed to the bill, capriciously decided to thwart him by supporting it. New Zealand women later went to Britain to help their suffragette sisters. But women were allowed to stand for parliament only in 1919, and the first female MP, Elizabeth McCombs (1873–1935), was elected only in 1933.

Maori Affairs

THE 'YOUNG MAORI PARTY'

Around 1858 the populations of Maori and settlers were equal, at about 60,000 each, but until the 1890s Maori population continued to fall while European population increased steadily. Maori loss of land was both a cause and an effect of depopulation, but diseases such as a measles epidemic and endemic tuberculosis contributed. By the 1890s the population was only about 40,000, but from that time it has continued to expand, very rapidly since World War II.

In the 1890s a new kind of Maori leader appeared and led a revival. There were three main figures: Apirana Ngata (1874–1950), Te Rangi Hiroa/Peter Buck (1877?–1951), and Maui Pomare (1875/6?–1930). All were influenced by the Maori Sir James Carroll (1858–1927), Seddon's government advisor on Native Affairs, and acting prime minister for a time in 1909 and 1911. Each was a member of a group of talented young men who had passed through the Anglican Te Aute College. Their headmaster, John Thornton, taught them virtue, but equally important the need to adapt to European ways if the Maori were to gain true equality. The group acquired the name 'Young Maori Party' though they were not a party as such. They met regularly from 1897 to 1910, and tried to improve Maori life in four ways: to increase education and health, to foster Maori farming on a communal basis, to stop further sales of Maori land, and to support chiefly status though they rejected the superstitious aspects of mana and tapu. They formed a loose alliance with Seddon and his Liberals and Ngata, Hiroa/ Buck, and Pomare all became members of parliament. But they opposed the Liberals' continuing acquisition of Maori lands, the largest since the 1860s. Around this time the first Maori newspapers also appeared.

The Young Maori Party may have been 'too Pakeha' for some modern Maori critics, but they showed through example that Maori were perfectly capable of rising to the highest ranks of the professions, a fact which both races needed to be aware of. They also showed and made explicit how the attitudes of both peoples had to change if the Maori people as a whole were to become equal members of modern New Zealand society.

Polynesian studies were pioneered by men such as S. Percy Smith (1840–1922) and Eldon Best (1856–1931), in the 1890s. New Zealanders were exceptional amongst Pacific peoples in organizing their own learned institution, the Polynesian Society (1892), and in involving indigenes such as Hiroa/Buck in the research. The Society published the (still flourishing) *Journal of the Polynesian Society*.

THE MAORI IN EUROPEAN ART

In the 1890s early 1900s striking portraits and group paintings by Gottfried Lindauer (1839–1926) and the much younger Charles Goldie (1870–1942) captured key activities and figures of the Maori, and celebrated the meeting of the two cultures. Many Lindauer paintings were commissioned by the Auckland businessman Henry Partridge. These include such works as *Tohunga under Tapu* (1901), *The Tohunga-ta-moko at Work* (1903), *Happy Days* or *Maori Children playing Knucklebones* (1907) and *As Cook found Them* or *Digging with the Ko* (1907). Lindauer depicted people, customs and ways of life. Even if, as has been claimed there is no drama in his work, in his groups there is often a restrained wit or whimsicality.

Lindauer had grown up in Bohemia and studied in Prague. Goldie was born in Auckland, had his first art lessons there, but learned his craft in Paris in the mid-1890s. Returning to Auckland in 1898 he rapidly established himself. His work is less ethnographical than that of Lindauer. Some still held a view that Maori were a dying race, and Goldie's paintings are expressive of this morbidity, the work *Memories* (1905), for example. Here an elderly upper class Maori woman, with moko, in a magnificent green dress is wistfully contemplating the past. Strangely, Goldie seems to have ignored the contemporary renaissance in Maoridom being achieved by people such as Ngata, Buck, and Pomare.

National Identity in an Imperial Polity

New Zealand national feeling was always of a kind which allowed New Zealanders to be Britons, just as English and Scots and Welsh were Britons.

NEW ZEALAND BRITONS

As the New Zealand Wars were drawing to their close, the novelist Anthony Trollope visited the country. In his 1873 book *Australia and New Zealand*, he nicely captured the nineteenth-century European New Zealanders' attitude with the following words:

> The New Zealander ... is more English than any Englishman at home. He tells you he has the same climate – only somewhat improved; that he grows the same produce – only with somewhat heavier crops – that he has the same beautiful scenery ... only somewhat grander in scale and more diversified ... that he follows the same pursuits and after the same fashion – but with less of misery, less of want, and a more general participation in the gifts which God has given to the country.

Despite a growing nationalism, Trollope's words would still have described many European New Zealanders until the 1970s. New Zealanders never felt any great pressure to be fully 'independent'. They were content to know that was available at any time they so desired.

The New Zealand Wars had an interesting effect. Some colonial troops claimed to be superior in bush fighting to regular army British troops. This conception fitted into the Trollope view of themselves as a *superior* Southern Hemisphere South Pacific Briton.

British sentiment was demonstrated when Seddon called on parliament to vote unanimously to send a contingent to support the Empire in South Africa at the end of the century, in what became known as the Boer Wars. The vote was fifty-four to five, and proportionately public support was probably similar. New Zealand in fact despatched about 6,500 troops including Maori, and 8,000 horses, as large a proportion as Britain herself, and a much larger proportion than from other colonies and dominions such as Canada. The New Zealanders gained a reputation for athleticism and stamina and with other colonial troops became a highly effective mobile force, and the folks at home were proud of the New Zealand effort.

NEW ZEALAND *V* AUSTRALIA

In part, New Zealand identity crystallized in reaction to the presence of the islands' nearest neighbours, the six Australian colonies. The Tasman Sea, 1200 miles/1900 ks, which separates the two lands, has always been wider literally and metaphorically than people in other countries realize. New Zealand national identity was forged in particular by the growth of the movement towards federation of the Australian colonies in the last decade or so of the nineteenth century, which occurred in 1901.

Many people in the Australian colonies at the time thought New Zealand would join. The possibility is still enshrined in Australia's Constitution. New Zealanders seriously considered the proposal, and leaders such as Sir George Grey had taken an important part as delegates in early federation discussions. Still, probably a majority agreed with Ballance and Reeves and Hall that 1,200 miles of ocean were a good argument against, and New Zealanders decided not to join.

They based their decision on their feeling of difference from Australia. Besides some convict ancestry not found in New Zealand, the Australian colonies had a much larger proportion of Irish and Roman Catholics. The cultural differences between Aboriginal Australians and Maori were also clear to all New Zealanders, and the Maori considered themselves superior. By 1900 there was no longer a significant market in the Australian colonies. Overwhelmingly New Zealand's economic ties were with Britain, and New Zealanders felt economically secure enough to remain alone.

The 1900 Report of the New Zealand Federation Committee claimed: 'the climates of the Continent and the Colony are as unlike as are the landscapes, and some people think that the two branches of the Anglo-Saxon race which inhabit them are already developing different characteristics'. It is as if Reeves and others were somehow aware of the facts about plate tectonic movement discovered seven decades later: that proto-New Zealand had been drifting away from Australia for 80,000,000 years. So why join it politically! New Zealanders were not Australians but temperate-climate, island-based, South Pacific Britons. It is significant that the term 'Australasia', which referred collectively to both places, became less used after 1901.

The decision to reject federation in effect committed the Maori and the European settlers to continue the evolutionary process/programme/agenda of becoming New Zealanders.

For these South Seas Britons the South Pacific was their 'backyard' and they believed the contribution of the Maori, and their own understanding of Maori, made New Zealanders experts in dealing with other Polynesians, and so gave the right to expand New Zealand influence. Vogel, Seddon, Reeves, all wanted increased British control. Vogel saw in the New Hebrides (Vanuatu), Fiji, Tonga, and Samoa, an island empire ripe for the taking. Their loyalties, like those of many contemporaries, lay not with Britain as such nor with New Zealand as such, but with the British Empire. In fact Seddon anticipated that one day New Zealand would take its place in a federated empire. Such men joined with Australian statesmen of similar views to pressure Britain. But British Prime Ministers were not persuaded. In 1901 Seddon was able at least to annex Niue as well as the Cook Islands, an annexation supported by many Maori, who felt ethnic consanguinity with Cook Islanders.

New Zealand feeling was encouraged by early success at rugby and tennis. Frederick A. Wilding (1883–1915) won the Wimbledon tennis title from 1910 to 1913, and was in the Davis Cup-winning team in 1907, 1909 and 1914 (playing for Australasia). But it has been in rugby and identification with the national rugby team the 'All Blacks' (refers to their uniform not their skin) that national feelings have most strongly coalesced. The New Zealand Rugby Football Union was established in

1892, but the earliest provincial associations were Canterbury and Wellington in 1879. The first overseas tour was to the eastern Australian colonies in 1884. For a century now a frisson of excitement and pride has passed through New Zealanders when their Rugby team performs the haka, *Ka Mate!* (Appendix 3), prior to the start of an international match.

LITERATURE

Nineteenth-century New Zealand literature was national only in the sense of using a New Zealand background. Until well into the 1900s most writers aimed at a British Isles, rather than a local readership, and made use of, and sometimes distorted, the exotic aspects of their environment. Several worthy chronicles and autobiographical narratives were produced such as Frederick Manning's *Old New Zealand* (1863), Samuel Butler's (1835–1902) *A First Year in Canterbury Settlement* (1863), and Lady Mary Anne Barker's (1883) *Station Life in New Zealand*. There were also writers of verse such as sometime premier, Alfred Domett (1811?–87), who wrote a romantic epic poem *Ranolf and Amohia* (1872). The best work towards the end of the century was in history, Reeves's elegant *The Long White Cloud* (1898), and the writing of ethnographers Smith and Best, which also helped define New Zealanders' self-conceptions.

Despite its literary lapses, the most remarkable New Zealand novel to come from century's end was written in 1889 by the former premier, Julius Vogel. *Anno Domini 2000* subtitled *Woman's Destiny* was a futuristic tale which Vogel published in London. As prophet he was correct in suggesting that New Zealand would have a female prime minister, that large dams would be a source of hydro-electric power, and that tourism, fishing, horticulture and wine would be important sources of New Zealand foreign exchange; several of his technological predictions are in general correct such as air conditioning and air travel in 'lightweight aluminium air cruisers'. Out of print for more than a century the novel was republished in New Zealand in the year 2000. Given that Vogel's future world was run mostly by able and admired women, a rather fantastic idea in 1889, it is very interesting to note that in the real year 2000, New Zealand women would in fact hold the following leading positions: Governor-General, Prime Minister, Leader of the Opposition, Attorney-General, Chief Justice, and CEO of the largest company.

New Zealand Technology and Science

Not all dwellers in these islands were farmers, miners, politicians, and businessmen. Some were inventors of new machines, others pursued pure scientific knowledge.

New Zealanders give one the impression that with a length of No. 8 fencing wire (0.16 ins/4mm), they can make or fix anything. Do-it-yourself, improvisation, arrived with the first settlers when they had to repair machinery and the nearest spare-parts store was in Sydney or Britain. Here are three of the most notable of the many inventors from the later nineteenth and early twentieth centuries.

Ernest Godward (1869–1936) wished to leave Invercargill and see the world. In 1901 he invented a spiral shaped hairpin, much superior to the straight variety: 250,000 were soon bought in Melbourne alone. He sold the patent to a US company for £20,000, which was a fortune then. He also invented a forerunner of the modern carburettor and formed companies in USA and Britain. By the 1930s the US Army was using his carburettor on its multitudinous vehicles. Godward saw the world.

Tired of tearing off stamps in Wellington Post Office, in 1891 the teenager R.J. Dickie (1876–1960) decided it must be possible to make a stamp-vending machine. Years of working came to fruition in 1905 when the world's first patented and marketed machine went into use at Wellington, for one penny stamps. About 4000 had been sold when another 'genius' worked out that one could insert something shaped and weighing like a penny, and still receive a stamp! Some quick modifications were made. For fifty years Dickie's was the most successful stamp machine in the world.

But the blue riband must go to Richard Pearce (1877–1953), a south Canterbury farmer, who may have flown a heavier-than-air machine before the Wright Brothers. Pearce, like the Wrights, worked for a time as a bicycle mechanic. Too poor to go to engineering school he was self-taught. From bamboo, steel tubes, canvas and wire, he constructed a monoplane, closely resembling modern microlight aircraft. It used a light-weight two-stroke engine Pearce had also designed and constructed. He took off in front of some local people and travelled perhaps 100 yards before crash landing. Because Pearce was a loner, misunderstood and maligned, accurate records were not kept. So when did this event occur? In letters he wrote years later he said he flew in February or March 1904. However, the best estimate, from circumstantial evidence says 31 March 1903. Orville Wright flew on 17 December 1903. Pearce made several later similar 'flights' or 'jumps'. Did Pearce really fly more than eight months before the Wrights? Though it had wing flaps and a rear elevator, the plane lacked lateral control, so by modern definition his effort does not count as guided flight. But for one man working by himself without funds, his plane was a product of astonishing practical genius.

New Zealand science also began early. Amongst the leaders was Alexander Bickerton (1842–1929), an outstanding London lecturer who brought science alive with dynamic demonstrations, and became first Professor of Chemistry at Canterbury College. Others were Richard Maclaurin (1870–1920), who arrived in New Zealand at age five, became foundation Professor of Mathematics at the new Victoria College (now University) in Wellington in 1899, and was later president of Massachusetts Institute of Technology, which he saved from being absorbed by Harvard University; and Frederick White who became chairman of the Commonwealth Scientific and Industrial Research Organization (CSIRO), Australia's greatest research institution. Julius von Haast and Ernest Rutherford were the greatest of the early scientists and will now be considered in some detail.

JULIUS VON HAAST (1822–87)

Haast, who learned his science in Germany, came to New Zealand in 1858. Following some early geological work in Auckland and Nelson provinces, he was asked to do a survey of Nelson's western areas. He made known the extent of the western coalfields, and showed that alluvial gold was carried by West Coast rivers, information which led to the goldrush.

Haast became involved with the Canterbury provincial government and his geological opinion was crucial for the Lyttelton Railway Tunnel. In 1861 he became a British subject and was appointed Provincial Geologist. In mapping provincial mineral resources, he explored all the Canterbury rivers to their sources, correctly predicted the presence of artesian water beneath the Canterbury Plains, and was the first to explore systematically the Mt Cook region. His expeditions also produced much new botanical information.

His pet project was to establish a world-class museum in Christchurch. The fortunate 1865 discovery of the huge pile of moa remains in Glenmark Swamp, some of which he exchanged for exhibits from around the world, made this dream a reality, and he became the museum's first director. He was also instrumental in the foundation of Canterbury College and became its first professor of geology.

A plethora of international honours came his way including a British, and an Austrian knighthood (giving him the right to use 'von'), and fellowship of the Royal Society. Ever enthusiastic, versatile, and a role-model, he is usually seen as the progenitor of New Zealand science.

ERNEST RUTHERFORD (1871–1937)

Rutherford was one of the *four or five most extraordinary scientists in the history of the world*. As the *Encyclopedia Britannica* directly puts it: 'Ernest Rutherford, ... is to be ranked in fame with Sir Isaac Newton and Michael Faraday.' If Newton (1643–1727) is the father of the laws of motion and Faraday (1791–1867) of electricity, then Rutherford is equally the father of our knowledge of the atom. He fundamentally altered our understanding of nature on three different occasions: explained the basis of naturally occurring radioactivity; discovered the structure of the atom; and was the first to transmute one chemical element into another.

Even his lesser achievements would have made a man famous. To mention merely three: early in his career he had the record for the longest-distance radio transmission; during World War I he headed the research on acoustic methods for detecting submarines, and when the USA entered the war in 1917 led the delegation which visited the US to present the British knowledge to the Americans; and he worked out the age of the earth, by developing methods now routinely applied by geologists.

Rutherford was born near Nelson in South Island, and won scholarships to Canterbury University College, Christchurch, graduating BA and MA in mathematics and physics. Encouraged by Professor Bickerton, his innovative post-graduate research on the high-frequency magnetism of iron, for which he constructed his own apparatus, took him to the forefront of contemporary physics. In 1895 he was awarded the single biennial scholarship for research overseas. He chose to work at the famous Cavendish laboratory of Cambridge University in England, then headed by J.J. Thomson (1856–1940), and was the first ever non-Cambridge graduate accepted as a research student. Thomson, who detected the existence of the electron, came to esteem him highly. After Roentgen discovered X-rays in 1895, Thomson invited Rutherford to share his research on how gas, an electrical insulator, could be made a conductor of electricity. This could be done using X-rays and ionizing rays from radioactive materials. Rutherford's enquiring mind now began examining radioactivity itself. He studied the ionizing effects of the radiation detected by Henri Becquerel (1852–1908) and Marie (1867–1934) and Pierre (1859–1906) Curie, and distinguished between alpha and beta forms of radiation.

At the tender age of 27, by now one of the world's leading physicists, Rutherford was appointed to head the physics department at McGill University in Montreal, Canada. Within three short years Rutherford had become the world leader in radioactivity. In Montreal, Rutherford and a young English chemist, Frederick Soddy (1877–1956), proposed in 1903 their disintegration theory of radioactivity, which said that atoms in a radioactive element (e.g., thorium or radium) slowly but spontaneously decay into lighter atoms of another element. This conception rejected the view held in one form or another since the time of ancient Greece that atoms are the indestructible basics of matter. It was also the first scientific conception of transmutation of chemical elements and seized the attention of the world. Further study from 1904 to 1907 showed that decaying radioactive elements finish as lead. For his work in Canada, Rutherford was awarded the Nobel Prize

New Zealand $100 note featuring physicist Ernest Rutherford. The note has been slightly modified for use in a bank campaign.

'for his investigations into the disintegration of the elements, and the chemistry of radioactive substances'.

In 1907 he returned to Britain to lead the physics department at Manchester University where he and his assistant the German Hans Geiger (1882-1945) developed an apparatus to measure the rate at which particles are emitted by radioactive materials. This Rutherford–Geiger detector was later improved to become the Geiger–Muller tube, 'Geiger Counter' we know today. Its new evidence, together with Rutherford's earlier data that alpha particles produce helium, proved that helium atoms are double charged alpha particles, or conversely, that the alpha particle of alpha radiation is the helium atom stripped of its two electrons.

When Geiger had trained undergraduate Ernest Marsden in radioactivity techniques, Rutherford gave him the task of seeing if alpha particles fired at metal foils could be scattered through large angles. Marsden found they were scattered, even for angles greater than 90 degrees. With his gift for analogy, the surprised Rutherford explained that this was like firing a large naval cannon at a piece of paper and having the shell bounce back!

In 1911, to the astonishment and initial disbelief of the scientific world, he explained that it meant that the positive charge and almost the total mass of an atom is concentrated in a relatively small region of 'space' which he called the nucleus, itself an 'object' a thousand times smaller than the atom's outside 'perimeter', while the negatively charged electrons circle this nucleus in fixed orbits. This is the model of an atom which every schoolchild now learns, but it took brilliant research combined with the leaping imagination of genius to conceive of it.

In the period 1917–19 he developed the implications of his model of the atom, and showed that when the nucleus of the element nitrogen is bombarded with alpha particles it disintegrates into hydrogen and oxygen nuclei. This was the first actual artificial transmutation of one element into another. For a thousand years alchemists had searched forlornly for 'the philosopher's stone' to achieve this. In 1919 Rutherford succeeded Thomson as director of the Cavendish Laboratory and made it the world's greatest physics research centre.

Rutherford's passion for science and the limited possibilities for doing frontier research in his homeland at that date forced him to pass the most productive part of his life overseas. He returned to New Zealand on four extended visits, and during that of 1923 stated, 'I have always been very proud of the fact that I am a New Zealander.' He was knighted, was later raised to the peerage as Lord Rutherford of Nelson, and, like Newton, was elected not just a Fellow, but President of the Royal Society. When he died in 1937 the *New York Times* wrote, '. . . It is given to few men to obtain immortality, still less to achieve Olympian rank during their own lifetime. Lord Rutherford achieved both.'

Rule by Farmers: the Reform Party of W.F. Massey

FALL OF LIBERALS, RISE OF LABOUR

By the end of the nineteenth century, political ideas advocating forms of socialism, confrontation, strikes, and in the case of those who later called themselves Communists, class revolution, were influencing many working people in the industrialized world. Inevitably they reached New Zealand. Books and pamphlets, particularly those of the leftist Chicago publishers C.H. Kerr, were influential, as were visiting lecturers, journalists and union leaders such as Tom Mann, Ben Tillett, Harry Bennett, and Charles Russell. Some stayed, such as the Australian H.E. (Harry) Holland (1868–1933), who later became leader of the New Zealand Labour Party. Radical ideas also entered with immigrants who had a union background, such as Australian-born Michael J. Savage (1872–1940), a later prime minister, Robert (Bob) Semple (1873–1955), and Patrick (Paddy) Webb (1884–1950).

These men began to exploit dissatisfactions which had been accumulating. For pragmatic short-term gains and for long-term socialist aims many New Zealand unionists became militant. After the death of Seddon the Liberal Party continued to lose its attraction for working people and small farmers. It was now led by the more pedestrian personality of Joseph Ward (1856–1930), and Reeves's brain-child the Arbitration Court had allowed wages to fall behind price rises, and was increasingly though probably inaccurately seen as pro-employer.

In 1907 there were twelve strikes. In 1908 there was an illegal but successful strike of West Coast coal miners at the intense little town of Blackball. This town became well known because of the presence of agitators such as Semple, because the strike leaders were able to gain control and form a militant Federation of Miners, and because in 1909 they established a more powerful Federation of Labour (FOL) overseeing the miners and other unions (and colloquially called the 'Red Feds'). The Liberal government alienated workers by increasing the penalties for striking if an agreed award decided by arbitration already existed. In 1911 the FOL adopted the revolutionary aims of the American Industrial Workers of the World (IWW). The IWW plan was eventually to instigate a general strike of all workers which would destroy the capitalist economic system and replace it with a union-based utopian socialist society.

In 1910 the various Trades and Labour Councils formally established a New Zealand Labour Party independent of fellow-thinkers in the Liberal Party. Five Labour MPs were elected in 1911. (The present Labour Party was established in 1916.)

A parallel growth of employers' organizations also occurred – the single organization in 1896 had become 122 by 1908, with almost

4,000 members. The parliamentary opposition reorganized itself a year later in 1909 under the name 'Reform Party'. It was led by William F. Massey (1856–1925) a farmer from Mangere near Auckland. It promised to leave intact the Liberals' reforms. But it also believed that socialists had become too powerful and that the Liberals were too accommodating. Its supporters were drawn from employers, small businesspeople, and most important, from the large farming population. Farmers had formed their own union in 1899 and gradually became better organized and an increasing force in New Zealand politics.

'MASSEY'S COSSACKS' *V* 'RED FEDS': THE GREAT 1913 WATERFRONT STRIKE

All movements in politics come to an end. In 1912 several Liberals 'crossed the floor' to support the new Reform Party, and so brought it to power. Massey would remain in office for thirteen years until his death.

Industrial disputes increased in 1912. In 1913 to achieve a united front, two new labour organizations were formed, the Social Democratic Party (SDP) whose aim was to introduce socialism by parliamentary means; and a new umbrella body of unions, the United Federation of Labour (UFL), also known colloquially as the 'Red Feds'. The UFL intended to use strikes, but not as a means to revolution.

By mid-1913 there had been two years of continual bickering and strikes. Matters took a serious turn in what would become the long May–November strike of goldminers at Waihi on the Coromandel Peninsula, which ended in fighting between unionists and police. In October strikes by the Wellington Watersiders' Union (wharf labourers/dockers) and disputes over use of non-union labour brought further conflict.

Massey's government became alarmed. It called for volunteer special constables. Farmers, concerned that their hard-won produce would soon be rotting on the wharves, responded to the call.

When poorly disciplined special constables batoned a taunting crowd, they inflamed unionists' grievances and earned the constables the ironic sobriquet 'Massey's Cossacks'. Naval ratings paraded on the wharves. Streetfighting broke out. In November, after the UFL ordered the waterside workers to strike, protected by troops, about 1700 farmers occupied the wharves in Auckland and they and other non-union labour loaded the ships. There were similar actions in Wellington. The union militants seethed.

Employers encouraged non-union labour to replace the strikers by legally forming a new wharf labourers' union within the laws of the Arbitration Act. In response the UFL called a General Strike of all non-registered unions and eighteen registered unions – mostly wharf labourers, miners, and seamen. But this UFL General Strike was undermined from the beginning because 55,000 members of registered unions refused to strike. The refusal of the two core unions of shearers and railwaymen also turned out to be crucial.

Key union leaders were arrested and special constables opened the wharves. Within weeks the seamen gave in, and in January the miners returned to work, forced to form a new union under the Arbitration Act. With the failure of their Waterfront Strike of 1913, the SDP and UFL collapsed. Workers as an industrial class would be unified only in the mid-1930s.

The combination of resolute leadership from Massey, farmers' power, united business, and the country's rejection of extremism had been too strong. And farmers were now the largest occupational group in parliament.

The Great War

The First World War is arguably the most traumatic event in New Zealand's history. The total New Zealander casualties in the four-year Great War, as it came to be known afterwards, would be appalling, much greater than that of Belgium, a country with six times the population, which was itself a battlefield. Some 16,317 died in action, and 41,262 were wounded – this was about a third of all men in New Zealand aged between twenty and forty. The war was the nation's first large involvement in international affairs (the South African War had been intra-Empire affairs) and had a profound impact on the whole community. It also radically altered the world context within which New Zealand was evolving.

On 4 August 1914 in order to attack France by the most favoured route, Germany declared war on Belgium and invaded her territory. Because Britain had agreed to protect Belgium's neutrality (as had Germany) she declared war on Germany. In respect to other British countries such as New Zealand the constitutional situation was assumed rather than specifically spelled out. In any case whether to go to war was academic because most of the population instinctively supported Britain – from sentiment, values, and consanguinity, and because they considered themselves British.

Within three days the New Zealand government had offered to send an expeditionary force. New Zealanders were clear where they stood. Here was a fight between democracy and its freedoms and autocracy and its greed. Though New Zealanders believe today that the moral lines were not quite as obvious as they then thought, there was a clear difference.

BLOODLESS SAMOA

Besides the returned soldiers from the South African War, New Zealand through part-time training of territorials and cadets had developed a relatively large number of men with some military experience. When the British government requested that New Zealand seize the wireless station in the German colony of Samoa, New Zealand was able to respond immediately. A volunteer force of 1400 men from North Island territorial units sailed on August 15. They captured German Samoa for the British Empire without having to fire a shot. This was in fact the first Allied victory of the war. Western Samoa remained under a rigid military government for the rest of the war.

A full-scale Expeditionary force under the command of General Sir Alexander Godley (1867–1957), nephew of the founder of Canterbury, departed in October, with almost 8,600 men and over 3,800 horses on ten transports. Their distinctive head-dress was the peaked hat, the 'lemon squeezer' as it was affectionately called. They joined with the Australian Imperial force (AIF) and together sailed for Europe. Because Japan was then an ally of Britain, the convoy was escorted by a destroyer of the Imperial Japanese Navy.

BLOODY GALLIPOLI

On 31 October the Turkish Empire came into the war on the side of the Central Powers, Germany and Austria, so, rather than proceeding to Britain, the ANZACS (Australian and New Zealand Army Corps) as the joint force was known, disembarked in Egypt to help protect that country and the Suez Canal from Turkish attack from Palestine, then part of the Turkish Empire.

By the end of 1914 stalemate had occurred on the Western Front, and Allies and Central Powers found themselves confronting one another along an enormous line of trenches. The Allied leaders decided that the opening of another war front was imperative.

As a result the New Zealanders became part of a famous, bloody and unsuccessful campaign on the Gallipoli Peninsula. The aim was to capture the Peninsula in order to control the narrow passage, the Dardanelles, which passed through Turkish territory and led to the Black Sea and Russia. Russia, an ally of Britain and France, but now showing signs of collapse, could thus be reinforced. Moreover, the Turkish capital, Constantinople (Istanbul), just to the north could be captured.

The campaign seems to have been ill-fated from the beginning. On 25 April 1915 the first ANZAC assault troops were carried some miles north of their intended landing place. Given its effect on the whole campaign the cause has been debated for ninety years. It may have been strong currents, or merely a misjudgment by a midshipman commanding a steamboat towing the assault troops. Instead of arriving at a broad beach leading to a plain, the troops had to attack a narrow beach and precipitous rugged hillsides, comparatively easy for the Turks to defend. Horrendous fighting occurred, but the ANZACS held their beachhead with 2000 casualties by midnight of the first day.

Soon the Turks, and the Allies, British, French and ANZACS were at a stalemate. Hoping for a breakthrough, the Allies remained too long. Heroic actions on both sides yielded little result. Quinn's Post and Chunuk Blair were the sites of marvellous New Zealand deeds. Finally, in a very successful nightime manoeuvre in January 1916 all Allied troops evacuated. Some 2,700 New Zealanders had died.

For New Zealand (and Australia), Gallipoli became a military legend, the legend of ANZAC, a campaign in which the country's soldiers had proved their valour. After the war, the anniversary of the landing, named ANZAC Day, became celebrated each year as the national day solemn above all others, and sacred in a secular way. As the years passed and New Zealanders fought in other wars, the ANZAC Day commemoration came to absorb their significance as well.

The Gallipoli campaign is today more meaningful than ever in New Zealand, and thousands of New Zealanders, a high proportion young people, travel each year to Gallipoli to honour the dead of their nation.

THE SHIFTING SANDS OF PALESTINE

From 1915 a New Zealand Mounted Rifles Brigade fought with great distinction as part of the Australian and New Zealand Mounted Division of the British Army in Palestine fighting the Turks. Riding skills perfected on the farms and sheep runs of up-country New Zealand proved tactical winners in the open-manoeuvring war in the desert.

They were under the command of the daring tactician, Brigadier-General Edward Chaytor (1868–1939), a New Zealander experienced in the South African War. The New Zealanders had great success at Romani in 1916, and Rafa in 1917. In 1918 they were part of a combined New Zealand, British, Jewish, and Indian force under Chaytor's command, which crossed the Jordan River on an 18 mile/30k front, captured the Jordanian town of Amman, and took more than 10,000 Turkish prisoners.

THE MID-WAR AFFAIR OF RUA KENANA, MAORI PROPHET

In April 1916, while the monstrous Battle of Verdun was being fought on the Western Front in France, in the isolated Urewera Mountains of North Island there occurred a peculiar confrontation.

The tradition of Maori prophets such as Haumene and Te Kooti continued into the twentieth century, in the persons of Rua Kenana and T.W. Ratana (below). Te Kooti had prophesied that he would be followed by another 'chosen one'. Rua Kenana's (1869?–1937) oratory, coupled with his spectacular 'visions', eventually persuaded the Tuhoe tribe that he was indeed that one. Rua claimed he was the brother of Christ and the son of the Holy Spirit. Maori prophets were neither tohunga (priests/experts) nor from chiefly families, but ordinary men who appealed to plain folk who were increasingly landless and sometimes at odds with their tribes.

Developing out of Te Kooti's Ringatu, Rua's religion identified the Maori with the Jews, another chosen people who had lost their lands. With plenty of Old Testament precedent, Rua took multiple wives. For a time he had seven – one drawn from each of the Tuhoe sub-tribes – as he explained a way of bringing unity to his people. Eventually there were twelve. He established a prosperous farming community

The Maori prophet Rua Kenana

called Maungapohatu in the rugged Urewera Mountains. Perhaps its most extraordinary feature was the circular two-storey courthouse and meeting house, decorated outside with playing card symbols of clubs and diamonds.

He had more visions. One prophesied that the rulers of the world would arrive to bring the millennium. Rua would be seated on the high throne above them all, including King George and the German Kaiser. A pacifist, Rua also discouraged his people from volunteering for military service. Although the Great War called forth immense heroism and sacrifice, it also created a climate of intolerance. Rua's pronouncements and actions were interpreted by the government as pro-German, and the newspapers built Rua into a sort of pro-German guerrilla working evil from his mountain hideout.

Finally, seventy-seven armed and mounted policemen were sent to arrest and charge Rua with sedition. The soon-to-retire Police Commissioner invited a newspaper reporter and photographers along to record the adventure. Rua was being handcuffed when a shot was fired, by whom no one knows. Sporadic firing followed during which a constable was wounded and Rua's eldest son, and a staunch friend, were shot dead. A forty-seven-day trial followed, famous for the way in which Rua's lawyer pointed out that in New Zealand someone could be arrested on a Sunday only for a felony, not for sedition! Though the jury found Rua not guilty of sedition, merely guilty of 'morally resisting arrest', the judge passed a draconian sentence of a year's hard labour and eighteen months of reformative detention.

When Rua returned from gaol he found his settlement in disarray, disillusioned, and in debt. Still he had visions. On his death in 1937, 600 followers assembled, many believing he would rise on the third day. Rua's efforts can be seen as the last Maori attempt to develop a separate polity. During Rua's last years another prophet was rising, T.W. Ratana, who, as we shall see, shared some of his aims but used very different methods. For Ratana played the Pakeha at their own game.

THE HELLISH TRENCHES OF FRANCE

On the Western Front troops of both sides dug themselves into defensive positions behind barbed wire, and in deep trenches. They lived in filth and mud, with lice and rats, destruction and death their constant companions.

When the New Zealand troops, including a Maori brigade, arrived in this hell in northern France in April 1916, they formed a separate unit, the New Zealand Division, commanded by Major-General Sir A.H. Russell, born in Napier, but trained at Sandhurst in England. At home, conscription for active service was introduced in 1916. Previously all New Zealand soldiers had been volunteers.

The Division went into battle near Armentières in May 1916. In September and October it was used further south in the area of the Somme River and was part of the disastrous attack launched on 15 September in the First Battle of the Somme. They went 'over the top' in an offensive that became infamous for its casualties and lack of progress. In the winter of 1916-17 they were involved in the flat area of the Lys River facing the Aubers Ridge. In June 1917 they played an important part in the successful attack at Messines. Some months later there occurred the slaughter of the Third Battle of Ypres. Amongst the many fine young men who died there was Frederick F. Wilding, the Wimbledon tennis champion.

At Passchendaele the New Zealand Division suffered catastrophically. Within a few hours in the abortive attack 2,700 men had been wounded and 800 men and forty-five officers killed. It was the greatest day's disaster in New Zealand history, worse than anything in the Musket Wars, and the single time the New Zealand Division failed to reach its objective in a planned assault.

Winter of 1917–18 was spent maintaining the Allied position east of Ypres. In 1918 the New Zealanders were involved in a desperate defensive effort to 'plug a gap' in the line, when the magnificent German Spring Offensive threatened to break through and change the course of the war. They not merely held their ground, but together with an Australian infantry brigade advanced, and inspired other sections of the Allied Line.

Towards the end of the war, from August 1918, the New Zealanders made a successful sweep from Bapaume to near Cambrai. They captured the mediaeval fortress of Le Quesnoy in the last week of the war, with its 60 feet/18m high walls. The townspeople within jubilantly welcomed the New Zealanders.

Something of the New Zealander's martial quality is shown in the fact that throughout the war only four New Zealand officers and 352 other ranks were captured by the enemy, whereas the New Zealanders took prisoner 287 officers and 8745 other ranks on the Western Front alone.

Today, the guns are silent. There are merely cemeteries. Immensely moving. They tug at the stomach. Mile upon mile of serried white crosses in deep green fields. Line upon appalling line to the horizon. The care in perpetuity of the graves, and memorials to New Zealanders in France and Belgium, is the responsibility of the Commonwealth War Graves Commission. Like the governments of other members, the New Zealand government makes a substantial annual contribution.

INFLUENZA EPIDEMIC AND PROHIBITION

In July 1918 a massive influenza epidemic hit Germany, then in rapid succession all the European countries, killing millions. It moved on to Africa, Asia and the Americas, then Australia and finally in October crossed the Tasman Sea to New Zealand. The bacteria flooded the lungs, and, in effect drowned their victims. War-weariness and inadequate nutrition had lessened people's resistance. In New Zealand about 8,500 people died in a population of some 1,160,000.

In April 1918 New Zealanders approved a referendum to prohibit all alcoholic beverages. The result was reversed by the more than 40,000 troops still overseas (by almost 3 to 1). Nevertheless some electorates and the Maori King Country remained 'dry' (no alcohol) areas. The closing of bars at 6pm, introduced as a (temporary!) wartime measure, lasted until 1967.

CHAPTER TEN

New Zealand from 1920s to 1945

New Zealand in the 1920s

Then came the 'Roaring Twenties' as the decade has been labelled. In New Zealand it was a muted roaring. Still, like other peoples New Zealanders responded enthusiastically to the new inventions, international telephone calls, wireless (radio), increasing use of motor cycles and cars, traffic lights on main city intersections, motion-pictures with sound ('talkies'), Australia–New Zealand flights, Britain–Australia flights, cross-Pacific flights. They enjoyed new kinds of music like Jazz, new dances like the Charleston.

During the war New Zealand had been prosperous, the countryside especially so. For the British government guaranteed to buy at good prices the entire farm production, wool, beef, mutton, lamb, butter, and cheese not required by the New Zealand domestic market. But by 1921 the world economy was in recession, and the New Zealand government economized. Salaries of public servants were cut, and unemployment increased.

Returned soldiers who so desired had been given land grants, but by 1925 a quarter of the 9,000 soldier-settlers had been forced to give up. Bankruptcy amongst small business was also high. In contrast, to improve production and coordinate marketing the government established Meat (1922) and Dairy (1926) Boards, and by 1930 dairy exports were actually three times the volume they had been in 1921.

VERSAILLES, THE LEAGUE, AND REBELLIOUS SAMOA

The Versailles Peace Treaty formally ended the war, and New Zealand, like Canada and the other self-governing British Dominions, signed it separately from Britain. Though Massey was reluctant because of the implicit separation from Britain, in 1919 New Zealand joined the newly formed League of Nations as a full and separately voting member. In the League's redistribution of former German colonies, New Zealand, as occupier, was awarded a Mandate over Western Samoa, but accepted this responsibility with considerable reservation. It also shared a joint mandate over the phosphate-rich island of Nauru. And in 1925 Britain transferred Union Island (Tokelau) to New Zealand. So, together with Niue and the Cook Islands, New Zealand was by then responsible for four Pacific territories. As we have seen, Samoa had a long tradition of difficulties of government, and the mandate became increasingly problematic.

The crux seems to have been the appointment of a singularly unsuitable person for such a delicate task: Major-General Sir George Richardson (1868–1938). Although Richardson was an outstanding army administrator, he showed little understanding of or sympathy for Samoan culture and was indifferent to its political traditions. Although the funds derived from German property seized in World War I were spent on an infrastructure of roads and hospitals, Richardson's administrative manner was unacceptable. Increasingly autocratic, he enjoyed meting out humiliating punishments to leading Samoans, felt threatened by European residents, and deported the Samoans' chosen leader, the part-Samoan businessman O.F. Nelson.

The grass-roots resistance movement, the 'O le Mau', which had opposed the German administration resurrected itself and became almost an alternative government. It organized demonstrations: 'Samoa for the Samoans', and 'Government of the People by the People, for the People' were typical slogans. The damage had been done, and matters worsened despite Richardson's recall. In 1929 during a peaceful anti-government demonstration, it seems some people tried to avoid being arrested for tax offences, and New Zealand policemen fired upon the crowd. Eleven Samoans including a high chief, Tupua Tamasese, were shot dead. Repression followed and key Mau were forced to hide in the hills. A large petition sent to the League of Nations asking for transfer to another nation such as Britain was ignored. There was some improvement after 1935 with the election of the Labour government in New Zealand which promised independence in due course.

MAORI AFFAIRS: PROPHET RATANA AND PRINCESS TE PUEA

Renewed interest in Maori welfare, such as the settling of some grievances over land sales began with the appointment of Gordon Coates as Minister in 1921, and even more so when Apirana Ngata became Minister of Maori affairs in 1928. Ngata was able to secure government aid for Maori farmers comparable to that paid to Europeans.

Contrastingly, in the same year that Apirana Ngata became Minister, the influential Maori prophet Tahupotiki Wiremu Ratana (1873–1939) declared that his spiritual mission was complete and that he was now beginning his political mission. Ratana's senior kinswoman (similar to a godmother) Mere Rikiriki had her own church. In 1912 she prophesied that he would become a spiritual leader. In due course on 8 November 1918 Ratana said he had a vision and believed himself selected by God. Inexplicable phenomena were claimed to have occurred over the following weeks, such as his placing in piles the clothing of several relatives saying they belonged to the dead; these relatives all died soon after in the influenza epidemic.

From that day Ratana preached that the Maori were God's chosen people. He gained attention from many well-publicized acts of faith healing and soon a village of believers, Ratana Pa, was growing around the house of 'the mouth of God'. Travelling throughout New Zealand he led a considerable religious revival. Many Anglican and Methodist ministers supported him. On the other hand there was much debate at the time as to whether the healings happened, and probably a large majority of New Zealanders thought him a charlatan.

Ratana denied the importance of whakapapa (genealogy) and the Maori class hierarchy of chiefs and princesses, and rejected Maori tribalism. He deliberately desecrated places supposedly tapu. He promoted cleanliness, and condemned the tohunga, sorcery, tapu and other things he considered superstitions. He believed he had to take his message to the world, so visited Britain, USA and Japan, and seems to have come to the conclusion that Maori and Japanese were two of the Lost Tribes of Israel. In 1925 the Ratana Church was formally set up. Other Christians broke with him over two issues. He took a second, young wife, supposedly to protect him from infatuated young women; and the godhead now consisted not of the trinity but was quadripartite: the Father, the Son, the Holy Spirit, and Ratana.

In 1928 after the dedication of Ratana Temple, Ratana's move into politics proper began. By circulating a petition of about 30,000 signatures, the church tried to have the Treaty of Waitangi ratified as a statute-based law. On this issue Ratana was perceptive and prescient, anticipating the legal moves of the Waitangi Tribunal which would be established in 1985. During the next decade or so Ratana gained control of the four Maori parliamentary seats. Their occupants kept alive the idea of ratifying the Treaty. With his egalitarian ideas he forged some links with the Labour Party, and after Labour won the 1935 election a formal agreement between Labour and Ratana was sealed.

The Ratana Church achieved its largest proportion of members in the mid-1930s when it attracted something like 20 per cent of Maori. Today it attracts perhaps 10 per cent. Ratana's real success was to have established a Maori church that successfully blended both religious and political affairs – something never achieved before.

Also in the 1920s a Maori from the other end of the social scale became politically important, Princess Te Puea (1883–1952), one of the most powerful women not just in Maoridom but in New Zealand as a whole. Like Rua, Te Puea first gained notice with her 1917 campaign against Maori conscription. A grand-daughter of the pacifist second Maori King, Tawhiao, she was ever aware of the injustice of government confiscation of the lands of the Waikato Tribe in the 1860s. Maori were particularly devastated by the 1918 influenza epidemic and Te Puea gained kudos through her compassionate nursing work and her attempts to improve Maori living conditions. In the old Kingite capital of Ngaruawahia on the beautiful Waikato River she worked to establish a centre where the Waikato people could find self-respect. This became Turangawaewae Marae, eventually the largest

Princess Te Kirihaehae Te Puea

marae in New Zealand. From the early 1930s Ngaruawahia was increasingly a national Maori meeting place, not just a Waikato one.

Te Puea encouraged cultural activities as a way of bringing Maori together, and cooperation with Apirana Ngata led to land development schemes. Te Puea knew most of the political leaders of New Zealand, and of the Pacific Islands. She disagreed with Maui Pomare's view that Maori progress rested on their adoption of European culture and her aristocratic conceptions and belief in the significance of whakapapa made any cooperation with Ratana impossible. By the time she died Princess Te Puea had shown the Maori that it was possible for some to adapt to the European way of life while retaining many of the most significant dimensions of Maoridom.

From the days of Hongi Hika three ways for Maori to respond to settlers had been possible. They could reject European culture completely and follow the Maori way. They could reject Maoridom entirely and adapt to what they called the Pakeha world. Or they could try some middle road, retaining what they valued in Maori culture but being Pakeha in their professional lives. At least from the end of the New Zealand Wars the first response was never entirely possible. Few took the second route. Most have accepted some degree of compromise, but the cultural proportions vary enormously. Princess Te Puea was at one end of the continuum, the men of the Young Maori party at the other. The Te Puea approach has become more common in recent decades.

The 1930s Depression Years

Within a year of the 1929 United States stock-market crash the New Zealand economy was worsening. The government responded with orthodox deflationary policies. Despite two cuts of 10 per cent in wages, unemployment continued to rise.

To compound New Zealanders' concern and remind them of their precarious geography, the Hawkes Bay earthquake and accompanying fires destroyed much of Napier and Hastings in February 1931 and killed 250 people. In a few years, with government guidance and private capital, Napier was rebuilt in the contemporary Art Deco style. Today it contains one of the most significant groups of Art Deco buildings in the world.

The new United Party prime minister, George Forbes (1869–1947), and his cabinet, like others overseas, were unable to devise new economic approaches. Forbes's response was to form a coalition government with Reform, which proved equally powerless. By mid-1932 between 7 per cent and 8 per cent of the workforce were unemployed though neither Maori nor women featured in the figures.

Relief schemes of public works had been implemented, and were continued. At least at the beginning much useful work was performed, building roads, improving city parks, and planting the great renewable *Pinus radiata* pine forests of the Volcanic Plateau. In 1935, five unemployed men with picks, shovels and wheelbarrows, also began the Homer Tunnel, which penetrates the Southern Alps! Here the altitude is about 3,000 feet (900m) the rainfall 250 ins/6350mm a year. Mechanization was introduced after World War II and the tunnel completed in 1953. Now traversed by tens of thousands of tourists annually, Homer links the picturesque lake country of north Otago to the spectacular inlets of Fiordland.

RIOTS IN DUNEDIN, AUCKLAND, WELLINGTON

As conditions worsened, normally moderate, well-mannered and law-abiding New Zealanders became desperate. In Dunedin the Unemployed Workers Movement (UWM) galvanized the people with protests and demonstrations. Harry Holland, the Labour Party leader, was happily predicting a workers' uprising.

On 8 April 1932 in Dunedin women were in the vanguard of a march which erupted into riot over food handouts. The city remained tense and on the 11th there was another riot connected to the UWM. On the 14th a riot was narrowly avoided in Auckland, and on the 15th perhaps 20,000 protesters gathered in the main street. Police seem to have misinterpreted a speech by Jim Edwards, the Communist leader of the Auckland UWM, batoned him, and a riot followed. The government improved relief payments but also increased the powers of the police. These measures failed to stop a third riot which broke out in Wellington on 10 May.

The press blamed rowdies and Communist agitators, the Labour Party opposition blamed the UWM, the government blamed the Labour Party. Historians generally agree that although New Zealand Communists hoped that discontent might lead to revolution and no doubt encouraged the mayhem, the riots were unplanned and mostly the result of pent-up frustration.

The great majority of New Zealanders were shocked, direct action was again discredited, and unemployed people looked to the Labour Party and amelioration through acts of parliament to change parts of the economic and social system. The Labour Party seized the chance to proclaim itself the only organized group capable of making the necessary changes.

Unemployment was at its greatest in 1933 at around 100,000, some 15 per cent of the workforce. Many people experienced poverty and hardship never seen before or since. Hardworking farmers lost their life's work when they had to walk off their bankrupt properties. 'Swaggers' (tramps) crossed the countryside in search of handouts or a day's work.

In fact the coalition United/Reform Party government did more than the unemployed or its political opponents ever acknowledged. It guided the reconstruction of Napier and Hastings, allowed many mortgages to go unpaid, and devalued the New Zealand pound, which helped exports. It established a reserve Central Bank in 1933 and when it lost office to Labour in 1935 left a balance of payments in substantial credit.

BOOKS AND PAINTINGS

Social realism has tended to dominate the New Zealand novel. This was especially so in the disillusioned 1930s, with some powerful books depicting individual struggles. These were the years when a national writing tradition first appeared.

Hoping to shock and shame the country into changing the economic system, John A. Lee, the Labour MP, scathingly exposed the consequences of poverty in his *Children of the Poor* (1934) and *The Hunted* (1936), and John Mulgan in his 1939 *Man Alone* also showed his sympathy for his solitary hero battered by forces beyond his control. Robin Hyde, the third novelist of this 'school', had written outstanding investigative articles. Her two moving novels follow the life of James Douglas Stark as he is affected by World War I and the Depression. Such books drew a poignant contrast between the promise of the Liberals' 1890s and the penury of the 1930s. Such writers were nationalists – in the sense of wanting to explore New Zealand themes. Frank Sargeson (1903–82) examined what it was to be a New Zealander, in such works as his 1936 *Conversations with My Uncle*.

Rejecting the nineteenth-century idea that poetry should evoke natural beauty, Alan Curnow, Denis Glover, R.A.K. Mason, Charles Brasch, and A.R.D. Fairburn developed a poetic tradition sensitive to problems of New Zealanders and their ethos – though they were influenced by and respected, leading English-speaking poets overseas such as T.S. Eliot and W.H. Auden.

In painting too, New Zealand was no longer the land of languid lakes and picturesque peaks – or if so the peaks had a hard edge. The stylized landscapes of Christopher Perkins are typical: *Silverstream Brickworks*, and *Taranaki* (a stark dairy factory set against a plastic Mt Taranaki), as are the industrial landscapes of Rita Angus. Russell Clark (*Saturday Night* and *Late Night*), showed the bland lives of town workers. Romanticism was killed for a generation. Though Frances Hodgkins (1869–1947) grew up in Dunedin where she learned her early techniques, and is New Zealand's best-known painter, she spent the Depression and her mature years abroad.

LABOUR IN GOVERNMENT, AND THE WELFARE STATE

New Zealand turned left at the 1935 election and voted in the Labour Party with its moderate socialist model of government intervention. Labour would hold power until 1949. Led by Michael J. (Micky) Savage (1872–1940), and his deputy Peter Fraser (1884–1950), Labour's social makeup was overwhelmingly working class. Four Labour MPs had served prison terms for subversion or encouraging violence. Six had belonged to the defunct 'Red Feds'.

Measuring the moment, Labour began as it meant to go on – by giving the unemployed a Christmas bonus! It nationalized the Bank of New Zealand, protected dairy farmers against fluctuations in income, helped agricultural labourers, and introduced a 40-hour working week. Large-scale hydro-electric installations were constructed on South Island lakes and rivers.

The spirits of depressed New Zealanders were lifted by the exploits of a female New Zealand pilot, Jean Batten (1909–82). Rotorua-born Batten was a sort of 'Garbo of the skies'. She was the essence of derring-do, and glamour, who kept her personal life mysterious. Flying was still wondrous and outside the experience of ordinary people, and female flyers something marvellous. In 1934 she smashed the England–Australia flight time by six days. In 1935 she was the first woman to fly the reverse route from Australia to England. In 1936 she made the first direct flight between New Zealand and England and the fastest ever flight from Sydney to New Zealand. She wore a glamorous white flying suit often topped off with a striking coloured scarf, and always appeared well made-up. Flying was massively expensive, and her fund-raising efforts were less well-known. Encouraged by her male-embittered mother she accepted huge amounts from infatuated men.

Worldwide attention, as in the days of Seddon and Reeves, was attracted by the 1938 Social Security Act. This extended unemploy-ment benefits, and began a scheme of universal superannuation. The Bill had been intended to introduce a completely free medical scheme, but professional concerns by the doctors to do with doctor–patient relationships modified this substantially. The final form appearing only in October 1941.

These developments continued the programme of Seddon and Reeves and moved New Zealand into the modern Western world of the Welfare State. As we have seen, the new government inherited a budget in credit including a large fund of sterling which it spent on public works, and it was also fortunate that the international economic situation began to improve from the mid-1930s on.

Opposition parliamentarians were however concerned about the huge bill for all these innovations, and the new government did have some learning to do. Wild statements about costless credit took capital out of the country and frightened away British investors. In 1938 and 1939 only disciplined and determined economic diplomacy by the treasurer Walter Nash (1882–1968), later a prime minister (1957–60), staved off serious trouble, perhaps national bankruptcy.

NEW ORIENTATION TO INTERNATIONAL RELATIONS

Under the previous government, the most important decision of the 1926 Imperial Conference in London of prime ministers of British countries was the report made by the committee chaired by Lord Balfour. Known as the Balfour Report, it declared:

> The United Kingdom and the dominions [i.e. New Zealand, Australia, Canada, etc.] are autonomous communities within the British Empire, equal in status, in no way subordinate to one another in any respect of their domestic or external status, though united by a common allegiance to the

Crown and freely associated as members of the British commonwealth of Nations.

These international relationships were formalized in the 1931 Statute of Westminster passed by the British parliament. It recognized the right of each country to control its own domestic and foreign affairs, to establish its own diplomatic corps, and to join international bodies. New Zealand had always been less insistent upon her freedom of action than some of the other countries and only ratified the statute in 1947.

Previous governments had neglected the League, but Labour was determined to state its own position on international issues and appointed William (later, Sir) Jordan (1879–1959) as High Commissioner to Britain and Ambassador to the League of Nations. Jordan won an admiring international audience with his criticisms of devious Old World diplomacy. During the 1930s New Zealanders watched the growth in Europe of German Nazism and Italian and Spanish Fascism with deep concern. One end of the political spectrum of reaction to depression, few New Zealanders identified with them, and at the London Imperial Conference in 1937 Savage castigated appeasement of the dictators Adolf Hitler (1889–1945) and Benito Mussolini (1883–1945) and discussed defence issues such as the building of the Singapore naval base. On the left, the Communist alternative offered by Stalin's command economy USSR seemed attractive to some, though few were aware of the murderous political purges of many millions of Soviet citizens throughout the 1930s which were a part of it.

World War II

No one in New Zealand was surprised when, after Hitler invaded Poland, Britain finally declared war on Germany. Though Savage, the prime minister, was ill with terminal cancer, he forthrightly stated the New Zealand position: 'Both with gratitude for the past, and with confidence in the future, we range ourselves without fear beside Britain. Where she goes, we go, where she stands, we stand.' In its context this was not jingoistic but realistic. Britain was not merely the crucial economic partner of New Zealand, but a beacon of democracy in an increasingly totalitarian world, and the source of most of New

Zealand's cherished ideals. It was however Peter Fraser who would be the key figure and lead New Zealand through the war.

As in World War I, as it now became known, New Zealanders were again involved in an early naval action. In December 1939 the New Zealand light cruiser HMS *Achilles* and two other Royal Navy cruisers engaged the German battleship raider *Admiral Graf Spee* in the Battle of the River Plate near Montevideo, Uruguay. Rather than allow his ship to be captured, the German commander scuttled her. *Achilles* returned to New Zealand early in 1940 to an enthusiastic welcome.

Though Fraser had opposed conscription during World War I, he was no pacifist. Aware that there was now a clearly defined Nazi–Fascist enemy, he supported conscription (the draft) in 1940. By that time the Winter 1939–40 phase of the 'phoney war', as the neutral Americans called, it had passed, the Nazi Blitzkrieg had forced the surrender of Denmark in a few hours, the Netherlands in five days, Norway in a few weeks, France in a month, and Britain itself was being attacked by the Luftwaffe (German airforce). USA would not enter the war for another year and a half, and Russia was Hitler's ally. In addition to Britain, the only nations at war with Hitler were other British Commonwealth countries such as New Zealand, Australia and Canada. From a New Zealand point of view, with Japan becoming ever more aggressive in the Pacific, the world looked dark indeed.

The first New Zealanders to become involved were the young men who travelled to Britain before the war began, to join Britain's Royal Air Force (RAF). One of the earliest was Edgar J. Kain (1918–40), born in Hastings.

'COBBER' KAIN; THE BATTLE OF BRITAIN; NZ AIRMEN

Kain was a 'natural'. He learned to fly at 16. Flying was his only love and to join the RAF his only ambition. Accepted into the RAF in December 1936 at age 18, in July 1939 he began flying the new Hawker Hurricane fighters and, just turned 21, was promoted to Flying Officer. Immediately the war began he was made a section leader in defensive patrols over northern France. He acquired the nickname 'Cobber' from his fellows. Within a month he had downed a German

Edgar 'Cobber' Kain, the ace New Zealand RAF pilot

Luftwaffe Dornier Do 17 light bomber at 27,000 feet, at that time the highest altitude fight in history.

Kain's good looks and congenial, ebullient nature made him ideal material for war correspondents. Here was a man! After shooting down a Messerschmitt fighter in March 1940 he crash-landed, his cockpit in flames. In another 'dogfight' he downed two more fighters, but, burned himself, had to parachute to safety. By this time he was acknowledged as the RAF's first ace, and had become a 'celebrity'. During Hitler's invasion of Belgium, the Netherlands and France, Kain played a key role in harassing the German airforce. By June 1940 he had downed 17 aircraft and was ordered to go on leave. To say *au revoir* he performed an aerobatic display over a French aerodrome. His plane crashed and he died, already a legend.

To invade Britain successfully Hitler had to keep the Royal Navy out of the English Channel; to do that he needed command of the air over the Channel in order to deploy his superior air power; and for that he had to destroy the RAF. Thus began one of the great battles of world history from July to October 1940 between RAF Fighter Command and Hitler and Hermann Göring's (1893-1946) Luftwaffe, known as the Battle of Britain. The outnumbered RAF fighter pilots achieved a killing rate of 1,733 to 915 and repulsed the Nazi attempt.

Of the New Zealanders in the battle the most prominent was Air Vice Marshal Sir Keith Park (1892–1975), from the little town of Thames, who went to Britain and joined the RAF in 1922, and in the late 1930s helped devise a coordinated defensive plan of aircraft, radio, and radar. His skilful control of the key south-east quadrant of Fighter Command was crucial to success. In 1948 he returned home and became active in local government. Some 127 New Zealanders fought for Fighter Command during the Battle of Britain, of whom 18 were killed. After the battle it was calculated that a fighter pilot's life expectancy was 87 flying hours.

The greatest New Zealand ace of the whole war was Group Captain Colin Gray (1914–95) who in the Battle of Britain and other theatres shot down 27 aircraft, shared another, and either damaged or destroyed a further 22. Almost as successful was Wing Commander Alan Deere (1917–95) from Wanganui, who destroyed 21 enemy planes.

During World War II as a whole an astonishing 10,950 New Zealanders were pilots, navigators, and gunners in the RAF, and more than 3,000 died. Many trained under the spectacular Empire Air Training Scheme in Canada, thousands of miles from Nazi planes and bombs.

There were not just two categories of airmen – living and dead. There were also the horribly wounded, often sickeningly disfigured. The greatest of surgeons who treated these men was Archibald (later Sir) McIndoe (1900–60), a New Zealander, and pioneer of what we now call plastic surgery. He had learned the rudiments of facial work during World War I, inspired by the surgeon Sir Harold Gilles (1882–1960), another New Zealander

REARGUARD IN GREECE AND CRETE

A New Zealand Expeditionary Force again sailed for Egypt, this time as a unique entity, under the command of Major General (later, Sir) Bernard Freyberg (1889–1963). Freyberg exuded charisma and enjoyed command. He had served in World War I as an officer in the Royal Naval Division, was wounded in Gallipoli, won a Victoria Cross (VC) (the highest British Empire and Commonwealth military award) during the First Battle of the Somme, and in all suffered eight other battle wounds. As part of the New Zealand force, the Maori had their own battalion under Maori command. Arapeta Awatere (1910–76) rose rapidly through the ranks and commanded the Battalion for much of the war. Lieutenant Moana-nui-a-Kiwa Ngarimu won a post-humous VC.

All of continental Western Europe was now either under German control, allied to Germany, collaborating, or neutral. The Mediterranean became a war zone when Italy joined Germany in June 1940. The first major New Zealand action was in Greece in 1941. Mussolini, expecting an easy victory, had invaded the country but was forced into an embarrassing retreat. To reinforce the Italians and also to secure their southern flank for the secret coming assault on the USSR, the Germans captured most of Greece. The New Zealand effort was part of a hastily arranged, under-manned holding operation together with British, Australian and Greek troops, against great odds, and losses were significant.

The Allies then evacuated to the Greek island of Crete. Their task was to hold the island against a German offensive based upon history's greatest airborne parachute invasion till that date. Two engagements by the Maori Battalion were memorable, Malerne Airfield, and especially that in late May. Surprised by a German attack while they were resting, the Maori sprang into instant action with a brief haka and a bayonet charge with war cries, killed about 100 Germans for four Maori dead and 10 wounded, and the remaining Germans fled. But the campaign as a whole was disastrous for the New Zealanders who had no air cover, and though they fought hard, suffered a casualty rate of about 50 per cent. Though British prime minister Winston Churchill (1874–1965) and several British generals highly praised the New Zealanders, New Zealand prime minister Fraser, and Freyberg, insisted that the New Zealanders would not again be used in similar engagements. Many German paratroopers were killed in Crete, and Hitler never again launched a paratroop-based attack.

DESERT BATTLES IN EGYPT AND NORTH AFRICA

From Crete the New Zealanders evacuated to Egypt. For the remainder of 1941 the New Zealanders joined other British and British Commonwealth troops fighting in the deserts of North Africa. At first this involved action against the Italians advancing towards Egypt from Italian-controlled Libya. Many Italian soldiers, unconvinced by Mussolini's imperial ambitions, had little desire to fight, and demoralized, surrendered in their tens of thousands. By February 1942, however, fighting against the well-equipped and disciplined *Afrika Korps* troops commanded by German Field Marshal Erwin Rommel (1891–1944) was a different matter. Italian resistance was also stiffened. However the New Zealanders adapted enthusiastically to the war of rapid manoeuvre across hundreds of miles of desert.

The British breakthrough came at the great Battle of El Alamein about 140 miles (225k) west of Cairo in October/November 1942. British, New Zealand, Australian and Indian troops attacked Rommel's Axis forces. The planning and professionalism of a new and inspirational British commander Lieutenant-General Sir Bernard Montgomery (1887–1976) provided renewed leadership and dispelled the New Zealanders' disillusion after two earlier poorly planned operations. The return of General Freyberg to their command also restored morale, and the British forces were now receiving more and improved military materiel. The New Zealanders were crucial in the frontal attack of four divisions, and a few days later in Operation Supercharge, the Second New Zealand Division led the attack which breached the Axis line. Soon after, the Axis forces were either surrendering or in headlong retreat.

SLOGGING UP ITALY

Those troops who were not repatriated to New Zealand were sent to Italy in September 1943. At first it had been thought that capturing Italy would be relatively easy. In fact it had backward roads, rugged terrain, capricious rivers, and harsh mountain winters, all of which wistfully reminded the New Zealanders of home. Such complex terrain joined to the fact that it was the retreating Germans rather than the lukewarm Italians who were the chief foe, turned Italy into one of the most difficult campaigns of the war.

The New Zealand forces were strengthened by an echelon of eager new recruits. Better equipped than ever, more than 14,500 troops of the 2nd New Zealand Division joined the British Eighth Army and the Eighth Indian Division.

After the stalemate of Orsogna, the New Zealanders joined in the famous Battle of Casino under the joint leadership of Montgomery and, because the USA had now entered the war, the American general, Mark W. Clark (1896–1984). The Germans held against waves of Allied attacks and casualties were high. Even the ferocious Maori Battalion failed to secure its objectives. As a disillusioned Freyberg said, 'Reminds you of Passchendaele, doesn't it?'

The New Zealanders were not chosen to share in the enthusiastic liberation of Rome, but fought on up the peninsula. Houses more often than not hid retreating German troops rather than welcoming Italian peasants. Fighting around Florence was difficult as were actions at Monte Lignano, San Michele, la Romola and the Senio River. The New Zealanders took Bologna in April 1945, then Venice. Freyberg was now ordered to capture the important port of Trieste, which he did. Tito's Communist Yugoslav partisans also wanted Trieste and some awkward moments ensued, but Tito retired in June. Despite the frustrations, New Zealand morale in the Italian campaign was generally good.

In North Africa and Italy the New Zealanders had done a fine job. In fact Montgomery, Anthony Eden (1887–1967) British foreign Minister, even Rommel, rated them the best unit in the British Eighth Army.

Captain Charles H. Upham (1908–94) was New Zealand's outstanding World War II soldier. He won the VC twice, for his gallantry on Crete in 1941 and for his heroism at Ruweisat Ridge in North Africa in 1942. Immobilized by his wounds, Upham was taken prisoner at Ruweisat and spent the rest of the war in prison camps. Only two other men in the history of the British Empire and Commonwealth won the VC twice, and Upham was the only combat soldier. Self-effacing, after the war he became a sheep farmer in north Canterbury.

TUIS

War was not quite all fighting. After deciding that the Cairo Club was 'dreadfully drab' with its all-male staff, General Freyberg, insisted that his troops should have a place with a civilian feel. So innovative New Zealand all-ranks Forces Clubs were established wherever troops arrived in large numbers. They were staffed by New Zealand female volunteers knows as 'Tuis'. (The Tui is a New Zealand honeyeater; of shiny blue-green plumage, it mimics.) Later they became part of the Women's Auxiliary Army Corps. The Rome Club for example occupied a de luxe hotel. Two days before New Zealanders arrived it had been a German Luftwaffe hotel. The Italian hotel staff just took a day's rest and then switched instantly to the Allied side! Göring, the gross, drug-addicted Nazi air chief, had occupied a suite with two enormous double beds and a colossal marbled bathroom. Now it was used by Tuis.

Tuis served in the canteen, and created a homely, welcoming atmosphere. They gave personal attention and psychic comfort when exhausted or homesick troops needed a sympathetic listener. Sometimes this attention was more traumatic. One Tui recalls visiting a dying young New Zealander: 'We sat with this boy, he just, you know, held on to us. We knew he was dying, he knew he was dying, but somehow it helped him to think he was holding on to two New Zealand girls.'

NEW ZEALAND AND THE PACIFIC WAR

In December 1941 the Japanese bombed the United States naval base at Pearl Harbor in the Hawaiian Islands and the USA was drawn into the war. Immense and righteous anger was the response, which increased when the Japanese soon after captured the American-controlled Philippines, much of New Guinea and other Melanesian islands. The Japanese aim was to cut communication lines between the Allies, the USA on one side of the Pacific and New Zealand and Australia on the other; to form a boundary for the southern flank of their Empire; and to make possible the conquest of New Zealand, and Australia should that be deemed desirable.

With the fall of British Malaya and the naval base at Singapore, with Britain's own fight for survival, and her navy needed in the Atlantic, Britain could no longer guarantee to protect New Zealand from Japanese invasion. Early in 1942 when New Zealand's crack troops were needed in North Africa, the New Zealand government looked to the USA for protection and agreed to a United States proposal that it be defended by an American division. In 1942 a series of US and Australian sea and land victories halted Japanese expansion and secured New Zealand safety.

From August 1942 about 20,000 troops made up a third New Zealand Division for the Pacific. Under the command of Masterton-born Major-General (later Sir) Harold Barrowclough (1894–1972), one of New Zealand's most illustrious citizen-soldiers, they were supported by the 15,000 men of the Royal New Zealand Airforce (established 1937) and 5,000 of the Royal New Zealand Navy (formed 1941). The Division fought in three successful amphibious assaults in the western Solomon Islands, of Vella Lavella, Treasury Islands, and Green Islands. Significant numbers fell ill from debilitating tropical diseases. Fortunately new medical techniques such as use of penicillin and Atabrin tablets saved many lives. It was better not to be taken prisoner by the Japanese. As with other Allied prisoners of war, New Zealanders suffered disease, starvation, and torture.

THE HOME FRONT

During the first few years of the war New Zealand was defended by a poorly equipped Home Guard of about 123,000 men, elderly, unfit, too young, or men who worked in key industrial and farming occupations. The 1000 or so conscientious objectors received little sympathy from the government, most being interned.

Between 1942 and 1944 the presence of the US troops was both comforting and curious. American manners, accents and military incomes were a revelation. To meet the needs of the newcomers milk bars and coffee shops were opened, a vigorous nightlife developed in Auckland and Wellington, and providers of recreational fare, restaurant owners, florists, taxi drivers, hotel keepers, and jewellers prospered.

The Americans' smart uniforms and free-spending overwhelmed many New Zealand women, and caused much anguish amongst New Zealand troops fighting half a world away. Though most relationships were transient, unwanted pregnancies occurred, and about 1,400 New Zealand women married Americans and, as 'war brides', departed after the war to live in the United States. Unsurprisingly, there were occasional brawls between American and New Zealand servicemen, such as the so-called 'Battle of Manners Street' in Wellington – mostly brutally crushed by military police.

The heavy industry begun with the railway workshops of the 1870s had further developed in the following decades. During World War II it produced armaments, munitions, and small ships.

With so many men fighting, women had to do their jobs: from sawmilling, to driving buses and trucks, to working in machine shops; more than 2,000 laboured as 'land girls' on farms. Nearly 9,000 such as the Tuis joined the women's army, navy, and air force auxiliary armed forces. All kinds of voluntary organizations complemented government effort. To boost supplies going to Britain, food rationing was introduced.

One of the values agreed upon by the Western leaders, Britain's Winston Churchill and America's Franklin Roosevelt (1882–1945) early in the war, was that they were fighting for democracy. There was a different kind of fight for democracy at the University of Canterbury in Christchurch. The Austrian philosopher, Karl Popper (1902–94) who fled his homeland before the Nazis took control, taught there from 1937 to 1945. During that time Popper produced perhaps the two greatest books ever to come out of New Zealand, *The Poverty of Historicism* and the two-volume, *The Open Society and its Enemies*. He wrote them from 1938 to 1943, first while war was looming and then when Germany and Japan were capturing Europe and South East Asia, and the outcome looked bleak indeed for democracy. Popper explains the illusory attraction of totalitarian ideas of right and left, in particular the thoughts of Plato, Hegel, and Marx. He points to the self-defeating nature of suppressing criticism, and the logical impossibility of developing a *science of history* as claimed by Nazis and Marxists. He argues instead for liberty in its widest sense, and the establishment and defence of political institutions which will minimize the inevitable errors of all rulers – those of an open society.

Japan of the late 1930s and 1940s was the opposite of an open society. The Japanese belief in the values of their closed society was demonstrated when 800 well-treated Japanese prisoners of war attempted a mass escape from their camp in the Wairarapa Valley near Wellington in February 1943, and 40 had to be shot dead and 80 wounded.

END OF WAR AND OCCUPATION OF JAPAN

The war against Hitler ended in May 1945, but that against the tenacious Japanese continued. Plans were prepared for a massive invasion of the Japanese homeland. Suddenly everything ended when the newly developed atomic bombs were dropped on Hiroshima and Nagasaki. Some 11,600 New Zealanders had died in the war, and 15,700 were wounded.

Under the command of General Douglas MacArthur, Japan was occupied by the Americans and a smaller British Commonwealth Occupation Force. This included about 12,000 New Zealanders (Jayforce), volunteers from the Italian campaign and others brought from New Zealand, together with Australian, British, and Indian troops. The New Zealanders were allocated the most south-westerly region of the main island of Honshu, with early work on demilitarization and demobilization. They landed in February 1946 and most had departed by the end of 1948.

CHAPTER ELEVEN

Prosperous South Pacific Nation: New Zealand 1945 to 1980s

Economic and Political Developments

After the war, the Labour government of Fraser wished to avoid an economic slump and to regulate the postwar boom. To do so it made some wartime powers permanent, e.g., in 1948 it passed the Economic Stabilization Act. It also wished to continue supplying food to Clement Attlee's Labour-governed Britain, now struggling to recuperate from the economically disastrous war – which was a noble aim. But many New Zealanders, anxious to get on with their peacetime lives, were dissatisfied at the resulting shortages, and in the 1946 General Election Labour clung to office only through the support of the MPs in the four Maori electorates.

Fraser and Nash had been prematurely aged by the war. In contrast, though he had fought in World War I, Sidney Holland (1893–1961), leader of the opposition National Party, appeared youthful, energetic, and full of ideas. He had been the main force in reconstructing the party out of the moribund United and Reform Parties. Holland learned much from the dynamic R.G. Menzies, his Australian equivalent. They were both strong royalists and democrats, convinced of the moderating role of the British Empire, pro-American, and deeply disturbed by the increasingly aggressive stance of the Soviet Union under Communist dictator Joseph Stalin (1879–1953). In fact both would win power within a few weeks of each other in 1949.

The war had made New Zealanders a little more nationalistic. In 1947 the Statute of Westminster was finally ratified by the New

Zealand parliament. In 1953 to regularize constitutional arrangements, the New Zealand parliament passed an act making Queen Elizabeth II formally and explicitly Queen of New Zealand.

THE NATIONAL PARTY GOVERNMENT, THE NZWWU AND THE 151-DAY WHARF STRIKE

Despite the temporary controls, compared with Britain and Europe, which took years to recover from wartime devastation, New Zealand, its homeland untouched by the war, was prosperous and had one of the world's highest standards of living.

When regulations were removed, price rises kept somewhat ahead of increases in wages awarded by the Arbitration Court, and though standards were still high, unions began to complain and strike.

As in Massey's time thirty years earlier, most of the trouble was on the wharves. Led by their militant president Harold (Jock) Barnes and secretary Toby Hill (1915–77) during the years 1946 to 1949, the New Zealand Waterside Workers Union (NZWWU) organized sudden stop-work meetings, bans on working overtime, 'go-slows', and numerous strikes, creating problems for the government out of all proportion to its size.

Some NZWWU members belonged to the Communist Party, dedicated to the destruction of free enterprise capitalist economies, and the NZWWU belonged to the Moscow-based, Communist-front World Federation of Trades Unions. Such facts worried Labour Government leaders. Bob Semple, former organizer of the UFL and opponent of military conscription, but now Fraser's Minister of Defence, called Barnes 'a wrecker ... ambitious for personal power ... a real threat to the industrial peace and general welfare of the people'. Meanwhile Holland's National Party opposition had seized the political initiative, decrying the strikes and Communist influence in the unions, and promising to curb the NZWWU. They were also able to point to the bellicose acts of the USSR internationally. In the 1949 election National defeated Labour by 46 seats to 34.

During its first year the National Party government was ultra-conciliatory. Even the Labour Party opposition complained that the government was making too many concessions to the NZWWU! In October, Barnes, now supremely confident, overreached with new demands, and refused to cooperate with a Royal Commission convened to consider waterfront conditions, claiming the terms of reference were too narrow. After some months of convoluted negotiations stalemate ensued. By this time the NZWWU had lost the support of other unions, the farmers were angry at lost exports, the general public were frustrated, and the press published furious editorials demanding the waterside workers be controlled.

The Holland government was patient no longer, and after the NZWWU again struck, in February 1951 implemented the powerful 1932 Public Safety Conservation Act. A state of emergency was declared, the strike was made illegal, and the NZWWU was deregistered and new waterside working unions were registered by the Arbitration Court. The NZWWU finally capitulated after 151 days on 11 July. Strikes had been endemic for seven years and this last one, the worst strike in New Zealand's history, had lost the nation 1,100,000 working days and cost the economy dearly. The 'big blue', as New Zealanders often called it ('blue' meaning fight/squabble), cast a long political shadow. It strengthened people's will to oppose Communism, and may have helped keep National the leading political party for the next forty years.

GOOD TIMES

Holland took advantage of the general frustration by calling an early election at which the Nationals again triumphed, defeating the Labour Party by 50 seats to 30. For the next thirty-four years, in domestic politics both Nationals and Labour tried to keep to the political middle ground. Until the 1970s, when overseas events added new political complexities, the two parties also shared much common ideology in international politics.

By the early 1950s Britain and Europe had largely recovered, Britain was paying record prices for New Zealand produce, and the prosperity continued. The unions now more moderate, there was nothing to sabotage economic prosperity and the 1950s and 1960s were good years for almost all New Zealanders.

As a sign of the times, in 1951 the New Zealand airline, Tasman Empire Airways Limited (TEAL), predecessor of Air New Zealand, began its legendary 'Coral Route' from New Zealand to Fiji, the Cook Islands, and Tahiti, by Solent seaplane. One of its advertisements read: 'Only 6½ hours [from Auckland] by TEAL Solent to restful Fiji! A short [!] flight in a fast, luxuriously appointed flying boat and there you are.' Fiji to the Cook Islands, and from there to Tahiti, each took a day's flying time. This was then Tahiti's only air link to the outside world.

In 1953 Edmund Hillary (1919–) and the Sherpa, Tensing Norgay (1914–86), became the first men to climb the world's highest peak, Mt Everest in the Himalayas. The whole country bathed in the warm glow of this massive achievement, and the pride felt by the rest of the British Empire and Commonwealth. Until that day Everest had been a last frontier, equivalent to the moon. It is difficult to describe its significance to post-1953 generations. Seventeen well-equipped expeditions straddling fifty years had tried to climb it and all had failed, with many deaths, so for a New Zealander to do this was something glorious. Heightening the intensity was the dramatic announcement of the achievement on the very morning that Queen Elizabeth II was being crowned in Westminster Abbey. Juxtaposed, the two events seemed to hail a new Elizabethan Age for New Zealand and the British Commonwealth.

Hillary became a New Zealand icon – *the* New Zealand icon. He is the only living person on the country's banknotes. He opens parks in tandem with governors-general. He epitomizes what 'Kiwis' value: a pioneer, leanness, fitness and good health, a knight (in 1954) but still a man of the people, gentlemanly with a mischievous streak, modest, adventurous, courageous, practical, and a model family man.

It was in the later 1950s and the 1960s that Hillary went on to other great achievements. He had humbled bush, snow, and mountains, and now he would humble the Antarctic ice cap. During the same decades there were stable New Zealand governments and stable but developing international relationships with other non-Communist powers, especially the USA, as we shall now see.

Foreign Policy

UNITED NATIONS AND OTHER INTERNATIONAL BODIES

The New Zealand Labour government had enthusiastically supported
the establishment of the United Nations. It believed that this would be
an international forum in which small countries such as New Zealand
would have a larger voice. It therefore opposed the move to give the
'Big Five', USA, Britain, France, China, and the USSR, a veto over
UN initiatives with which they disagreed. The New Zealand fear of
the veto proved prophetic. In the immediate post-war years the Labour
government was disillusioned by the uncooperative Soviet attitude in
the UN as exemplified in its relentless use of the veto.

One development which affected New Zealand was the change
from League 'mandates' to UN 'trust territories'. The principle of
national self-determination still applied, but the UN Trusteeship
Council was more active in pushing countries like New Zealand to
accelerate independence. Post-war relationships between New
Zealand and the Trust Territory of Western Samoa were generally
harmonious, and independence was achieved in 1962.

In 1950 the foreign ministers of the British Commonwealth countries met in Colombo, Ceylon (Sri Lanka). There emerged the six-year
Colombo Plan of self-help and foreign aid to raise the standards of
living of peoples in all the South-East Asian countries. New Zealand
contributed £1,000,000 a year and provided technical training.

Increasingly aware of its geographical position, New Zealand also
sponsored the South Pacific Commission, first proposed during the war
as an organization of colonial government. Established in 1947, it
undertook research projects related to Pacific island countries but had
little power.

REACTIONS TO COMMUNIST EXPANSION

The Fraser Labour government noted how the USSR's masterly
manoeuvring succeeded in installing Communist governments
throughout Eastern Europe, which, except for Tito's Yugoslavia, took
their orders from Moscow. It saw how East Germans were 'voting with

their feet' by fleeing in hundreds of thousands to West Germany, and how Stalin had tried in 1948 to blockade the West into submission over West Berlin.

For such reasons, in the developing Cold War as it became known, the New Zealand government strongly supported Britain, USA and other Western democracies. So concerned was the New Zealand government at the world situation that in 1948 Fraser, who had gone to jail for opposing conscription (the draft) in World War I, now introduced it in peacetime. Recognizing Britain's limits, and remembering the might of the USA in repulsing Japan, the Labour government sought more tangible ways of allying itself with the USA. With that policy Holland's National Party strongly agreed.

THE KOREAN WAR

In June 1950, secretly supported by Stalin, North Korea invaded South Korea. For reasons that are unclear, the USSR boycotted the UN Security Council, so without Soviet veto, a resolution was passed calling on member countries to support the South. The USA would provide most of that support but other Western nations such as New Zealand, Britain, and Australia contributed contingents. The New Zealand response seems to have been for two reasons. New Zealanders believed that Communist expansion needed rebuffing. They also understood that in an Asian-Pacific world newly dominated by the Soviet and Chinese Communist giants, their own security lay squarely under US protection. To support the United Nations and the Americans in Korea was therefore sound international politics. There was almost no opposition within New Zealand to such involvement. In a four-year period nearly 4,000 troops fought in Korea, all volunteers, with 112 casualties, including 33 killed.

Because of the Korean War the USA became anxious to conclude a peace treaty with Japan to ensure her alignment with the non-Communist West. But New Zealand and Australia were fearful of Japanese resurgence and refused to sign a peace treaty without some kind of United States guarantee of security. At the point when an overwhelming United Nations victory in Korea looked clear, the sudden successful Chinese intervention in December 1950 induced a special urgency into all these issues.

THE ANZUS PACT

The new relationship was formalized in the signing by the Holland government in San Francisco in September 1951, mid-way through the Korean War, of what became known as the ANZUS Treaty (**A**ustralia, **N**ew **Z**ealand, **U**nited **S**tates). The main provision of ANZUS was that the three countries would consult if their territories, island territories, armed forces, ships, or planes were attacked 'in the Pacific area'. Such an attack would be treated by each country as 'dangerous to its own peace and safety'. As such, ANZUS was weaker than the NATO agreement that an attack on one was an attack on all. Also unlike NATO, no treaty organization was established, but joint military exercises were held at regular intervals, and ANZUS was envisaged as applying indefinitely. Most helpful was the regular military, diplomatic, and cabinet contact which resulted, something unthinkable as recently as 1950. ANZUS would remain the bedrock of New Zealand foreign policy until 1985. This was the first time New Zealand had joined any international organization without British membership and was politically a fore-runner of the slow dissolution over the coming decades of formal New Zealand–British political and economic ties. In the same week New Zealand signed the peace treaty with Japan.

SEATO

As part of the general commitment to forward defence in South East Asia, New Zealand also became a founding member of the South East Asia Treaty Organization (SEATO) in 1954, which included Britain, Australia, France, Thailand, Pakistan, the Philippines, and the USA, and had its headquarters in Bangkok. The Treaty was part of the broad Western effort to contain the spread of Communism. The pact, which required unanimous agreement if a common danger within the area were to be met by military response, was never really effective, for the signatories drew different interpretations of their commitments. Its last joint military exercise was in 1975 and SEATO dissolved in 1977, actually a long time for an international treaty.

MALAYA AND INDONESIA

Alongside other British Commonwealth troops (including Fijians), New Zealand helped in the Malayan Emergency (1949–60), fighting against a Communist insurgency. This was a response to an attempt by the Malayan Communist Party (mostly Malayan Chinese) to over-throw the British colonial administration, despite or because of the British intention to give Malaya independence. New Zealand forces first became involved in 1949 and more directly so after 1955. From 1954 the guerrillas were increasingly on the defensive. To the fasci-nation of rural Malayans, there was a New Zealand battalion concert party, which performed hakas. Malaya provided the chance to develop the skills of jungle warfare, which proved to be the basis of later, effective New Zealand action in Indonesia and Vietnam. Defeat of the Malayan Communists was also history's first successful elimination of Communist guerrillas.

Then in 1963 Indonesia's intransigent president Achmed Sukarno (1901–70) began what he called *Konfrontasi* (Confrontation). As part of its withdrawal from empire in Asia, Britain had announced plans to federate Malaya (which then included Singapore) and the several British territories in Borneo which shared a 1,000-mile (1,600k) boundary with Indonesia, to form the new state of Malaysia, a popular conception in the countries involved. Sukarno seems to have seen an attack on this idea as a way of distracting the public from the appalling state of his own economy, and preventing the formation of a new and powerful Islamic rival in the region. He threatened Malaya and sent infiltrators across the border in Borneo and saboteurs into Singapore. Though they saw this as unjustified aggression against another Commonwealth country, New Zealanders were reluctant to become involved because of potential long-term antipathies. Eventually responding to British and Com-monwealth pressure New Zealand did send planes, an SAS detachment, and minesweepers to patrol the Malacca Straits. A coup in Indonesia heralded a power change, Sukarno was sidelined, and Indonesia quietly abandoned Confrontation. Malaysia and Indonesia signed a peace treaty in 1966. Though New Zealanders inflicted substantial losses on the enemy, they suffered no fatalities.

THE VIETNAM WAR AND ITS POLITICAL EFFECTS

The collapse of the European empires in South East Asia during and after World War II caused great instability. As part of this, Vietnam was divided into a Communist-controlled North and an anti-Communist South. During the 1960s the USA became involved in a civil war between the South Vietnamese government and Communist guerrillas (Vietcong) who wished to establish Communism in the South. The guerrillas were supported increasingly by the regular North Vietnamese army, and both were supplied by the USSR. The war was New Zealand's longest and most controversial military engagement of the twentieth century.

In 1964 New Zealand had sent a non-combatant engineering team and medical unit to help the South, and in response to US overtures in May 1965 combat troops were despatched in the form of an artillery battery linked to the Australian infantry already in Vietnam. In 1968 SAS troops were deployed. Holyoake's National government was always reticent about this involvement so kept the contribution small, and confined to volunteers. The New Zealanders operated in conjunction with the larger Australian forces. Perhaps the most famous engagement was the support by New Zealand gunners for the Australian infantry which gained a spectacular victory against great odds at the Battle of Long Tan (1966). About 3,500 men served, either regular army or volunteers, with no more than 550 involved at a time. Casualties were somewhat larger than in Korea: 222 with 35 dead.

This limited involvement was still sufficient to provoke a massive negative reaction at home. Knowledge of the bloodletting in Vietnam and of growing protests in the USA came directly into New Zealand sitting rooms via television, and had repercussions in anti-war demonstrations. The country became emotionally polarized, and the traditional two-party agreement on foreign policy dissolved. The main opponents of the war were young, educated, middle class, affluent. The supporters tended to be older. For the first time, large protest marches became a *recurring* feature of the New Zealand political scene. Such opposition unsettled the National government, and its small commitment became even smaller. Prime Minister Holyoake and his cabinet however rejected the criticisms of the anti-war movement. They strongly defended the help they were giving to a small country under Communist threat, and their policy of forward defence in alliance with the United States. The National Party was twice victorious at the polls during this Vietnam period, though Labour under Norman Kirk (1923–74) was elected in 1972. By this time the US was itself withdrawing from the war, and the Kirk Labour government then brought the few remaining troops home. The overwhelming consensus of twenty years earlier of a special relationship with the USA no longer existed, and the war had set in motion further fundamental changes in the country's foreign policy.

In 1971 New Zealand had become party to a five-power defence arrangement (with Britain, Australia, Malaysia, and Singapore) to protect Commonwealth countries in the region. Under evolving arrangements, New Zealand forces carried out exercises with those of the other nations into the 1990s, by which time the original Communist threat no longer existed.

New 'Solutions' in a New World Order

In an extraordinary period of about twenty years from the early 1970s New Zealand passed through several of the most radical political and social changes in its history.

By 1973 New Zealand was prosperous, partly based on a temporary boom in world prices for agriculture. Immigration from the Pacific Islands and Britain was increasing. Cook Islanders and Niuean immigrants, because of the special political arrangements had evolved that were also New Zealand citizens. But ethnic tensions were aroused by Samoans (the main source) and Tongans, non-citizens, who preferred New Zealand to their tiny islands and overstayed their visas and work-permits. Though the government was within its rights in deporting many of these people, they felt it unfair. In Auckland, gangs of Maori and Pacific Islanders developed, and brawled with one another.

The New Zealand dollar was revalued. Then owing to a cartel organized by Arab producers the price of oil suddenly quadrupled. The previous large positive balance of trade became a huge deficit. A Liquid fuels Trust Board was formed to consider fuel options. And as in other Western democracies, New Zealand now began to experience an unexpected economic condition called 'stagflation', namely, stagnant economic growth accompanied by increasing unemployment and rising inflation.

These developments had been unanticipated in the prosperous 1960s, when government confidence had been demonstrated in the planning and construction of the new town of Porirua, on the west coast just north of Wellington, the largest 'new town' ever developed in the country. From 1961 and into the mid-1970s Porirua grew rapidly.

To avoid inflation, the Labour government resorted to massive overseas borrowing and all kinds of local regulations. It tried a scheme to fix maximum retail prices. To keep people in work it added wool, mutton, lamb, milk, the railways and the post office to the already large number of industrial subsidies. New Zealand industries were the most subsidized of all the Western capitalist democracies, and New Zealand became probably the most economically regulated country outside the Communist bloc.

Kirk died and was replaced by Wallace (Bill) Rowling (1927–95), who produced a complex superannuation scheme for all citizens. But the opposition under Robert Muldoon (1921–92) promised to intro-duce a scheme which proved much more attractive to voters (and more problematic to pay for), and at the 1975 election Muldoon's Nationals regained office.

NATIONAL ADOPTS LABOUR PARTY ECONOMIC IDEOLOGY: A SURPLUS OF SUBSIDIES

The fact that for much of the time he was also his own Minister of Finance made Robert Muldoon one of the most powerful prime ministers ever, his only historical rivals being Seddon and Fraser. Raised in poverty by his mother in the Depression, he possessed the sort of personality that produces adulation in supporters and deepest antipathy in opponents. His foreign policy was based on membership of the British Commonwealth and adherence to the US alliance, ANZUS, and SEATO, though the latter ended soon after he took office.

Robert Muldoon: Prime Minister and Minister of Finance from 1975–84

The ethnic conflicts had been distractions from the key issue of the economy. The late 1970s witnessed very high rates of inflation, and New Zealand began to slide down the scale of the most wealthy nations per capita. Many professional and skilled people migrated to Australia and elsewhere, which was a serious loss.

Though there had existed a Labour–National welfare state consensus since the later 1930s, the National Party had always regarded itself as the party of free enterprise, even if often more in rhetoric than reality. But Muldoon entirely ignored such traditions and produced greater peacetime control than any government before or since. Millions of dollars went to subsidize farmers, who increased their production of mutton and lamb, much of which then became unsaleable and had to be changed into fertilizer. Employing powers awarded in the 1948 Economic Stabilization Act, in 1982 there was a 'wage and price freeze', which allowed the government to regulate rent, the fees paid directors, and dividends to shareholders. The second world oil crisis in 1979 following the fundamentalist Muslim takeover in Iran raised inflation and import prices. As a positive response to New Zealand's economic problems the Muldoon cabinet developed a policy called 'Think Big'.

THINK BIG: PETROCHEMICALS, STEEL, ALUMINIUM

One result was the development of power sources previously rejected as unviable, and a new petrochemical industry grew up. There were natural gases, ethane, propane, and butane, in Taranaki in the Kapuni field south of Mt Egmont/Taranaki and the off-shore Maui Field to the south-west (only discovered in 1969). Given economic need, it was known that these gases could be turned into petroleum (gasoline).

The oil crisis created the need. When construction of the Motunui synthetic fuel plant, just north of New Plymouth, began, 85 per cent of New Zealand petroleum came from imports, but the plant would reduce this to 50 per cent. In 1980 the government reached agreement with petroleum companies to build the plant and in 1982 the New Zealand Synthetic Fuels Corporation (later Petrocorp) was established, 75 per cent state owned.

Many units of the plant were prefabricated in Japan, shipped to New Plymouth and moved by road to Motunui. Some of these units weighed 650 tons (588 tonnes), fifteen times the maximum weight allowed on the road! Part of the road had to be reconstructed to take the weight, and money was budgeted to repair any parts of the remainder of the road which were damaged.

The plant was constructed to the latest environmental standards, with special attention to noise reduction and recent developments in resisting earthquakes. It was the world's first large-scale use of the zeolite process to produce petroleum. In two stages the plant first reduced the gas to methanol, and then the methanol to petroleum. Ten years later, when world oil prices were low, production was ended.

'Think Big' included expansion of the New Zealand Steel Mill at

Glenbrook, 40 miles (65k) south of Auckland, which, in a unique process, makes steel from local black iron sand first noticed in 1769 by Captain Cook. There were also complex plans to further develop near Bluff, on the southern tip of South Island, a large aluminium-producing industry based upon the hydro-electric power of the Lake Manipouri power scheme. (In 1996 there was a major upgrading of the smelter.) Such developments, despite their achievements, were enormously expensive, and there were rumblings of discontent in the National Party. New political parties began challenging 'Think Big', and ate away at National's support.

A considerable economic coup was a free-trade agreement with Australia in 1983. But when Muldoon lost his tiny parliamentary majority after a National MP voted against his government over visits by nuclear-powered ships, he called a sudden election. To his surprise, with votes captured by the new small parties, National lost to Labour 37 to 56.

THINK LATERALLY: TRANQUILLIZER GUNS, SPACE ROCKETS

As we have seen, New Zealanders were 'thinking laterally' and displaying enterprise long before the term 'think big' was used by the government, for they are 'do it yourself professionals'. Since World War II the private sector has continued to develop an enormous range of inventions, many of them economically significant. Let us consider a few of the most ingenious.

There is the tranquillizer gun of Timaru's Colin Murdoch (1929–), used by game wardens, farmers, and zoologists around the world. A pharmacist who owned a veterinary practice and had repaired all sorts of guns during World War II, Murdoch combined the perfect background experience. He travelled the world testing his tranquillizer-charged dart guns, which are now exported from his Timaru factory to more than 150 countries. Murdoch also invented the disposable, sterile, plastic medical syringe, and a host of other helpful products such as medicine bottle lids which are child-proof.

The electric fence does the opposite of tranquillizing, but is equally effective for its purpose. This brainchild of Waikato farmer Bill

Gallagher developed in a rudimentary form in the late 1930s from an electric triggering device which sent a shock through the family car when the farm's horses scratched themselves on it! By the early twenty-first century Gallagher's group had over 100 worldwide patents and their fences surrounded sheep and cattle, and around the world, antelope, kangaroos, and zebras.

Then there are the sector navigation lights designed by optical physicist Norman Rumsey who worked at the Department of Scientific and Industrial Research (DSIR). In many parts of the world sector lights have replaced the old system of two harbour lights, one behind and placed higher than the other, which captains line up to guide their ships in. The idea developed from a problem at the harbour of Porirua, which as a growing new town was increasing its harbour traffic, and where harbour cliffs made the standard system impossible to apply. Rumsey created a modified light-focusing projector which sends forth three beams of colour, a narrow white beam in the middle, with a wider beam of green to the left and red to the right. As long as the captain sees only white light ahead he knows he is on course. The DSIR licensed the system to commercial companies and it is now a good export earner.

The most spectacular technological invention of our time has been the space programme, and a New Zealander born, bred and schooled was central to its achievements. William Pickering (1910–) was born in Wellington and attended Havelock Primary School near Nelson – which Rutherford also attended! After studying engineering in New Zealand he took a doctorate at CalTec, was unable to find employment in his homeland, returned to USA, and in an amazingly short time became director of the national Jet Propulsion Laboratory (JPL).

When NASA was established in 1958 Pickering and the JPL were given vast funds. He soon became a key figure in the massive American space achievements of the 1960s. The three high points were: the Mariner II expedition to Venus in 1963 and Ranger VII to Mars in 1965, Ranger VIII which photographed the moon's surface in 1966, and Apollo XI which placed Neil Armstrong (1930–) as the first man on the moon in 1969.

Less spectacular than Pickering's space vehicles, but more economically useful to New Zealand have been a multitude of other inventions such as: the electronic petrol/gasolene pump; the Waipuna non-chemical weed-control system (just water or biodegradable foams); the Barmac rock crusher; spreadable butter (i.e. without certain fatty acids/triglicerides which keep it hard in the refrigerator); the Baeyertz Tape, a simple non-technical method for accurately estimating when baby will be born; the Hamilton jet boat which reaches thrilling speeds in a few inches/centimetres of water – so popular with tourists to New Zealand. The list could continue for pages. And although some New Zealanders may not know it, computer software written by their own people earns the country as much in overseas currency as does the wine industry.

NEW ZEALAND WINES

Of the late nineteenth-century winemakers, the Hawkes Bay companies descended from H.S. Tiffin (1816–96) at Church Road and John Chambers (1819–93) at Te Mata are still producing commercially. Many of the early growers came from wine-making regions in Continental Europe, amongst whom Vidal in Hawkes Bay and also Corbans just west of Auckland have survived as large efficient modern companies.

In the early 1900s the government for the first time showed some (temporary) interest, with the appointment of a government viticulturist. But after 1908 it was government restrictions rather than encouragement that were the norm. In 1927 the Customs Department had allowed foreign brandy to be imported at reduced duties to fortify local wines, but the Health Department prosecuted the winemaker for the same action! Because of a compromise over prohibition in the 1893 Alcoholic Liquor Sale Control Act, some electoral districts were 'dry' (no alcohol), others 'wet'. Corban's winery was in a dry district. They set up a shop a matter of yards/metres away across the railway line in the adjacent wet district!

Licensing laws changed in the 1960s, allowing wine in restaurants and to be sold in shops, and in the next two decades Busby's 1830s hopes for a flourishing wine industry were at last fulfilled. Over a hundred wineries now produce more than 95 million pints (45 million litres) a year. New areas have been opened in Marlborough, Canterbury, and the Wairarapa. And in the last few years an area of microclimate, north-sloping, dry and warm, in the barren uplands of central Otago has proved excellent.

Sauvignon blancs, for which new Zealand's climate is ideal, were the first to gain an international reputation. Chardonnays also do well. The best reds come from Hawkes Bay, such as the Te Mata Estate revitalized in the 1980s, especially the cabernet sauvignons. There has also been rapid development in excellent sparkling wines, with liaisons being forged with leading French champagne houses.

The Arts

New Zealand population is large by Pacific Island but small by world standards, and its artistic culture reflects this fact. It has nevertheless produced a number of creative people of world rank. Since the 1940s the state has increasingly subsidized the arts. The Queen Elizabeth II Arts Council awards annual grants to theatre, music, modern dance, ballet, and opera, and the New Zealand Literary Fund subsidizes writers and publishers.

For its size New Zealand publishes a large number of novels. Since World War II literary themes have diverged. Janet Frame, born in Dunedin in 1924, is widely agreed to be New Zealand's outstanding novelist. Morbidly, her poverty-stricken childhood, the deaths of two sisters, and sessions in psychiatric wards provided content for her work. During her hospitalizations she compulsively read the classics and then began to write. Her three autobiographical works, *To the Is-land* (1982), *An Angel at my Table* (1984), and *The Envoy from Mirror City* (1987) are best known. Though her work is hardly uplifting, it is accomplished and has won international awards such as the Commonwealth Writers' Prize for fiction and Britain's leading Booker Prize.

Other novelists of note are Maurice Shadbolt (1932–), Maurice Gee, Witi Ihimaera (1944–) and Keri Hulme (1947–), the last two Maori. Frank Sargeson (1903–82) produced short stories, but the most admired short-story writer is Katherine Mansfield (1888–1923). In her tales, what happens to the characters takes second place to what is felt. Though she wrote mostly before World War I and as an expatriate,

Katherine Mansfield, New Zealand's most admired writer

Mansfield remains a perennial favourite for New Zealanders, and her work continues to sell and be studied as though she were a contemporary. Probably her best work was still to come when she died aged 34. Margaret Mahy is a top writer of children's stories. Dame Ngaio Marsh (1899–1982), who divided her time between London and Christchurch, and produced Shakespearean repertory theatre in the latter, was for decades one of the world's most popular writers of detective fiction.

In the 1950s and 1960s James K. Baxter (1926–72), regarded by some as New Zealand's greatest poet, more fully refined the New Zealand tradition first developed in the 1930s by Curnow and others.

In the 1970s and 1980s effective professional theatre companies were established, such as the Downstage in Wellington, and The Mercury Theatre in Auckland, and, later, the Fortune Theatre in Dunedin. But professional theatre has always struggled in New Zealand. The first local figure to inspire New Zealand biographical drama was the missionary Thomas Kendall, with plays by Sargeson and Bruce Mason (1921–82). More recently, Stuart Hoare wrote *Rutherford*, and in 2002 *The Face Maker* about Sir Archibald McIndoe, the surgeon who rebuilt the disfigured faces of RAF pilots.

Until the last decade or so, the best performing artists had to go overseas to blossom and be recognized. Oscar Natzke (1912–51), born in the King Country, spent his teenage years as a blacksmith's striker, in which job he developed a physique to match his deep bass voice. His scholarship to Trinity College in London launched him into an international career. Of his performance in *The Magic Flute* in 1947 the London *Daily Telegraph*'s critic wrote, 'Here is majesty; and the young who have heard him this season will remember him all their lives.' His short life is a good example of the possibility of upward social mobility in New Zealand. Natzke was the role model for later singers such as Inia Te Wiata, Donald McIntyre and Dame Kiri Te Kanawa (1944–), the most famous of all. The crystal-voiced Te Kanawa has performed opera across the world. She sang at the wedding of Prince Charles and Lady Diana Spencer, and at Queen Elizabeth II's Jubilee in 2002. Ballet dancers such as Rowena Jackson (1926–) also sought fame in Britain.

In the 1960s a booming 'art scene' emerged, begun by painters such as Colin McCahon (1919–87) and Don Binney, aided by the growth of private galleries and the country's general prosperity. Influenced by international movements, they used specifically New Zealand subjects.

A National Film Unit was established during World War II and in 1971 to encourage local film-makers the New Zealand Film Commission. It may be films which have achieved the greatest international interest. *Goodbye Pork Pie* (1980), about 'blokes' on the run, was the film which gave New Zealand film-makers the confidence to be themselves, earning acclaim at home and a profit overseas. Jane Campion's *The Piano* (1993) won at Cannes, and at the Hollywood Academy Awards with Oscars for child supporting-actress and screenplay, to New Zealand girl Anna Paquin (aged 9), and to Campion. That it had mostly New Zealand actors, a New Zealand male lead (Sam Neill) who was becoming Australian, and was an Australian-produced, French-financed, New Zealand expatriate's view of New Zealand, showed just how integrated the film world was becoming. It also showed that New Zealanders could now hold their own with the best.

The same year, Peter Jackson's (1961–) *Heavenly Creatures* was an artistic and commercial success at home and overseas. *Once were Warriors* (1994), based on Alan Duff's novel of harsh Maori urban life, achieved box office records in New Zealand, encouraged a cult following in Maori fashion, and was popular at foreign film festivals. But that which truly put New Zealand on the cinematic world map was the spectacular success of the American-financed films of J.R.R. Tolkien's *Lord of the Rings* trilogy beginning in 2001. Using New Zealand-made laser technology and directed and filmed in New Zealand by Peter Jackson, they benefited from a native son's masterly use of the country's magnificent scenery from Tongariro National Park to Fiordland, for which it was probably the best advertisement ever.

Sport

Playing and watching sports are however the main leisure activity for most of the population. Rugby football, as already mentioned, is still the most popular sport, both for players and spectators. In the 1970s and 1980s tensions were raised by the desire of the New Zealand Rugby Union to organize tours to and by South Africa, whose teams were selected racially. This involvement had repercussions first abroad and later at home. Because New Zealand's sporting contact with South Africa was interpreted as support for that country's Apartheid policy, New Zealand was widely criticized abroad, and the African nations boycotted the Montreal Olympics because New Zealand attended. New Zealanders saw this as rank hypocrisy by regimes many of which were themselves military or one-party dictatorships.

In 1981 the New Zealand government allowed a South African rugby tour of New Zealand. The result was huge street processions of anti-Apartheid 'Stop the Tour' demonstrators who tried to prevent the matches. The resulting antipathies between demonstrators and rugby supporters exceeded anything in the Vietnam years. The demonstrations succeeded, for this was the last South African rugby tour prior to the demise of Apartheid.

New Zealanders were happy to see Apartheid end and to be able to play the South Africans without controversy. For rugby is regarded as the national sport, and to have been an All Black is an honour hoped for by just about every New Zealand schoolboy. In recent years resident Pacific Islanders have begun to form, with Maoris, an increasingly larger part of national teams. Polynesian physiques seem specially suited to the game. The massive Jonah Lomu (1975–), ethnic Tongan, is the most famous player in recent decades, during which period rugby has been professionalized. There have also been changes in rugby's social class makeup and it is more working class than previously.

As a sign of the times and television influence, the main competition is no longer the formerly fanatically-fought-for inter-provincial Ranfurly Shield, but the Super 12, a new competition between the main New Zealand provinces, Australian states, and South African provinces. International matches, including the Rugby World Cup, which New Zealand was the first nation to win, are as popular as ever. Rugby League and Soccer also have enthusiastic followings. Cricket has come of age in recent decades, with New Zealand able to hold its own with the world-leading Australians. Basketball and hockey are popular with both sexes, and net-ball is easily the most important winter sport for women. Horse racing is a popular spectator sport. New Zealand has a fine history of competitive Athletics with 8 Olympic Gold Medals won.

New Zealanders have long been active yachtsmen, and recent decades have witnessed much dedicated support for the country's successful team in the America's Cup yacht race, based in Auckland.

In recent decades there has been a proliferation of water sports such as canoeing and white water rafting, and of locally invented 'sports' such as bungy jumping, paragliding, and adventure caving.

Pure Science since World War II

Though there is the technological development and the admirable scientific research of the DSIR, and though increasingly much fundamental research work goes on in the science departments of the universities, New Zealand's small population and economic resources have never been able to sustain a large scientific community. This has meant that even in the second half of the twentieth century many of the leading scientists have been forced, like Rutherford, to go overseas. Several have become world leaders in their fields.

The cosmologist Beatrice Tinsley (1941–81) was an outstanding student at New Plymouth Girls High School and Canterbury University, who went to Dallas in 1961. Though her Ph.D. in astronomy was extraordinary, she encountered prejudice against women scientists. Only during the last five years of her short life was she fully recognized. She produced new and profound ideas about the evolution of stars, galaxies, and the universe itself. She established that galaxies evolve more rapidly than hitherto suspected, provided convincing models of that evolution, and suggested what galaxies might look like in their infancy. Her fame is now worldwide, with several astronomical prizes named after her.

Maurice Wilkins (1916–) was born in the isolated hamlet of Pongaroa in the Wairarapa. Though his parents took him to England at age six, he always claimed to be a New Zealander. His X-ray crystallography images gave Francis Crick and James Watson the foundational clues in their successful search for the structure of DNA, the key biological discovery of the twentieth century and perhaps of all time. Wilkins and they all received the Nobel Prize in 1962.

Allan Wilson, the biological evolutionist (1936–91), was born in Ngaruawahia, took degrees from Otago University then went to the University of California at Berkeley, where he remained for the rest of his academic career and turned ideas of biological evolution upside down. He deduced that our earliest hominid ancestors evolved only five million years ago, about fifteen million years less than then accepted. Even more controversially, by further DNA analysis he produced the 'Out of Africa' Theory which argued that the first true human evolved in Africa around 270,000 years ago rather than millions of years ago.

Alan MacDiarmid (1927–) was awarded the Nobel Prize in 1999 for his and his colleagues 'discovery and development of electronically conductive polymers' – special kinds of plastics. Growing up in the Hutt Valley during the Depression and World War II, MacDiarmid acquired a large dose of work ethic. Working part-time he put himself through his BSc and MSc degrees at Wellington's Victoria University College. After gaining a PhD at Wisconsin he wanted to return to New Zealand, but fate took him to the Chemistry Department at the University of Pennsylvania where, ever-youthful, he has researched and taught on polymers to the present day. His continuing New Zealand contacts and vacations have resulted in work with colleagues at his *alma mater* in Wellington. Collaboration of this kind between expatriates and local New Zealand scientists is increasing.

While winemakers, writers, artists, playwrights, inventors and scientists were contributing to their country and the world, the political and economic culture of New Zealand was going through its own extraordinary changes. We have examined some of these in discussing 'Think Big', but even more radical changes in economic and foreign policy were to follow.

CHAPTER TWELVE

Radical Changes at Home and Abroad: New Zealand post-1980

New Foreign Policies

In the 1984 election there was more than just a change of parties, there was a generational change. Many of the new parliamentarians had no memory of the Great Depression or World War II, and had been active in the anti-Vietnam War demonstrations. The new Labour cabinet members were young, mostly in their forties, mostly professional, and contained few of the kind of trade union leader who had established the party and had been so significant in earlier Labour governments.

A NEW RELATIONSHIP WITH THE USA

Labour's campaign policy had expressed the intention to close New Zealand ports to all nuclear-powered or armed ships of all countries. In effect this meant US ships. In contrast, the rapidity of the election had allowed Labour to be vague about its economic intentions – as we shall see, a portentous omission.

The crisis broke soon after Labour took office, during the meeting in Wellington of the ANZUS Council. President Reagan's (1911–) US Secretary of State, George Schultz, and Australia's Foreign Minister, Bill Hayden (1933–) discussed defence policy with David Lange (1942–), the new prime minister. It was pointed out that unless American vessels could enter New Zealand ports the ANZUS Treaty was meaningless. Now Schultz's irresistible force met the Lange's immovable object. For security reasons the United States refused to say whether or not its ships were nuclear, and Lange said his government would refuse to allow them in unless it was clear they were not. After thirty-one years as a bulwark of New Zealand foreign policy ANZUS was nearing its end.

The Labour-led parliament passed a Nuclear Free Zone Control Act in 1987, which banned nuclear-powered and/or armed ships. The government also signed a South Pacific Nuclear Free Zone Treaty in November 1986, as did most South Pacific island states, although not French Polynesia, of course, because the French were still carrying out atomic tests there. Though these actions was seen by many New Zealanders as a sort of 'declaration of independence' there were serious repercussions. Threats of trade sanctions were made by United States congressmen over the nuclear ban, but more crucial, the United States government announced that New Zealand membership of ANZUS was ended.

Servicemen stationed in Singapore under the Commonwealth Five Power Agreement were withdrawn, though joint exercises were continued. For the first time since World War II there were no New Zealand troops abroad except some UN observers in the Middle East.

New Zealand now looked to the South Pacific as its special concern, a region where it already had responsibilities for the Cook Islands, Niue, and Tokelau. A 'Ready Reaction Force' was developed to respond to acts of terrorism or hijackings. In 1997 and 1999 the Royal New Zealand Navy acquired two fast new Anzac Class modular-structure frigates built in Melbourne, part of an agreement for co-ordinated defence arrangements with Australia (the Australian navy bought eight). The frigate deal involved large-scale New Zealand private enterprise. More than 400 New Zealand companies won contracts to work on the ships' construction. In some cases this led to orders for similar equipment for projects elsewhere. One company won contracts for its filter systems for ships being constructed in Hong Kong, Kuwait, and Britain.

ANTIPATHY FOR FRANCE

Meanwhile the nuclear story took another turn. From 1972 on, New Zealand had protested at the United Nations and to the French government over continuing above-ground atomic tests at Mururoa

Atoll on the southern tip of the Tuamotus in French Polynesia. Her protests were joined by those of Australia, and the countries of the South Pacific Forum, for fall-out was carried by the prevailing winds across most of them. Eventually the French agreed to end above-ground tests. They then sank vast shafts into the atoll's base to continue conducting tests underground from 1975 on, though they were galled by the continuing protests.

Many members of government and many other New Zealanders were strong supporters of the private environmental organization, Greenpeace, founded by David McTaggart (1933–2001). Greenpeace had sent a protest vessel into the test area and was about to do so again with the *Rainbow Warrior*. In July 1985, docked in Auckland Harbour it was sunk by explosives. A photographer was killed. Within days, Dominique Prieur and Alain Mafart, two French secret service agents in New Zealand, were arrested for this act of terrorism. At first the French government denied everything. In fact the attack followed the

The sinking of Greenpeace's *Rainbow Warrior* in Auckland Harbour by French agents in 1985

explicit orders of the President of France, François Mitterand (1916–96). Prieur and Mafart were sentenced to ten years' gaol for man-slaughter. The French pressured New Zealand to allow the two to serve their sentences in the French Tuamotus, but when this was granted soon reneged, and the terrorists returned to France and honour. Meanwhile Greenpeace received enormous free publicity and support across the world, and New Zealand–French relations were at an all-time low. When France resumed underground testing in 1995 to worldwide protest, New Zealand for a time ceased all diplomatic relations with that country.

New Domestic Policies

Lange was a lawyer, a large man with a wit to match. The deputy prime minister was another lawyer, Geoffrey Palmer and the finance minister was businessman Roger Douglas (1937–). In the next six years they would turn the New Zealand economy upside-down in a manner shocking to most traditional Labour supporters.

A CHANGING WORLD MARKET

The oil price rises of the 1970s and the entry of Britain into the European Economic Community (EEC/EU) in 1973 sent shockwaves through New Zealand. Britain, recognizing that New Zealand was a dependent small economy, forced her new economic partners to allow New Zealand some concessions, with special adjustments to its British Commonwealth preferential trade arrangements during a transition period. (Meetings between the New Zealand foreign minister and EU officials have occurred regularly since 1975.) New Zealand made the most of this extra time, working hard at diversifying her export markets. She increased exports of forest products, fish, horticultural produce, and temperate fruits, especially Kiwi fruit. Originally New Zealanders called the latter 'Chinese Gooseberry' but in USA that name was used for another fruit. The name was changed to 'melonette' – cute, but melons attract heavy US duty. Because the single word foreigners associated with New Zealand was 'Kiwi', the name became 'Kiwi fruit', and biological research improved its quality. Deer farming for venison and goat farming to produce mohair and in recent years, organic foods, also diversified New Zealand's exports.

The 'big four' of wool, meat, butter and cheese provided only half of exports by 1984, and only about 9 per cent of exports went to Britain (cf. over 80 per cent in the 1930s). Within a decade Australia, the USA, and Japan were all larger markets than Britain although New Zealand encountered agricultural protectionism in all three. But manufacturing had grown little and imports of manufactured goods were increasingly expensive. The standard of living and New Zealand's rank in the list of developed economies had fallen from number 4 in the 1950s to about number 20. 'Think Big', despite its achievements, had not halted this decline. The new government decided to move far and fast – very fast in the opposite direction.

LABOUR REJECTS ITS ECONOMIC IDEOLOGY: 'ROGERNOMICS'

Roger Douglas, bringing together ideas from the Treasury and from personal advisors and aware of monetarist theory and practice elsewhere, decided on a radically different kind of government. He introduced the 'Think Small' (though that was not the term used) of deregulation, privatization, and encouragement of free enterprise, and Lange allowed him the freedom to implement this conception.

Suddenly the statist principles of Seddon and Reeves's Liberals and Savage and Fraser's Labour Party were discarded and the period 1984 to 1987 witnessed a multitude of profound changes. Most democracies believe that upper houses act as a check upon extreme and untested legislation. But New Zealand had abolished its Legislative Council in 1950. This fact made both the radical interventionism of Muldoon and the radical deregulation of Lange–Douglas easy to implement.

Under what became known as 'Rogernomics' by friend and foe alike, one of the world's most controlled and rigid economies outside the Communist bloc became one of the most free. The financial market was deregulated. New banks were allowed. Early in 1985 the New Zealand dollar was floated. Controls were removed from transactions on foreign exchange. Income tax, amongst the world's highest, was slashed, and a Goods and Services Tax (GST) introduced. There had been nothing comparable to these tax changes since income tax was begun in 1891.

Consumers' electricity subsidies, subsidies to farmers, government incentives for exports, and import licences were all ended, and tariffs, state controls on marketing, and the number of employees in government organizations were radically reduced. State-owned, often subsidized enterprises in coal mining, electricity, forestry, and lands were changed into commercial state corporations and expected to run at a profit.

Business people were thrilled by Rogernomics. They had been both cosseted and constrained for fifty years, and now they were free. Investors were optimistic and in 1986 there was a stockmarket boom. Muldoon warned that prices were unrealistic, but was ignored. At the election in 1987 the Lange government was returned.

Then troubles began. As in other parts of the developed world there was a stockmarket crash in late 1987, especially severe in New Zealand. Companies large and small went bankrupt, but much inefficiency was also removed. Still unemployment continued to rise. Some economists, and many in the Labour Party, said it was time to end Rogernomics, which, with its disorienting change had caused much anguish, while the economy had not developed as expected. In response Douglas could point to a much lower rate of inflation, a budget surplus for the first time in more than twenty years, a declining trade deficit, and much-improved balance of payments. Enormous divisions appeared in the cabinet and in the party.

In a bitter replay of the Seddon–Reeves disagreement of ninety years before, Lange wanted to slow down while Douglas wanted to accelerate. Douglas wrote to Lange claiming that, 'New Zealand is now a country led by a government paralysed by your inability to work with me.' He was dismissed. In 1989 in less than a year the Labour Party caucus reinstated Douglas to the cabinet (but not to Finance) so Lange, his authority overruled and his health failing, immediately resigned. Geoffrey Palmer became prime minister. A new star was also in the ascendant, that of former political science academic, Helen Clark

(1950–) who became deputy prime minister, the first New Zealand woman in so high an office.

But the ghost of Rogernomics still haunted. Soon the Labour government sold Air New Zealand, the Development Finance Corporation, New Zealand Steel, Petrocorp, the Post Office Bank, and the Shipping Corporation. New Zealand education also changed. The Education Department reduced administrative staff from around 2500 to about 500. The century-old Education Boards were abolished, and elected Trustees in about 2,400 communities replaced school committees and took on many of the functions of the former Boards, e.g., in hiring, firing, and promotion.

It was a much trimmer, more efficient New Zealand economy which entered the 1990s.

Maori Renaissance and Waitangi Tribunal

The Te Maori exhibition held in Wellington in 1986 aroused great interest in Maori art. The exhibition was both a celebration of a new beginning and a lament for lost possibilities. It was part of a renaissance in Maori life and spirit that had begun slowly in the 1960s, and which government supported from the 1970s. From that decade onward, carving, plaiting and weaving had a resurgence, as a new generation, with government encouragement, became aware of its artistic traditions, and considered new ways of expressing *Maoritanga* (Maoriness). Since 1972, first at the spectacular Whakarewarewa thermal area in Rotorua, there has occurred the increasingly popular biennial Aotearoa Traditional Maori Performing Arts Festival. In the last decade some tribes have even developed morale through building and maintaining huge war canoes (waka).

For the first time there developed a distinct Maori approach to writing. In the 1970s the success of Witi Ihimaera with his short stories and novels encouraged others. The greatest international acknowledgement came with Keri Hulme's Booker Prize-winning novel *The Bone People*.

Paralleling the Maori literary rebirth in English, there was a movement to save the Maori language. In the last twenty years Maori language and culture have been given unprecedented exposure in the curriculum of all state schools and in special schools. Departments of Maori Studies were established in all universities. There were now radio stations broadcasting in Maori. Maori was for the first time made an equal official language with English. Government buildings and departments now listed their titles in both languages. There was increasing use of Maori words in place names (Mt Cook/Aoraki) even in the nation's name, Aotearoa-New Zealand. In some cases Maori superceded English. Thus the great new national museum in Wellington is colloquially known as 'Te Papa' rather than as 'Our Place' or the 'Museum of New Zealand'.

When World War II ended, about 88 per cent of Maori lived in the country areas; dramatically, by the early 1980s more than 80 per cent resided in towns and cities. Urbanization also brought social problems, as the Maori tried to adjust to a very different environment. As differences between Pakeha and Maori achievement and lifestyle widened, Maori radicals captured an audience more willing to listen and protest about their grievances than in the past. Body tattoos were more common. Since the 1990s and early third millennium, facial 'moko' have been adopted by some young Maori proud of their culture, using traditional motifs which tie them to their ancestors. An extreme had been reached in 1984 when Donna Awatere, a Maori psychologist and writer, called for the establishment of a separate Maori state.

Discontent focused overwhelmingly on loss of land, and the way in which the Treaty of Waitangi had been ignored. Through the combination of early European purchases, confiscation during and after the New Zealand Wars, the judgments of the Native Land Court, and continuing buying by the government to make farmland available to settlers, Maori tribal lands had shrunk from something like 66 million acres in 1840 (i.e., the whole country), to 7 million in 1911, to 2,995,000 acres (1,212,000 hectares) in 1975. At that point many Maori said no more land must be lost. (There was of course other *privately owned* Maori land.)

In 1975 protest was centred on a month-long, 696-mile (1120k) land march by hundreds of Maori and Pakeha supporters from near

Cape Reinga, the most northerly point, to Wellington. led by 80-year-old (later, Dame) Whina Cooper (1895–1994). Despite traditional Maori prejudice against women she had become a leading voice from the 1930s onwards. Activists began occupying selected sites and gaining maximum media coverage. In 1977 in a much-publicized action, for 17 months the Ngati Whatua occupied Bastion Point in Auckland, the last remnant of their Auckland lands, which had been taken for gun emplacements in World War II on the promise of being returned when not so used. Maori had reacted to a plan to sell it for luxury housing. Finally they won their case and today their marae occupies the site. Another high-profile and destructive occupation was Moutoa Gardens in Wanganui for months in 1995. In the same year the arson of famous Takahue School near Kaitaia harmed the Maori cause. From the 1970s, the New Zealand national day, Waitangi Day, previously a time for celebrating cultural togetherness became a time for protest by some sections of Maori.

THE WAITANGI TRIBUNAL AND RELATED ISSUES

A mighty achievement for the Maori was the Waitangi Tribunal, established in 1975 to consider Maori grievances relating to the application of the principles of the Treaty of Waitangi, but excluding issues and claims arising prior to 1975. After much debate and persistent Maori protest, in 1985 the Tribunal's authority was extended so it could make decisions and recommendations involving all years back to 1840. Claims were registered quickly, some 140 by 1987, all concerning longstanding grievances.

General Maori discontent grew from beliefs that between the end of the 1850s and the 1940s and despite the efforts of people like the Young Maori Party, Maori had been marginalized; that in losing their land they had lost their culture and their capacity to participate in modern society and the economy on equal terms; that the school system was unsympathetic to Maori special needs and aspirations; and that they had been consistently discriminated against by government departments, as in the 1890s government loans to European settlers but not to Maori, and pensions that favoured Europeans prior to World War II.

In the past Maori had been unable to argue for Treaty rights in legal cases because the Treaty was not included in acts of parliament. But in 1986, the courts began to set precedents which made it clear that the Treaty, after decades of neglect, had legal status in New Zealand particularly in cases of land and resources. The High Court, for instance, reversed a conviction of a Maori man for taking undersized shell-fish. The decision said he had a customary right to shell-fish which outweighed contemporary fishing regulations. In 1987 the Court of Appeal ruled that 'the principles of the Treaty of Waitangi override everything else in the State Owned Enterprises Act'. Many Maori saw such changes as a profound judicial breakthrough.

The Tribunal's proceedings have seemed snail-like to people unaware of the complex and time-consuming historical research which must go into adjudication of claims, and years can pass between the findings of the Tribunal and a final settlement by the government (accompanied by an apology) with claimants. A point often misunderstood is that the opportunity to air grievances and have them heard is, from a Maori point of view, itself crucial to the process of reconciliation.

Some members of the National government of James (Jim) Bolger (1935–), which took office in 1990, were sceptical of Maori Treaty claims, believed the Waitangi Tribunal encouraged new grievances rather than resolved old ones, and so wanted what they saw as a divisive business to be completed as rapidly as possible. They therefore established an alternative process, the Office of Treaty Settlements, for the government to conduct direct negotiations with tribes for reparations.

When the Treasury became alarmed at the size of awards being allocated, and recommended that there be a ceiling of a billion dollars over a decade, the government accepted this suggestion and put forward the concept of a 'fiscal envelope' of this amount. Foreign observers also thought some kind of statute of limitations seemed reasonable. But Maori, radical and moderate, rejected this suggestion, saying it had been decided unilaterally. While many Maori leaders acknowledged that there were limits to what New Zealand could afford, they claimed that an average $100 million a year over a ten-year period was derisory, and many awards would necessarily be small. The government withdrew the idea.

In 1996 the Whakatohea and Taranaki tribes were awarded $44 million and $135 million respectively. As Bolger's government feared, some settled claims have generated other discontents. The Taranaki settlement left nearly 300 Taranaki leasehold farmers angry at the inadequate government compensation they received for loss of their own livelihoods. Let us consider two cases in some detail, Ngai Tahu of South Island and Tainui of North Island.

NGAI TAHU

Ngai Tahu claims were of long standing, arising from government purchase of South Island in the 1850s in twelve main transactions for very small sums. Moreover, as time passed, government promises for reserves for hunting and gathering, and rights to resources such as greenstone were not honoured. As a result Ngai Tahu said they found themselves unable either to maintain their traditional way of life or to participate fully in the settler economy.

The Waitangi Tribunal reported on the main land claims in 1991, stating that the government had failed in its obligations, though not all claims were accepted. In 1998 the Ngai Tahu Claims Settlement Act passed through parliament with an award of money and property valued at $170 million.

Because they had always been a fishing people, Ngai Tahu also made a separate claim regarding fisheries, stating they had lost their customary fishing rights mentioned under Clause 2 of the Treaty of Waitangi. As part of a wider settlement of Maori fishing claims, the government recognized that the Waitangi Treaty had acknowledged Ngai Tahu rights to fishing around their former territory. Under the Treaty of Waitangi (Fisheries Claims) Settlement Act of 1992 (often called the Sealord deal) the government provided $150 million for Maori to purchase 50 per cent of Sealord Products, the country's largest fishing company with its 20 per cent of the government-determined com-mercial sea-fishing quota. The Sealord deal itself became contentious among Maori because North Island tribes believe Ngai Tahu received a disproportionately large share. (Maori were also guaranteed non-commercial, customary fishing rights.)

The shrewd and charismatic Ngai Tahu leader Sir Tipene O'Regan (1939–) said the settlement payment had enabled the tribe to 'step out of grievance mode'. At present Ngai Tahu are prospering, the awards have energized them, and they are now an important player in the South Island economy.

To what extent customary fishing rights from 1840 can be rationally adjudicated now in a different world of modern fishing techniques is itself a nice historical and philosophical point not lost on contemporary European New Zealanders. A 1987 political cartoon shows fish holding a meeting. The chairman fish declares, 'OK, this meeting supports the return of traditional fishing grounds to the Maori – provided they return to their traditional fishing methods ... the wooden spear! The flax net! And the bone hook!'

TAINUI

The Tainui claim was based on confiscation of their Waikato land during the New Zealand Wars. That this confiscation was unjustified was established by the Sim Commission in 1928 and payments were made and trust funds set up during the 1940s. But Tainui remained dissatisfied. Direct negotiation with the government via the Office of Treaty Settlements produced a 1995 reparations payment of $170 million. One Tainui leader said, 'We have caught the development bus and left the grievance bus behind. There's now a different mind-set among the majority of our people.' The Tainui then bought forests in Canterbury, fishing companies, hotels in Hamilton, Pauanui and Sydney, townhouses in Wellington, subdivisions in Hamilton, land at Kawhia, and the Auckland Warriors Rugby League team (a big loser of money). They spent $800,000 on educational scholarships, used $500,000 to upgrade their marae, and built a $10,000,000 post-graduate college. But much was ill-advised and by the year 2000 the tribe was being split by a corrosive dispute over heavy losses from disastrous investments and was struggling to stay solvent. Fortunately for future Tainui, the chastened tribal leadership managed to regroup and reorganize its investments.

Many non-Maori, who believed that the policy of assimilation had been working in the 1950s and 1960s have been bewildered at the implication that little had been done for Maori – what, they said, of hospitals, schools, welfare payments, state-provided housing? Sceptics suggested that all compensation claims are problematic because miscegenation has made it almost impossible for any Maori today to be pure-blood, so that Maori ethnic identification is now culture-based rather than genetic anyway.

Some Maori were also beginning to question the payments and current interpretations of the Treaty. Alan Duff (Maori mother, Pakeha father), the author of *Once were Warriors*, argued that Maori should pay their own way and attacked Maori leaders for 'constantly putting their hands in the public trough'. Winston Peters (1945–), the Maori leader of the New Zealand First Party, prefers integration to bi-culturalism. Even Sir Tipene O'Regan has pointed out that the Treaty is being used where other forms of political argument are needed. There is in fact a wide range of Maori views.

MMP and Other Developments

As prime minister, Geoffrey Palmer was never popular and in an extraordinary move, a mere seven weeks before the 1990 election, he was replaced by Mike Moore (1949–). Bolger's National Party won in a landslide with a record 67 seats to Labour's 29. The electorate had shown very clearly what it thought of Labour's Rogernomics, and many of its instigators lost their seats.

But within two years, National's attempts to use high interest rates to damp inflation had been only moderately successful and there was a slowing in economic growth and an increase in unemployment. Also unpopular were cuts in social security, and tinkering with the health system. To accommodate the country to the new employment world, the important Employment Contracts Act ended compulsory union membership and award wages, and, reduced to the status of incorporated societies, unions lost the unique importance they had enjoyed since Reeves's Act of 1894. Union membership declined substantially, part-time work increased, and employees made new contractual arrangements with employers. But National popularity plummeted, and internal factionalism surfaced with criticism from the cabinet member Winston Peters, who eventually formed his own party, New Zealand First. Labour under Moore tried to renew itself in opposition. But the most powerful attacks came from a new left-of-centre grouping calling itself the Alliance, consisting of New Labour led by Jim Anderton, the Green Party, Mana Motuhake (separate identity/autonomy/independence), a new Maori party, and the Democratic Party, which metamorphosed from Social Credit. The common values holding this diverse group were opposition to the policies of the two major parties and hope of a change in the electoral system towards proportional representation.

Internationally and importantly, Bolger mended the relationship with the USA, and New Zealand prime ministers were once again welcome in Washington, but as friends rather than as allies like Australia. The fact that the Cold War had ended made the nuclear ship issue less significant.

THE 1987 CONSTITUTION ACT

A constitutional issue in these years was the formalising of the New Zealand constitution itself. This was not because of any momentous national danger or constitutional crisis. In New Zealand Parliament had always been sovereign and remained so, but the government wished to make explicit the rules relating to handover of governmental authority, and to bring together formally in one Act and under one document the most important statutory constitutional provisions.

The Constitution Amendment Act came into law on 1 January 1987. The preamble reads:

> An Act to reform the constitutional law of New Zealand, to bring together into one enactment certain provisions of constitutional significance, and to provide that the New Zealand Constitution Act 1852 of the Parliament of the United Kingdom shall cease to have effect as part of the law of New Zealand.

In New Zealand the Governor-General is the representative of the Sovereign (presently Queen Elizabeth II of New Zealand and the

United Kingdom) and exercises the royal powers derived from statute and general law (prerogative powers). The Sovereign appoints the Governor-General on the Prime Minister's recommendation, normally for a term of five years. The powers of the Governor-General were explicitly set out in the Letters Patent 1983, and it is for the courts to decide on the limits of these powers. The Governor-General's main constitutional function is to arrange for the leader of the party with the most support in Parliament to form a government.

The Governor-General's assent is required before bills can become law. The Governor-General is required, however, by constitutional convention and the Letters Patent, to follow the advice of government ministers. In extraordinary circumstances, under what is called the Reserve Power the Governor-General can reject advice if convinced that a government is intending to act unconstitutionally.

There remain a number of British acts (referred to as imperial acts) which are in force as part of New Zealand law. Some are historic constitutional acts, such as Magna Carta 1215, and the Habeas Corpus Act 1679.

REGIONS

In 1989 sub-national government was reorganized when Regions were established (see map), boundaries based upon water catchment areas, and their elected Councils were given responsibility for preservation of natural resources, which previously had been the task of a variety of different national and local bodies. In some cases Regions approximate to the boundaries of the old provinces and many have the old provincial names. But with no responsibilities for the courts, the police, or education, Regions are not politically analogous to, say, American or Australian states or Canadian provinces. The duties of Regional Councils vary slightly, and they coordinate with City and District Councils.

MIXED MEMBER PROPORTIONAL REPRESENTATION

In 1984 a Royal Commission had examined the electoral system. Surprisingly, it recommended an approach modelled on Germany, Mixed Member Proportional Representation (MMP), rather than the

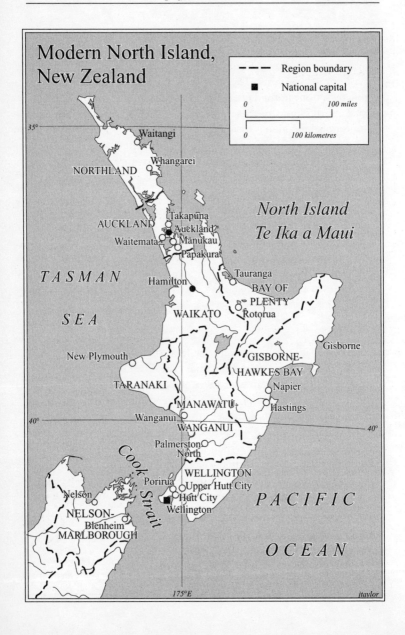

Modern North Island, New Zealand

- – – – Region boundary
- ■ National capital

0   100 miles

0   100 kilometres

35°

Waitangi

Whangarei

NORTHLAND

North Island
Te Ika a Maui

Takapuna
AUCKLAND   Auckland
Waitemata   Manukau
Papakura

T A S M A N   Hamilton   Tauranga
                BAY OF
S E A   PLENTY
         WAIKATO   Rotorua

New Plymouth   Gisborne
               GISBORNE-
            HAWKES BAY
TARANAKI   Napier
      MANAWATU-   Hastings
40°   Wanganui   *40°*
         WANGANUI
       Palmerston
        North

Cook Strait

      Porirua   WELLINGTON
Nelson   Upper Hutt City
         Hutt City
NELSON-   Wellington
   Blenheim
MARLBOROUGH

P A C I F I C

O C E A N

175°E   jtaylor

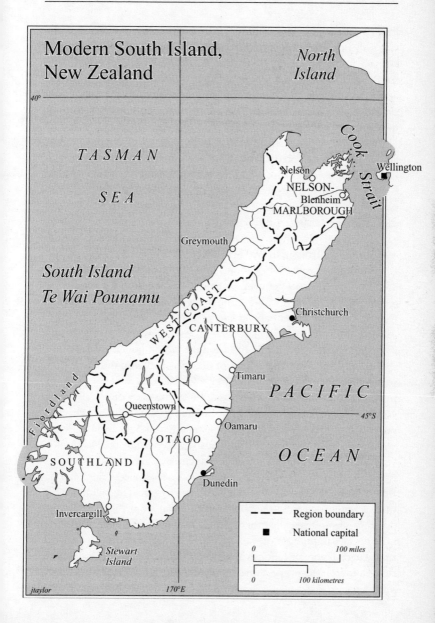

Modern South Island,
New Zealand

*North
Island*

40°

T A S M A N

S E A

Nelson

Cook Strait

Wellington

NELSON-

Blenheim

MARLBOROUGH

Greymouth

*South Island
Te Wai Pounamu*

WEST COAST

CANTERBURY

Christchurch

Fiordland

Timaru

P A C I F I C

Queenstown

45°S

Oamaru

OTAGO

O C E A N

SOUTHLAND

Dunedin

Invercargill

*Stewart
Island*

- - - Region boundary

■ National capital

0   100 miles

0   100 kilometres

jtaylor

170°E

First Past the Post (FPP) system used since the very first elections. Labour was unhappy with the idea and shelved it. But the idea of MMP had escaped from any government control and was running loose in the nation, and an influential private body, the Electoral Reform Coalition, kept it in the news. Seeking to appear conciliatory, both main parties promised to hold a referendum on MMP if they won the 1990 election, though both leaders assumed a referendum would confirm FPP.

The National government held a referendum in 1992. A turnout of about 55 per cent voted. About 84.7 per cent voted for some sort of change from FPP, and about 70.5 per cent indicated this change should be to MMP. Perhaps this result was to be expected because those who wanted change would be more keen to vote. The major parties were dismayed; the Alliance was overjoyed. The second step was to organize a straight referendum between FPP and MMP, which occurred during the 1993 General Election. In a 80 per cent turnout of voters National won the election 50 seats to 45 Labour, and MMP won the referendum by 1,032,919 votes, 53.9 per cent, to 884,964 votes, 46.1 per cent.

MMP supporters were aware that a single-chamber parliament set few restraints on government power except through triennial elections, and understood that MMP would make it less likely for a single-party majority government rapidly to introduce radical policies.

The Alliance, with 18 per cent of the vote, had won only two seats, making it even more determined to exploit the new MMP system at the next election. Like 1894, 1935, and 1949, the election of 1993 was crucial in New Zealand history. The political ground rules had changed enormously. Suddenly, minor parties could have political clout. There was every indication that governments would have to be coalitions.

Under MMP the new House of Representatives has 120 members, 65 from the now much enlarged general and Maori electorates, and 55 from lists supplied by the registered political parties. The ballot consists of two votes, one for a member of parliament from the electorate in which a person lives, the other for the party preferred. The total party vote decides its number of seats, provided it achieves at least 5 per cent of the overall vote or captures a single electorate. List MPs are allocated seats to top up the proportional representation as indicated by the total party votes.

There was much to learn. Previously impossible tensions were introduced within the major parties as colleagues jockeyed for electorate seats. It now took weeks to finalize election results and to form governments. Bolger faced the coalition problem directly by suggesting that some National MPs form a minor party or parties but continue to support the government if elected. New parties proliferated. At the 2002 election there were twenty-one parties, from National and Labour through the smaller parties like New Zealand First and the Greens, to tiny single-issue parties such as the Christian Heritage Party, and Outdoor Recreation New Zealand.

Jenny Shipley, New Zealand's first woman prime minister in 1997

After the 1996 election and the longest time taken in forming a government in the twentieth century (eight weeks), the National Party under Bolger finally formed a coalition government with the New Zealand First Party of Winston Peters. Bolger was prime minister and Peters deputy. In the meantime the economy drifted without government control. Internal party politicking led to Bolger's resignation in November 1997 and the appointment of the first female prime minister, Jenny Shipley (1952–)

MINORITY GOVERNMENT

In November 1999 Labour won most seats and formed a coalition with the Alliance led by Jim Anderton. Helen Clark became New Zealand's second female prime minister. A former academic without experience of hardship, Clark was regarded suspiciously by many. But her attention to detail and growing confidence continually increased her support.

To outraged opposition in parliament and dismay in the country, in mid-2000 Clark's Labour–Coalition government scrapped the country's 34 fighter planes, leaving merely transports and helicopters. Air Force personnel were shocked. This was the first time since the RNZAF was established in 1938 that the nation no longer possessed combat aircraft, and meant reorganized defence rearrangements with other countries, particularly Australia. In contrast, from 2000, New Zealand contributed to the UN peace-keeping force in newly independent East Timor and helped to develop the country's government infrastructure. In late 2001 Clark sent a small contingent of SAS troops to help the USA look for Muslim terrorist Osama bin Laden and defeat the Taliban in Afghanistan, and sent peacekeepers in 2002.

By early 2002 the coalition agreement had collapsed and Clark called an early election. Labour won 52 out of 120 seats. Coalition arrangements were made with the Progressive Coalition for two more seats, so Clark led a minority government of 54 seats. In order to make government possible, agreements were also made with rightist United Future's eight MPs to support Labour on votes of no confidence and supply. But United Future family and economic agendas were so different from those of Labour that legislation still looked problematic.

The anticipated coalition with the Green Party became impossible with the latter's rigid rejection of genetically modified foods.

A GROWING CONFIDENCE

During the 1990s there seemed to be a new nationwide optimism, in part perhaps because Maori grievances were at last being resolved, and because of New Zealand's self-confident independent international stance. Government and private companies enthusiastically promoted the country with its superb natural assets as a tourist destination. Characteristic of this confidence were two extraordinary new buildings, one from the public sector, the other private.

The Museum of New Zealand, *Te Papa Tongarewa*, in Wellington was constructed between 1993 and 1998. The large triangular structure, about 395×625 feet/120×190m across and 75 feet/23m high, rose on earlier reclaimed land which required special 'dynamic consolidation' compacting. The previous occupant, a hotel, was safely removed to an adjacent site. Because the site is so close to the Wellington and Wairarapa earthquake faults, special anti-quake techniques were required. A base-isolation system of special rubber/lead bearings was installed to take the main weight and allow for lateral movements of up to 40 cm, and teflon/stainless steel bearings to counter uplifts of 7.6 cm. Te Papa, as it is colloquially called, was also constructed to resist freak 1-in-2000 year gales. The architects employed complex shapes and the structure contained huge internal spaces for striking, innovative, modern museum displays.

The Sky Tower in Auckland at 1,094 feet/333.6m, is the tallest structure south of the Equator. Constructed between 1994 and 1997 with innovative techniques, it can withstand Force 8 earthquakes, and 1-in-1000 year gales of 125mph/200kmh. Lightning was another hazard. A 350mm gold-coated conductor ball on top of the mast draws lightning down a triaxial cable to earth; the structure's reinforcing steel was also built as a Faraday cage to trap and conduct electrical energy to earth; and twelve lightning rods around the windows of the viewing pod provide protection from side strikes. Because a descent of 1200 steps in an emergency is impossible for the elderly and disabled, there are special fire refuge areas constructed on the lower floor of the pod.

The pod itself has high capacity sprinkler and smoke containment systems.

Early in 2002 New Zealand's independent foreign policy was again demonstrated when Helen Clark took the lead with Australia's John Howard and Britain's Tony Blair in trying to expel Zimbabwe from the Commonwealth because of the fraudulent election of Robert Mugabe to the presidency. In her view the Commonwealth stood for little if it allowed such a dictator to remain a member. Later in the year she tried again to draw the matter to the world's attention at the World Summit on Sustainable Development. At both meetings her initiatives were frustrated by a coterie of African leaders.

Meanwhile the South Pacific island states had been trying to find a role in a world increasingly out of their control, and it is to their evolution and tribulations that we now turn.

CHAPTER THIRTEEN

'The Pacific Way': South Pacific Islands since 1901

South Pacific Colonial Government

By 1901, with the main exceptions of New Caledonia and Fiji, European control in Melanesia was still mostly limited to coastal areas, and the remaining several million Melanesians went about their lives much as they had done for thousands of years. In Polynesia, though there was much more contact and influence, and greater involvement in the world's commercial economy, the majority of people also followed traditional ways of providing food, through subsistence gardening, cultivation, and fishing.

However, in Polynesia during the previous hundred years, four great changes resulting from Western contact had made life different from all earlier centuries. People now used iron tools, and iron utensils for cooking their subsistence-produced food. With the exception of Easter Island and large parts of the French territories, some variety of Protestant Christianity, though modified by local mores, was all pervasive. Tribal warfare had been largely brought to an end by Christian teaching, and the administration and pacification programmes of colonial governments. And lastly, as a result of native disunion, and the efforts of settlers and traders, with the exception of Tonga, each island group was now ruled by European or American colonial governments with varying degrees of native participation.

MELANESIA AND POLYNESIA TO 1939

In 1883 the colony of Queensland in Australia had pressed Britain to annex all of eastern New Guinea (the Dutch claimed the west), but was refused until Germany annexed the north-east. Such a brouhaha then erupted in Queensland and other Australian colonies that Britain agreed to annex the south-east (Papua) in 1884. In 1906 this British New Guinea (Papua) was transferred to the recently federated Common-wealth of Australia. The new Lieutenant-Governor was Sir Hubert Murray (1861–1940), who would rule the territory for the long period until the outbreak of World War II. Murray was deeply principled but paternalistic; little else than paternalism and minimal development was possible given the diverse nature of the territory and people, and the tiny funding he was allowed by the Australian government. The long-term good of the native peoples was his overriding concern, and slowly, annual patrols made the highland tribes aware of the colonial government in the capital hamlet of Port Moresby, which, in the early 1900s consisted of Murray's verandahed house, a handful of huts, and a wharf. Murray slowly brought tribal warfare to an end, and substituted games such as rugby and cricket, which were enthusiastically adopted.

North-east New Guinea remained German until captured by Aus-tralian forces in 1914 at the beginning of World War I. After the German Imperial government had taken control early in the century, a benevolent paternalism was implemented by the governor Albert Hahl – unlike the authoritarianism of the previous administration by German commercial companies.

In the New Hebrides (Vanuatu), in the latter 1800s, Australian Presbyterian missionaries and planters invested heavily, both of whom were continually imploring the British government to annex the archipelago. French planters in larger numbers challenged this putative British control. A British/French joint naval agreement was made in 1887, and later, the compromise 1906 'Condominion' was formed, which gave the citizens of the two imperial nations equal rights, and established two separate, antagonistic administrations. Cynics, with some accuracy, referred to these as the 'Pandemonium'.

In the 1830s the first LMS mission arrived in New Caledonia, a French Roman Catholic mission in 1840. Using the killing of missionaries as a pretext, France annexed the islands in 1853. The territory was ruled by military governors until 1884 and was a penal colony from 1864 to 1897. Among these convicts were many of the

7,500 prisoners from the unsuccessful 1871 Paris Commune revolt. The main island,Grand Terre, has the world's largest known nickel deposits, about 25 per cent of world reserves, mined since 1875, at first by convicts. Settlers were brought from France and large tracts of land were taken over for cattle ranches, which destroyed Kanak farms and ancient irrigation systems. A revolt broke out in 1878 against the French. After it was put down the *indigenat* system was introduced which exploited the Kanaks, placed them outside normal French law, and turned them into peons. Many were forced into reservations in mountainous areas which they could leave only with police permission. By 1901 only about 10 per cent of the land, most of it mountainous or poor, remained in Kanak hands. Kanak population continued to decline. During World War I Kanaks had to fight for France (about 400 were killed) but a Kanak revolt in New Caledonia itself forced the French to maintain a strong military presence for the rest of the war. The *indigenat* system was periodically reviewed, but officials always decided that the Kanaks had not evolved sufficiently to warrant citizenship!

In Fiji Sir Arthur Gordon's solution remained largely intact until World War I. The arrival of more indentured Indian labourers, with their high rate of reproduction, added to racial tensions. In 1914, a non-combatant labour unit was voluntarily recruited in Fiji. Fiji was also the scene of the single World War I economic development which unsettled a colonial regime. This was the Viti Company founded by Apolosi Nawai, who, claiming religious visions, realized that by co-operating, Fijians could raise capital and run commercial companies just like the European settlers or the CSR. Fijians were attracted to this idea, and national feeling began to develop as a natural accompaniment. The European-dominated government became concerned for its commercial supremacy and perhaps for its political control. In 1917, in a drama which reminds one of the Rua Kenana affair in New Zealand, Nawai was accused of sedition, found guilty, and exiled to the distant island of Rotuma.

Nevertheless the Fijian chiefs strongly supported the British and considerable progress of the Fijian population resulted, e.g., most children of school age received tuition by the mid-1920s. The same was not so for the Fijian Indians, alienated by political marginalisation and the land system which allowed them to lease only, or buy a little of the limited freehold. They found it enormously frustrating to watch land which they had cleared and worked hard to produce economic crops, returned to the Fijian owners who then allowed it to revert to scrub.

In Western Samoa the German governor, Wilhelm Solf (1862–1936), saw Samoa as a legitimate part of the German Empire and supported the commercial activities of the DHPG (German Trading and Plantation Company). Though he was also mindful of Samoan welfare in resisting pressures by settlers to buy land. Inconsistently Solf's regime largely ignored Samoan traditions, and the Mau a Pule, an indigenous political resistance movement, developed. Fearing revolt, Germany sent warships in 1909, and the Mau leaders were exiled to Saipan in Micronesia which was then German territory. When New Zealand captured German Samoa in World War I the German plantation estates were confiscated and the profits used for Samoan public works, health and other services. Some land was redistributed to Samoan owners, and gave the Samoans an economic base.

American Samoa was governed by the United States Navy from 1900 to 1951, with the islands' role as a strategic naval base the priority. The naval-officer governor ruled as an autocrat. With ample funds available, village health and education were improved and many Samoans were employed by the navy, which was generally seen as benevolent.

Tonga, the nearest thing to an independent Pacific polity, ambled along contentedly under British protection, its internal affairs run by the native monarchy begun by King George Tupou I, respected by Tongans and foreigners alike. In 1918 Queen Salote (1900–65) succeeded her brother and began one of the most popular reigns in history, not just in the Pacific but in the world.

In 1888, much to the relief of the New Zealanders who were worried they might be taken by an unfriendly power, the closest unclaimed Polynesian groups, Niue and the Cook Islands, at the wish of the inhabitants, became British protectorates. Giving in to pressure from missionaries and traders, in 1892 and 1893 respectively, Britain also annexed the Gilbert and Ellice Islands, and the Solomon Islands.

Between 1882 and 1914 Tahiti and French Polynesia were ruled by no fewer than twenty-four, often bored French governors. This fact suggests the unimportance at that time of these islands in French political thinking. The governors' main concern was to keep the phosphate coming from Makatea Island in the Tuamotus.

During World War I Australian and New Zealand forces occupied the German colonies in the South Pacific, and military regimes took control for the duration of the war. German cruisers and armed merchantmen sank the French cruiser *Zelee* and lobbed shells into Papeete market, and Tahitians and Cook Islanders joined French and New Zealand forces in Europe.

THE LEAGUE OF NATIONS' MANDATES

Significant for the future was an ideal which had been gestating in the minds of Western intellectuals for several decades. The conception was 'national self-determination', stated most explicitly by President Woodrow Wilson (1856–1924) of the United States during debates which produced the Treaty of Versailles after World War I. The ambiguous concept of 'nation' was however never analysed, and political and economic reality and power politics made anathema any discussion of the national aspirations of some peoples and groups. France, and the USA (even during Wilson's presidency), either paid lip service to or ignored the principle in respect to their own South Pacific colonies.

Nevertheless the League of Nations did establish a Permanent Mandates Commission, which allocated German Samoa to New Zealand, Nauru and German New Guinea to Australia. The principle underlying the conception of a 'mandate' was rather like a wardship over a human being, i.e., to govern the territory for the benefit of the indigenous inhabitants, until, at some time in the future they were ready to govern themselves. Despite the ambiguities, mandates were a noble conception, something new and relatively altruistic in the world's selfish political history. Though reality fell far short of ideal, the idea of mandates had unspoken future implications for all colonial territories.

World War II in the South Pacific

The Melanesian islands were deeply affected by World War II. Japanese forces occupied large parts of New Guinea, the Bismarck Archipelago, and Solomon Islands. The massive military and economic reaction of the USA to the Japanese attack on Pearl Harbor made it inevitable that the islands, seas, and skies of Melanesia would become one vast battlefield.

Backed by billions of dollars, the rapidity and size of the American advance was astonishing to New Zealand and Australian troops. It was a series of unending miracles for Islanders. Airstrips were constructed in days, huge planes landed, floating drydocks became portable ports for ship repairs, army camps the size of towns went up in a week, and later, disappeared or were abandoned even faster, and massive quantities of noisy machinery, trucks, fuel carriers, troop carriers, bulldozers, jeeps, and tens of thousands of troops worked all through the day and night.

In battle areas Islanders saw their gardens flattened, palm trees blasted, relatives killed, villages destroyed. Many parts of New Guinea and Solomon Islands suffered up to two years of Japanese occupation. Specific treatment varied, but it was often arrogant and authoritarian, and, as they began to lose the war Japanese behaviour became more brutal. Some of the most vicious fighting of the war occurred here, as at Guadalcanal in the Solomon Islands.

INDIGENOUS CONTRIBUTIONS TO THE ALLIES

Thousands of New Guineans worked as porters and labourers for the Australian and US armies. Here was social and political revelation. For these white men showed friendship, and mateship, and were not bosses like the Japanese or the pre-war Mandated Territory plantation owners. Five battalions of New Guinea troops fought for the Allies in the New Guinea jungles, and a battalion of Fijians fought in the Solomon Islands. Both gained first class reputations as jungle fighters.

From 1942 New Caledonia became a US military base and American construction of roads and airfields began the modernization process of that territory. Farther east and south-east, Fiji and the Polynesian islands were not affected physically by the war except for defensive gun batteries. Fijians were very pro-British, and about 10 per cent of their population engaged in active service or labour units. In 1943 the Fijian military forces included about 6,400 Fijians, 800 expatriate New Zealanders, but only 260 Indians. Fijian private donations paid for a Royal Navy destroyer, HMS *Fiji*, and for several RAF Spitfires. With enthusiastic local support, Nadi became a significant Allied airport. The Fiji Indians, bitter at their second class status, mostly refused to help, Indian labourers even going on strike in 1943. Such different attitudes further alienated the two communities. For a time Fiji and the Samoas sustained American garrisons and were used in the military build-up. The army's purchase of local supplies and the free-spending habits of US troops brought boom times. To a lesser extent the same thing occurred in islands further from the military action such as Tahiti, the Cook Islands and Tonga. The Tongan people paid for a Spitfire for the RAF, named *Queen Salote* after the monarch.

CARGO CULTS, JON FRUM

One fascinating side-effect of the war in Melanesia was the rebirth of cargo-cults, a phenomenon first recorded in the late 1800s. These movements, which resemble Christian millennialism, promoted belief in a new age to be begun with the arrival of 'cargo' (money and factory-made material goods) sent to earth by supernatural forces or beings. The vast amounts of American military equipment encouraged the revival. Such cults, like any religious sect in times of rapid and disorienting change, provided stability and hope.

One of the most fascinating was Jon Frum on Tanna in Vanuatu. One account goes something like the following. In the mid-1930s, increasingly resentful of Presbyterian regulations the people of western Tanna began to talk about a mysterious person, Jon, who had emerged *from* the sea and presented himself to several kava drinkers. Jon explained that there would soon be food and wealth in abundance and no more epidemics.

During the war, about a thousand workers from Tanna, many Jon believers, were employed by the American army. They were impressed by the seemingly endless supplies: from chocolates to steel ships. They noticed how generous the troops were, particularly the Black Americans.

They noted the medical units with red crosses on vehicles and tents. Perhaps the mysterious Jon had come from the USA. From that time Jon Frum believers have tried various ploys such as constructing a rough airfield in the scrub to tempt planes full of cargo to land; soon after the Americans departed, large numbers of red crosses were erected across Tanna, in hope of medical treatment. But Jon Frum has failed to come. Surely since the mid-1930s is rather a long time to wait? Not at all say the cultists: Christians have been waiting for nearly 2000 years.

Independence and After

King George Tupou's Tonga (and King Kamehameha's Hawaii) were the first Pacific Island polities to resemble in some degree a modern independent state. But for most of Melanesia and Polynesia, independent statehood/nationhood remained abstract and unconsidered ideas until after World War II. Independence came to the South Pacific not because of indigenous pressures as had occurred in Western Samoa, but because of United Nations power politics and the British decision to give independence to the colonial empire. Neither France not the USA encouraged independence in their territories, but sought some form of interdependence with the metropolitan power.

'THE PACIFIC WAY'

In the late 1960s and the 1970s, at the time independence was being introduced, a popular slogan, 'the Pacific Way', first articulated by Ratu Sir Kamisese Mara (1920–) of Fiji, was used by Pacific Island leaders to identify the manner in which (so it was claimed) they made government and institutional decisions. Disagreements were dissolved and without rancour or dispute a consensus was to be reached which left no one feeling a loser. After all, it was said, this was the traditional manner of making decisions in Oceania. As we have seen, in the days of chiefly power prior to European contact that latter claim was at best partly true, or more true of decisions at the village level. 'The Pacific Way' was thus a wishful illusion – but a nice aspiration.

What may have contributed to the idea was the peaceful and consensual manner in which so much independence was achieved. But as shown by the struggles in New Caledonia and French Polynesia, peacefulness of political change depended on the willingness of the colonial power to withdraw. Of course myths of indigenous nation-building make useful political capital, especially for the foundation Presidents/Prime Ministers and their parties.

PACIFIC INDEPENDENCE ARRIVES

South Pacific independence arrived in the following order. First was Western Samoa: the New Zealand UN trusteeship was ended, and independence came in 1962. In 1965 the Cook Islands became self-governing 'in association with' New Zealand. The latter looked after foreign affairs for the first few years, with the Cook Islands Ministry of Foreign Affairs taking over progressively. Nauruans had been offered the option of occupying either of two fertile islands off the Queensland coast, one about forty times, the other about twenty times the size of Nauru, with local autonomy but Australian citizenship. The Nauruan government wanted the Queensland island *and* Nauruan independence. When this was refused, they took the independence option in Nauru itself in 1968. Fiji gained independence in 1970, and Tonga came completely out from under the shade of the British protectorate the same year. Little Niue, like the Cook Islands, became self-governing in association with New Zealand in 1974.

Also in 1974 the Australian colony of Papua in the south-east and the UN trusteeship territory of New Guinea in the north-east became the self-governing country of Papua-New Guinea (PNG). Not long before, the Australians had been thinking that for the good of the native peoples these territories would require decades of careful tutelage before they could become viable. But the Australian government bowed to UN pressure. Solomon Islands, Tuvalu, and Kiribati gained independence in 1978, and the New Hebrides as Vanuatu in 1980. Whether independent nationhood, or some alternative like the Cook Islands' relationship with New Zealand was best for these countries was never considered by the United Nations.

New Caledonia and French Polynesia were given a degree of internal self-government and in 1977 American Samoa gained the right to elect its governor and legislature.

Politically, South Pacific countries have many similarities. Their governments are centralized with common procedures, similar bureaucracies, similar problematic elections, insufficient constraints on political corruption, and often venal leaders. They are members of the same international bodies, and receive ideas from the same sources and aid from the same or similar donors for the same reasons.

Many play the same sports. In all the British Commonwealth island colonies (governed by Britain or Australia, or New Zealand) organized sport was introduced either deliberately in order to replace local rivalries or warfare, or as the indigenes copied games played by administrators and traders. As a result in Papua-New Guinea, Fiji, Tonga, Samoa, and the Cook Islands, rugby or rugby league is the main men's sport, with intense rivalry at every level. Cricket too is played, though in some islands it has been radically modified: in Samoa teams and supporters may consist of whole villages; in the Trobriand Islands (PNG) teams of up to 60 men magically decorate themselves, paint their shins white to look like cricket pads and play in competitions which may take weeks. In the same region, in the last two decades netball has become the chief women's sport. In the French islands, soccer, boule and other French games prevail.

There have also been differences within the similarities, and something brief will now be said about these.

PAPUA-NEW GUINEA

With over 5,000,000 people PNG is easily the largest polity in the South Pacific islands. There are multitudinous languages, minimal formal education, a weak government infrastructure, rich pockets of minerals whose profits are unevenly shared, and hundreds of isolated, often mutually hostile mountain tribes. PNG shares a 500-mile border (a straight line on a map crossing snow-covered mountains and malarial swamps) with West Papua, where there is a disastrous Melanesian independence revolt against the Indonesian occupiers. That PNG has held together in any form for over 30 years is remarkable. The copper-rich island of Bougainville tried to break away during a bitter civil war from 1989 to 1997, leaving 20,000 dead and 40,000 refugees. The islands of New Britain, New Ireland, and Manus also tried (peacefully) to secede in 1974. And the PNG military have attempted several quasi-coups – defeated by the fact that no single ethnic or political group is sufficiently strong to dominate.

On almost any set of criteria, PNG is worse off than before independence. Tribal warfare in the highlands had been largely suppressed by the Australian administration, but flared up after independence and is at times out of control. PNG is now deep in graft: a former chief justice of PNG said in 1992: 'If we charged everyone who is corrupt, we would probably have no one to run the place.' In the 2002 national election, which took months, many electors were unable to vote owing to problems with the electoral roll, and dozens were killed. History came full circle when Sir Michael Somare, who had been the first prime minister, again took office – though his party held only about 10 per cent of seats. Fortunately, 70 per cent or more of the population still relies on subsistence farming.

SOLOMON ISLANDS

This state, with its resources of minerals and timber, looked promising at independence, but government roguery over two decades encouraged by venal pressures from international logging companies have ruined the economy. Formal education is chaotic. There have been running internal tensions and threats of secession. In 1999 the Guadalcanal Revolutionary Army attacked, intimidated, and killed people from other islands and deported some 20,000 – Guadalcanal is the site of the capital, Honiara. Fearing similar oppression, non-natives on other islands returned to their homes. By 2003 government had virtually collapsed. The international airport at Honiara had to be closed for a time because the government had not paid the insurance. Warlords were in control of large areas, people, including children, were being shot dead on whim, and, as used to happen a century earlier, a Seventh-day Adventist pastor had his head cut off. Again, only local subsistence farming kept food in most people's bellies.

VANUATU

Over a hundred languages are spoken in Vanuatu ('Land Eternal'), with one or two thousand speakers each. There are also Indian, Fijian,

English, French, Chinese, Vietnamese, Tongan, and Kiribati minorities.

Supported by Britain and opposed by France, the Vanua'aku Party had worked for independence since the 1960s. Led by Anglican priest, Father Walter Lini (1942–99), the party won government at independence in 1980 and governed until 1991. To local delight, as promised, the government confiscated all foreign-owned land, with no compensation, and redistributed it. Plantation productivity plummeted to almost zero and the local economy plunged disastrously. Just prior to the election, with clandestine French encouragement, two separatist rebellions broke out, on Tanna Island and Espiritu Santo, which Lini was able to suppress by calling in the aid of the PNG Kumel Force. Owing to French intransigence, Vanuatu, alone amongst the new Pacific countries, can claim it had to fight for independence.

Though the Vanua'aku Party promised freedom of expression, fair shares of the country's benefits to all citizens, and honest government, Vanuatu soon became a nepotistic state. Governments have changed, but dissimulation and double dealing are endemic – though Lini also modestly suggested that any middle-sized nation should be able to function efficiently under a political leader and about six competent civil servants! There is real opportunity for economic growth if politics can settle, for tourism could grow enormously. Some of the scenery is magnificent and the active volcano on Tanna and the twin volcanoes on Ambrym are among the most spectacular and unusual sights in the South Pacific.

Rural life remains much the same, and on islands such as Tanna one can still meet villagers with penis-sheaths and grass skirts. Here almost everyone is still engaged in subsistence production (though there are cash crops too). The splendid forests provide a multitude of resources: food, building materials for houses and boats, and natural medicines. More food is produced than needed, and the surplus is given away in ostentatious public gesture. Though towns like Vila and Luganville are growing, many people after a time return to their own villages, where life is more social and certainly cheaper. Taboos of menstruation and childbirth remain strict.

FIJI

In the 1960s Britain, pressured by the United Nations, insisted on independence for Fiji, though the inhabitants themselves were content to remain a colony. The Fijians assumed they would be in control, the Fiji Indians anticipated equal political rights. So a compromise constitution was patched together, with equal representation in the lower house but a larger number of seats to Fijians in the nominated senate.

From long before independence, governments had been controlled by the Alliance Party under Ratu Sir Kamiese Mara, with Fijians most significant in Alliance cabinets but with some membership of Indians and Europeans. The Indians frustratedly acquiesced in their subordinate status.

In 1987 the racial reality of politics in Fiji became clear to the world. The National Federation Party, mostly Indians, formed a coalition government with the Labour Party, also mostly Indians. Together they held 28 seats to the opposition Alliance Party's 24 seats held by Fijians. Nevertheless a quarter of the 28 government seats were Fijians and the new prime minister, Dr Timoci Bavadra (1935–89), was also Fijian. Still, because only a small percentage of Fijians had voted for the government, it had really come to power on Indian votes. A situation in which three-quarters of the ruling party was Indian was intolerable to many Fijians, but especially the chiefs. The new government had *constitutional* authority, but Fijians held the *power*: except for an odd Indian, the army was entirely Fijian, and disproportionately large for a Pacific country; the police force too was predominantly Fijian. After only six weeks Colonel Sitiveni Rabuka (1948–) took his troops into parliament, arrested Dr Bavadra and his cabinet, and took control.

New Zealand and Australia strongly protested against the coup, but most island governments considered that indigenous rights were politically more important than democratic form and Tonga recognized Rabuka's coup within days. Rabuka brought back Mara as head of government, with himself a severe presence behind the throne. In the next ten years more than 60,000 Indians emigrated, to New Zealand, Australia, Canada and USA. Because they were descended from lower castes almost none returned to India where caste, though illegal, still

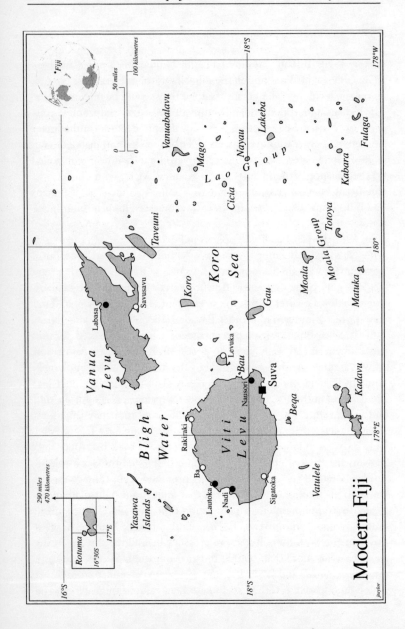

Modern Fiji

rules. This exodus represented a huge proportion of the professional people. Fijians became a majority of the islands' population once again. Rabuka allowed civilian government after some months, under a new Fijian-controlled constitution, but still dissatisfied, instituted another coup later in the year.

Rabuka ordered the efficiently run National Bank of Fiji to make generous loans to Fijians. Dealings soon became corrupt, with large amounts to set up businesses lent to people who knew nothing about business. By 1997 it was bankrupt, leaving Fiji a debt of something like US$160 million.

In 1999, because Indians voted almost entirely for the Labour Party, they again held a majority of seats. To forestall another coup, new prime minister Mahendra Chaudhry (1942–), the first Indian in that post, gave most cabinet positions to Fijians. The situation was still unsatisfactory to Fijian nationalists and in May 2000 another coup was instigated by a failed businessman, George Speight, who kept the prime minister and cabinet prisoner for 57 days. It is now obvious to the world that the Fijians will for the foreseeable future never again allow a government to be or even appear to be dominated by Fijian Indians. The 'Fijianization' of recent decades has given greater self-respect to native Fijians, but has been of little economic benefit.

Almost everyone is religious. The Indians are overwhelmingly Hindu, about 15 per cent Muslim, with a few per cents of Christians and Sikhs. The Fijians are mainly Methodist, and that church is politically powerful. Rabuka himself is a lay preacher.

TONGA

Authority and power have always rested heavily in royal and aristocratic hands. Post-1970 and full independence have seen little change. Though the monarchy is still popular, in the 1980s a democracy movement developed, made up of most of the elected MPs. In 1998 it took the name Tonga Human Rights and Democracy Movement. The Movement wins most of the minority of parliamentary seats which are elected by the people (in comparison to the majority representing the Tongan nobles and appointed by the king).

In clinging to its royal traditions Tonga accepted the idea of parliament, but not of the responsibility of cabinet to parliament. This makes Tonga's claims to be a constitutional monarchy questionable. Unlike other real *constitutional* monarchies such as New Zealand and the Netherlands, the monarch, the nobles, and nepotism rule. Not a single *elected* MP has ever been made a cabinet minister. It is a crime to criticize the royal family or to anger a public servant (because they are constitutionally the monarch's servants).

Still, from the visitor's point of view the Tongan monarchy makes the country intriguingly different from other island nations. The monarchy is able to act quickly and enforce changes sometimes difficult in republics. In 1979, for instance, the king banned humpback whaling in Tongan waters. As a result whales have increased in numbers and

Queen Salote of Tonga on the way to open her parliament in 1945

whale-watching tourism has grown significantly. Tonga also diversified into some small specialized industries to do with woollen goods and luxury yachts, and launched two satellites (from Kazakhstan!) for leased foreign telecommunications use.

Religion also rules. The king is head of the state church. No planes are allowed to land on Sundays, and it is a criminal act to work on Sunday except for essential services. It is also illegal to play organized sport – though swimming is allowed. Tonga is a physically safe destination for the visitor, and from the early 1990s has tried to catch up with the other Polynesian countries in attracting tourists. Meanwhile Tongans have been migrating to New Zealand, USA and Australia.

SAMOA

Those who know the South Pacific tend to agree that Samoa ('Western Samoa' until 1997) is Polynesia at its purest. With the possible exception of Tonga, it has kept its identity better. And in Apia it has one of the Pacific's most charming spots. Samoans are proud of their country and almost every village is neat and clean and, though incomes are low by Western standards, there seems to be little poverty. Each village has its green (malae), where, at the end of the day people gather to chat, or play kirikiti (Polynesian cricket) or volleyball. Rugby, boxing, and netball are all popular.

But the visitor may miss the undercurrents. Samoa, led by two papa title holders, the first fully independent country, also had the first disillusioned people. Merely two years after independence, the Samoan author Albert Wendt was complaining about Samoan leaders who preach austerity, hard work, thrift, honesty, integrity and godliness, but in practice ignore them and 'maintain themselves in power, comfort, and privilege'.

Samoa accepted representative politics but not universal franchise and resented United Nations emphasis on the latter, because it disregarded Samoan traditions. Discontent is not about representation (although only chiefs may stand for parliament, about every second Samoan male over thirty years of age is a chief) but about malfeasance. At one point the Samoan government failed for seven years to present audited accounts to parliament. If Samoa has economic problems, corruption contributes to them. The third part of the Mau's 1920s slogan, 'Government of the people by the people *for the people*', now looks like irony.

Junk foods have taken a toll of modern Samoan health: cans of corned beef are now as common as taro. The traditional Samoan house, the fale, is still widespread though now often roofed with corrugated iron. Though over a third of the population is under fifteen, net growth rate is small because of emigration to New Zealand, Australia and the USA. But it is still true that people are generally friendly and welcoming to visitors, and most travellers are delighted by these islands.

AMERICAN SAMOA

Until the Americanization of the early 1960s, life was similar to that in the rest of the archipelago. In 1961 *Reader's Digest* published the article 'America's Shame in the South Seas'. The writer mistook the simple subsistence extended family life of the Samoans for economic deprivation, and thundered that American Samoa was a national disgrace. Homely family values, absence of crime, community cooperation, the easygoing culture, were nowhere factored into the simplistic economic equation. Soon President John Kennedy (1917–63) had appointed H. Rex Lee (1910–2001) as governor and told him to put things right.

American Samoa was hit with a tidal wave of development. North American-style houses replaced the simple, environmentally friendly fale, asphalted roads covered walking tracks; there were new electricity generators, sewerage projects, harbour construction, a large hospital, modern American-style school buildings, an international airport to bring in the outside world, tuna canneries (to replace the economic base of the US Navy which had shipped itself to Honolulu and Long Beach), dependence on the state, and fast food. And North America's social problems arrived too.

In 1951 control had been transferred from the US Navy to the US Department of the Interior. The American Secretary of the Interior appointed a governor with full administrative powers. After 1961, fearful of losing their welfare state, the people preferred an appointed governor until 1977, when Peter Coleman (1919–97), a Samoan, was elected. Electoral procedures for a territory House of Representatives

(Fono) were set up; but the members of the Senate are nominated through the Samoan system of chiefs or 'Matais'. American Samoa is also allowed an elected, non-voting delegate to the US Congress, and except for defence, American Samoans run the country's affairs. American Samoans are American 'nationals' and passport holders, but not American citizens although they travel freely between American Samoa and the USA, but can vote in mainland elections only if resident there.

The USA continues to pay for mainland-standard services for the Islanders. The territory government, tuna canning, and tuna fishing each employ about a third of the workforce. Average earnings are something like four times as much as in Samoa and increasing. Some thoughtful American Samoans are trying to find a middle way which allows for more Polynesian values, but talk of independence is almost zero.

COOK ISLANDS

When the Cook Islands became independent in 1965, New Zealand was providing 65 per cent of government income, but by the early 2000s this had dropped to around 10 per cent. Tourism was actively promoted and the islands now attract about five times their total population each year. Black pearls began to be cultured in the northern islands of Manihiki and Pehrhyn, and are the country's main export. Though the population of the Cook Islands have dual Cook Islands–New Zealand citizenship, that status is not reciprocal, and the Cook Islands are in no way controlled by New Zealand.

For its first quarter century or so, the Islands contracted little government or private debt and achieved the highest income per head in the South Pacific Islands. But in 1989 Sir Geoffrey Henry (1940–) was returned to office, because of, according to a Pacific watcher, 'almost hallucinatory visions and unachievable promises'. Within a year the government was plunged into horrendous debt through dubious deals. In Avarua, the little capital on Rarotonga Island, a US$6 million National Cultural Centre, a personal project of Henry, was constructed with foreign money. It stands proudly, but deteriorating. In 1996 to try to balance the books, Henry sacked about half the country's public servants and reduced all public salaries by 50 per cent. Massive migration to New Zealand followed.

The only way for a Cook Islander to acquire land is to inherit it, or lease it. This policy has retarded economic development, for land is owned in many tiny, usually scattered parcels inefficient for farming, though a natural food source of lush local tropical fruits exists in cornucopian proportions.

The main island of Rarotonga stands magnificent, an extravagant green, its interior largely untouched, and many visitors find the Cook Islands ideal places for relaxing holidays and excellent snorkelling and diving.

NEW CALEDONIA AND FRENCH POLYNESIA

Many of the political problems in the French territories since World War II have resulted from the fact that France continued to regard overseas lands as part of France not as colonies or small nations in the making. Some local political activity developed during World War II. Political parties evolved in New Caledonia in the 1940s and in French Polynesia in the 1950s. But the fact that in each case there were two different racial groups who wanted greater autonomy, the French settlers, and the indigenous Melanesians or Polynesians, meant that political advance was impeded. Though nothing like the bloodshed which had occurred in Algeria, another French colony of settlement with an indigenous population, politics in the two territories could be nasty.

The most famous statesman of French Polynesia was the blond-haired Pouvanaa a Oopa (1895–1977), who fought in World War II in the Free French Pacific Battalion. In 1949 he founded the Rassemblement Democratique des Populations Tahitiennes (RDPT). For ten years he was a huge annoyance, opposing French rule, and agitating for employment of Polynesians in government. Populist and Protestant, he attracted Polynesians who saw in him a father figure who could restore their dignity and challenge the arrogance of French 'metropolitans'. Strangely, it was the push for independence elsewhere in the world which undid him.

The Algerian War and the world trend to independence made

President Charles de Gaulle (1890–1970) aware that the relation of France and its overseas territories had to be redefined. In 1958 he held an empire-wide referendum in which the choice was either independence and no more financial help, or continued association with France with economic benefits with political strings. By significant majorities made possible by the votes of the French settlers, New Caledonia and French Polynesia preferred to remain associated. Pouvanaa a Oopa's party was in shock. Riots broke out in the capital, Papeete. Pouvanaa was made the convenient scapegoat, charged with and found guilty of arson and sentenced to eight years in jail. The RDPT declined. Construction of an international airport at Faaa on the outskirts of Papeete in 1961 ended Tahiti's relative isolation.

The RDPT was at an extreme disadvantage because the colonial government dominated the media; the government has always employed about half the working population; and from 1962 on the French began their series of atomic tests and constructed the vast Centre d'Experimentation du Pacific which poured billions of francs (more than a billion US dollars a year) into the Polynesian economy. Usually a step ahead of unrest, reforms of 1977 and 1984 allowed greater local control of budget and policy, and were extended in 1990 and 1996. The Assembly of French Polynesia has councillors from each of the five archipelagoes and is elected every five years. Head of government is elected by and from the Assembly. French Polynesians return two deputies to the French National Assembly in Paris. Nevertheless, riots against the atomic tests shook Papeete in 1987 and 1995, and, the Polynesian population outraged by the extension of tests, the independence party of Oscar Temaru made large gains in the 1996 election, but had reduced support in 2001. When the bomb-testing facilities at Mururoa Atoll were dismantled after 1996, unemployment began to rise dramatically, though France promised to subsidize the territory until 2006.

In the Society Islands conduct is a blend of Polynesian and Gallic – it is common for women to greet each other with a kiss on each cheek. As in the rest of Polynesia, the Christian religion remains powerful and ubiquitous. Tahiti and the other Society Islands are heavily Protestant, with Roman Catholics stronger in the outer archipelagoes.

In New Caledonia, post-war agitation for more local autonomy was led by a French settler, Maurice Lenormand. He managed to develop a bi-racial party, the Union Caledonienne (UC) of Caldoches (French settlers) and Kanaks, supported by the religious missions and the unions, which performed strongly in the elections for the territorial assembly. A socially unsettling nickel-mining boom occurred in the 1950s and 1960s, bringing in new immigrants from Vanuatu. This prosperous New Caledonia gave renewed confidence to Kanaks and Caldoches, leading to the violent political agitations of the next twenty years.

The first Kanak university graduates who returned from France (and the 1968 Paris student uprising) made a political impact. In 1977 the successor to the UC, the Front Uni de Liberation Kanak (FULK) and another independence group made independence and return of Kanak land issues in the Assembly election of 1977. Because of this continuing agitation for independence and land rights for the Kanaks, France withdrew some of the earlier concessions. Immigration of French settlers and other groups such as Vietnamese was promoted, and the bi-racial agreements of earlier years floundered. There was sporadic violence between Kanaks and settlers. By the later 1979s the Kanaks were in a minority, and aware of independence in neighbouring Melanesian countries became deeply frustrated. Depending on metropolitan French politics, concessions and regressions were made. In 1984 the pro-independence parties merged to form the FLNKS (Front de Liberation Nationale Kanak), led by the dynamic former Catholic priest Jean-Marie Tjibaou (1936–89). 'Les Evénements' (the Events), as the next two years of chaos became known, had begun. FLNKS boycotted the Assembly elections and proclaimed a provisional government of Kanaky. A few days later ten Kanaks were shot by mixed-race settlers. Factions armed and civil war looked imminent. FLNKS rejected a hastily prepared proposal for a referendum on independence and self-government 'in association' with France. The shooting of an FLNKS leader led to riots. French paratroopers were flown in, and a six-month state of emergency declared. As a concession four regional councils were tried in 1985, but when three of them fell under the control of Kanaks who wanted autonomy, their authority was reduced.

During the 1988 French presidential election, Kanak nationalists kidnapped French hostages. In an electoral show of force President Mitterand sent in the commandos, and in a complex and confused situation of fighting and parleying the militants were killed. Returned to power, Mitterand agreed to a new political arrangement. The independence and FLNKS leader Tjibaou, the leader of the Caldoches and the RCPR, Jacques Lefleur (1932–), and French PM, Michel Rochard (1930-) signed the Accords de Matignon which agreed on amnesties for former political crimes, the equivalent of billions of US dollars to accelerate Kanak economic development, three semi-autonomous provinces, and a referendum on independence in 1998. In May 1989 Tjibaou and his deputy were killed by a Kanak political opponent.

In 1998 Lefleur, the new leader of the FLNKS, and the French prime minister Lionel Jospin (1937–) signed the Accords de Noumea, which agreed to a protracted transfer of power from France to New Caledonia, with development of accompanying currency, flag, name (most likely 'Kanaky'), etc. The promised referendum was held, and 72 per cent endorsed this agreement. A referendum (again!) on full independence would be held within twenty years. The situation is complex, and the French still value their prestige as the only nation in the European Union with substantial Pacific Basin commitments, so it may be *plus ça change, plus c'est la même chose*.

Dependent Independence

Even New Zealand, with more than 150 years of complex economic development and with the largest and most sophisticated economy in the South Pacific Ocean, had problems adjusting to a changed world economic system in the 1970s and 1980s. So the new South Pacific countries expected and received continuing economic support from their former colonial masters, and, decades later, because island expenses far exceed island incomes it looks as if heavy dependence will continue indefinitely. (Aid to Fiji and PNG have tended to be the lowest.) Moreover, there had to be mutually satisfactory agreements about foreign-owned investments. Vanuatu's high-handed expropriations

The basilica of St Anthony of Padua in Nuku'alofa, Tonga

were the exception rather than the rule. Not one of the new countries had sufficient numbers of educated public servants or administrators or technically skilled workers to run government, infrastructure, and an effective economy, and this meant expatriates had to remain until indigenes could be trained. Nowadays many expatriates are Asians.

All South Pacific countries faced similar problems. Though some countries had one or two other products, e.g., Fiji sugar, PNG coffee tea and cocoa, it was copra, *a product of their common natural environment*, that was for decades (much less now) the single sustainable market staple of the region. The Islands also competed in world markets, and many of their citizens had now acquired tastes which only outside contacts could supply.

To encourage cooperation, the islands and their former colonial masters supported the development of regional organizations, which will be described later. Island governments also asked the advice of the same experts from the Asian Development Bank, the World Bank, and the International Monetary Fund. But options were limited, and they received the same advice: to diversify economically and to promote tourism.

ECONOMIC DIVERSIFICATION?

Diversification was easy to recommend, but a limited possibility in the tiny economic and physical base of the smaller islands. As a result some island leaders have been tempted to indulge in quasi-legal enterprises. In 2000 the OECD criticized the Cook Islands, Nauru, Niue, Tonga, Vanuatu, and Samoa, for being tax havens which harmed their own trade and investment. There has however been progress in timber, minerals, and fishing.

In recent decades the Melanesian countries have developed large timber industries, with much exported to Japan. With insecure governments anxious for quick returns, short-sighted deals with multi-national logging companies have denuded huge regions of forest, with inadequate reafforestation. While the small islands of Polynesia have little mineral wealth, minerals account for more than 70 per cent of the income of Melanesian countries, with the vast quantities of copper and gold in PNG and nickel in New Caledonia. Fishing is second to mining as income earner for the South Pacific as a whole. Income results chiefly from tuna fishing and from licence payments from foreign countries whose trawlers use the islands' Exclusive Economic Zones. Policing foreign fishing fleets is however difficult. And preventing disastrous overfishing by Japanese, Korean, Taiwanese and United States fleets with their massive modern techniques is even more so.

EXCLUSIVE ECONOMIC ZONES

In 1992 a United Nations convention promulgated a new Law of the Sea. It recommended an extension of each nation's territorial limits from 3 to 12 nautical miles off the coast, and claims to the resources of continental shelves in Exclusive Economic Zones (EEZs) to 200 miles. Many aspects of the Law had been accepted in practice long before. In 1976, for instance, the South Pacific Forum of Pacific Island countries

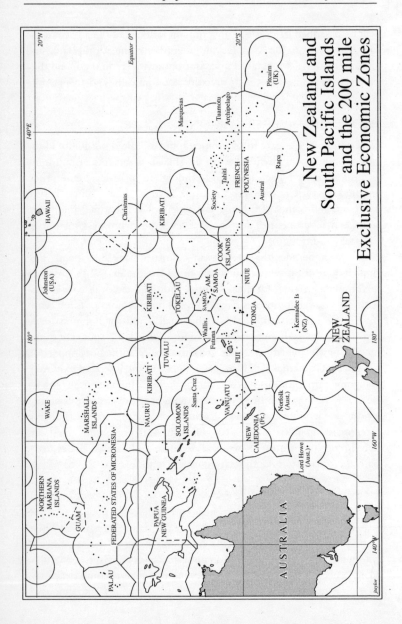

New Zealand and
South Pacific Islands
and the 200 mile
Exclusive Economic Zones

had agreed upon an EEZ for each of its members. EEZs refer mainly to fisheries and undersea mineral exploitation. Freedom of navigation to ships of all nations is guaranteed. The Law of the Sea increased immensely the areas controlled by South Pacific countries, and potentially, their political and economic clout. Combined South Pacific island EEZs cover something like fifty times their total land areas, and there are known to be vast mineral resources on the ocean floor.

TOURISM

Expanded tourism looked promising. It would be based on the exotic natural environment and cultures. These aspects had captured the Western imagination from the beginning. Drawing upon these costless sources, it appeared that tourism, like some perpetual-motion machine, would require only commonsense to produce endless income. The developing programmes soon exposed the shortcomings.

Perhaps a little over 40 per cent of net earnings from tourism actually remains in the islands. The rest goes on salaries for expatriate management, repatriated profits, costs of imported goods such as fuel to drive the tourists around in coaches and boats, and to power the generators needed to run the hotels. To attract hotels for tourists, governments must offer tax concessions and build airports and roads and communications. Construction can cause erosion of beaches, resort sewerage pollutes lagoons, and some imported foods such as beef are required to meet the preferences of tourists. Native culture is changed and often debased to fit tourist schedules. Cheap handicrafts distort tradition to meet skewed tourist demands, with imitation New Guinea masks being made and sold in Fiji, and tikis in Tonga which copy those of Hawaii. Though locally produced items can be an important proportion of souvenirs, there have always been imported tourist 'bargains' made in South Korea, Taiwan, or China. On the other hand, it is only tourist demand that keeps some valuable indigenous arts in existence.

Meanwhile the magnificent oceans, reefs, and lagoons, the high green islands, and the beaches are the major attractions, for swimming, surfing, snorkelling, scuba diving, and just lying in the sun. For nowadays it is the Pacific Islanders who wear trousers and long dresses and the European, Australian, New Zealand, and US visitors who go half-naked. Modern Polynesian dress codes are strict. Revealing shorts, halter or tank tops, and swimming costumes away from the water are considered vulgar in Tonga and Samoa. So deeply embedded is fundamentalist Christianity that in some islands even modest bathing suits are considered risqué for women. French Polynesia and New Caledonia are an exception, where beach fashions at the large hotels and resorts look like Polynesia before the missionaries arrived.

South Pacific leaders talk about conservation to preserve an environment which amongst other things will lure tourists, but they can be self-destructively inconsistent. In 1995, to help protect the sea turtle from becoming extinct Pacific island countries observed 'the Year of the Turtle'. In 1996 the South Pacific Forum held its meeting in the Marshall Islands (in the North Pacific). Many sea turtles were killed to feed the visiting heads of government, with not a sign of protest from them! Though tourist numbers continue to increase, hopes of economic independence based upon tourism seems to be unlikely.

LOSS OF SUBSISTENCE FARMING

Subsistence farming was largely independent of the world economy and terms of trade. One of the tragedies of post–World War II Polynesia has been the loss of this 'subsistence prosperity' as countries have been lured into the markets of the industrial world and their people and governments to that way of thinking. The economic criteria of the developed world misread the nature of this prosperity.

Less barter and subsistence farming have also meant less social support for families and a disquieting drift into the towns. The most developed islands now have considerable urbanization. More than half the population of each island country lives in towns such as Pago Pago (American Samoa), Noumea (New Caledonia), and Papeete (French Polynesia), and about a third in Nuku'alofa (Tonga). In many capitals there are high levels of unemployment and accompanying social problems. Though Port Moresby has the lowest capital population proportion of any Pacific country, it is the largest Pacific Islands city, with by far the greatest social problems.

Working for wages, growing cash crops, creeping individualism, all have lessened the support networks which were normal in all South Pacific villages, especially in Polynesia. In Melanesia, however, there are still large areas where what is mainly subsistence farming is still very significant. Women do much of the hard labour, tending family gardens, cooking, cleaning, looking after children, collecting water. Men do perhaps as much in hours but their work is more interesting – fishing, hunting or raising pigs, boat building, carving artifacts, discussing village matters.

In Polynesian islands, with their small areas, population growth has been high and without emigration would have proved devastating. New Zealand, Australia, Canada, Hawaii, and mainland USA have all absorbed Polynesian excess population. By the 1980s more Cook Islanders and Niueans were already resident in New Zealand than in the home islands, and the trend has continued. There are also several times as many American Samoans in the USA (including some thousands in Alaska!) as in American Samoa. There are something like 250,000 Island Polynesians in New Zealand, and considerable numbers in USA and Canada.

Regional Cooperation: Literature, Arts, and Games

Pacific oral tradition told stories of warriors of low birth who won wealth and rank through their exceptional character and abilities, of low-status women who became influential wives of paramount chiefs, and of younger brothers who challenged unworthy elder siblings. After European contact, some of these tales were written down by interested Westerners and an occasional newly literate Islander. But for 150 years South Pacific literature was produced by Westerners such as Hermann Melville (1819–91), Pierre Loti (1850–1925), Jack London (1876–1916), W. Somerset Maugham (1874–1975), and James A. Michener (1907?–97).

Prior to the 1960s, storytelling by South Pacific Islanders was an oral tradition. Though some modern writers use the oxymoron 'oral literature' there was virtually no literature as such by native Pacific Islanders. The first real indigenous literature developed with initiatives from the University of the South Pacific. Its student magazine, *Unispac*, included stories by Pacific Islanders. Even more significant, were the 1973 establishing of the South Pacific Creative Arts Society with its magazine, *Mana*, and the first Festival of Pacific Arts held in Suva in 1972 which stressed the uniqueness of indigenous culture. There then appeared a literature which discussed indigenous themes. Writers criticized colonialism and materialist values for their destructive impact, and lauded South Pacific difference from the rest of the world. With time, a more critical attitude to their own cultures has also emerged.

The most famous writer has been the Samoan Albert Wendt (1939–) who exposed the far from idyllic manipulation and conformity of his own islands in a string of novels such as *Pouliuli* and *Leaves of the Banyan Tree*. Wendt now works as a leading professor at the University of Auckland. The Tongan short-story writer and poet Epeli Hau'ofa has satirized various aspects of Island life: 'Our people work so hard on Sunday it takes a six-day rest to recover.' Other writers include Jaoh Saunana of the Solomon Islands, Raymond Pillai and Sudesh Mishra of Fiji, and Fata Sano Malifa and Sia Figiel of Samoa.

The quadrennial Festival of Pacific Arts, originally promoted by the South Pacific Commission, is the major cultural gathering for the whole region, and has brought about a revival or development of interest in all the arts indigenous and introduced. Each Festival convenes at a different city: following Suva were Rotorua, New Zealand, 1976; Port Moresby, PNG, 1980; Papeete, Tahiti 1985; Townsville, Australia, 1988 (Australian Aborigines take part); Avarua, Cook Islands, 1992; Apia, Samoa, 1996; Noumea, New Caledonia, 2000; and Palau, Caroline Islands, Micronesia is scheduled for 2004. Thousands of colourfully dressed Islanders carve, tell stories, make tapa, tattoo, cook in earth ovens, firewalk, and demonstrate other activities in almost limitlessless variety.

Organized sport is a high South Pacific priority. Tonga, Samoa, and Fiji have played one another in rugby for decades. Volleyball is popular throughout the islands. Tahiti is the leader in Pacific soccer. Body building and martial arts are intensely practised in even small islands. And the quadrennial South Pacific Games (and an inter-Games mini-Games!) bring together the sports elite of 22 countries/territories/

islands in a gathering which parallels that of the Festival of Arts. The twelfth meeting is planned for Suva in 2003. Both Festival and Games are vehicles for expressing pride in indigenous cultures and abilities. Of immense long-term significance, they are also creating a pan-Pacific Island fellow feeling.

COMMONWEALTH AND UNITED NATIONS

All the former British colonies and quasi-colonies remained in the Commonwealth, except when Fiji withdrew for a time after the military coup. The Commonwealth offers a glamorous stage upon which leaders of these mini-states can talk as equals with New Zealand, Nigeria, Australia, India, Britain, South Africa, and Canada, and look good at home; and it provides a natural contact with the countries of the Third World. It also provides special economic aid.

On British and New Zealand initiative, in 1968 the University of the South Pacific was established, based in Suva, Fiji. Paid for by most of the island governments, it was planned as a regional university to benefit all the islands. Innovative distance and extension education programmes were begun, with branches in many countries, and visits by central staff. But in practice Fiji continued to benefit disproportionately and dominated academic appointments. Substantial funding support came from outside, especially Commonwealth countries, including the cost of all the university buildings.

For reasons of prestige most Pacific countries have joined the United Nations. Though it occasionally allows their leaders to strut upon the world stage when the president or prime minister speaks to the General Assembly, they can ill-afford this luxury.

SECRETARIAT OF THE SOUTH PACIFIC AND PACIFIC ISLANDS FORUM

The South Pacific Commission, with headquarters in Noumea, New Caledonia, set up in 1947, was the first organization to promote *regional economic* development. Now consisting of 22 Pacific Island countries, plus, because of former or current colonial interests, USA, Britain, France, Australia and New Zealand, it meets annually. The first four countries listed provide about 90 per cent of the budget. In

1997 its name was changed to the Secretariat of the Pacific Community.

The second organization which attempted to coordinate South Pacific economic interests was the Pacific Islanders Producers' Association, begun in the early 1960s by Fiji, Tonga, and (then, Western) Samoa to help market their produce. In 1971, partly as a deliberate alternative to the South Pacific Commission, the Association was enlarged, and reorganized into the South Pacific Forum. Including New Zealand and Australia, it is now the most important regular meeting place for Pacific heads of government of 16 independent countries to consider a range of common interests. In 2000, now having North Pacific Micronesian membership as well, it was renamed the Pacific Islands Forum. Forum coordination much reduced the disadvantages of isolation. In 2001 it began discussing the idea of a free-trade agreement among members.

The Forum also established a civil aviation agency, a shipping line, a shipping council, a maritime development programme and the Forum Fisheries Agency, headquarters in Honiara, Solomon Islands. The last was to strengthen their hand in developing fishing in the 200-mile EEZs, and to protect themselves against the depredations of foreign fleets.

A South Pacific trade commission was set up based in Australia to promote exports there, and later a broader Regional Trade and Economic Cooperation agreement provided for improved access to the New Zealand and Australian markets. But trade within the region has always been minimal and dominated by the Melanesian countries.

The signing by Forum countries of the South Pacific Nuclear Free Zone Treaty in 1986 gave a feeling of regional solidarity as did co-ordination of diplomatic protests against French atomic tests at Mururoa Atoll. Fiji and Vanuatu were banning visits by nuclear vessels as early as 1982.

Australia and New Zealand each pay a third of Forum operating costs. Australia provides more than New Zealand for Forum projects. By 2002 Australia was beginning to demand value for money. At the meeting in Suva, Prime Minister John Howard (1939–) made plain Australia's intention to link money with democratic standards. 'We have a perfect right to say to a country that we will provide aid but in return we would like certain standards of governance to be met.' This is a delicate issue. Heads of government of Pacific Islands countries are easily offended. In times of crisis they look to Australia to rescue them, but they resent it when Australia calls for order. By the end of 2002 these failing mini-nation states of the Pacific desperately needed reorganization. Otherwise collapse like that of the Solomon Islands threatened to occur elsewhere, especially in other parts of Melanesia.

Despite problematic politics, the convention of leaving office when voted out has been widely accepted in Melanesia and Polynesia. In this respect, other post-World War II independent countries in Africa and South East Asia (as well as long-established Latin American ones) are put to shame. So there is *some* sense in which the Island Pacific shows respect for constitutional authority. So far there have been successful *coups d'états* only in the Melanesian countries of Fiji and Vanuatu, and (except for the American settlers' overthrow of the Hawaiian monarchy in the late nineteenth century) Polynesia has had none.

New Zealand and the South Pacific Today and Tomorrow

In many ways, compared with a decade or so ago, New Zealand is a much more interesting country to live in and to visit. With the liberalization of shopping hours, gaming and liquor laws, no longer can overseas visitors superciliously complain that New Zealand is shut at the weekend. Still, such comments were made by people unaware of the positive family and social values, physical and mental health, and community welfare that such regulations enhanced. And these things have suffered under the changes. New Zealand government was transformed by the privatization of the 1980s and 1990s, streamlined and made more efficient, but the full results of these changes are still to be seen. It is undoubted that New Zealand is now a country of greater freedom economically and individually, but concomitantly has greater inequality. Whether this freedom has resulted in more creativity is also a moot point. A social climate of greater individual initiative and change also necessarily produces greater insecurity and hardship for some, and this has happened. But at least New Zealand has been brought into the mainstream of Western social economy.

Reaction to Britain joining the European Union forced the country's economic diversification, so that the chief market became the Pacific–Asia region. Though old staples like wool and mutton are still of major importance, with lamb, for instance, exported to 90 countries in 2002, many of the destinations have changed and some are Islamic. There has also been a new confidence and independence in foreign policy especially *vis-à-vis* the USA.

Achievement in the traditional sports of athletics and rugby has remained high, while successes in cricket and basketball have brought a new optimism. The Kiwi penchant for invention has taken new forms in the computer age, and there is no longer a 'cultural cringe' in the arts.

MMP massively changed the parliamentary and legislative scene, and in 2002 politicians and governments were still coming to terms with the new situation. Government introduction of radical change such as 'Think Big' or 'Rogernomics' now seemed to have been in a different historical era.

The decisions of the Waitangi Tribunal and direct negotiation with the government changed the economic status of many Maori tribes, suddenly making them big players in the nation's business world. Concomitantly, new tensions were introduced into Maori–Pakeha relations. A decade after the first large payments, it is obvious that for their own economic advancement, and to lessen government concerns and public criticism, some Maori tribes need to be more circumspect in their investments.

Relaxation of immigration regulations which brought in substantial numbers of Asians also changed the country, adding the diversity, interest, challenges, and social, religious, and ethnic tensions that multiculturalism inevitably brings. New Zealand was also rapidly being 'Polynesianized' by the high Maori birth-rate and by increasing immigration from Polynesian islands. It was a sign of the times when in August 2002, for the first time in the country's 700 years of political and religious history, Islam had been allowed to penetrate to such a degree that a member of parliament was allowed to swear allegiance on the Cour'an.

Thus the New Zealand political/social/economic scene changed enormously in the last twenty-five years of the twentieth century. Values and ways of doing things cherished for more than a century were overturned. Within two generations New Zealanders exchanged a British Empire and Commonwealth milieu for a South Pacific and global one.

At least a majority of New Zealanders still had faith in their country's future. This cannot be said for some of the Pacific Island nations. Though the indigenous Fijians believed in themselves, Fiji continued to be beset by ethnic hatreds. Samoa, and Tonga, despite their internal political problems, still believed in their own ethnicity. But smaller countries such as the Cook Islands and Niue were struggling to exist as separate entities. Tokelau and Tuvalu were wondering whether a rising ocean would sink them completely, and Niueans worry whether there will be anyone remaining on their island in a decade. French Polynesia faced an uncertain future, with future independence from France fraught with economic difficulties.

But Melanesia, except for New Caledonia, looked even more problematic. The New Zealand Ministry of Foreign Affairs was warning of horrendous problems 'from ethnic tensions, widening socioeconomic disparities, failures of governance, economic stagnation, population growth, and the impact of wider global trends'. Even worse, their vulnerability makes them (and these points apply to Polynesia too) soft targets for drug trafficking, people-smuggling into New Zealand and Australia, money laundering, and perhaps international terrorism.

Political independence did not lead to economic independence, and the desire of many Islanders for Western lifestyles brought disillusion and large-scale emigration which shows no sign of ending.

The pressure of the United Nations, which led to independence for so many of these fragile island states and mini-nations in the 1960s and 1970s, now looks at best problematic and doctrinaire.

On a positive note, there are some signs that this fragile independence may in time give way to a larger, perhaps federal political and economic entity encompassing all the now independent states of the South Pacific. The cooperation shown by the various pan-Pacific bodies such as the Pacific Islands Forum is a solid intimation of this. If the combined mineral riches resting untapped on the ocean floor of all their immense EEZs were fully exploited, the wealth of such a federation could be enormous.

As the early chapters of this book have shown, Pacific Islanders do share a common past: perhaps they may also share a common future.

Notes

Notes

Firewalking in Fiji

Firewalking has been practised for religious reasons in several parts of the Pacific such as, Fiji, and the Society Islands (Tahiti). Today Fiji is the home of ritual firewalking.

Various explanations for firewalking have been believed. It will ensure a good harvest, or it will purify the participants, or it is a test of guilt. According to Fijian legend, a warrior from the island of Beqa was given this power by a spirit god, and his descendants still have the power to firewalk. Traditionally fire-walking was done only on special occasions. Fijian participants followed (and still follow) rules of tapu (taboo) such as sexual abstinence and not eating coconuts. Today native Fijian firewalking is performed mostly for commercial reasons at several resort hotels, and tapu periods and preparations are shorter. Native Fijians walk on heated local stones with a fractured structure. Some Fijian Hindus also firewalk in a colourful ceremony, on red hot coals. Both groups of walkers believe that those who do not ritually prepare will be burned. Hindu walkers also believe that those who lack faith will be burned, the faithful spared.

BEQA FIJIAN FIREWALKING ON HOT STONES

In Beqa a 12/15 feet diameter pit of river stones is prepared. These stones, 12 or more inches in diameter, are heated for 6 to 8 hours by burning logs on top. Organized by a ritual leader, chanting young men clear the remnants of the logs away, and then flatten out the stones with a taut, thick vine. Bundles of special leaves and of long swamp grass are laid around the outside of the pit. They then stand in a circle outside the pit, leaving a gap for the walkers to enter. The actual firewalk consists of a brisk single-file walk around the circumference stones. At a shout the leaves and grass are tossed into the centre of the pit and the firewalkers remain for some seconds of chanting in the centre, then walk off. Following the walk, various ritual acts take place, the pit is covered with earth, and four days later further ritual acts occur. The firewalkers believe that unless every aspect of the sequence is precisely followed they will be burned.

HINDU FIJIAN FIREWALKING ON RED HOT COALS

To give thanks for the blessings of power and long life, Hindu firewalkers prepare with fasting and prayer. They then bathe in the Pacific, afterwards covering themselves with tumeric powder and ash. They pierce their bodies with sharp pieces of metal like a coil of wire through part of the skin of the throat, a neat metal trident through the ear-lobe (parts of the body where there are fewer nerve cells). Then they walk a mile or two to a temple. The whole sequence ritually prepares and, they unquestioningly believe, protects them for their ordeal. The walkers focus their minds upon the Divine Mother, and the actual firewalk consists of several brisk five-second walks over a bed of red-hot coals about 20 feet long. Ritual chanting and drumming accompany the walkers.

'The coals were hot enough to grill chicken,' observed a gullible modern travel writer, 'even at my considerable distance from them.' This is correct, but as we shall see, irrelevant.

Presumably the preliminary preparations, their faith, focusing on the Mother, the power given by the spirit of Beqa, the proper sequence of ritual, protect the walkers from pain and injury? Not at all.

FIREWALKING BY EVERYONE: IT'S JUST PHYSICS

As Dr John Campbell of Canterbury University, New Zealand, the doyen of Western firewalkers, says: 'IT'S JUST PHYSICS, FOLKS!' Each year Campbell conducts many firewalks to encourage scientific understanding and to fight superstition. In July 2002, in the middle of the city of Dunedin, New Zealand, after he had explained the simple physics principles involved, about 500 ordinary New Zealanders of all ages, with no special preparation, walked barefooted across a bed of red-hot coals.

No special mental state, no religious faith, no psychological preparation is needed. It is not a matter of mind over matter, indeed mind doesn't matter at all. To understand what is happening we need to distinguish (1) between temperature and heat and (2) between heat conductors and heat insulators.

A very small piece of matter can have a very high temperature but contain very little heat and not burn us when we touch it. People who have open fires in their hearths know that if a piece of red-hot charcoal spits out onto the carpet, they can pick it up and throw it back into the fire without getting burned, even though the temperature is very high.

Of course the beds of stones or coals in the firewalks reach a very high temperature, as much as $1470°F$ ($800°C$), and also contain large amounts of heat. But whether the bed of stones/coals will burn us depends not on the temperature or the amount of heat, but on whether enough heat can quickly penetrate into our feet.

Some materials are good conductors of heat, some are poor conductors, i.e., are good insulators. The first point to note about firewalking is that the surface of our skin is just dead skin cells and these dead cells are thickest on the soles of our feet, so our soles have a relatively low capacity for conducting heat, i.e., are reasonable insulators. The second point is that during a brisk firewalk it is only for a *short time* that each of the walker's feet is in turn *actually in contact* with the stones/coals for about half a second. So the soles of our feet are sufficient insulators for the time they are in contact.

Though the stones/coals are at a high temperature, and though there is an immense amount of heat in the bed, and though the stones/coals feel hot, and though some heat is transferred, insufficient heat is transferred at each step to injure firewalkers. Only a relatively thin layer of the charcoal is actually burning. When we step upon it, heat is transferred from this layer into the dead cell layer of our feet, and the surface fire temporarily even goes out, so the temperature of the surface drops. This is the reason why walkers' feet leave dark footprints in the charcoal for a few seconds. There is a parallel effect with the heated stones.

Anyone with normal feet can walk at normal pace four or five steps over red hot coals or heated stones without ill effect.

The key fact is the slow transference of heat, not the very high temperature or the total amount of heat in the beds. The high temperature of the stones/coals, which will cook a chicken if we leave it lying there, and which so impresses everyone, is an irrelevant distraction to understanding.

People can firewalk only on a few selected materials such as rocks with a fractured structure (as the native Fijians of Beqa do) or charcoal (as the Fijian Hindus do). People cannot walk on a bed of red-hot metals at the same temperature, for metals are good conductors. The heat energy lost from the metal surface into the layer of dead skin on our soles is replaced extraordinarily rapidly, so the surface temperature of the metals remains high, large amounts of heat are transferred, and we are badly burned in a fraction of a second.

Provided the native or Indian Fijian firewalkers don't dawdle, or mid-way stand still for too long to check their faith, they will firewalk successfully. Because native Fijians go barefooted so much of the time, they also have a thicker layer of dead cells on their soles than do people who wear shoes, and so can experience a longer safe period of time remaining in contact with their hot stones.

Choose *the facts of physics over superstition* and you too can firewalk. Of course, in Fiji the locals will try to stop you! After all, to claim that mysticism is involved keeps power in their hands.

The Treaty of Waitangi

Her Majesty Queen Victoria of the United Kingdom of Great Britain and Ireland regarding with Her Royal Favour the Native Chiefs and Tribes of New Zealand and anxious to protect their just Rights and Property and to secure to them the enjoyment of Peace and Good Order has deemed it necessary in consequence of the great number of Her Majesty's Subjects who have already settled in New Zealand and the rapid extension of Emigration both from Europe and Australia which is still in progress to constitute and appoint a functionary properly authorized to treat with the Aborigines of New Zealand for the recognition of Her Majesty's sovereign authority over the whole or any part of those islands – Her Majesty therefore being desirous to establish a settled form of Civil Government with a view to avert the evil consequences which must result from the absence of the necessary Laws and Institutions alike to the native population and to Her subjects has been graciously pleased to empower and to authorize me William Hobson a Captain in Her Majesty's Royal Navy Consul and Lieutenant Governor of such parts of New Zealand as may be or hereafter shall be ceded to Her Majesty to invite the confederated and independent chiefs of New Zealand to concur in the following Articles and Conditions.

Article the first

The Chiefs of the Confederation of the United Tribes of New Zealand and the separate and independent Chiefs who have not become members of the Confederation cede to Her Majesty the Queen of England absolutely and without reservation all the rights and powers of Sovereignty which the said Confederation of Individual Chiefs respectively exercise or possess, or may be supposed to exercise or possess over their respective Territories as the sole sovereigns thereof.

Article the second

Her Majesty the Queen of England confirms and guarantees to the Chiefs and Tribes of New Zealand and to the respective families and individuals thereof the full exclusive and undisturbed possession of their Lands and Estates Forests Fisheries and other properties which they may collectively or individually possess so long as it is their wish and desire to retain the same in their possession; but the Chiefs of the United Tribes and the individual Chiefs yield to Her Majesty the exclusive right of Preemption over such lands as the proprietors thereof may be disposed to alienate at such prices as may be agreed upon between the respective Proprietors and persons appointed by Her Majesty to treat with them in that behalf.

Article the third

In consideration thereof Her Majesty the Queen of England extends to the Natives of New Zealand Her Royal protection and imparts to them all the Rights and Privileges of British Subjects.

[signed] W. Hobson Lieutenant Governor

Now therefore We the chiefs of the Confederation of the United Tribes of New Zealand being assembled in Congress at Victoria in Waitangi and We the Separate and Independent Chiefs of New Zealand claiming authority over the Tribes and Territories which are specified after our respective names, having been made fully to understand the Provisions of the foregoing Treaty, accept and enter into the same in the full spirit and meaning thereof in witness of the which we have attached our signatures or marks at the places and the dates respectively specified.

Done at Waitangi this Sixth day of February in the year of Our Lord one thousand eight hundred and forty.

Haka: A Living Tradition

by Maria G. Figueroa

During the last fifty years interest in haka has increased considerably as Maori have reclaimed their heritage, and haka have become a phenomenon uniting Maori and Pakeha New Zealanders. It is fascinating that at the beginning of a new century, the young are expressing their pride as New Zealanders through practising this ancient *taonga* (treasure) of Maori culture.

POINT AND MYTHICAL ORIGIN

Maori dances were a way of expressing every emotion, used on such occasions as birth, marriage, and death, for divination and at new seasons of the year, in joy and sorrow, victory and defeat, for receiving visitors, going to war, and making peace. Dances and their accompanying songs or chants demonstrated the strong rhythmic sense of the Maori. According to their subject, dances could be slow and graceful or fierce and energetic.

In Maori legend, Te Ra, the Sun God, had two wives: Hineraumati, the essence of summer, and Hinetakurua, the essence of winter. Te Ra and Hineraumati lay together and gave birth to a son called Tanerore, whose dancing for his mother began haka. The trembling air or dancing light on shimmery hot summer days is Tanerore dancing, and the trembling of the performers' hands during a dance is Tanerore's reflection, captured in the proverb: *Te haka a Tanerore* – 'the quivering of the air on a hot day'.

There has always been a male or female leader. The leader is like a conductor or musical director giving time to music, movement and the accompanying song solos and chorus parts. Both men and women dance. However, while the poi dances with their graceful expressiveness were/are exclusively for women, the haka can be performed by both. In many haka today, the men are to the fore, with the women lending vocal support in the rear. A common feature of all haka is the use of the whole body whether performed while standing, sitting, or kneeling.

DEFINITION

As with any living institution, distinctions become blurred, interpretations change, experts may differ and their categorizations may conflict. Nowadays categorization is itself a matter of intense debate. Even the word 'haka' is used in different ways. One school of thought says that 'haka' is really a generic name for all Maori dance. A second view is that the term refers specifically to the vigorous posture dances, the *taparahi* and *peruperu*, in which case other popular performances such as poi dances, powhiri, and action songs, though forms of Maori art of great traditional value and significance, and no less importance, are not haka. (*Taparahi* were/are performed without weapons, *peruperu* with weapons.) To prevent ambiguity, this second view will be adopted in the following discussion.

What the general public, especially outside New Zealand, often misleadingly calls 'the haka' is merely one specific dance, the *Ka Mate!* haka. Moreover, they think the *Ka Mate!* haka is a war dance (*peruperu*). To classify *Ka Mate!* as a war dance is to be ignorant of the history and sophistication of haka. This false idea may be the result of seeing performances by New Zealand's national rugby team, the All Blacks, who perform *Ka Mate!* prior to an international match *as though the match were a battle*. In fact *Ka Mate!* is an example of *haka taparahi*, i.e., haka without weapons. *Haka taparahi* are posture dances, which may express any public or private sentiment. (Most haka seen today are *haka taparahi*.)

HAKA PERUPERU OR WAR DANCES

The purpose of *haka peruperu* was to intimidate the enemy and reach the necessary level of excitement for battle. Performing such haka warriors became insensible to any possible threat or real challenge from the enemy, or, as they poetically put it, their 'angry friends'. The music created by *peruperu* was crucial in the effect. The stamping rhythmic ferocity of these haka was to freeze the enemy's blood and stir one's own. The haunting echo of *putatara* conch trumpet or *pukaea* war horn along with the resonant booming of the *pahu* tree gong, contributed to the art of Tu, the god of war.

Lieutenant-Colonel Arapeta Awatere, who led the Maori Battalion towards the end of World War II, said that *peruperu* was the true war dance, pointing out that, '*Peruperu* is the intensive form of *peru* "anger" and this is how the war-dance got its name, and that is its psychological purpose which no other form of haka could match in the past, can match now, or ever will.' The anthropologist Elsdon Best claimed that *peruperu* were performed on occasions such as: (1) *arrival of visitors* because part of the ritual of encounter was based on the assumption that intentions were unknown. Whether they came in peace or not, the war party's preparedness and the war dance accompanying the ritual helped determine the intentions of the visitors; (2) *preparation for war or imme-diately before a battle* performed to determine the omens, to learn the opinion of the gods of war in relation to the expedition; the performance of the warriors helped to divine whether success or defeat lay ahead of them; a faultless haka implied good fortune; (3) *conclusion of a successful battle* after the enemy had fled the field. This war dance was a demonstration of superiority, success and the joy of victory. Replicas of weapons from pre-European and nineteenth-century wars are the ones used in *peruperu* today.

Some experts distinguish between *peruperu*, *tutu ngarehu* and *whakatu waewae* – all being war dances. They say *peruperu* is characterized by high leaps with legs folded under, whereas in *tutu ngarahu* the warriors jump from side to side, while in *whakatu waewae* there is no jumping.

FURTHER VARIETIES OF HAKA

According to different experts there are many other varieties of *haka taparahi*. A few of these are described here. *Ngeri* is a short haka with no set movements, which allow the performers freedom to express themselves in various ways. It is used, as one expert says, 'to stiffen the sinews, to summon up the blood', to enthuse the dancers. It is a short, sharp wake-up call to action of various sorts. *Manawawera* like *Ngeri* has no set movements, and is performed at funerals, unveilings, ceremonies connected with the dead. *Kaioraora* are formal means of expressing hatred. Literally the word means to eat alive. Every tribe has composed them, and every tribe has inspired them. To be the inspiration of *kaioraora* was and still can be an honour. So today, *kaioraora* tend to be preserved by the tribe that is hated or whose ancestor is hated! (Mostly they have been composed by women.) There are also varieties of haka specific to tribes, heard by outsiders, if at all, only at festivals.

As will be seen from the descriptions already provided, categories and varieties of haka can be based on function, or on the manner of performance, or on how performers are grouped, and so on.

TECHNIQUES

Haka involve a series of rhythmical movements of the whole body accompanied by a song or a series of short refrains. Haka portray the passion and vigour of the race. They are a message of the soul expressed through words and movement. In performing them the whole body comes into play, particularly the face. The expression of the face graphically illustrates the meaning of the words.

Essential features are: (1) *pukana*, used in all forms of Maori dance, which involves *dilating the eyes* so that the whites are exaggerated and the pupils barely seen, performed by both sexes; (2) *whetero* or the *protruding of the tongue to full length*, performed by the men only; (3) *potete*, which is the *closing of the eyes at different points in the dance*, performed by the women only. It is essential that only some dancers in the group *pukana* and do so with grace and style. In the case of the female, the *pukana* accompanied by a knowing smile can do much to beguile and to allure. While the male does not smile in quite the same way as the female, there is much that is attractive about the male *pukana* and *whetero*.

Since thoughts are expressed using the tongue, it is highly honoured in Maori culture, as shown in the exaggerated stylized carvings of male ancestors. The message of every haka might be elementary or profound, but for that message to be fully expressed the tongue is of the utmost importance. In Maori culture it is the male who stands on the marae to express the personal and collective thoughts of his people. Depending on his mastery of the word, their mana rises or falls. It is essential to be able to display this mastery of the tongue. Women do not *whetero* in haka because they are not principal speakers on the marae. Similarly the eyes are of central importance because Maori believe that the eyes are the windows of the soul; they express what the rest of the body cannot.

Other traditional terms are: (4) *whakapi*, contorting the body and facial features; (5) *were*, pouting or projecting the lips; (6) *potete*, grimacing. Meanings of these terms may vary from tribe to tribe.

Although *haka taparahi* and other dances interpreted many social events which were peaceful in intent, because they were not a mere pastime but a custom of high social importance, they, just like *haka peruperu*, had to be *performed* with energy. Competitors at present-day haka events are advised that if they still have energy at the end, then they did not perform properly!

KA MATE!

Below are the most famous lines from the *haka taparahi* performed by the New Zealand rugby All Blacks, and nowadays by many other New Zealand international sporting teams. It is widely believed that *Ka Mate!* was composed by Te Rauparaha (see Chapter 6), the terrifying fighting chief of the Ngati Toa, who as a young man was hiding in a kumara storage pit while fleeing pursuing warriors. It tells the simple tale of his vacillating emotional state as the warriors searched for him: from fear of capture and death to the sunlike exhilaration of escape.

> *A, ka mate! Ka mate!*
> *Ka ora! Ka ora!*
> *Ka mate! Ka mate!*
> *Ka ora! Ka ora!*
> *Tenei te tangata puhuruhuru*
> *Nana nei i tiki mai whakawhiti te ra!*
> *A, hupane! A, kaupane!*
> *A, hupane! A, kaupane!*
> *Whiti te ra!*

> 'Tis death! 'Tis death!
> 'Tis life! 'Tis life!
> 'Tis death! 'Tis death!
> 'Tis life! 'Tis life!
> Behold! There stands the hairy man
> Who will cause the sun to shine!
> One step upwards, another step upwards!
> One step upwards, another step upwards!
> The sun shines!

THE FUTURE

For much of the twentieth century it was the male Maori boarding schools that ensured the continued performance of haka of a variety of themes. While many of the allusions and references were unknown to the younger performers, haka were preserved and disseminated.

The main nationwide vehicle for expressing the importance of haka today is the biennial Aotearoa Traditional Maori Performing Arts Festival begun in Rotorua in 1972. A very positive outcome of this extraordinary Festival is not just the immense stimulation and popularity it has created for haka, but that many haka have been composed with widely diverging themes – haka continue to grow and diversify! This growth necessarily includes healthy controversy, such as questioning whether it is appropriate to perform *Ka Mate!* prior to international sporting events.

The majority of the Maori population are young, 40 per cent being under fifteen years of age. This younger component of the Maori population wish to be heard and to be considered in the decisions which impinge on their futures. Despite the problems of contemporary life, many of these young people have a strong feeling for, and an active interest in, tradition and custom, and haka are central to these *taonga*.

APPENDIX 4

Moko: Maori Facial Tattoo

by C.J. Chambers

Unlike in most of Polynesia where body tattoo was so important, in New Zealand it was the moko, the facial tattoo, which acquired greatest cultural and religious significance, and became in the created individual patterns a unique art-form. That the practice was ancient is indicated by the fact that bone chisels have been found in two of the country's oldest archaeological sites.

THE MALE MOKO

The male Maori accepted the moko in the prime of life, and wore proudly that which, as a core part of his identity, was 'at once an image of beauty and an image of ferocity', as Michael King says. Moko-wearers knew their patterns in detail and used them like signatures. On the Treaty of Waitangi essential parts of moko were used as signatures. As one old man told the journalist-historian James Cowan,

> You may lose your house ... your wife and other treasures. You may be robbed of all your most prized possessions. But of your moko you cannot be deprived, except by death. It will be your ornament and your companion until your last day.

The facial moko designated a person's standing in society, his pa group, and was intimately bound up with his fighting prowess.

The first Europeans to see the moko of such warriors were James Cook and his ship's company. Sir Joseph Banks observed that '...of a hundred tattoos which at first sight could be judged exactly the same, no two on close inspection proved alike.' It was this individuality which in New Zealand helped such tattoo to become *tapu* (taboo).

Each moko was chiselled in the traditional manner, preferably using the wingbone of an albatross, producing deep grooves in the skin, to which the ground black charcoal-derived dye was applied, which became blue when viewed through the skin. Spirals were characteristic of moko, and ancestral and lifeforce connotations were subsumed in the symbolism of the pattern. There were two elements in the patterns: standard designs, and those particular to each head which enabled the person to be recognized from his tattoo (often the sections inscribed on the forehead and in front of the ears).

A Maori warrior wearing a bird feather cloak with his face painted in a traditional moko design

The incising of a moko was accompanied by day-long ceremonies and chants with mystical and religious rites. For moko, like other aspects of Maori culture, was but one element in a unified view of life involving art, religion, food gathering, recording genealogies, birth and death, war, and so on. This *Maoritanga* (Maoriness/culture) involved a coming-to-grips with mundane ordinary life, but on another level was directed by unseen forces of Polynesian cosmogony.

The procedure was also excruciating and caused dreadful swellings. In the 1830s one observer wrote, 'The process was one of intense pain, the recumbent figure of the victim wincing and writhing at every stroke of the operator and quivering upon the torments inflicted.' The incisions, says another, 'caused a great deal of blood to flow which they kept wiping off with the side of the hand, in order to see if the impression were sufficiently clear. When it was not they applied the bone a second time to the same place.' In some cases there were permanent distortions of the features. To make sure their moko was never obscured, *Maori men plucked out every facial hair.*

Because the face and blood were involved, those being tattooed remained tapu, and had to be given food and drink by others. 'During the time of tapu', writes a minister, 'he could not be touched by anyone, or even put his own hand to his head.'

As male ornamentation became less acceptable under European and Christian influence, the patterns of moko became less varied and creative, and moko themselves less and less common. Cowan said he could find no male who acquired a moko later than 1865. Maori masculinity took on a European cast, with chiefs turning Christian and wanting no further part in warfare. They therefore refused the moko, and instead adopted beards and moustaches.

THE FEMALE MOKO

Maori myth and story-telling and reports by early European observers mention female warriors. There was Moenga, an 'Amazon', who 'fought with a paiaka, and hewed the enemy down on every side.' There was also the brave chieftainess, Maraea, who defended the gateway of Te Tapiri Pa and saved her people. And Hurihia the female *tohunga* (priestess), who had run miles to get help to defend her village, and who eventually acquired such mana and status she performed ceremonies prior to battle. There were women and girls of the *rangatira* (aristocratic) class who might possess consanguineous rights and responsibilities belonging to more than one tribe and who became crucial as peace envoys – it was acknowledged that such a 'female peace' was firm and reliable because gender and genealogy made it valid. It was these women, and the daughters of paramount chiefs, who were granted 'the blue privilege' of wearing a moko, and its acquisition was a time for special ceremony. But unlike the total facial tattoos of the men, women's moko concentrated on the lips and chin.

But with the decline in male moko, it was not just aristocratic women, but ordinary women and girls who decided to preserve parts of their culture through the visibility of the moko – the torture of the tattoo.

In time bone chisels were replaced by metal, and later still, by 1910, tattooing was even done with darning needles. The application of moko continued into the period between the world wars into the 1940s, indeed even into the 1950s. Special practitioners of the art drew and cut moko on women of all ages, and a prestigious specialist such as Tame Poata would progress all around North Island, travelling by train and car, and where they could not reach, by horseback.

The Maori ladies he and others tattooed thereby acquired a cloak of dignity and authority recognized by the Maori world. It lasted throughout their lives and affected all those who came into contact with them, including the men like Michael King who interviewed them in old age and made them the subject of their books and photographs. It was these women who preserved the spirit and significance of moko while much of the Maori world paid it little heed.

TODAY

Now the wheel has come full circle, and it is once again men, in this case young men, who are wearing permanent moko. As one explains,

> Not everyone can wear one. I had to get permission from the elders in my clan. And I prayed to my ancestral spirits to grant me the strength to wear a moko. Every moko is unique to the wearer. In my case every line tells a story. My moko reflects 480 years of my ancestry.

And at gatherings such as the Aotearoa Traditional Maori Performing Arts Festival, temporary moko are worn proudly as part of dance and haka competitions by both sexes.

The world too has started to take notice of moko. Though some Maori find foreigners' adaptation of moko (in fashion, for example) insulting, others welcome this acknowledgement of their unique art form. For many of them, moko are like haka in showing the world that New Zealand exists and has a creative indigenous culture of its own. As the writer/editor of a recent photography book on moko says, '*Ta moko* exposes more than the revival of a tradition – it reveals the beauty of Maori past and the promise of Maori future.'

Largest Islands, South Pacific

(First figure sq. miles, second figure sq. ks)
New Guinea (Indonesia/Papua New Guinea) 309,000/820,000
South Island (NZ) 57,900/151,000
North Island (NZ) 44,300/114,000
Grande Terre (New Caledonia/France) 6,250/16,192
New Britain (Papua New Guinea) 4,100/10,619
Bougainville (Papua New Guinea)3,600/9,324
Viti Levu (Fiji) 3,179/8,234
New Ireland (Papua New Guinea) 2,240/8,650
Vanua Levu (Fiji) 2,145/5,556
New Georgia (Solomon Islands) 2,116/3,365
Isabela (Galapagos Islands/Equador)2,060/5,300
Guadalcanal (Solomon Islands) 2,047/5,302
Isabel (Solomon Islands) 1,772/4,590
Espiritu Santo (Vanuatu) 1,550/4,015
Malaita (Solomon Islands) 1,500/3,885
Makira (Solomon Islands) 1,204/3,188
Choiseul (Solomon Islands) 980/2,538
Malekula (Vanuatu) 793/2,053
Manus (Papua New Guinea) 750/1,943
Stewart (NZ) 674/1,746
Savai'i (Samoa) 660/1,710
New Hanover (Papua New Guinea) 596/1,545
Fergusson (Papua New Guinea) 519/1,345
Lifou (New Caledonia/France) 500/1,296
Tahiti (Society Islands/France) 402/1,042
Upolu (Samoa) 384/1,114

Monarchs, Governors-general, Governors, Presidents, Prime Ministers

NEW ZEALAND

Governors

Sir George Gipps (also Governor of New South Wales) 30 Jan 1840–3 Jan 1841
Captain William Hobson 1840 (Lieutenant-Governor to 3 Jan 1841)
Willoughby J. Shortland (administrator) 1842
Captain Robert FitzRoy 1843
Sir George Grey 1845 (Governor-in-chief Jan 1848–Mar 1853)
Robert Henry Wynyard 1854 (acting)
Thomas Gore Browne 1855
Robert Henry Wynyard 1861 (acting)
Sir George Grey 1861
Sir George Ferguson Bowen 1868
Sir George Alfred Arney (acting) 1873
Sir James Fergusson 1873
George Augustus Constantine Phipps, Marquess of Normanby 1874
James Prendergast 1879 (acting)
Sir Hercules George Robert Robinson, 1879 (acting to 17 Apr 1879)
James Prendergast (acting) 1880
Sir Arthur Hamilton Gordon 1880
James Prendergast (acting) 1883
Sir William Francis Drummond 1883
James Prendergast (acting) 1884
William Hillier, Earl of Onslow 1889
James Prendergast (acting) 1892
David Boyle, Earl of Glasgow 1892
James Prendergast (acting) 1897
Uchter John Mark Knox, Earl of Ranfurly 1897
William Lee, Baron Plunket 1904
Sir Robert Stout (acting)1910
John Poynder Dickson-Poynder, Baron Islington 1910

Sir Robert Stout (acting) 1912
Arthur William de Brito Savile Foljambe, Earl of Liverpool 1912

Governors-general

Arthur William de Brito Savile Foljambe, Earl of Liverpool 1912
Sir Robert Stout (acting) 1920
John Rushworth, Viscount Jellicoe of Scapa 1920
Charles Fergusson 1924
Sir Michael Myers (acting) 1930
Charles Bathurst, 1930 (from 1935 Viscount Bledisloe of Lydney)
Sir Michael Myers (acting) 1935
George Monckton-Arundell, Viscount Galway 1935
Sir Michael Myers (acting) 1941
Sir Cyril Newall, Baron Newall 1941
Sir Michael Myers (acting) 1946
Sir Bernard Cyril Freyberg 1946 (from 1951, Baron Freyberg of Wellington)
Sir Humphrey O'Leary (acting) 1952
Sir Willoughby Norrie 1952 (from 1957 Baron Norrie)
Sir Harold Eric Barrowclough (acting) 1957
Charles John Lyttelton, Viscount Cobham 1957
Sir Harold Eric Barrowclough (acting) 1962
Sir Bernard Fergusson 1962
Sir Richard Wild (acting) 1966
Sir Arthur Porritt 1966
Sir Richard Wild (acting) 1972
Sir Denis Blundell 1972
Sir Richard Wild (acting) 1977
Sir Keith Jacka Holyoake 1977
Sir Ronald Davidson (acting) 1980
Sir David Stuart Beattie 1980
Sir Paul Reeves 1985
Dame Catherine Tizard 1990
Sir Michael Hardie Boys 1996
Dame Sian Elias (acting) 2001
Dame Silvia Cartwright 2001

Premiers and Prime Ministers (since responsible government)

Until the time of John Ballance, premiers did not lead parties in the modern
sense. They were supported by loose coalitions and factions based upon shifting
local and sectional interests. Though they might dub themselves 'Liberals' or
'Conservatives' these were at best general labels.

The word 'Premier' was used until 1906, when reference was first made to Seddon as Prime Minister.

Henry Sewell 1856
William Fox 1856
E.W. Stafford 1856–61
William Fox 1861–62
Alfred Domett 1862–63
Frederick Whitaker 1863–64
F.A.Weld 1864–65
E.W. Stafford 1865–69
William Fox 1869–72
E.W.Stafford 1872
G.M. Waterhouse 1872–73
William Fox 1873
Julius Vogel 1873
Daniel Pollen 1875–76
Sir Julius Vogel 1876
Harry A. Atkinson 1876–77
Sir George Grey 1877–79
John Hall 1879–82
Frederick Whitaker 1882–83
Harry A. Atkinson 1883–84
Robert Stout 1884
Harry A. Atkinson 1884
Sir Robert Stout 1884–87
Sir Harry Atkinson 1887–91
John Ballance (Liberal) 1891–93
Richard J. Seddon (Liberal) 1893–1906
William Hall-Jones (Liberal) 1906
Joseph G. Ward (Liberal) 1906–12
Thomas MacKenzie (Liberal) 1912
William F. Massey (Reform) 1912–25
Francis H.D. Bell (Reform) 1925
Joseph G. Coates (Reform) 1925–28
Joseph G. Ward (United) 1928–30
George W. Forbes (United-Reform) 1930–35
Michael (Mick) J. Savage (Labour) 1935–40
Peter Fraser (Labour) 1940–49
Sidney G. Holland (National) 1949–57
Keith J. Holyoake (National) 1957
Walter Nash (Labour) 1957–60
Keith J. Holyoake (National) 1960–72

John R. Marshall (National) 1972
Norman E. Kirk (Labour) 1972–74
Wallace (Bill) E. Rowling (Labour) 1974–75
Robert D. Muldoon (National) 1975–84
David R. Lange (Labour) 1984–89
Geoffrey Palmer (Labour) 1989–90
Michael (Mike) K. Moore (Labour) 1990
James (Jim) B. Bolger (National) 1990–96
James (Jim) B. Bolger (National/NZ First) 1996–97 (first MMP election)
Jenny Shipley (National/NZ First) 1997–99
(minority government from August 1998)
Helen Clark (Labour/United) 1999–2002
Helen Clark (Labour/Progressive) 2002 (minority government)

AMERICAN SAMOA (since election of governors)

Governors

Peter T. Coleman (Republican) 1978
Aifili P.L. Lutali (Democrat) 1985
Peter T. Coleman (Republican) 1989
Aifili P.L. Lutali (Democrat) 1993
Tauese P.F. Sunia (Democrat) 1997

COOK ISLANDS (since independence)

Prime Ministers

Albert R. Henry (Cook Islands Party) 1965
Sir Thomas Davis (Democratic Party) 1978
Geoffrey Henry (Cook Islands Party) 1983
Pupuke Robati (Democratic Party) 1987
Sir Geoffrey Henry (Cook Islands Party) 1989
Dr Joseph Williams (Coalition) 1999
Dr Terepai Maoate (Coalition) 1999
Dr Robert Woonton (all-party Coalition) 2002

FIJI (since independence)

Governors-general

Sir Robert Sidney Foster 1970
Ratu Sir George Cakobau 1973
Ratu Sir Penaia Ganilau 1983

Presidents

Ratu Sir Penaia Ganilau 1987
Ratu Sir Kamisese Mara 1993 (acting to Jan 1994)
Ratu Josefa Iloilo 2000

Head of the Interim Military Government

Josaia Voreqe 'Frank' Bainimarama 2000

Prime ministers

Ratu Sir Kamisese Mara 1987 FA
Timoci Bavadra NFP 1987
Sitiveni Rabuka 1987 (military coup d'etat)
Ratu Sir Kamisese Mara FA 1987
Sitiveni Rabuka FPP-SVT 1992
Mahendra Chaudhry FL 1999 (from 19 May 2000, captive of Speight)
George Speight (coup d'etat) 19 May 2000–13 Jul 2000
Ratu Tevita Momoedonu (acting for Chaudhry) 27 May 2000 (hours)
27 May 1940–4 Jul 2000 (Vacant)
Laisenia Qarase Non-party (interim) 2000
Ratu Tevita Momoedonu 14 Mar 2001–16 Mar 2001
Laisenia Qarase FPP-SVT 2001 (interim) 2001

Party abbreviations: FA = Fijian Association (Fijian nationalist); FL = Fijian
Labour Party (ethnic Indian, social-democratic); FPP-SVT = Fijian Political
Party/Soqosoqo ni Vakavulewa ni Taukei (ethnic Fijian nationalist); NFP =
National Federation Party (social-democratic)

FRENCH POLYNESIA (since autonomy)

High Commissioners (also presidents of the council of ministers to 14 Sep 1984)

Alain Robert Ohrel 1983
Bernard Gérard 1985
Pierre Angéli 1986
Jean Montpezat 1987
Michel Jau 1992
Paul Roncière 1994
Jean Aribaud 1997
Michel Mathieu 2001

Presidents

Gaston Flosse TH-RPR 1984
Jacques Teuira TH-RPR 1987
Alexandre Léontieff HM 1987
Gaston Flosse TH-RPR 1991

Presidents of the Territorial Assembly

John Teariki UP 1986
Frantz Vanisette UF 1987
Jacques Teuira TH-RPR 1987
Jean Juventin PUP 1987
Emile Vernaudon AA 1991
Jean Juventin UP 1993
Justin Arapari UP 1996

Party abbreviations: PUP = Partie Union Polynésienne (Polynesian Union Party); TH-RPR = Tahoeraa Huiraatira-Rassemblement pour la République (People's Rally for the Republic, conservative/gaullist); AA = Ai'a Api/ Nouveau Terre (New Land, centrist, autonomist); HM = Haere i Mua (Polynesian Party); UF = Uni Front (United Front); UP = Union Polynésienne (Polynesian Union, moderate autonomist, includes Te Tiarama and Here Ai'a parties)

PAPUA NEW GUINEA (since independence)

Governors-general

Sir John Guise 1975
Sir Tore Lokoloko 1977
Sir Kingsford Dibela 1983
Sir Ignatius Kilage 1989
Sir Serei Eri 1990
Dennis Young (acting) 1991
(Sir) Wiwa Korowi 1991
(Sir) Silas Atopare 1997

Prime Ministers

Michael T. Somare PNGUP 1975
Sir Julius Chan PNGUP 1980
Paias Wingti PDM 1985
Rabbie Namaliu PNGUP 1988
Paias Wingti PDM 1992
Sir Julius Chan PPP 1994
John Giheno (acting) PPP 1997
Sir Julius Chan PPP 1997
Bill Skate PNC 1997
Sir Mekere Morauta PDM 1999
Sir Michael T. Somare NAP 2002

Party abbreviations: NAP = National Alliance Party; PDM = People's Democratic Movement; PNC = People's National Congress; PNGUP = Pangu Pati (Papua New Guinea United Party); PPP = People's Progress Party

SAMOA (since independence)

Heads of State (*O le Ao o le Malo*)

Malietoa Tanumafili II and Tupua Tamasese Mea'ole 1 Jan 1962–5 Apr 1963
Malietoa Tanumafili II 5 Apr 1963

Prime Ministers

Tupua Tamasese Lealofi IV Non-party 1972
Mata'afa Mulinu'u II Non-party 1973
Tupua Tamasese Lealofi IV Non-party 1975
Tupuola Taisi Tufuga Efi CDP 1976

Va'ai Kolone HRPP 1982
Tupuola Taisi Tufuga Efi CDP 1982
Tofilau Eti Alesana HRPP 1982
Va'ai Kolone HRPP 1985
Tofilau Eti Alesana HRPP 1988
Tuilaepa Sailele Malielegaoi HRPP 1988

Party abbreviations: CDP = Christian Democratic Party; HRPP = Human Rights Protection Party; SNDP = Samoan National Development Party

SOLOMON ISLANDS (since independence)

Governors-general

Baddeley Devesi (from 1980, Sir Baddeley Devesi) 1978
Sir George Lepping 1988
Moses Pitakaka (from 1995, Sir Moses Pitakaka) 1994
Sir John Lapli 1999

Prime Ministers

Peter Kenilorea SIUPA 1978
Solomon Mamaloni PAP 1981
Sir Peter Kenilorea SIUPA 1984
Ezekiel Alebua SIUPA 1986
Solomon Mamaloni SIUPA 1989
Francis Billy Hilly Non-party 1993
Solomon Mamaloni GNUR 1994
Bartholomew Ulufa'alu SILP 1997 (5 Jun–27 Jun 2000 held hostage by MEF)
Manasseh Sogavare PPP 2000
Sir Allan Kenakeza PAC 2001

Party abbreviations: SIUPA = Solomon Islands United Party; SILP = Solomon Islands Liberal Party; NAP = National Action Party; PAC = People's Alliance Party (social-democratic); GNUR = Group for National Unity and Reconciliation (Solomon Islands National Unity, Reconciliation and Progress Party); MEF = Malaita Eagle Force (paramilitary, ethnic Malaita islander regionalist); PPP = People's Progressive Party

TONGA (since constitutional government)

Monarchs

King George Tupou I 1875
King George Tupou II 1893
Queen Salote Tupou III 1918
King Taufa'ahau Tupou IV 1965

Prime Ministers (all Non-party)

Tevita Unga 1875
Rev. Shirley Waldemar Baker 1881
Sir Basil Thomson (acting) 1890
George Tuku'aho 1890
Jiosateki Toga 1893
Jione Mateialono 1905
Tevita Tu'ivakano 1912
Uiliami Tupou-lahi Tungi 1922
Salomone Ata 1940
Prince Taufa'ahau Tungi (became Taufa'ahau Tupou IV) 1949
Prince Fatafehi Tu'ipelehake 1965
Baron Vaea of Houma 1991
Prince Lavaka Ata Ulukalala 2000

VANUATU (since independence)

Presidents

Ati George Sokomanu VP 1980
Frederick Karlomuana Timakata (acting) VP 1984
Ati George Sokomanu VP 1984
Onneyn Tahi (acting) VP 1989
Frederick Karlomuana Timakata VP 1989
Alfred Maseng (acting) UPM 1994
Jean-Marie Léyé Lenalcau Manatawai UPM 1994
Nipake Edward Natapei (acting) VP 1999
John Bennett Bani UPM 1999

Prime Ministers

Walter Hadye Lini VP 1980
Donald Kalpokas Masikevanua VP 1991
Maxime Carlot Korman UPM 1991

Serge Rialuth Vohor UPM 1995
Maxime Carlot Korman UPM 1996
Serge Rialuth Vohor UPM 1996
Donald Kalpokas Masikevanua VP 1998
Barak Tame Sopé Maautamata MPP 1999
Edward Natapei VP 2001

Party abbreviations: VP = Vanua'aku Pati (Party of Our Land, Socialist, anglophone); UPM = Union des Partis Modérés (Union of Moderate Parties, authoritarian, francophone); MPP = Melanesian Progressive Party

Chronology of major events New Zealand ('NZ' = New Zealand)

1838	First Catholic mission arrives (Pompallier).
1839	British Colonial Office decides to intervene in NZ; Col. William Wakefield of NZ Co. arrives, 'buys' 8 million hectares/31,000 sq.mls of Maori land.
1840	Capt. William Hobson as Lt.-Governor; NZ jurisdiction separated from New South Wales; Treaty of Waitangi signed; NZ claimed by British; capital shifted to Auckland; Wellington settled by NZ Company.
1841	First settlers in New Plymouth (Taranaki).
1842	First settlers in Nelson; first merino sheep arrive (from Australia).
1843/46/47	Isolated skirmishes at Wairau, Wanganui, and Wellington.
1844	Honi Heke at Kororareka begins Northern War; beginning of North Island sheep industry.
1845	Honi Heke and Kawiti sack Kororareka; Northern War a draw.
c.1845–1860	era of Maori/settler cooperation.
1846	Gov. Grey kidnaps Te Rauparaha; Col. Despard at Ohaeawai.
1847	Wellington colony granted a Lieutenant-Governor.
1848	Free Church of Scotland settlers at Dunedin (Otago).
1850	Anglican settlers at Christchurch (Canterbury).
1851	Pastoralism first profitable in Canterbury.
1852	British parliament passes NZ Constitution Act; central parliament and 6 provinces with assemblies; gold in Coromandel.
1853	Foundation of Oamaru.
1854	First national parliament meets; steamer for coastal trade arrives from England.
c.1854–58	Commencement of Maori King Movement.
1855	Provinces allowed control of land; huge earthquake in Wellington region; foundation of Invercargill.
1856	Responsible government introduced; Henry Sewell first premier; foundation of Napier
1858	Te Wherewhero first Maori king (as Potatu I) in King Country.
c.1858	Settler and Maori population equal.
1859	Foundation of Timaru.
1860–64	Main clashes of NZ Wars, in Taranaki, Waikato.
1861	Gold rush in Otago; Bank of NZ set up; *The Press* (Christchurch) established.
1862	First Maori schools set up.
1864	Defeat of Maori at Orakau; defeat of British at Gate Pa; West Coast gold rush; beginning of Hamilton; foundation of Hastings.
1864–72	Skirmishing between settlers/Maori Prophets; NZ Wars end.

1865	Capital moved to Wellington; establishment of Native Land Court.
1866	Foundation of Palmerston North.
1867	Maori right to vote; 4 Maori seats in parliament; completion of first tunnel (Lyttelton–Christchurch railway).
1868	Introduction of NZ standard time.
1869	Colonial Treasurer, Vogel, begins 10-year 'Vogel Boom', massive capital borrowing for public works/immigration; Otago University NZ's first.
1869–80	massive expansion of communications; natural increase/ immigration double population.
1876	Provinces abolished; Wellington linked by cable to Sydney (and thence London).
1877	Compulsory primary education.
1882	First shipment of frozen meat to Britain; first dairy cooperatives.
1882–90	Manufacturing boom in Dunedin.
1884	Married Women's Property Act; Maori King Tawhiao visits Queen Victoria.
1885	Commencement of Wellington–Auckland Railway.
1888	Scandal over sweated labour in Dunedin.
c.1890–1910s	Lindauer and Goldie paintings of Maori life.
1891	Liberal Party under John Ballance in government.
1892	Employers' Liability Act; establishment of NZ Rugby Football Union.
1893	Richard Seddon becomes Liberal leader and premier; women given vote.
1894	Industrial Conciliation and Arbitration Act; Shops and Shop Assistants Act restricts trade on weekends.
c.1896–1921	Prosperity based on small family farms.
1897	Queen Victoria's Diamond Jubilee; foundation Victoria University College, Wellington; 'Young Maori Party' forms.
1898	Old Age Pensions and Divorce Acts.
1899	NZ troops to Boer War.
1900	Deserting husbands forced to pay maintenance.
1901	NZ rejects federation with Australian colonies; NZ annexes Cook Islands, Niue.
1903?	Richard Pearce flies first heavier than air plane?
1905	Triumphal All Black rugby tour of Britain.
1907	NZ granted dominion status.
1908	Rutherford wins Nobel Prize for Chemistry; Quackery Prevention Act.
1909	Reform Party set up; Federation of Labour established.

1910/11/12/13	Wilding wins Wimbledon tennis title.
1911	Widows pensions introduced.
1912	First Reform Party government, under Massey.
1913	Waterfront strike, intense government–union confrontation.
1914	NZ declares war on Germany, captures German Samoa.
1914–18	In World War I 17,000 men killed, 56,000 wounded.
1915	NZers as ANZACS take part in Gallipoli Campaign in Turkey – first great foreign battle; Palestine campaign begins.
1916	Maori Pioneer Battalion established; NZ troops on Western Front; Labour Party formed.
1917	Battle of Passchendaele; 6pm closing of bars (until 1967).
1918	Influenza pandemic.
1919	NZ member of League of Nations.
1920–29	'Roaring Twenties'; expansion of communications, electricity; marketing boards; Ratana Church develops.
1925	Coates first NZ-born PM; Tokelau passed by Britain to NZ.
1928	Ngata first Maori Minister.
1930	Great Depression begins to bite; Ratana links with Labour.
1931–36	Massive unemployment, national trauma; writers explore NZ themes.
1931	Napier–Hastings earthquake.
1932	Depression Riots in Dunedin, Auckland, Wellington.
1933	McCombs first woman MP.
1935	First Labour Party victory under Savage; commencement Homer Tunnel.
mid-1930s	Female pilot Jean Batten smashes aviation records.
1939	NZ declares war on Germany; Maori Battalion formed under own command; social security legislation.
1940	Centenary celebrations; NZ airmen in Battle of Britain.
1941	NZ declares war on Japan; NZers serve with distinction in Greece, Crete.
1942	Battles of Minqar Quaim and El Alamein; US marines arrive in NZ (to 1944).
1943	Italian campaign begins; NZ troops fight in South Pacific.
1944	Battle of Cassino in Italy; NZ begins Pacific withdrawal
1945	Trieste captured; NZers serve with Allied occupation forces in Japan; NZ foundation member of UN; nationalization of Bank of NZ.
1947	NZ ratifies Statute of Westminster; *Landfall*, literary journal established; baby-boom begins.
1948	Economic Stabilization Act.
1949	Resounding National Party electoral victory under Holland.

1949–63	NZ troops help fight Malayan Communists, Indonesian Confrontation against Malaysia.
1950	NZ troops with UN to Korean War (to 1953); Legislative Council abolished; NZ supports Colombo Plan.
c.1950–1970	NZ economic prosperity.
1951	Bitter 151-day waterfront strike; ANZUS Pact signed; Maori Women's Welfare League established.
1953	Hillary first man to climb Mt Everest; Ruapehu crater lake bursts, kills train travellers.
1964	NZ troops to Vietnam.
c.1970 on	Maori cultural, economic, political renaissance.
1971	Protests against Vietnam War reach peak; NZ Film Commission set up; NZ joins 5-Power defence arrangements.
1972	NZ troops withdraw from Vietnam.
1973	Massive oil price-rise; Britain joins EEC (EU), forces economic rethinking; NZ protests against French atomic tests.
1973–85	Search for new markets; diversification of factories, horticulture, fishing; increasing government economic controls.
1974	Franchise extended to 18-year-olds.
1975	Waitangi Tribunal established to determine Maori land claims; Whina Cooper leads Maori land march to Wellington.
1977	First great Maori occupation, Bastion Point in Auckland; contraception, sterilization, abortion made legal.
1978	CER (Closer Economic Relationship) with Australia.
1981	Controversial South African rugby tour of NZ.
1982	Synthetic petroleum plant begun.
1985	Massive deregulation and free-market policies instituted by Labour; Greenpeace's *Rainbow Warrior* sunk in Auckland by French agents; jurisdiction of Waitangi Tribunal retrogressive to 1840.
1986	NZ Constitution Act; large-scale corporatization of government departments; Yacht KZ7 wins America's Cup; homosexual law reform.
1987	Nuclear Free Zone Control Act effectively ends NZ role in ANZUS; NZ All Blacks win first Rugby World Cup.
1989	Regions established; new Ministry of Maori Affairs; Bastion Point returned to Ngati Whatua; steel and coal privatized; radical changes to school governance.
1990	Dame Catherine Tizard, first female governor-general; Nationals election win with NZ's largest ever majority.
1991	Abolition of compulsory unionization; NZ troops in Gulf War.
1992	Fisheries Settlement Act awards Maori 10% commercial fishing quota; massive chunk of Mt Cook/Aoraki topples.

1993   MMP (proportional representation) in elections; NZ Rail sold to US interests.

1994   NZ troops as peace-keepers in Bosnia; Waitangi commemorations disrupted by Maori extremists; first legal NZ casino.

1995   Maori rejection of Treasury's proposed 'Fiscal envelope'; $170 million reparations awarded to Tainui; ship *Tui* sent to protest against French Pacific nuclear tests, NZ cuts diplomatic relations with France; Mt Ruapehu erupts.

1996   First MMP election, small parties significant; $145 million to Taranaki Maori, $40 million to Whakatohea; National and NZ First form coalition.

1997   Jenny Shipley NZ's first female PM; *Skytower* opened.

1998   *Te Papa* opened; $170 million awarded to Ngai Tahu as reparations.

1999   Labour wins election, Helen Clark, NZ's second female PM.

2000   America's Cup retained; NZ troops in UN peacekeeping force to E. Timor; RNZAF fighter planes scrapped.

2001   NZ governed by women: PM, Governor-General, Leader of the Opposition, Chief Justice, Attorney-General (and chief executive of largest company).

2002   NZ peacekeepers to Afghanistan; Labour forms minority government.

Chronology of major events
South Pacific Islands ('SP' = South Pacific)

BC

c. 50,000 BC	Ancestors of Melanesians enter Pacific.
c. 8000 BC	Papuans reach Solomons.
c. 2000–1300	Lapita Cultural Complex evolves in Bismarck Archipelago/ Solomon islands.
c. 1200 BC	Proto Polynesians (Lapita People) reach Vanuatu, Fiji, Tonga.
c. 1000 BC	Proto-Polynesians (Lapita People) settle Samoa.

AD

c. 300	Polynesians settle Marquesas.
c.700	Settlement of Easter Island?
c. 950	Tongans conquer Sava'i and Upolu in Samoa.
c. 1000	First settlers of Cook Islands.
c.1000 on	Regular tribal warfare in Fiji.
c. 1200–1300	Heyday of moai (statues) building, Easter Island.
1520	Magellan, first European to sail Pacific.
1567	de Mendana finds the Solomon Islands.
1595	de Quiros finds Espiritu Santo in Vanuatu.
1605–6	de Quiros and de Torres find south-east coast of New Guinea.
1642–43	Tasman, from Batavia (Djakarta) voyages along west coast of NZ and through Tonga and Fiji.
1722	Dutchman Roggeveen lands on Rapanui, calls it Easter Island.
1760s on	Rise of Pomares in Tahiti.
1767	Englishman Samuel Wallis and crew, searching for *Terra Australis Incognita*, find Tahiti; beginning of noble savage idea.
1769–71	Cook's first Pacific Voyage: through the Tuamotu Archipelago; 6 weeks in Tahiti to observe Venus; searches for *Terra Australis*; circumnavigates NZ; along east coast of Australia.
1772–75	Cook's second Pacific Voyage: sails anti-clockwise, visits NZ twice; penetrates beyond Antarctic Circle to disprove existence of *Terra Australis*; visits Easter Island, Cook Islands,

	Tahiti, Tonga, Fiji, New Caledonia; home via Cape Horn.
1774	Tahitian war fleet attacks Moorea.
1776–79	Cook's third Pacific Voyage: sails anti-clockwise through NZ to Cook Islands, searches for passage north of North America or Asia; to Hawaii where Cook is killed.
1788–89	Frenchman de Bougainville explores Pacific.
1789–90	Mutiny on HMS *Bounty*; mutineers to Tahiti and Pitcairn Is.; deposed Captain Bligh sails 4,000 miles in ship's boat to Timor.
1791	First SP whaling fleet of 5 ships leaves Sydney.
1797	Protestant missionaries to Tahiti.
1799–1840	Civil wars in Tonga.
1801	HMS *Porpoise* from Sydney begins Tahitian trade in pork.
1812	Pomare II of Tahiti converted to Christianity, followed by subjects.
1815	Pomare II wins Battle of Feipi; (Protestant) Christianity accepted in Tahiti.
1820	Village of Suva (later capital of Fiji) relocates from Nauluvatu to present position.
1821	Protestant missionaries to Cook Islands.
1822–29	Dumont d'Urville explores SP, categorizes Micronesia, Melanesia, Polynesia.
1830	Rev. John Williams to Samoa.
1836	Catholic missionaries to Tahiti.
1839–41	Wilkes US Exploring Expedition charts Pacific islands.
1842	French make Tahiti protectorate, with Papeete capital.
1843	Siege of Suva by Rewa and allies; beginning of Great Fijian War to 1855, Ba v Rewa, and Cakobau's rise to power.
1845	George Tupou I, king of Tonga.
c.1845	Whaling at its height.
1847	Tongans invade eastern Fiji.
1853	France annexes New Caledonia.
1854	Cakobau turns Christian.
1855	Cakobau allied to King George Tupou I of Tonga wins Battle of Kaba in Fiji.
1857	Godeffroys of Hamburg begin trading in Samoa in coconut oil.
c.1860–70	European settlers in larger numbers in Samoa, Tonga, Fiji.
1860s	Height of indentured labour trade for plantations; slave trading from Peru and Chile destroys cultures of Penrhyn (Cook Islands), Easter Island.
1862	Tongan King George's Constitution.
1864	First sale of Samoan land to foreigners – Godeffroys; New

	Caledonia becomes French penal colony, nickel discovered (mined from 1875).
1869	*Fiji Times* begins publication.
1869–73	Civil war in Samoa.
1871	Cakobau as leader of Fiji announces government; Cakobau's authority reinforced by arrival of HMS *Cossack*.
1873	Cakobau battles the Kai Colo hill rebels.
1874	Offer of Fiji to Britain, by Cakobau and Council of Chiefs is accepted; Levuka first capital; Gordon first governor.
1875	Measles epidemic kills 40,000 Fijians; rebel hill tribes pardoned.
1876	Tongan–German treaty of friendship, gives German use of port.
1878	Kanaks (New Caledonia) revolt against French rule.
1879	Tongan–British treaty of friendship gives British use of port; first indentured labourers from India to Fiji.
1880	France fully annexes Tahiti, begins annexing other archipelagoes (last, Australs in 1901) to form French Polynesia; end of reign of last Tahitian king, Pomare V.
1880s	Colonial Sugar Refining Co. constructs sugar mills in Fiji.
1882	Suva new capital of Fiji.
1883	Queensland's (Australia) annexation of east New Guinea disallowed by Britain.
1884	Germany annexes north-east New Guinea; Britain annexes south-east New Guinea (Papua).
1893	Solomon Islands a British Protectorate
1888	Chile annexes Easter Island; Cook Islands become British Protectorate after petition.
1889	Power struggles between Germany, Britain, USA in Samoa result in compromise appointment of king.
1899	USA and Germany annex and divide Samoa.
1900	Cook Islands to NZ control.
1902	Trans-Pacific cable links Fiji etc. to Australia, NZ, North America.
1906	Papua passes to control of Australia; British–French 'Condominion' in New Hebrides (Vanuatu).
1908	Mau Movement in Samoa resists German rule.
1914	World War I begins; German Samoa captured by NZ.
1915	Fijian, Tahitian, Kanak troops sail to World War I.
1917	Kanak revolt against French rule.
1918	Salote Queen of Tonga.
1919	Former German Pacific colonies become League of Nations mandates to Australia, Britain, NZ, (Japan in N. Pacific).

1920s (to 1935)	Political struggle between Samoan Mau and NZ.
1928	First trans–Pacific flight – by (Sir) Charles Kingsford Smith and Charles Ulm.
1929	Fijian Indians achieve Legislative Council representation; 11 Samoans killed by NZ police during demonstration.
1932	Fijian gold rush.
1939	World War II begins; Pan American commences trans–Pacific flying–boat service.
1941–45	Pacific Islanders work as labourers for Japanese and Allies; New Guineans/Fijians/Tahitians in Allied Forces.
1942	Japan invades New Guinea and Solomon Islands.
1947	SP Commission established.
1953	Queen Elizabeth II visits British Commonwealth Pacific islands.
1959	Kenneth P. Emory proposes that Polynesian origins were in Tonga–Samoa.
1960s	Imitation voyages help establish facts of Polynesian colonization.
1962	Western Samoa independent from NZ; 1962 on, expansion of French nuclear Centre d'Experimentation; 1962–6 Americanization of American Samoa.
1963	First Fijian Indian political party.
1965	Cook Islands independent in association with NZ.
1966	France begins atomic tests at Moruroa Atoll.
1968	University of SP established; Nauru independent.
1970	Fiji independent; Tonga fully independent.
1971	SP Forum set up.
1972	First Festival of Pacific Arts (Suva); birth of SP literature.
1974	Papua–New Guinea independent; Niue independent in association with NZ.
1977	First elected governor of American Samoa.
1976	SP Forum agrees on upon Exclusive Economic Zones (EEZs).
1978	Solomon Islands, Tuvalu, independent; Fijian troops as peacekeepers in Lebanon (and 1982 in Sinai).
1979	Kiribati independent.
1980	New Hebrides (as Vanuatu) independent.
1980 onwards	Democracy movement in Tonga.
1983	Monasavu hydro–electric power station opens in Fiji.
1984–6	*Les Evénements* disturbances in New Caledonia.
1986	SP Nuclear Free Zone Treaty.
1987	Two bloodless military coups in Fiji, declared republic; withdraws from Commonwealth; over decade 60,000 Indian Fijians emigrate.

1988	Provincial autonomy in New Caledonia.
1990	Race-based Fijian constitution; universal suffrage in Samoa.
1992	UN promulgates Law of the Sea; recommends 200-mile EEZs.
1996	French halts atomic tests.
1997	Western Samoa becomes 'Samoa'; new Constitution in Fiji.
1998	Noumea Accords signed in New Caledonia, substantial autonomy, setting independence referendum for 2018; revolution in Solomon Islands.
1999	Mahendra Chaudhry, first-ever Indian PM in Fiji.
2000	Coup in Fiji by Speight; tourism and trade affected; OECD criticizes Cook Islands, Nauru, Niue, Tonga, Vanuatu, Samoa, as tax havens harming trade/investment.
2001	New government in Fiji with all-indigenous-Fijian cabinet.
2002	African/Caribbean/Pacific summit in Fiji; Solomon Islands bankrupt.

Further Reading

General Histories, New Zealand

BELICH, JAMES, *Making Peoples* (Auckland & London/Honolulu, 1996, Penguin, University of Hawaii Press) long, witty, modern interpretation of evolution of Maori and Pakeha (settler) New Zealanders to c.1900

BELICH, JAMES, *Paradise Reforged* (Auckland & London/Honolulu, 1998, Penguin, University of Hawaii Press) modern interpretation of evolution of Maori and Pakeha (settler) New Zealanders since c.1900

BROOKING, TOM, and ENRIGHT, PAUL, *Milestones: Turning Points in New Zealand History* (Lower Hutt, 2nd ed. 1999, Mills Publications) 23 readable high-points of NZ history; large number of excellent, little-seen illustrations; annotated reading list

REEVES, WILLIAM PEMBER, *The Long White Cloud* (London, 1898/1924; London, 1998, Tiger Books) classic account of NZ development, by inspirer of NZ welfare state legislation

SINCLAIR, KEITH, *A History of New Zealand* (Auckland, revised ed., 2000, Penguin) short, stylish, cleanly written account

SINCLAIR, KEITH, (ed.), *The Oxford Illustrated History of New Zealand* (Auckland, 2nd ed. 1997, Oxford University Press) readable, modern chronological sequence by 15 specialist historians

MCKINNON, MALCOLM (ed.), *New Zealand Historical Atlas* (Wellington, 1997, David Bateman & NZ Department of Internal Affairs) spectacular coffee-table size book; innovative visual displays of political, economic, social history; idiosyncratic index

New Zealand's Wars

BELICH, JAMES, *The New Zealand Wars* (Auckland, 1986/1998, Penguin) reinterpretation by modern expert of wars between Maori and settler – formerly 'the Maori Wars'

CROSBY, R.D., *The Musket Wars: A History of Inter-iwi Conflict 1806–45*

(Auckland, 1999, Reed) first book-length description of epochal Maori civil wars; well illustrated and mapped

MCGIBBON, IAN (ed.), *The Oxford Companion to New Zealand Military History* (Auckland, 2000 Oxford University Press) readable encyclopaedia, alphabetically listing people, facts, and battles

Treaty of Waitangi

CHRISTIE, WALTER, *Treaty Issues* (Christchurch, 1997, Nationwide Book Distributors) sympathetic treatment of European/Pakeha viewpoint

ORANGE, CLAUDIA, *The Treaty of Waitangi* (Wellington, 1989, Bridget Williams Books) short, illustrated account explaining key points of view re NZ's foundational treaty

WARD, ALAN, *An Unsettled History* (Wellington, 1999, Bridget Williams Books) sympathetic treatment of Maori viewpoint

New Zealand and South Pacific Lives

BEAGLEHOLE, J.C., *The Life of Captain James Cook* (London, 1974, A. & C. Black; Stanford, 1998, Stanford University Press) culmination of life's work; masterful account of the greatest of all explorer-seamen, by the doyen of Pacific historians

BURNS, M.G., *Cobber Cain* (Auckland, 1992, Random Century) biography of the exuberant first air ace of World War II

CAMPBELL, JOHN, *Rutherford: Scientist Supreme* (Christchurch, 1999 AAS Publications) the biography of the extraordinary Nobel Prize scientist, by a modern NZ physicist; corrects much misinformation; illustrated

DALZEIL, RAEWYN, *Julius Vogel* (Auckland, 1986, Auckland University Press) life of the brilliant 19th-century treasurer and premier of NZ

DEVALIANT, JUDITH, *Kate Sheppard – a Biography* (Auckland, 1992, Random Century) life of talented leading NZ suffragette

KING, MICHAEL, *Te Puea: a Biography* (Auckland, 1973, Auckland University Press) life of Maori princess, most influential Maori female of 20th century

SINCLAIR, KEITH, *William Pember Reeves: NZ Fabian* (Oxford, 1965, Oxford University Press) story of restless statesman responsible for radical 1890s welfare state legislation

VON HAAST, H.F., *The Life and Times of Sir Julius von Haast* (Wellington, 1948) life of polymath who laid foundations of NZ science

The Dictionary of New Zealand Biography 5 Vols. (Wellington, 1990–2002, Ministry of Culture) vast resource for descriptions of deceased New Zealanders; about 3000 detailed biographies; some biographies of early Maori are genealogically problematic
Also available at www.dnzb.govt.nz/dnzb/

NZEDGE: biographies of many famous New Zealanders living and dead: www.nzedge.com

General Histories of the South Pacific

BEAGLEHOLE, J.C., *The Exploration of the Pacific* (London, 1966, A. & C. Black) the best Pacific historian in an early work

CAMPBELL, I.C., *A History of the Pacific Islands* (Berkeley, CA & Christchurch NZ, 1989/1996 University of California Press/Canterbury University Press) short, readable account by a world expert; good on early history and individual islands.

CROCOMBE, RON, *The South Pacific* (Suva, 2001, University of the South Pacific) distillation of a lifetime's travel and study of history and culture; fascinating details; specially good on period since World War II; earlier versions of this book in many libraries

IRWIN, GEOFFREY, *The Prehistoric Exploration and Colonization of the Pacific* (Cambridge, 1992/96, Cambridge University Press) archaeologist author argues that Polynesian colonization was relatively rapid purposeful and systematic, with continually improving methods

JENNNGS, J.D. (ed.), *The Prehistory of Polynesia* (Cambridge MA, 1979, Harvard University Press)

KIRCH, PATRICK, *The Evolution of the Polynesian Chiefdoms* (Cambridge, 1984, Cambridge University Press) discusses cultural differences between islands

LEWIS, D., *We, the Navigators* (Honolulu, 1972, University Press of Hawaii) remarkable reconstruction; essential reading for understanding Polynesian navigation

MAUDE, H.E., *Slavers in Paradise* (Canberra, 1995, Australian National University) account of capturing and enslaving of Pacific Islanders by Peruvians in 1860s; scholarly *and* readable

Histories of Individual Pacific Islands

BAHN, PAUL & FLENLEY, JOHN, *Easter Island, Earth Island* (London, 1992, Thames & Hudson) modern account, with moral

CAMPBELL, I.C., *Island Kingdom: Tonga Ancient & Modern* (Christchurch, 1992, Canterbury University Press) most authoritative modern Tongan history

DE BOVIS, EDMOND, *Tahitian Society Before the Arrival of the Europeans* (Laie, Hawaii, 1976/1980, Institute for Polynesian Studies, Hawaii Campus; Brigham Young University) translation of short account written in the 1840s; naval officer author key figure in the French annexation of New Caledonia

HOWE, K.R., *The Loyalty Islands* (Honolulu, 1977, Hawaii University Press) account of life of island chain east of New Caledonia

KING, MICHAEL, *Moriori* (Auckland, 1989, Penguin) story of ill-fated Moriori of the Chatham Islands east of New Zealand

MAC CLANCY, JEREMY, *To Kill a Bird with Two Stones* (Vila, 1990, Vanuatu Cultural Centre Publications) lucid account of Vanuatu from early times to independence

MELEISEA, MALAMA, and others, *Lagaga: A Short History of Western Samoa* (Suva, 1994, University of the South Pacific) definitive work on Samoa, by Samoan authors

SCARR, DEREK, *Fiji: a Short History* (London/Sydney, 1984, George Allen & Unwin) readable work by historian long resident in Fiji

SCOTT, DICK, *Years of the Pooh-Bah: a Cook Islands History* (Rarotonga & Auckland, 1991, Cook Islands Trading Corporation & Hodder and Stoughton) illustrated, readable account with emphasis on period of British and New Zealand control

TJIBAOU, JEAN-MARIE, *Kanake – the Melanesian Way* (Papeete, 1978, Les Editions du Pacifique) imaginative illustrated distillation of New Caledonian native (Kanak) history and way of life by a cultured independence leader

VAN TILBURG, JO ANNE, *Easter Island* (Washington D.C., 1994, Smithsonian Institution) scholarly account with latest interpretations

Historical Gazeteer ('NZ' = New Zealand)

Numbers in bold refer to the main text

AMERICAN SAMOA

Shares pre-1900 history with Samoa (q.v.). Became a separate polity in that year, when the Samoan Islands were divided with Germany. More dramatically beautiful than Samoa. Tutuila, the narrow 19-mile (30k) main island (200 inches/5,000mm rain yearly) is like some lush green dragon lying languidly in the ocean. From a plane or from the ridge of Rainmaker Mt (Mt Pioa) above the capital of **Pago Pago** the scene is breathtaking. Since dramatic Americanization of early 1960s, local agriculture has declined. Despite a flourishing tuna fishing industry, the economy is heavily reliant on the United States government. After previously being either US naval officers, or civilian governors appointed by the Secretary of the Interior, in 1978 the office of governor became elective. In recent decades thousands have emigrated to Hawaii and mainland USA.

The three **Manu'a Islands** to the east were traditionally believed to be the first lands created by god Tagaloa, and the paramount chief of this sacred place, the Tui Manu'a, was held in high esteem. The islands now being

American territory, the last Tui Manu'a, who died in 1909, stipulated that the title should end with him. The National Park of American Samoa (dedicated 1997) boasts shining, palm-fringed, white sand South Ofu Beach, which some connoisseurs claim to be the loveliest in the world. **114–18, 126, 300–301**

AUCKLAND AND REGION

NZ's and the Pacific Islands' largest city stands between deep **Waitemata Harbour** on **Hauraki Gulf** to the east and shallow **Manukau Harbour** to the west, on an isthmus produced by eruptions of more than fifty volcanoes during the last 50,000 years. Located at a similar latitude south to San Francisco and Athens north, Auckland enjoys a temperate climate. Aucklanders can indulge themselves on dozens of nearby beaches on mainland and Gulf islands. The rich marine and bird life and fertile volcanic soil of the Auckland Isthmus, were highly prized by early Maori, and caused recurring feuding. In the mid-1700s the Ngati Whatua from the north invaded and conquered much of the area and remained in control. In the Musket Wars of the early 1800s another Auckland tribe, the Ngati Paoa, which held land a little to the south of the isthmus, was massacred by the invading Nga Puhi from the Bay of Islands (q.v.) and fled southwards to the Waikato Region (q.v.), returning only in the 1830s.

From the early part of the 1800s, European and US whalers frequented Hauraki Gulf. The first European establishment was a sawmill in 1833. Missionaries arrived in the area by 1834. The Treaty of Waitangi was signed by several local chiefs in 1840, and at the invitation of the Ngati Whatua the village of Auckland was established by Lieutenant-Governor Hobson in 1840 as the first capital of British–Maori NZ. It was named after Hobson's superior, George Eden, 2nd Earl of Auckland (England), First Lord of the Admiralty, later Governor-general of India. A sailing regatta celebrated the occasion, repeated yearly ever since on Auckland Anniversary Day, which helped establish the city's enthusiastic sailing tradition. About 500 Scots settlers boosted the population in 1842. Substantial growth occurred during the NZ Wars of the early 1860s when Auckland became the base for the British campaign. Auckland continued to grow steadily to become NZ's largest port and city, overtaking Christchurch (q.v.) in 1897; by 1911 it had nearly doubled its 1897 population to over 100,000. It has continued to outpace the other cities, and by 2000 its metropolitan area was more populous than that of the other four biggest cities combined.

In 1959 the Auckland Harbour Bridge linked the city with the fast-growing North Shore suburbs and with **Devonport**, the chief naval base and dockyard of NZ. The inner suburb of **Parnell** has restored old houses and shops: *Kinder House* (1857) and *Ewelme Cottage* (built of kauri in the 1860s) are early structures. Other early homes are *Acacia Cottage* (1841) near One Tree Hill, *Alberton* (1862) in Mt Albert Road and *Highwic* (1862) in Epsom, all open to the public.

Auckland Art Gallery, NZ's first permanent gallery (opened 1888), holds some of NZ's earliest settler paintings, and Lindauer's and Goldie's portraits of Maori. *Auckland War Memorial Museum* in the Domain, sited on an extinct volcano, has extensive displays of Maori arts, including the splendid 1878 meeting house *Hotunui*, and the great war canoe *Te Toki a Tapiri* (Tapiri's battle-axe) c.1836. The *Museum of Transport and Technology* has remnants of Richard Pearce's original plane (which may have flown prior to the Wright Brothers) and his Utility Plane of the 1940s. The *National Maritime Museum* has imaginative displays.

South of the city centre, 654 feet 200m Mt Eden, like dozens of others in the area, was a former Maori pa (hill fort). The most extensive Maori earthworks are those of One Tree Hill; originally terraced gardens, they became important as fortifications sometime around the 1600s, capable of sheltering several thousand people, as outside tribes began to dispute control of the isthmus. Perhaps 600 years ago **Rangitoto Island**, the area's largest volcano (probably now extinct), erupted from the sea; there were Maori living on adjacent Motutapu Island at the time.

Notable private structures include the *Cathedral of the Holy Trinity* (in Parnell) and the 1,094 ft/333.6m *Sky Tower* (1994–97), constructed with innovative techniques to withstand Force 8 earthquakes, and 1-in-1000 year gales of 125mph/200kmh.

There are annual Pasifika Games of sports and dance competitions. Recent decades have seen substantial immigration of Asians and Pacific Islanders (such as Tongans and Samoans) who now make up about 14% and 13% respectively, and (together with Maori [11%]) have added richness and variety to the city's cultural heritage – and a level of ethnic tension unknown since the NZ Wars. **147, 148, 168, 171, 178–9, 223, 281, 287**

BAY OF PLENTY, VOLCANIC PLATEAU, CENTRAL PLATEAU

NZ's main volcanic area, which first became active about 2 million years ago, reaches in a broad band from active and growing **White Island** in the bay (for decades a sulphur mine), into North Island through the northern Bay of Plenty region to Rotorua and the Volcanic Plateau, south to Lake Taupo on the Central Plateau and the three great volcanic peaks.

The **Bay of Plenty** was named by Cook because of the prosperity of its Maori tribes and perhaps because he received ample supplies. CMS mission established at Te Papa in 1835. During the early years of the Musket Wars local tribes were devastated by campaigns of Nga Puhi from the Bay of Islands in Northland (q.v.), and involved in the mid-1860s in battles in the NZ Wars (Gate Pa, Te Ranga). **Tauranga/Mt Manganui**, are ports, manufacturing and resort towns, with attractive seaside and hill scenery, and centres for a rich fruit-growing area (main NZ kiwi-fruit region since 1970s).

To the south is the **Volcanic Plateau**, for long the homeland of the Te Arawa confederation. In 1823 Te Arawa were also invaded by Nga Puhi, took refuge on sacred **Mokoia Island** in **Lake Rotorua** (alt. 920 feet/280m) but were severely defeated. In the 1870s Te Arawa resisted government investigation of their lands, but increasing visitors to the local hot springs for therapeutic bathing, and to the gorgeous Pink and White Terraces of water-borne silica deposits near **Mt Tarawera** changed their minds; in 1880 the tribes agreed to development of a spa town at **Rotorua**. With the economic downturn of the 1880s, and the 1886 eruption of Tarawera (dormant for 500 years) which destroyed the Terraces (the explosion was heard in Auckland), development was retarded.

The 1894 opening of a railway link to Hamilton (q.v.) and Auckland (q.v.) spurred growth. In and near Rotorua ('Sulphur City') are the most energetic thermal areas in NZ, with gushing geysers, popping hot springs, pulsating mud pools, and sensational sulphur smells. The city itself grew on the south-west corner of 31sq. mile/ 80 sq.k Lake Rotorua, the largest of the regional lakes. In Ohinemutu, the lakeside Maori village section of Rotorua, are *St Faith's* Anglican Church with Maori decoration, and *Tamatekapua Meeting House*. In the Government Gardens by the lake, the impressive mock-Tudor former *Bath House* (1908) is now the *Rotorua Museum of Art and History*, storing Te Arawa treasures, historical displays and showing reconstructed spa rooms. **Whakarewarewa** ('Whaka'), 2k south, the largest and most-visited thermal area, has *Pohutu Geyser* and the *Polynesian Spa* (since 1886). Maori concerts and hangi (food cooked in traditional earth ovens) are a major attraction and a sort of living history. In 1972 this was the venue for the first biennial Aotearoa Traditional Maori Performing Arts Festival.

There are thermal areas farther out such as: **Waimangu Volcanic Valley** created by the eruption, with its Blue Lake, Green Lake, and buried Maori village; **Tikitere (Hell's Gate)**; and **Waiotapu**, 15.5 miles/ 25k south.

In the 1920s and 1930s huge areas of the Volcanic Plateau were planted with Monterey Pine (*Pinus radiata*) by government and private companies, and cobalt treatment of soils allowed expansion of mixed farming. Some decades later, milling and board production brought into existence such towns as **Kawerau** and **Tokoroa**.

About 30,000 years ago, farther south in the **Central Plateau**, a stupendous volcanic explosion threw more than 240 cubic mls/1000 cubic ks! of earth into the sky and across the countryside, leaving a huge depression. In AD 177 there occurred another explosion, earth's mightiest of the last few thousand years, with debris flung an estimated 40 miles (64k) into the atmosphere. (Its climatic effects were noted in China.) The hole produced by these explosions filled with fresh water to become **Lake Taupo**, 607 ft/185m deep, 25×15 mls/42×25k, NZ's largest. **Taupo** town grew from a military redoubt erected in 1869 by Lt. Col. J.M./Roberts's Armed Constabulary during the sporadic final phase of NZ Wars, and on land purchases from local Maori. A small town of less than 1000 people until after World War II, it now has a *Volcanic Activity Centre* and is a centre for boating, walking, rafting, and thanks to a batch of rainbow trout brought from California in early 1900s, also world famous for trout fishing. Nearby **Wairakei Thermal Valley** with the *Wairakei Geothermal Power Project*, (begun 1956, commissioned 1963) the world's second such project, generates about 5% of the country's electricity. Other considerable thermal areas are at nearby **Craters of the Moon** and the spectacular **Orakei Korako** about half way to Rotorua.

South of the lake is **Tongariro National Park**. In the early 1880s Te Heuheu Tukino, paramount chief of the Ngati Tuwharetoa, was worried about loss of his mana if parts of the great volcanic mountains in his region, sacred to Maori, were sold. His son-in-law, MP for Tauranga, suggested they be made, 'a tapu place of the Crown, a sacred place under the mana of the Queen'. From this idea emerged a deed of gift and the Tongariro National Park Act of 1894 which preserved the three volcanoes. Two of NZ's most spectacular walks: *Tongariro Northern Circuit* and *Tongariro Crossing* traverse the park. **Tongariro**, the most northerly volcano (6,457 ft/1968m), last erupted in 1926 and is active with several craters, coloured lakes, and hot springs. Geologically recent **Ngauruhoe** (6,983 ft/2291m) is a beautifully symmetrical cone with a single vent. Many-peaked **Ruapehu** (9,177 ft/ 2,797m), North island's highest mountain and most active volcano, has a crater lake. It erupts every few years. The special *Chateau Tongariro* tourist hotel near Ruapehu opened in 1929. **19, 137, 138**

CHATHAM ISLANDS

The Chatham Islands, about 500 miles east of the South Island of New Zealand, consist of a 348 sq. ml (901 sq. km) main island, a smaller one of 24sq ml (62 sq. km), 8 others, and a towering 566-feet pinnacle rising abruptly from the ocean. Much of the main island is covered by lagoons.

Probably around AD 1400, perhaps in a hopeful colonizing effort, a group of (South Island?) Maori found the Chathams, but lost contact with NZ. When the eponymous HMS *Chatham* rediscovered the islands en route to Tahiti (q.v.) in 1791 there were perhaps 1,600 Moriori, as they were then

called. Whalers and sealers began using the islands around 1800. In 1835 the peaceful Moriori existence was destroyed by an invasion of North Island tribes. The Moriori were murdered and enslaved and reduced to perhaps a tenth of their number. Maori and Moriori interbred. The islands were annexed to NZ in 1842. The local language ceased in 1900 with the death of the last Moriori scholar, Hirawanu Tapu. The last full-blooded Moriori died in 1933. Today about half the population claim Moriori descent, surviving on sheep farming, fishing, and crayfish processing. There are now regular flights from Wellington (q.v.). **140–41**

CHRISTCHURCH, CANTERBURY AND MT COOK REGION

'Puari', a Maori community of perhaps 800 Waitaha people and later, the Ngati Mamoe peoples, lived pre-1700 along what is now the western edge of downtown **Christchurch**. By the early 1800s the Ngati Tahu controlled the area. The first Europeans were sealers and flax traders. In 1831 **Banks Peninsula** was site of a massacre of Ngati Tahu by North Island's fearsome Te Rauparaha. The French made a colony there at **Akaroa** in 1840. But they had been preempted by British annexation, and were soon absorbed by the Anglican settlers of the Canterbury Association in 1850, who founded **Lyttelton** and Christchurch, implementing the systematic colonization ideas of E.G. Wakefield. Sheep farming on **Can-**

terbury Plains, and later wheat, became economic mainstays, and Christchurch and Canterbury Province prospered.

One of the great pleasures of Christchurch is its Victorian Gothic and neo-Gothic structures – the largest cluster in Australasia. Many are the work of Benjamin W. Mountfort, perhaps NZ's greatest architect. Examples are the striking *Provincial Council Buildings* (completed 1866), and the former *University of Canterbury* buildings (now the *Arts Centre*) with their cloisters (1865–98) – here is the early laboratory of physicist Ernest Rutherford. Mountfort also supervised *Christchurch Cathedral* (Anglican) (constructed 1864–1904) in *Cathedral Square*. A steep climb gives a view from the tower balcony. There is a society of bellringers which began in 1881. The spire has twice been damaged by earthquakes. The striking concrete neo-classical basilican Roman Catholic *Cathedral of the Blessed Sacrament* (consecrated 1905) designed by Francis W. Petre, stands in Barbados Street.

Because the names of the most prestigious English Anglican dioceses had been adopted for the streets of the port of Lyttelton, surveyed earlier, a mixture of lesser names from England, Ireland, Wales and the Empire were used for Christchurch streets. So today we find, Hereford, Armagh, St Asaph, Colombo, Montreal, and so on. Spanish-style *New Regent Street* opened in 1932 during the Great Depression. Today a boutique and cafe pedestrian mall, it remains the only street in NZ built to a single style. The 1980s building boom destroyed the architectural unity of the city. NZ's first tunnel, for a railway, was driven through an extinct volcano of the **Port Hills** by 1867. The statue of Canterbury founder, John Robert Godley, faces the cathedral. Statues to pioneers and early superintendents Fitzgerald and Rolleston, as well as to Queen Victoria, Cook, and Antarctic explorer, Scott, grace the city centre.

Canterbury Museum has good early colonial exhibits and a hall of Antarctic Discovery, with probably the world's most extensive display of genuine historical Antarctic artifacts. Most of the great Antarctic explorers, Scott, Shackelton, Byrd, Fuchs, and Hillary (even the Japanese Antarctic Expedition 1910–12), used Christchurch (and Lyttelton) as the base for departure. The *International Antarctic Centre*, near the airport, has excellent exhibits, and a unique Antarctic aquarium, all of which give vicarious experience of 'The Ice'. It is also HQ for supply to NZ, US, and Italian bases and programmes in Antarctica. The history of the RNZAF unfolds at the *Air Force Museum* at former *Wigram Base*. Suburbs to the west have long included numerous private houses with exquisite gardens.

In north Canterbury **Kaikoura** on **Kaikoura Peninsula** was a whaling station from 1842, and is now a mecca for wildlife enthusiasts. *Fyffe House* is an early whaler's dwelling (c.1860) and NZ's first company for whale watching was established in 1987. Here are many sites of Maori pa, where, in 1828 Te

Rauparaha slaughtered Ngai Tahu tribespeople.

To the west stands **Mt Cook/ Aoraki** (12,300 feet/3755m) NZ's highest peak (named for English explorer and Maori god) first climbed by local mountaineers in 1884. In 1991 a huge section cascaded from the summit. About two-thirds of **Mt Cook National Park** lies under permanent snow and ice. In the region are 16 other peaks above 10,000 feet (3050m). More than 300 glaciers have formed in the Southern Alps, many in this area, the largest the nearby **Hooker, Mueller**, and **Tasman Glaciers** (named for 19th-century scientists, and the Dutch navigator). At **Mt Cook Village** is famous *Hermitage Hotel*, perfectly positioned for viewing the mountain – 1884 first version destroyed by flood in 1913, rebuilt higher up stream and destroyed by fire in 1957, and rebuilt in its present form. Mountain climbing has resulted in more than 180 deaths. The family of Donald Burnett on their 30,000-acre high-country *Mt Cook Station*, has consistently produced the world's finest merino wool since the late 1800s.

Timaru (Maori 'Te Maru' – place of shelter) on rolling hills on the coast in South Canterbury began as the Weller Brothers' whaling, station c.1838, with the first 120 immigrants in the *Strathallen* in 1859. Its was one of few places early Maori canoeists could find some shelter along the east coast. An artificial harbour was begun in 1877. It is now a holiday town and service centre for fishing fleets. **20, 67, 156–62, 180, 192, 202–6, 236–7**

COOK ISLANDS

Though they may have been visited at an earlier date, the islands seem to have been settled around AD 1000 by Polynesians from the **Tahiti** (q.v.) area, with the northerly islands probably settled from Samoa. Fifteen main islands cover 240 sq.ks in a vast 2 million sq.ks of ocean. The largest, **Rarotonga**, an ancient submerged island, was volcanically resurrected about 2 million years ago. The northern islands are low coral atolls, at the mercy of the ocean during hurricanes. On Raratonga is a marae as old as settlement, and underneath the main asphalted inland road, a coral block road of similar age.

Each island was either a separate polity, or shared by several competing tribes, originally ruled by chiefs and cultural-cum-religious leaders, *taumga*, who were masters of woodcarving, farming, and sailing as well as religion. European navigators such as Alvaro de Mendana in 1595, and James Cook visited the southern islands (Cook thrice between 1773 and 1779). Russian navigators gave the islands their name.

Christian missionaries such as John Williams arrived in the 1830s, bringing the Bible and bacteria, which killed about two-thirds of the people. In 1888, concerned at the French occupation of Tahiti, the chiefs persuaded Britain to establish a protectorate. In 1901 NZ was given control, and in 1965 the Islands gained independence under PM

Albert Henry. Black pearls are produced in the north, and the government is actively promoting the archipelago as a relaxing tourist destination. The little capital, **Avarua**, stands on Rarotonga. Today all 18,000 Islanders share NZ citizenship, but not vice versa. Several times that number have migrated to NZ and Australia. English and Cook Island Maori are the official languages. **98, 199, 286, 301–2**

DUNEDIN, OTAGO, SOUTHLAND, STEWART ISLAND

Early Maori history in the Otago area was bloody, with three-way tribal wars. European and US sealing and whaling used some local Maori, but brought disease and Maori depopulation. The area saw several heroic actions during the Maori Musket Wars, such as the 1837 defeat and death of Te Puoho in Southland (below), after his 400-mile journey the length of South Island to conquer southern Maori.

First permanent European settlement was in 1848 by Scots of the Free Church. **Dunedin** (ancient name for Edinburgh) was made capital of new province of **Otago**. Development was boosted by discovery of gold in 1861. Dunedin became NZ's largest town with the first university (1869). Original architectural style was retained for all new buildings for 50 years. Central city was constructed around the unusual *Octagon: First Presbyterian Church* 1873, *St Paul's Anglican Cathedral* 1919; *Dunedin Town Hall* (1930). The ornate *Railway Station* of 1904 by 'Gingerbread' George Troup is decorated with lions and nymphs and the monogram of NZ Railways. The city missed high-rise development of 70s/80s and is still architecturally people-size.

The *Otago Museum* has displays of penguin, moa and other extinct birds; *Otago Settlers Museum* is good for local history. *Signal Hill* lookout has a 1940s centennial memorial.

Out of town stand impressive *Lanarch Castle* (completed 1886), constructed for a banker by 200 workmen over 15 years, and *Olveston* (built 1904–6) originally the home of businessman D.E. Thomin, patron of the arts, with elegant furnishings and art. Begun early, there are magnificent *Botanical Gardens*. Closeby **Otago Peninsula** provides a nice blend of natural and human history: with *Fort Taiaroa* and its Armstrong Disappearing Gun set up during a 19th-century Russian scare; and its albatross colony repopulated from 1938, one of the few in the world so near human settlement, and yellow-eyed penguins. Hooker's sea-lions are also now breeding naturally.

Inland in north Otago lies **Queenstown**, once a gold town (gold 1862). The first European to settle was William Rees – his statue adds interest to the shopping mall. From 1947 tourism took over because of rushing **Shotover River**, **Remarkable Mountains**, and breathtaking **Lake Wakatipu**. A multiplicity of adventure tourism gives the town an extraordinary youthfulness, zest, and attraction. To the south **Lake Te Anau** is almost equally beautiful.

In **Invercargill**, NZ's most southerly city, in the region of **Southland**, homely provincialism is an asset, as is the *Southland Museum and Art Gallery*. The port of **Bluff** (the departure point for the catamaran to Stewart Island)(below) houses the huge *Tiwai Point Aluminium Smelter* (1971, upgraded 1996). To the east, on the coast route to Dunedin are the absorbing **Catlins**, an area with some ancient NZ podocarp forest, fur seals and sea-lions. On the Otago north coast stands the port of **Oamaru** (1853), with a multitude of striking civic and private buildings constructed from attractive local sandstone (soft to saw, it hardens on exposure to air) – hometown of NZ's best-known novelist Janet Frame, and home to tiny blue and yellow-eyed penguins.

Stewart Island, the most southerly NZ island, was 'Rakiura' to the Maori, meaning the island of the glowing sky (the lingering summer sunsets, and/or the spectacular Aurora Australis of Winter). There were two ships' captains called William Stewart, the island being named after the second – who claimed the kudos of the first (who drew the first maps!). Some gold found in 1867. Shetland Islanders migrated here, but departed. **Oban** is the only settlement. Now mostly a nature reserve, and a paradise for trampers/hikers/bush walkers, birdwatchers. **148, 172–5, 223, 224**

EAST COAST (POVERTY BAY, HAWKES BAY)

Maori settlement is ancient. In the later 1800s European whaling and farming began, and missionaries arrived. During the early years of the Musket Wars the tribes of Poverty Bay were devastated by campaigns of Nga Puhi from the Bay of Islands (q.v.). and in the mid-1860s fought battles in the NZ Wars. Charismatic Maori prophet, Te Kooti, was captured and transported to Chatham Islands (q.v.). In 1868 Te Kooti escaped with 200 followers, brought his Ringatu religion to **Poverty Bay** and attacked Maori and settler. (Cook gave the name in 1769 because of difficulty in replenishing his stores.) The East Coast saw skirmishing in the last few years of the Wars, involving other Maori prophets fighting against settlers and allied Maori tribes. Te Kooti escaped into the Urewera Mountains.

The main town in the Poverty Bay region is **Gisborne** on the coast, centre of fruit growing and vineyards. Strong Maori influence is in evidence. *Gisborne Museum and Arts Centre* has Maori and colonial history and maritime exhibits, and at the river mouth are statues to Cook (near to where he first set foot in NZ) and to his cabin boy, 'Young Nik' (Nicholas Young), who first sighted the NZ coast in 1769. To the south is majestic **Mahia Peninsula**, once an island.

West of Gisborne is one of the country's most attractive untouched native forest areas **Urewera National Park**, in the Ureweras, home of the Maori Tuhoe. Beautiful **Lake Waikaremoana** (Sea of Rippling Waters) formed by a colossal landslide (5 miles/8k long) which blocked a river about 2,200 years ago, is popular for fishing, boating, and a famous walking track. Te Kooti's successor, the prophet Rua Kenana, inspired a thriving community for decades at **Maungapohatu** (4,500 feet/1366m), where there is a tiny remnant. At nearby **Ruatahuna** in its majestic valley, the *Mataatua Marae* commemorates Te Kooti.

To the south is the **Hawkes Bay** region, named after the British admiral, Edward Hawke, who saved Britain from French invasion. The largest town, the vacation resort and port, **Napier** (after British general and administrator, Charles Napier), founded 1854, suffered a disastrous earthquake and fire in 1931 (7.9 on Richter Scale). Government-guided, privately financed, the razed town was rebuilt in a few years in the Art Deco style popular at the time (e.g., *Hotel Central, Daily Telegraph Building*). Today it is possibly the world's best cluster of Art Deco. *Marine Parade* has a statue of Maori legend 'Pania of the Reef' and *Hawkes Bay Museum*. The airport stands on the huge piece of land the earthquake raised from the ocean.

Hastings (1864), 20k south, a centre for market gardens, fruit and vineyards, was also struck by the earthquake and rebuilt in Art Deco and Mission-style (*Westerman's Building*, the *Municipal Theatre*, the paved *Civic Square* with Art Deco *Clock Tower*). Hawkes Bay was a separate province in 1853–76 and is one of NZ's best wine-producing regions (chardonnay and cabernet sauvignon). Some 60 miles farther south is the much-photographed 83-letter AA road-sign of an area claiming the

world's longest place name. **19, 181, 222**

EASTER ISLAND (RAPANUI)

This high triangular Oceanic island, formed by successive volcanic eruptions, has no natural harbour or permanent streams. Colonized from Australs? Marquesas? Gambias? (q.v.) probably by accident, around AD 700. The colonists, the most isolated in the Pacific, probably lost contact with the rest of Polynesia. Famous for its monolithic stone statues (moai) Polynesia's largest.

Overpopulation and almost complete destruction of habitat produced clan wars, depopulation, and cannibalism. European navigators first visited in 1700s, the first, Dutchman Reggeveen, in 1722. Much of the remaining population was seized by Peruvian slavers in 19th century. Annexed by Chile in 1888, for decades it was leased as a sheep farm. In 1980s and 90s archaeological and other scientific research discovered the nature of the island's formerly mysterious and unknown early history, including deciphering the mysterious Rongorongo tablets. Modern Easter Islanders are now reclaiming their history, and since 1975 have celebrated in a the two-week-long 'Tapati Cultural Festival'. Increasing numbers of tourists are destroying historical areas such as *Orongo*, site of the Birdman Cult. **Hanga Roa** is the only town. **8, 52–9**

FIJI

For perhaps 1000 years from 1300 BC

or 1200 BC the 'Fiji Tonga, Samoa Crescent' formed the region in which proto-Polynesians and their culture first evolved from the original Austronesian-speaking Lapita people. The Fijian 'type' slowly evolved as waves of migration from the Melanesian islands to the north-west arrived. During the first millennium of the Christian era there seems to have been considerable coming and going between Fiji and the nearby evolving Polynesians. From the 13th century there was Fijian inter-tribal warfare, and large numbers of earthwork fortifications were built on the two main islands of **Viti Levu** and **Vanua Levu**. Fijian chiefs held absolute power of life and death over commoners. Many European seafarers avoided the archipelago after 1700 because of its fierce reputation.

In the 1700s endemic warfare reduced the tribal contenders to five 'confederations', and by the early 1800s the two most powerful were Bau, centred on tiny **Bau Island** off east coast of Viti Levu, and Rewa on the south-east corner. By this time Western sandalwood traders had introduced muskets, which stimulated the long war between these two powers. Bau, using its great double-hulled war canoes, 'druas', triumphed. Bau's Chief Cakobau then claimed hegemony over all Fiji, though in fact his power was limited. By mid-century, European, US, and Australian settlers had introduced coconut and sugar plantations and pressed for control in government. In 1858, to pay a debt alleged by some US citizens, Cakobau offered Fiji to

Britain, but she declined. Australian businessmen paid Cakobau's debt in return for land and influence, and more settlers arrived. Fiji was becoming anarchic, so Cakobau again offered the islands to the British, who finally agreed to take control from 1874.

The governor forbad further land sales to foreigners and involved the Fijians in their own governance. Because they did not want to work on the foreign sugar plantations, in time, 60,000 indentured Indians were brought in. Because (unexpectedly) so many remained, a new political problem developed. Fijians wanted to keep political control, Indians struggled for equal rights. Fijians were strongly pro-British in the World Wars. In 1928 on the first cross-Pacific flight, Australian Charles Kingsford Smith landed in Suva's Albert Park on the leg from Hawaii.

At independence in 1972, a compromise constitution was patched together, with equal Indian–Fijian representation in the lower house, but more Fijians in the senate. In 1987 a military coup ousted a new, mainly Indian-dominated government after only six weeks. A second military coup that year, and after a period of relative calm, a civilian-led coup in 2000, destabilized the country. Tens of thousands of Indians emigrated. Under a new Indian PM, Fiji remains politically problematic.

Levuka, on Ovalau Island, developed in the 19th century with the sandalwood and beche-de-mer trades, and was, after 1874, the first capital. Today, now dependent on fish packing, it has many quaint buildings from its heyday, and, like a place frozen in time, was designated an 'historic town' in 1989.

Suva, capital from 1872, developed on Suva Peninsula in the territories of Rewa. Hot, wet, humid for much of the year, Suva is multicultural with churches, temples, and mosques. The *University of the South Pacific* (1964) south-east of the city proper, was established to service the whole South Pacific. *Fiji Museum* in *Thurston Gardens* is a highlight, with fine examples of Fijian artifacts and history and a striking display of tapa cloth. Designed by Viti Architects, the new *Parliament Complex* (opened 1992) on the southern part of Suva peninsula, emphasizes the recent trend to traditional indigenous values, and integrates indigenous Fijian conceptions, materials and crafts, and modern architectural techniques.

In the 1970s, **Nadi** on the west coast developed as Fiji's chief airport and significant centre for tourism. Firewalking was brought to Fiji by the indentured Hindus, but was also practised by indigenous Fijians of Beqa Island south-west of Suva. Several tourist resorts offer fire-walking shows (Appendix 1). **59–62, 97, 109–14, 285, 295–7, 321–3**

FIORDLAND

In this misty, magnificent, almost uninhabited south-west NZ region of drowned glacier-carved valleys, the mountains rise straight from the waters of the fiords. Cook came here in 1769 and 1773. The famous sealing captain John Grono had a base in **Doubtful Sound** in 1809 and gave many of the names to the region, such as **Milford Haven**, after the Welsh port. In 1851 many of the fiords were first surveyed by HMS *Acheron*. With its narrow entrance, sheer cliffs and plunging waterfalls, **Milford Sound** (14 mile/22k long) is the pick of the fiords. The 'hermit' prospector Donald Sutherland built a shack in 1878 and did much to cut tracks, map, and open up the region.

In 1924 a serious proposal was made to harness the beautiful 500 feet/150m **Bowen Falls** for power (to make fertilizer!). Cruise ships appeared relatively early, in 1874, 77, 79, 81, 83, and 85. The first, a government vessel in 1874, had the NZ governor aboard. The Union Steamship Company in 1877 began the sequence of summer cruises. By 1883 the large *Tarawera* was carrying 300 passengers. In 1910, its successor, *Waikare*, struck an uncharted rock in Doubtful Sound and sank (without loss of life), putting an end to cruises until 1928. The World War I pilot, J.R. Dennistoun, made the first ascent of Milford's sheer **Mitre Peak** (5,561feet/1,695m) in 1911. Lake steamers began to carry walkers to Te Anau village, east of the mountains, to bring them to the tracks gradually being opened across to Fiordland. 'The Finest Walk in the World', an article published in the London *Spectator* in 1908, alerted Britons to the spectacular Milford Track and the beauties of Fiordland.

The first roads into the region were built with picks, shovels, crowbars, and wheelbarrows. An improved road was constructed with relief labour during the great Depression, surveyed by John Christie in 1933/34, and the **Homer Tunnel** through the mountains (originally proposed in 1889 by W.H. Homer) was begun in 1935 – again with pick and shovel! The first narrow link was pierced by 1940. World War II prevented further work until 1951. Walkers only were allowed through in 1947. Thousands of tourists now come in coaches via the road ˙and Homer Tunnel, to make day-trips on Milford Sound.

In the 1930s larger ships plied the sounds, including ss *Monowai*, which as HMNZS *Monowai* took part in the 1944 World War II D-Day landings. Ever since, cruise ships have visited in increasing numbers. Queen Elizabeth II in *Britannia* sailed here in 1978. **18, 20, 88, 223**

FRENCH POLYNESIA

French Polynesia's 1359 sq. miles (3520 sq. ks) of land in about a million square miles of ocean encompass every variety of South Pacific island from youthful high islands to ancient atolls, so the territory offers the traveller a splendid range of experiences. The lagoon and reef-ringed high **Society Islands** (the most famous being **Tahiti**) form the core of this huge ocean territory, together with other islands such as nearby Moorea, Huahine, Raiatea, and Bora Bora. The name 'Society' was chosen by Cook because of the islands' proximity. To the east are the atolls of the Tuamotus. Some 310 miles/500k

north-east again are the high, jagged Marquesas, and a similar distance south of Tahiti lie the Australs. South-east of the Tuamotus we find the isolated Gambia Archipelago.

The Marquesas were probably settled first, by Samoans, by about AD 300, and became the distribution point for colonizing the whole eastern South Pacific. From the Marquesas the eastern Tuamotus and Society Islands would have been colonized within a few hundred years. Legend claims that Tahiti was settled from Raiatea. The Gambias and eastern Tuamotus were likely settled from the Marquesas around AD 500. In the 900s Tahitians colonized the western Tuamotus, the Australs (and the Cook Islands [q.v.] about AD 1000). Evolving into a sacred centre, Raiatea became the chief Society Island.

For centuries social and trading expeditions were common, linking islands within the several archipelagoes, and less often, between archipelagoes. Disputes and wars troubled islands and island groups. (About the time the first European navigators were arriving, the fierce warriors of **Anna Atoll** spread horror across most of the Tuamotus.)

A search for *Terra Australis Incognita*, the supposed Unknown Southern Continent, brought the Europeans. In 1595 Spain's de Mendana de Neira found the north-east of the Marquesas – Las Marquesas de Mendoza, which he named after his patron, a marquis (i.e. *marquesa*), the Viceroy of New Castile (Peru). His chief pilot de Quiros found some of the

Tuamotus in 1606. Dutchman Rog-geveen chanced on several of the Society Islands in 1722. In 1767 Wallis and his crew in the British ship *Dolphin* were the first Europeans to see exotic Tahiti, anchored in **Matavai Bay** and began the legend. They were followed by many more including Bougainville and Cook.

At that time, like most other islands, Tahiti was divided into conflicting chiefdoms. Gradually the Pomare family came to dominate, helped significantly by the Bounty Mutineers, and later by Protestant missionaries, so the whole island was theirs by 1815. A few decades later, because Britain did not respond to the pleas of the Tahitian royal family for protection, France was able to declare an unwanted pro-tectorate in 1842, and by 1847 the queen was a French puppet. Little by little all the archipelagoes fell into French hands. With the exception of Maketa (below), the French neglected the islands. In World War I a German destroyer shelled Papeete in Tahiti, and in World War II Tahitians and others fought for the Free French forces on the Allied side.

In the late 1950s Tahiti's popula-tion was about 40,000; by AD 2000 it was over 150,000. The island is unchallenged as the political, eco-nomic, and cultural centre of French Polynesia. The capital, **Papeete** ('basket of water'), is an European creation which began with Wallace and even more Cook in 1769. Cook also anchored in Matavai Bay just to the north, which had easy access through the reef. Traders and whalers visited, and the French made Papeete

the administrative centre. By the 1860s it had developed its present form, with a settlement of Europeans along the waterfront and straggling into the valley behind. In the early 1900s population was less than 5,000, in the 1960s still not much more than 20,000, but by 2002 it was French Polynesia's 'big city' with over 100,000 people, attracting hopeful and hopeless from everywhere else in the French islands. In keeping with French ideas of centralization, Papeete has French Polynesia's only international airport at **Faaa** (1961).

Despite the central *Catholic Cathe-dral of the Immaculate Conception* (1869–75) close to the **Mission District** of Catholic and Protestant schools, Tahiti is predominantly Protestant, as is made clear every Sunday morning at *Paofai Church* west of the town centre. The *Territorial Assembly* and other government buildings stand on the site of the former Pomare Family 1883 royal palace, demolished because of ter-mites, in front of which is the statue of Tahiti's greatest indigenous leader, Pouvannaa a Oopa. The *High Com-missioner's Residence* stands nearby. Behind the two is the spring and pool the 'Queen's Bathing Place' because Queen Pomare used it. More recently erected is the *Presidential Palace*.

Cook's fort was constructed at *Point Venus*, the northern promontory of Matavai Bay. There is nothing to show the site today. There is however a memorial to the first LMS missionaries who came ashore there in 1797. Each year the world's champion surfers compete at *Teahupo'o*, a mighty dome of coral off *Passe Hava'e* at the south-west corner of **Little Tahiti's** barrier reef. Here gentle ocean swells rear up into killer waves.

Other Society Islands such as **Moorea**, **Bora Bora**, and **Raiatea** are the classic high islands of travel posters. Raiatea was for a thousand years the sacred island (its Marae Taputapuatea is the largest in French Polynesia), and its town of **Utuora** is the second largest after Papeete. Tourism on Moorea has boomed, with a third of all hotel rooms in French Polynesia.

Missionary-encouraged copra production was important from 1870s in the **Tuamotus**. For half a century from 1908 and until the deposits were worked out, **Makatea Island** mined and exported ever-increasing tons of phosphate to Japan, New Zealand, and Australia, and was the heart of the French Polynesian economy. Today, cultivation of black pearls is the Tuamotus' mainstay and important for the economy of French Polynesia. **Rangiroa** (47 × 15.5 miles/75 × 25k) is the world's second largest atoll, surrounding its immense 'lagoon' (Kwajalein in Micronesia is somewhat larger).

The isolated **Marquesas**, with no encircling reefs, have been sculptured into fantastic peaks and plateaux. In 1813 an American naval captain had designs upon the island of **Nuka Hiva** as a base. French annexation and contact with whalers brought disease and the population declined from perhaps 18,000 in 1840 to 2000 in 1920. Underdeveloped until the 1980s, recent decades have seen improved infrastructure. Copra cultivation is important, and more recently, noni, a fruit of claimed therapeutic use. Local culture has been reborn, handicrafts flourish and the population is increasing.

The varied, scattered, and relatively barren **Austral** Islands, 400k south, are somewhat cooler than the Society Islands, and were fully annexed only in 1901, and the long period of undisturbed English mission activity had ensured their Protestantism. **Raivavae** Island was almost entirely depopulated by disease in the 1830s, its culture destroyed.

Of similar latitude to the Australs, but 1650k south-east of Tahiti, the **Gambier   Islands/Archipelago** (main island **Mangareva**), named after a British admiral who supported the first Protestant mission, were annexed by France in 1881. Scene from 1834 to 1871 of a Catholic missionary-enforced   construction programme, culminating in the *Cathedral of St Michael*. Black pearls are cultured.

Britain, USA, and Russia ceased atmospheric atomic tests in 1963. In 1962 France began construction of the vast *Centre d'Experimentation du Pacific* at **Moruroa (Mururoa) and Fangataufa Atolls** in the eastern Tuamotus, which poured billions of francs (more than a billion US dollars a year) into the Tahitian and Polynesian economy. France continued to conduct atmospheric tests despite a 1973 World Court request to halt, and worldwide condemnation. In 1981 in spite of endless protests, though ending atmosphere tests, the

French drilled bomb shafts under the Moruroa lagoon and continued their tests underground. In 1995 President Chirac announced another round of tests. NZ and Chile broke diplomatic relations, there was worldwide outrage, and as in 1987 riots erupted in Papeete. France concluded testing in 1996. In 1998 the French admitted plutonium had leaked into **Moruoa Lagoon** and in 1999 that the two atolls' coral cones had cracks. Because the tests were only 250 miles/400k distant from Mangareva, a huge atomic fallout shelter was built – the forbidding *Maison Nucleaire*. **81–4, 85–7, 119–23, 262–3, 287**

NELSON & MARLBOROUGH

The Maori Ngati Tumatakokiri probably arrived in this most northerly part of NZ's South Island, from North Island in the 1500s. During the Musket Wars an alliance between North Island Ngati Apa and South Island's main tribe, Ngai Tahu, attacked and almost obliterated them and occupied their territory. Ngati Apa and Ngai Tahu were in turn almost destroyed by genocidal Ngati Toa invasions from the North Island in the 1820s and 30s.

The inter-island ferry from Wellington, which commenced its scheduled run in 1888, enters the superb fingered Marlborough Sounds to arrive at the port of **Picton**. About 50k north-west is **D'Urville Island** where the Dutchman Abel Tasman, the first European to see this region, anchored in 1642. Cook named the sound **Queen Charlotte** (after the

wife of King George III), visited it four times and established it as one of the best-known navigators' shelters in the Pacific. During the 1820s the Sounds were the site of bay whaling. In 1827 Frenchman Dumont d'Urville explored the Sounds on the expedition which helped him create the classification of Pacific Islands into Polynesia, Melanesia, and Micronesia. Here in 1840 Major Bunbury proclaimed British sovereignty over South Island.

In 1840 the NZ Company settled the **Nelson** district (named after Admiral, Lord Nelson, of Battle of Trafalgar fame), but the settlement almost perished from lack of organization and delays in surveying. In 1843 what is often seen as the first skirmish of the NZ Wars occurred in the **Wairau Valley** near Nelson (Wairau Incident/Massacre), when 22 settlers were killed by the formidable Te Rauparaha. To the east, the new province of **Marlborough** (after John Churchill, First Duke of Marlborough) was created when local settlers became discontented with funds from their land sales being used in Nelson town's development. The town of **Blenheim** (after Marlborough's victory over France in 1704) became capital in 1865. The province was dissolved in 1876 though the name was kept for the region. Blenheim is the centre of NZ's most famous and largest wine-growing district, with sauvignon blancs, chardonnays, and rieslings.

Nelson city, once capital of former Nelson province, is known for its beautiful beaches and bays, fruit growing, local artisans (especially pottery), and sunny days. Discovery of gold nearby helped its development in the 1860s. Nelson has the interesting Art Deco Anglican *Christ Church Cathedral* (begun 1925, consecrated 1972); restored workers' cottages; *South Street Gallery*; *Suter Art Gallery* (1895/1978); *Broadgreen House* (c.1855); and *Cawthron Institute* (since 1920), an independent ocean and freshwater research organization oriented to Nelson and NZ problems.

South of Nelson at **Brightwater** is the tranquil and informative circular open-plan memorial to the extraordinary physicist Ernest Rutherford, who was born in the village in 1871. About 30 miles/50k to the northwest is **Abel Tasman National Park**, developed in the 1940s, famous for its coastal 4/5-day walking track, the most popular in NZ with over 20,000 walkers a year. About the same distance away again is Farewell Spit, a wetland and bird sanctuary of international significance – for thousands of years migrating wading birds from the Arctic tundra have resided here in summer. **18, 182, 204–6**

NEW CALEDONIA

Lapita Ware, famous as the pottery which identifies the Lapita People, the first groups to migrate into the islands east of New Guinea, was first discovered here at Lapita on Foue Peninsula, and suggests settlement of the islands around 1300 BC, with influxes of Melanesian peoples soon after – Melanesian paddle ceramics from the Isle of Pines to the south-east have been dated to 900 BC. To the east of the main island of Grande Terre are the Loyalty Islands, Ouvea, Lifou, and Mare.

Cook landed in 1774, using 'Caledonia', the Roman name for Scotland. In the 1830s the LMS arrived, Roman Catholic missions in 1840. Adopting the killing of missionaries as a pretext, the French annexed the islands in 1853. The territory was controlled by military governors until 1884 and became a penal colony (1864–97). The main island, *Grand Terre*, has the world's largest known nickel deposits, mined since 1875 by convict labour. Settlers were brought from France and given Kanak land. A revolt broke out in 1878 against French control. The revolt was suppressed and many Kanaks were forced into reservations in mountainous areas. Kanak population went into severe decline. By 1901 only about 10% of the land, mountainous and poor, remained in Kanak hands. Kanaks were forced to join the French army during World War I and a revolt broke out again, in 1917. Only after World War II were Kanaks allowed to move freely and become French citizens. In 1958 the first local Assembly elections were held, increased in size in 1976. In the early 1980s the Kanaks pressed for independence. In 1985 further moves to independence were frustrated by French settlers (Caldoches) and official skulduggery, and when the Kanaks responded violently France took the opportunity for repression. Though there is again a considerable degree of autonomy, the next opportunity to vote for full independence has been postponed until 2018!

The superb **Isle des Pines** (Island of Pines) about 30 miles/50k south-east of Grande Terre, named by Cook, was also settled by Lapita People and has its own colourful history. In the 1600s its inhabitants were attacked by people from Lifou, who then interbred. In the first half of the 1800s the island was a centre for the sandalwood trade, and Catholic missionaries arrived. In the 1870s it became a convict settlement. Just prior to World War I the island was returned to its original tribal people, the Kunies, who have remained aloof from New Caledonia's politics. Nowadays the island is a tourist paradise with stunning white sand beaches. **Vao** is the only proper village, home of the chief and administration, with a Melanesian *mairie* (town hall) and an attractive *Mission Church* (1860).

Noumea (formerly Port-de-France), founded 1854, is easily the largest town and the capital. For a long time it was a shanty town; in 1890 visiting author R.L. Stevenson said Noumea was 'built from Vermouth cases'. During World War II the USA has a military headquarters here. As a result there are suburbs called *Receiving* and *Motor Pool*! Of historical/architectural significance are: the imaginative new (1995) *Headquarters of the Secretariat of the Pacific Community* (formerly South Pacific Commission, set up 1947), which uses materials from all its member countries; *St Joseph's Cathedral* (from 1888) constructed by convicts; good displays of local culture

in the *New Caledonian Museum*; architecturally extraordinary 8-hectare *Tjibaou Cultural Centre* (1998), named for the assassinated independence leader, east of downtown, which commemorates Kanak and Oceanic culture and ways of life. The huge nickel refining plant at nearby *Point Duiambo*, owned by SLN (Société Le Nickel) formed in 1880, makes Noumea one of the South Pacific's most industrialized towns. **7, 8, 97, 284–5, 302, 304–5**

NIUE

'Niu-e' means 'coconut-here' or 'behold: the coconut!' Only 100 sq.miles (259 sq.k) and 1370 miles/2200k north-east of NZ, Niue is a large, flat, re-emerged atoll, with most of the coastline rising sheer from the sea. Poverty of soil allows rain to filter through the limestone to form a multitude of caves, which were used as houses and for storage and burials. Over the aeons the rainwater has collected to form a 'cell' within the island, which floats on the seawater and which is accessible through some of the caves. No rivers run into the sea, which is crystal clear, and so diving and snorkelling are spectacular.

The island seems to have been settled by Tongans in the south and Samoans in the north, around AD 1000. For hundreds of years the people of the north and south were bitter enemies. Forests were laced with tracks cut by raiding parties looking for food and women. Social structure was less organized and hierarchical than most Polynesian societies – perhaps the last surviving example of the earliest

Polynesian societies. On his 1774 voyage Cook's landing party was ferociously repulsed.

The first missionary was Rev. John Williams in 1830, but most Niueans were converted by one of their own, Nukai Peniamina. Sunday has been serious for more than 150 years.

There was an appointed/elected monarchy organized by the missionaries, ending in 1900 with King Togia, when, under missionary pressure, Niue became a British Protectorate. In 1901 Niue was annexed to NZ, and until 1974 ruled by Resident Commissioners. After World War II self-government was gradually introduced. Niue is now independent in free association with NZ and more than 90% of Niueans now live in NZ (and Australia) (Niueans are NZ citizens, but not vice versa.) With less than 2,000 people and falling rapidly, Niue is the world's smallest parliamentary democracy, and its fourteen villages also have their own councils, but is heavily dependent (more than three-quarters of the budget) upon financial support from NZ.

Niueans are selective eaters, use their own version of the earth oven, and traditionally rejected the ubiquitous pawpaw (papaya), which was regarded as 'poor man's food'.

The capital village of **Alofi** is mainly a single road which stretches several miles along the coast.

NORTHLAND AND BAY OF ISLANDS

This most northerly region of NZ was occupied for hundreds of years by tribes such as Te Aupouri in the far north, through Nga Puhi, to Ngati Whatua in the south. Whaling ships frequented the area to trade for supplies especially in the magnificent Bay of Islands. European and Americans settled at Kororareka on the Bay, which became NZ's first European town, a base for whalers. Increasingly concerned about racial clashes, in 1833 the British sent James Busby to Kerikeri on the Bay, as official Resident to NZ tribes. Busby helped establish a loose, temporary federation of far north tribes.

The decades-long Musket Wars were begun from the Bay by the chief, Hongi Hika of the Nga Puhi, from 1818 onwards. Christianity arrived in 1814 with Rev. Samuel Marsden from Sydney. The earliest version of written Maori was created here by missionary Thomas Kendall. Kororareka is now the charming little town of **Russell** (after a British Colonial Secretary): its small *Museum* has maritime exhibits; white *Pompallier House* (1842) made of rammed earth, housed the Catholic Marist mission's printing works; *Christ Church* has sections dating from 1835 (graveyard of Maori chiefs, whalers, sailors); there is a famous flagpole on *Flagstaff Hill* above the town, whose first four versions were chopped down in 1844 by the chief, Hone Heke, in early skirmishes in NZ Wars. There are remains of Maori pa at **Kororipo** and **Ruapekapeka** from the same clashes.

A short ferry-ride across the bay is **Paihia/Waitangi**. Paihia is the site of an early mission station, now a tourist centre for the region. Wait-angi, just to the north, is the site of 1840 Treaty of Waitangi by which many Maori chiefs ceded NZ's North Island to Britain, represented by Lt. Gov. William Hobson. The Treaty of Waitangi was signed in a marquee beside the extant *Treaty House* (Busby's residence) (1833); nearby are the *Maori Meeting House* and NZ's largest war canoe, both built to commemorate 1940 centenary of Treaty. NZ Day is celebrated here each 6 February. At the north end of the Bay lies **Kerikeri** site of NZ's second mission. NZ's oldest wooden and stone buildings, *Kemp House* and the *Stone Store*, parts of the mission, still stand.

Whangarei, on large, deep Whangarei Harbour, first settled in 1839, abandoned in 1845, reestab-lished a few years later and incorpo-rated in 1896, is the largest town in Northland. Yachts from across the world moor in *Town Basin*. In the 1850s five ships of Gaelic-speaking Scots Highlanders settled at **Waipu** south of Whangarei. Their traditions live on in annual Highland Games. About 40 miles directly west of Whangarei across Northland penin-sula lies the **Kauri Coast**. Here in the second half of the 1800s a kauri timber and kauri gum industry flourished, cut and dug mostly by hard-working immigrants, many from Dalmatia, (a peak of about 20,000 workers), gen-erating a substantial proportion of NZ's trade. The protected, remaining great kauri trees in **Waipoua Kauri Forest** suggest in a small way how the whole coast used to look. One massive

tree of 16ft/5m diameter may be some 2,000 years old.

On the far northern tip of Aupouri Peninsula, **Cape Reinga** is the northern 'pilgrimage site' for people who wish to travel the length of the country. Still growing, on the very tip of Otawhiri Point is an ancient pohutukawa tree, lashed by the winds and spray, whose roots in Maori legend protect the entrance to the next world. **93, 105–9, 127–9, 131, 135–8, 144–7, 149, 162–3**

PAPUA NEW GUINEA

People have inhabited New Guinea, the world's second largest island, for at least 50,000 years. By 25,000 years ago there would have been hundreds of different tribes. Most of the huge island remained one of the world's last great unknown territories until well into the twentieth century.

It was dragged into the modern world of nation states when the new German Empire, a latecomer in the search for colonies, annexed the north-east corner in 1883. A year earlier, the Queensland colonists, in Australia, fearful of just such an action to their north, had annexed all of eastern New Guinea themselves (the Dutch claimed the west), but Britain disallowed this move. Pressed by Queensland and other Australian colonies. In 1884 Britain annexed the south-east, as Papua. In 1906 control of British New Guinea (Papua) was transferred to the recently federated Commonwealth of Australia. Slowly, from the tiny capital **Port Moresby**, government patrols made contact with the hundreds of tribes of the interior with their multitude of languages. German New Guinea was captured by Australian forces in 1914 at the beginning of World War I, and governed separately from Papua until after World War II, when a joint Australian administration of Papua New Guinea (PNG) was established. In the war PNG was the scene of bitter jungle fighting between the Japanese and Allied forces. The southward thrust of the Japanese was finally halted by the Australians in the key *Battle of the* **Kokoda Trail** in the **Owen Stanley Range**, and in the east by Australians and Americans at **Milne Bay** and by US forces at **Buna** and **Gona**.

PNG was given independence in 1974. The country is characterized by the most extraordinary contrasts. In the **Highlands** tribes still follow subsistence farming and engage in sometimes bloody mock battles; in lowland Port Moresby people make use of supermarkets and sports stores and use electricity generated by modern hydro-electric power stations. The government has had difficulty holding the country together, however, and from 1987 to 1994 the copper-rich island of **Bougainville** tried unsuccessfully to secede. Corruption is considerable and crime increasing.

During the twentieth century, **Port Moresby** grew from a governor's house surrounded by a few huts on the harbour to a sprawling city of about half a million people – mostly urban poor. Of architectural and historical interest are: the excellent *National Museum and Art Gallery*, and

Parliament House. A scenic drive up the impressive **Sogeri Gorge** north of the city reaches the beginning of the Kokoda Trail at *Ower's Corner*. It is possible to walk the trail – three tough days. There is a war memorial to New Guineans and Australians who died in the battle.

Rabaul, **Goroka**, **Madang** and **Lae** are other towns which have grown up to service sections of the country.

In the north-east, the 700 mile/ 1100k, deep **Sepik River** and its Valley attract increasing numbers of tourists to the striking indigenous culture, especially its art. **25, 26, 27– 8, 100, 283–4, 292–3**

SAMOA (FORMERLY WESTERN SAMOA)

Covered by lush green jungle (200 ins/5000 mm rain) these tropical islands 1,130 sq.miles/2934 sq.ks sit in the heart of the Pacific at 14S latitude. Remains of the earliest villages of the original Lapita People date to about 1000 BC.

By the European Middle Ages, wars and alliances had created four powerful families and titles, known as papa titles, akin to four royal lines. Genealogical tradition suggests that in the late 1400s all four titles were bestowed upon one person, a woman, Salammasina, who became the first ruler of all Samoa, though individual papa families remained strong. High chiefs possessed as many wives as they wished, and marriages by their virgin daughters were crucial in the system of alliances.

The first European explorer to visit

was Roggeveen in 1722, followed by Bougainville in 1768 and La Perouse in 1787. The largest island is **Savai'i**. Sailors and escaped convicts settled in small numbers in **Apia**, on the other large island of **Upolu**, and through whaling and trading Apia became the main town by the 1840s.

The greatest 19th-century influence was the Christian missionaries. German companies had success in developing coconut plantations for oil and copra. For the civil war of 1869–73 vast amounts of land were sold to pay for weapons. During the next 20 years rivalries and jealousies, local and international, resulted in 'governments' patched together by shifting coalitions of chiefs and settler leaders, and civil wars and rebellions. In the late 1800s USA, Britain, and Germany had designs upon Samoa. Conferences were held in the period 1885 to 1889, which decided Samoa should be a single kingdom with the king and top officials selected by the neutral king of Sweden, and consuls of USA, Britain, and Germany allowed advisory powers. For a few years Samoa was 'independent' under King Malietoa Laupepa. The country became ungovernable again and the three countries finally awarded Western Samoa to Germany and eastern to USA.

In the first weeks of World War I, NZ captured Western Samoa for the British Empire. After the war the territory was mandated to NZ by the League of Nations. NZ rule was disliked and was opposed by the Mau resistance movement. After World War II Western Samoa became a UN Trust Territory, and in 1962 was the first of the South Pacific island countries to gain independence. At the weekend *kilikiti* teams are supported by a *lapes*, a group of many singers and dancers. They confront one another and make fun of the opposing players. Singing is continual, with even more volume on Sundays.

Inland from Apia *Mount Vaea Scenic Reserve*, next to *Vailima Botanical Garden* (once estate of R.L. Stevenson), is popular with tourists. The *Stevenson Museum* is in the writer's home (restored 1994), which was used after his death by heads of state and governors. In the two large islands there exist about 140 'star mounds'. These raised platforms, of various heights, have multiple protrusions. Their significance is unknown – perhaps connected to the ancient chiefly sport of pigeon hunting, or else for religious activities. On Savai'i is the difficult-to-find *Pulemelei Mound*, the largest ancient monument in Polynesia (base 200 × 164 feet/ 61 × 50m; height 39 feet/12m). The mystery deepens because Samoan oral traditions make no mention of it. Archaeologists are seeking permission to examine it.

Manono Island between the two main islands is about as near as one can get to early Polynesian times. No roads, no vehicles, thatched fales, semi-subsistence lifestyle. **114–18, 218–19, 247, 286, 299–300, 312**

SOLOMON ISLANDS

Perhaps 25 million years ago the earliest of these volcanic islands rose from the ocean. Papuan-speaking hunter-gatherers were settling the islands by about 25,000 BC. Proto-Melanesians, who spoke Austronesian languages arrived about 4000 BC and the famous Lapita Culture came and evolved after 2000 BC. Spanish attempted colonization in the mid-1590s.

In the late 1700s British and French navigators arrived. Whaling to some extent, and sandalwood and beche-de-mer traders visited. The violence of traditional culture (murder, cannibalism, headhunting, and skull worship) antipathy caused by deaths from European diseases, and maltreatment by traders, made the Solomons extraordinarily problematic for Europeans. Missionaries were few and cautious.

Encouraged by traders, Britain created a protectorate over the southern islands in 1893, and extended this in 1897, 98 and 99. The suppression of the 1927 Kwaio Rebellion left a legacy of ill feeling towards Europeans. In 1942, after the panicked departure of Europeans for Australia, the Japanese captured the **Shortland** and **Treasury Islands** in the west and soon after took **Guadalcanal**. US forces counter-attacked and recaptured the island with tremendous casualties on each side. On many islands are leftovers from World War II battles. Thousands of Islanders worked for the Allied forces, and their experiences helped the rise of cargo cults, such as 'Marching Rule'. When the last US troops departed in 1950, Britain introduced regional assemblies. A

governing Council was elected in 1970 and independence arrived in 1978. Ethnically related Western Solomon Islanders became involved in Bougainville's failed ten-year-long struggle for independence from PNG. In the late 1990s anti-government rebellions broke out, and by 2003 the country was anarchic.

After World War II **Honiara** on Guadalcanal replaced **Tulagi** as capital. Here in 1568 Mendana, the Spanish explorer, raised a cross and claimed the island for Spain, and the main street today is Mendana Avenue. The town grew from a cluster of World War II Army Quonset huts, and expanded over some of the fiercest Pacific battlefields: the Mataniko River, which splits the town, was for a time the Japanese/US frontline. Worth noting are: *Solomon Islands National Museum* with good displays of cultural artifacts; large, conical *Parliament Building* (1993) overlooking the town, built with US funds by a Japanese company; headquarters of the *Fisheries Agency* of the South Pacific Forum; *US War Memorial* (dedicated 1992). Divers in offshore Iron Bottom Bay can observe wrecked World War II ships. **23, 79–80, 288, 293**

TAHITI (SEE FRENCH POLYNESIA)

TARANAKI, WANGANUI, MANAWATU

About half way between Wellington and Auckland, Taranaki, dominated by the huge regular cone of Mt Taranaki, juts into the Tasman Sea.

The volcano is dormant, the last eruption being about 350 years ago. Maori occupied the region from early times. In 1820s during the Musket Wars, fearful of attack by Waikato tribes, the local Maori fled in large numbers south. When European settlers arrived in 1841 the coast was almost deserted and the NZ Company purchased land from the Maori who remained. After the original Maori returned, problems arose. As the settlement at **New Plymouth** (from 1840) grew, more land was needed. Sale of ambiguously owned land caused the Taranaki War (1860–61) to break out. Settlers fled their farms and huddled in the town, and the war ended in a truce.

Of historical note in New Plymouth are: *Taranaki Museum* with local artifacts; *St Mary's Church* (1846), one of the oldest stone churches in NZ, with fascinating grave stones of early settlers, soldiers, and Maori chiefs; and the stone *Richmond Cottage* (1853).

In the final decades of the 1800s Taranaki became NZ's greatest dairying region. Whole milk was collected from farms and processed at a central location 'dairy factory', mostly cooperatives, by 1901. The province experienced another boom after the discovery of natural gas and oil at **Kapuni**, south of Mt Taranaki in 1959. To meet the NZ oil crisis of the 1970s an innovative synthetic fuel plant was constructed at **Motuni**, just north of New Plymouth, which produced petroleum throughout the 1980s using natural gas from Kapuni and the off-shore Maui Field to the south-west discovered only in 1969.

Egmont National Park, the second oldest in NZ, established in 1900, encircles the mountain. A ski site in winter, in summer Mt Taranaki takes a day to climb; weather is fickle, and like much of mountain NZ, can rapidly change from sunny to a raging gale. More than 50 people have died on it. From **Stratford**, 40k south of New Plymouth (many streets are named after Shakespearean characters), a heritage trail leads to Taumarunui in the King Country (q.v.) passing **Whangamomona** village, sites of old Maori pa, abandoned mines, and tiny local museums.

South of Taranaki lies the **Wanganui** area ('harbour' in Maori). The **Whanganui River**, its source 181 miles/290k away on the slopes of Mt Tongariro volcano (q.v.), flows to **Wanganui** town on the coast. In 1840 the town was founded by disappointed settlers from the Wellington colony, Col. William Wakefield's deed of sale being signed in what are now *Moutoa Gardens*. Historically the Whanganui, NZ's longest navigable river, was a major 'highway' for Maori between the ocean and the interior of North Island, through the native podocarp forest, with many Maori villages along its length – there still are. Confused conflict between Maori and settlers over land claims broke out in 1847. Maori near Wanganui supported the settlers, up-river tribes opposed them. After the founding of the town, European settlers gave the river heavy use, with the first commercial steamer service in 1886, and journeys all the way to **Taumar-**

unui. Voyages on 'the Rhine of NZ' were advertised in Australia and Europe and by 1905 about 12,000 tourists a year were making long river trips. Railways and roads eventually stole the river's tourists and trade.

After World War I, returned soldiers were granted land for farms on the riverbanks above **Pipiriki**, most of which proved disastrous. In recent years kayaks and jet boats have revived the river's fortunes. In 1995 Maori claims to and occupation of Moutoa Gardens generated ethnic tension. The fine buildings in central Wanganui town have been restored. The large *Wanganui Regional Museum* is one of the country's best; also *Wanganui Riverboat Centre and Museum*.

Farther south on routes to Wellington (q.v.), is the **Manawatu** area, with **Palmerston North** and its universities the main town in this farming region. *Massey University* (originated as Massey Agricultural College, 1927), named after the early twentieth-century farmer PM, has long been of significance for NZ agricultural research. Of historical interest are the new *Science Centre and Manawatu Museum* (1994) and the *NZ Rugby Museum*. **165–6, 167–8**

TONGA

The Lapita People arrived in Tonga around 1200 BC. The first ruler of Tonga, the Tu'i Tonga, is conventionally assumed to have begun his reign over the largest island of Tongatapu in AD 950. Over the centuries control was extended to other islands in the archipelago, and even at times to parts of Samoa and Fiji (q.v.). Additional hereditary titles, Tui Ha'atakalaua and Tui Kanokupolu, evolved, their holders intermarrying and sharing mana, responsibility, and power in complex patterns of control. As in other archipelagoes various European navigators such as Cook visited. Cook was so impressed with the Tongans he called the group 'the Friendly Isles'.

Between 1820 and 1845 Taufa'ahau Tupou, who converted to Christianity in 1834, became ruler of **Ha'apai** and **Vava'u**, two of the main islands, and succeeded to the Tongatapu Island title of Tui Kanokupolu (the other titles had languished). Thus he was possessor of the three most powerful titles in the Tongan archipelago. He had to subdue several reluctant Tongatapu chiefs before he could finally claim to control the whole archipelago in 1852, and now took the name and title King George Tupou. King George, with the help of the Methodist missionary, Shirley Baker, whom he made PM, modernized Tonga by introducing a string of reforms, though King George reserved final authority to himself. He died in 1893 at age 96. In 1901 Tonga became a British protectorate, though internally self-governing. From 1918 the long and intelligent reign of King George's grand-daughter Salote endeared her to the Tongans and to people in other countries. Her son, the present king, took control at her death in 1965. For most of this period the royal family maintained a residence in Auckland. In 1970 the light mantle of the British protectorate was removed and Tonga became completely independent again. Tongans are proud that they alone among all South Pacific island peoples were never fully colonized.

Much of the population of the country resides on **Tongatapu**, the largest island. It is the centre of Tonga's history, culture, and politics, and the seat of the government and Tongan royalty. **Nuku'alofa** is the capital and the only real town. It holds the *Royal Tombs*, and the *Royal Palace*, not open to the public, but easily seen. This enticing white frame structure with its red roof is like a mix of Hansel and Gretel's gingerbread house and some elaborate English provincial cricket pavilion. Prefabricated in New Zealand, it was assembled in 1867. Just west of Nuku'alofa town centre is the private *Atenisi Institute and University*, which has been the best university level institution for liberal arts in the South Pacific outside New Zealand.

At the eastern end of the island stands the mysterious *Ha'amonga Tri-lithon*, three huge coral stones each about 40 tons arranged in the form of a gate, probably constructed by the eleventh Tui Tonga in the 1200s. **10, 49, 80, 103–9, 247, 286, 297–9**

VANUATU (FORMERLY NEW HEBRIDES)

'Vanuatu' means 'Land Eternal', and the people call themselves, 'Ni-Vanuatu', i.e., 'of Vanuatu'. In 1774, James Cook, who made the first real charts of the islands, was reminded of the dark tree-covered islands of the

Hebrides, off Scotland's west coast. The first settlers arrived about 1500 BC. Today's population is a mixture of Lapita People and Melanesian groups moving over hundreds of years out of the Solomon Islands (q.v.). There also seems to have been some small settlement by Polynesians from the east. Throughout their history, and as is so today, Ni-Vanuatu lived in small, clannish villages, separated by the rugged terrain. There were the usual inter-tribe, inter-clan wars of Melanesia. More than 100 languages evolved. These are still spoken, together with the national language, Bislama, and English and French.

In 1606, the Spanish navigator de Quiros believed he had here discovered *Terra Australis Incognita* (actually it was **Espiritu Santo**, the largest island). William Bligh sailed through the northern islands in his famous open boat journey. The sandalwood trade flourished for several decades. The first missionary, John Williams, landed on **Erromango** in 1839 and was eaten. A Presbyterian mission under John Geddie arrived in the southern island of **Aneityum**, consolidated, and Presbyterianism became the chief Christian religion. Anglicans and Catholics followed. Today perhaps 90% of the people are Christian in some sense, others belong to the Jon Frum cult, or to traditional religions. Though accurate figures are unknown, European diseases ran rampant and disastrously reduced the population.

A handful of British and Australian

settlers, cattle ranchers, coconut harvesters, and (during American Civil War) cotton growers came, but were outnumbered by similarly motivated French. Pressed by the settlers, and to forestall any German territorial designs, an Anglo-French Joint Naval Commission was set up in 1887 to try to control the resulting near-anarchy, and a two-nation 'Condominium' was agreed to in 1906. World War II brought the US army to build bases to attack the Japanese in the Solomons. When these forces departed in 1945, immense quantities of surplus material were sold cheaply, or dumped into the sea. So-called cargo cults such as Jon From developed, in the belief that massive amounts of Western material goods like those of the US army would appear in some supernatural manner.

By the mid-1960s settlers claimed about 30% of land. Planned expansion led to Ni-Vanuatu discontent and moves for independence. Britain supported, France hindered these moves – even to the extent of encouraging separatist rebellions. In 1980 the new government called in the aid of the PNG military to restore its authority. Foreign-owned land was confiscated without compensation.

The archipelago has some of Melanesia's most fascinating scenery, such as the active volcano on **Tanna** and twin volcanoes on **Ambrym**. There are also unique cultural practices such as the amazing 'land diving' on **Pentecost** Island. Tourism is increasing, and some wealthy Australians maintain villas, but high costs

and a lack of infrastructure hinder development. The main town and capital is **Port Vila** on **Efate**. It climbs steep hillsides around the bay, giving superb green views, making it in many travellers' opinions the South Pacific's most attractive capital. **27–8, 85, 284, 293–5**

WAIKATO REGION & KING COUNTRY

The Tainui Maori long thrived in the **Waikato River** valley, one of NZ's most fertile farming regions. Fortified pas were constructed on strategic bends in the river. During the Musket Wars, northern warrior chief Hongi Hika invaded the Waikato and caused much bloodshed. Maori–British fighting occurred in 1863–64 during the NZ Wars, when troops mustered by Governor Grey and led by General Cameron, pushed south from Auckland (q.v.) and after victory at the Battle of Rangiriri captured the Kingite capital of **Ngaruawahia** and other places. (A phenomenon rare in NZ, there is a Rangiriri Battle Site Heritage Centre commemorating the 1863 encounter.) During the twentieth century **Turangawaewae Marae**, the largest in NZ, was constructed at Ngaruawahia. From the 1920s through the efforts of Princess Te Puha the marae became a rallying place for Maori cultural regeneration.

In 1864 two military redoubts, Hamilton East and West, were constructed on opposite sides of the Waikato to protect confiscated lands, soldier-settlers arrived, and two villages grew up. The villages were amalgamated in 1877 and joined by Union Bridge in 1879, to form what is now New Zealand's largest inland city, **Hamilton**, named after John F. Hamilton, popular master of HMS *Esk*, a vessel used in the NZ Wars. Five more bridges were built in the city in the 20th century. Though there was a road connection to Auckland by 1868 and a railway by 1879, the river remained economically important into the 20th century. Hamilton grew as cooperative dairy farming expanded into the Waikato lands, and as the links to Auckland, to the west coast, and east to Rotorua (q.v.) and the Bay of Plenty (q.v.) were made. In 1995 the government allocated $170 million to the Waikato Tainui tribe as compensation for seizing the lands of their ancestors during the NZ Wars.

The *Waikato Museum of Art and History*'s new premises (1997) make imaginative use of a riverbank site for its collection of regional Maori artifacts and NZ art. The large *Mormon Temple* at Tuhikaramea in southern Hamilton (dedicated 1958) was the first to be built in the Australia/South Pacific region. Spectacular gardens and emerald grasslands along the river banks have long been a delight.

Raglan (after Lord Raglan, the Crimean War general), on a pretty sheltered harbour to the west, is Hamilton's nearest beach, with art and craft shops. First sale of land to an European was in 1850. **Cambridge**, 12 miles/20k south-east of Hamilton, has an English-feel, with tree-lined avenues. St Andrew's Anglican Church, over 100 years old, has a carved wooden interior.

After the Waikato War, Kingite Maori led by King Tawhiao rallied for some decades in a virtually independent somewhat undefined area of perhaps 3,000 sq. miles (6475 sq.k) farther to the south, which became known as the **King Country**. It remained under (peaceful) Maori control longer than any other region. From 1884 to 1955 the Maori chiefs kept the King Country 'dry' (alcohol prohibited). The first real European penetration was the Auckland–Wellington Main Trunk Railway which entered the King Country in the 1890s.

Towns which gradually developed in the King Country are **Otorohanga**, **Taumarunui** and **Te Kuiti**. The extraordinary **Raurimu Spiral** of curves and tunnels completed in 1908 is south of Taumarunui on the Main Trunk Line. **Waitomo** is the small centre for the famous **Waitomo Caves** system. The most famous is *Glowworm Cave*, long known to Maori and shown to surveyor, Frederick Mace, in 1887 by the chief, Tinorau. Ever since there have been organized tours of the cave. **166–9**

WELLINGTON AND REGION

Wellington, at the extreme south of the North Island and strategically located at the geographical heart of the country, has been the national capital since 1865. The site and country to the north were originally inhabited by a sequence of clashing Maori tribes, especially during the Musket Wars, such as the Te Ati Awa, Ngati Mutunga and Ngati Tama and Ngati Toa. The nation's chief commercial, banking and finance centre and its second port, it grew around **Port Nicholson** (Te Whanganui-a-Tara – the great harbour of Tara) one of the world's best harbours. In 1839, a vessel of the colonizing NZ Company, trying to put into practice the systematic colonization concepts of E.G. Wakefield, arrived from England and chose a site at the mouth of the **Hutt River**. The settlers soon moved to the more suitable **Lambton Harbour** on the west shore. Much of downtown stands on reclaimed land. Nature too helped – the 1855 earthquake uplifted beaches into a platform.

Named in 1840 in recognition of the help given the Company by the first Duke of Wellington, the city has become hub of the nation's communications and transport, with railways and roads to all parts of North Island, ferry and steamship links to South Island, and air services to all parts of the country. Wellington and the adjoining towns of the Hutt River Valley such as **Hutt City** and **Upper Hutt City** (named for Sir William Hutt, NZ Company shareholder) and **Porirua** have heavy industry and produce consumer goods. Natural gas comes by pipe from the Kapuni field (q.v.).

Buildings include the huge innovative, earthquake-proofed *Te Papa – Museum of New Zealand* (1993–98);

War Memorial Carillon; the mixed historical styles of *Victoria University of Wellington* (founded 1897 to celebrate Queen Victoria's diamond jubilee). In Thorndon is a splendid government and cathedral complex all within a few blocks: *Old Government Building* (1876, one of the world's largest wooden structures); classical Parliament House by John Campbell (1922), elegant Gothic-revival *Parliamentary Library* by Thomas Turnbull (1899), with statues to Prime Ministers John Ballance and Richard Seddon in front; ultra-modern 'beehive' *Government Offices* (1980, by Sir Basil Spence); *St Paul's Anglican Cathedral*, opened by Queen Elizabeth II in 1995 (as in mediaeval England cathedrals were close to castles, so in modern Wellington Anglican Cathedral is alongside parliament); *Old St Paul's* – early English Gothic revival, consecrated 1866, built of native timbers, threatened with demolition in 1960s; Roman Catholic *Cathedral of the Sacred Heart* (by Francis W. Petre, 1901); *National Library* (including Alexander Turnbull Library), one of world's great sources of South Pacific research material; *National Archives* (copies of the Treaty of Waitangi and of the 1893 petition for women's suffrage). The *William Clayton Building* (opened 1982) was the world's first to use 'base isolation' of huge lead–rubber bearings to neutralize earthquake movement. A cable car, opened in 1902, ascends past the university to the Botanic Gardens.

Memorials to the two founders of Wellington are minimal: a neglected

The Beehive, Executive Buildings, Wellington

neo-classical drinking fountain to Col. William Wakefield beside Basin Reserve, and his gravestone in Bolton Street Cemetery; and two plaques to Edward Gibbon Wakefield on the site of his house, in *The Terrace* in Thorndon.

Wellington has become home of national arts organizations. In 1971 the NZ Ballet and Opera Trust amalgamated the NZ Ballet (1953) and the NZ Opera Company (1954).

To the north-west along the Tasman Sea coast is the quiet agricultural **Horowheneua** Region, with beautiful **Lake Horowheneua**. In 1823 the region was the scene of ferocious attacks on the local Muaupok'o

people by Te Rauparaha of the Ngati Toa. Off-shore stands **Kapiti Island** 6 miles × 1.2 miles (10 × 2k), seized by Te Rauparaha in 1823 as strategic base for his campaigns. In 1897 it became a quiet bird sanctuary, now controlled by the Department of Conservation, with access restricted to 50 people a day!

The **Wairarapa** ('Glistening Waters') is a great sheep-rearing and also mixed farming region of mountain and plain, north-east of Wellington, settled early by sheep farmers from Wellington, and rail-linked to the capital in 1880. **Masterton** in the north is the main town. It holds an annual 'Golden Shears' competition (since 1958) in which master sheep shearers from around the world compete. **138–40, 147, 150–7, 165–9, 183, 281**

WEST COAST

In this narrow half-pioneered coastal strip small crystal lakes reflect the great peaks, and the tangled bushland contains innumerable rusted relics of 160 years of mining gold and coal, and cutting timber. In the north the road through *Buller Gorge* from Nelson (q.v.) reaches the coast near **Westport**. Now a base for outdoor activities in nearby national parks (including underground rafting!), it began in the 1860s as a centre for nearby coalmining; its *Coaltown* museum is imaginative. Ten miles east, **Denniston** was until 1967 NZ's greatest coal mine, site of innovative 'self-acting' *Denniston Incline*. The road south threads hamlets which thrived 130 years ago during the gold rush. **Reefton** just to the east, named for its gold-bearing reefs, had NZ's first town electricity supply and street lighting in 1885. South-west on the road to coast, tiny **Blackball** (founded 1866) to service gold mines, was the coal town where the first NZ Federation of Labour organized in 1909 (colloquially the 'Red Feds').

On the coast 10 miles south-west at the mouth of the *Grey River* (after Gov. George Grey) **Greymouth** is the West Coast 'metropolis', once a site of a Maori pa. Its driftwood-clad beach like all the others presents the traveller with wild, wet, wistful seascapes. *History House Museum* and *Shantytown* (imitation 1880s gold town), to the south, preserve local history. Greymouth is the terminus of the *Transalpine Railway* from Christchurch (q.v.), which in about 4 fascinating hours passes through an extraordinary range of scenery – plains, rolling hills, sheer mountains, river valleys, gorges, and lakes.

Hokitika, 25 miles/40k along the coast, settled in 1861 as a port for imports and gold export, is now a centre for working greenstone. (Ancient Maori travelled into nearby mountains to gather greenstone for weapons and art objects.) Of some historical interest are the *West Coast Historical Museum*, *Custom House* and *Gibson Quay*.

About 75 miles/120k south lie Glaciers **Franz Josef** (after Austrian emperor) and **Fox** (after NZ premier), major tourist attractions served by villages of same names. Heavy rainfall, a vast accumulation zone, and steep valleys force these glaciers to move fast (for glaciers!). First explored in detail by Julius von Haast, founding director of Canterbury Museum (q.v.), they were in retreat for more than a century after Haast first measured them, but began growing again in 1985. About 13 miles/20k south again lies the beautiful **Haast Region**, a major wildlife refuge of great rainforests, wetlands, and seal and penguin colonies. Further south is Fiordland (q.v.). **202**

Index

NB NZ = New Zealand; SPI = South Pacific Islands